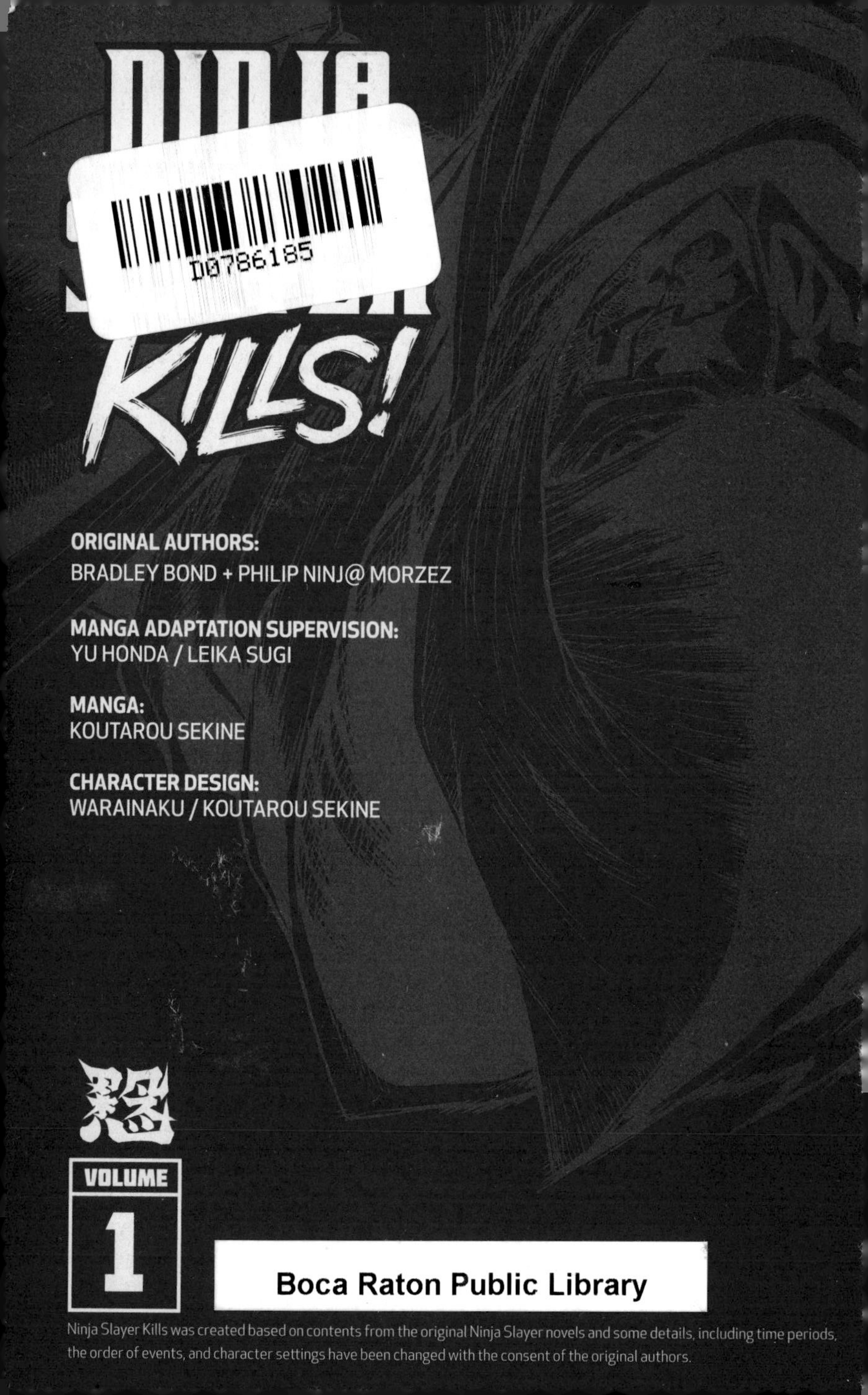

NINJA SLAYER KILLS!

ORIGINAL AUTHORS:
BRADLEY BOND + PHILIP NINJ@ MORZEZ

MANGA ADAPTATION SUPERVISION:
YU HONDA / LEIKA SUGI

MANGA:
KOUTAROU SEKINE

CHARACTER DESIGN:
WARAINAKU / KOUTAROU SEKINE

VOLUME 1

Ninja Slayer Kills was created based on contents from the original Ninja Slayer novels and some details, including time periods, the order of events, and character settings have been changed with the consent of the original authors.

怒

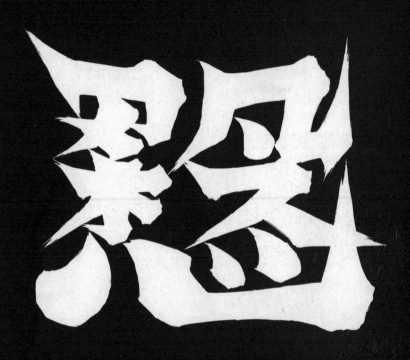

FOREWORD

Domo.
I am Truncator, the ninja editor of Ninja Slayer. Possessed by the dark soul of an ancient scribe, I utilize my literary *karate* to strike fear into those who dare besmirch the name of ninja through lackluster writing. All typos must perish!

It brings me great pleasure to present the story of Ninja Slayer to all manga reading ninja-heads out there and I—
What's this? Are you not a ninja-head? Impossible! *Namusan!* Oh my Buddha!

Before you can enjoy the world of Ninja Slayer, you must diligently build up your *wazamae* by studying the ways and history of the ninja, for the world of ninja is a treacherous one. Even something as innocuous as manga, when written and edited by true ninja, can send non-ninja-heads on a journey to the opposite shore of the Sanzu River.

To prevent your head from exploding upon reading these pages, I ask that you first behold the *kotodama* on page 202 of this book. These phrases and explanations will not only allow you to understand the ninja lingo used in this series, but the words themselves have been imbued with ninja soul energy to prevent madness. Heed my warning: those who read the tale of Ninja Slayer without knowing these *kotodama* are certain to descend into a blood-fueled madness that can only end in *hara-kiri*.

NINJA SLAYER KILLS!
CONTENTS

BONUS EXTRAS 特 別 収 録

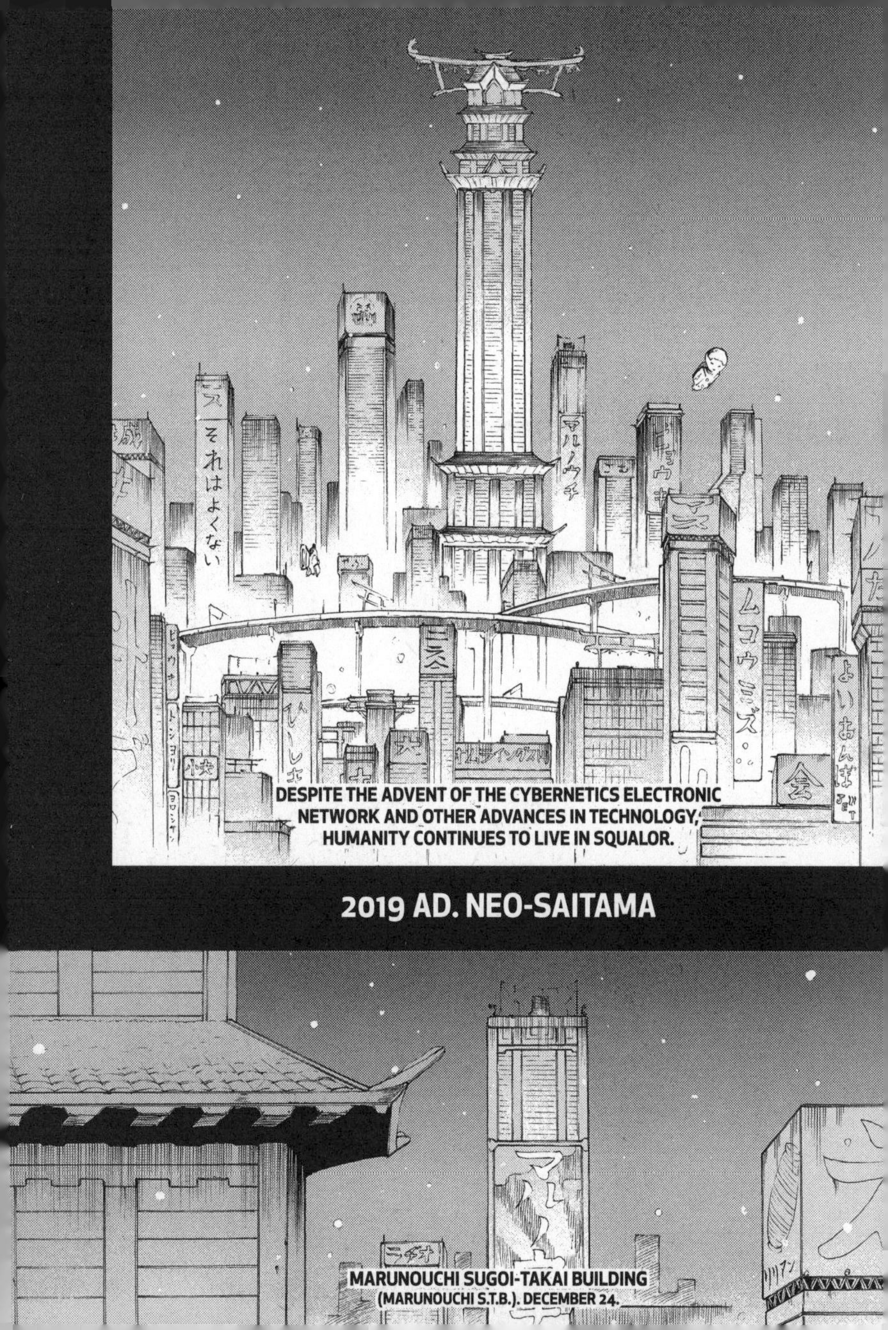
それはよくない
DESPITE THE ADVENT OF THE CYBERNETICS ELECTRONIC NETWORK AND OTHER ADVANCES IN TECHNOLOGY, HUMANITY CONTINUES TO LIVE IN SQUALOR.
2019 AD. NEO-SAITAMA
MARUNOUCHI SUGOI-TAKAI BUILDING (MARUNOUCHI S.T.B.). DECEMBER 24.

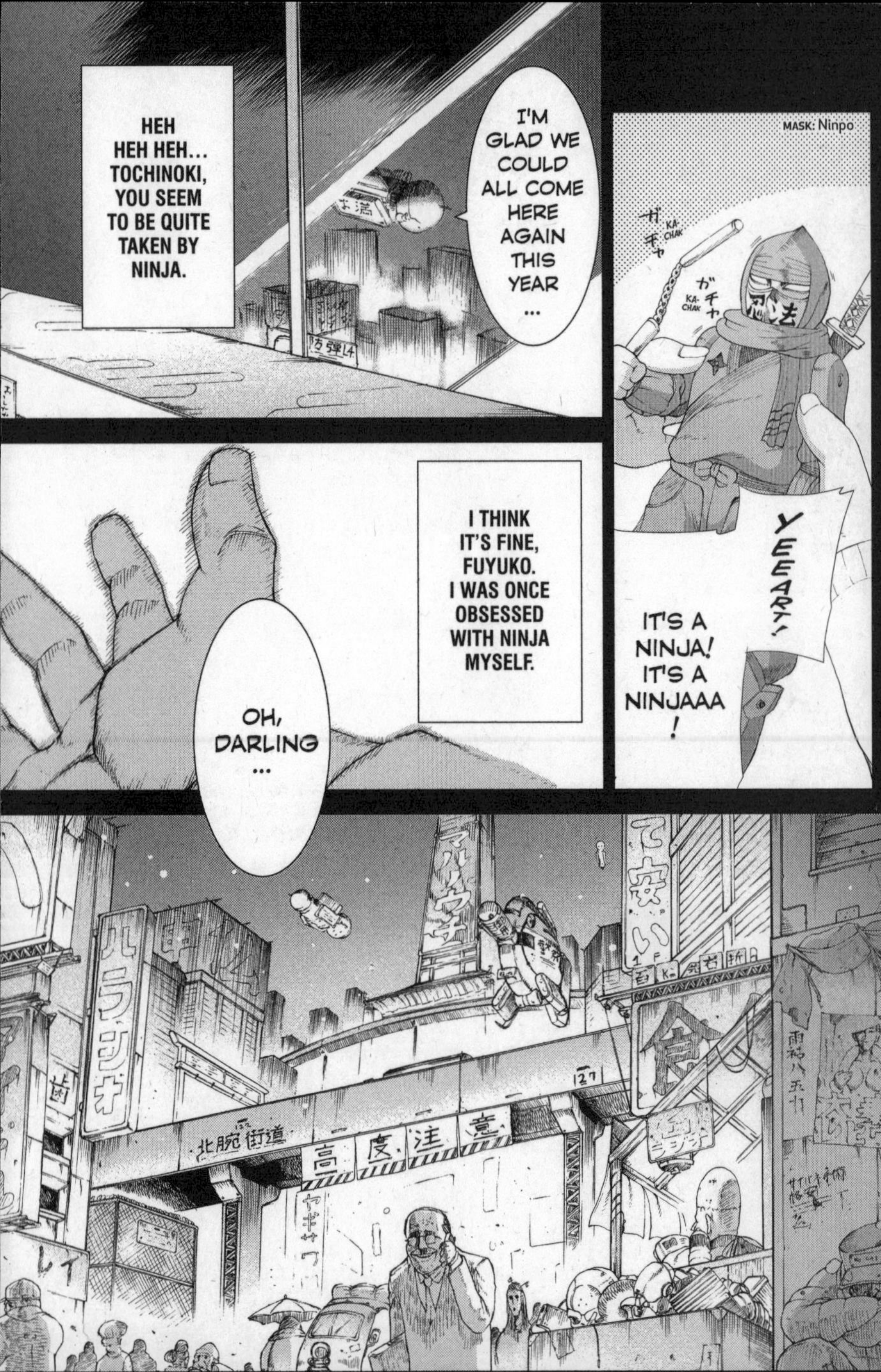
MASK: Ninpo
KA-CHAK
KA-CHAK
YEEART!
IT'S A NINJA! IT'S A NINJAAA!
I'M GLAD WE COULD ALL COME HERE AGAIN THIS YEAR...
HEH HEH HEH... TOCHINOKI, YOU SEEM TO BE QUITE TAKEN BY NINJA.
I THINK IT'S FINE, FUYUKO. I WAS ONCE OBSESSED WITH NINJA MYSELF.
OH, DARLING...
北腕街道
高度注意
127

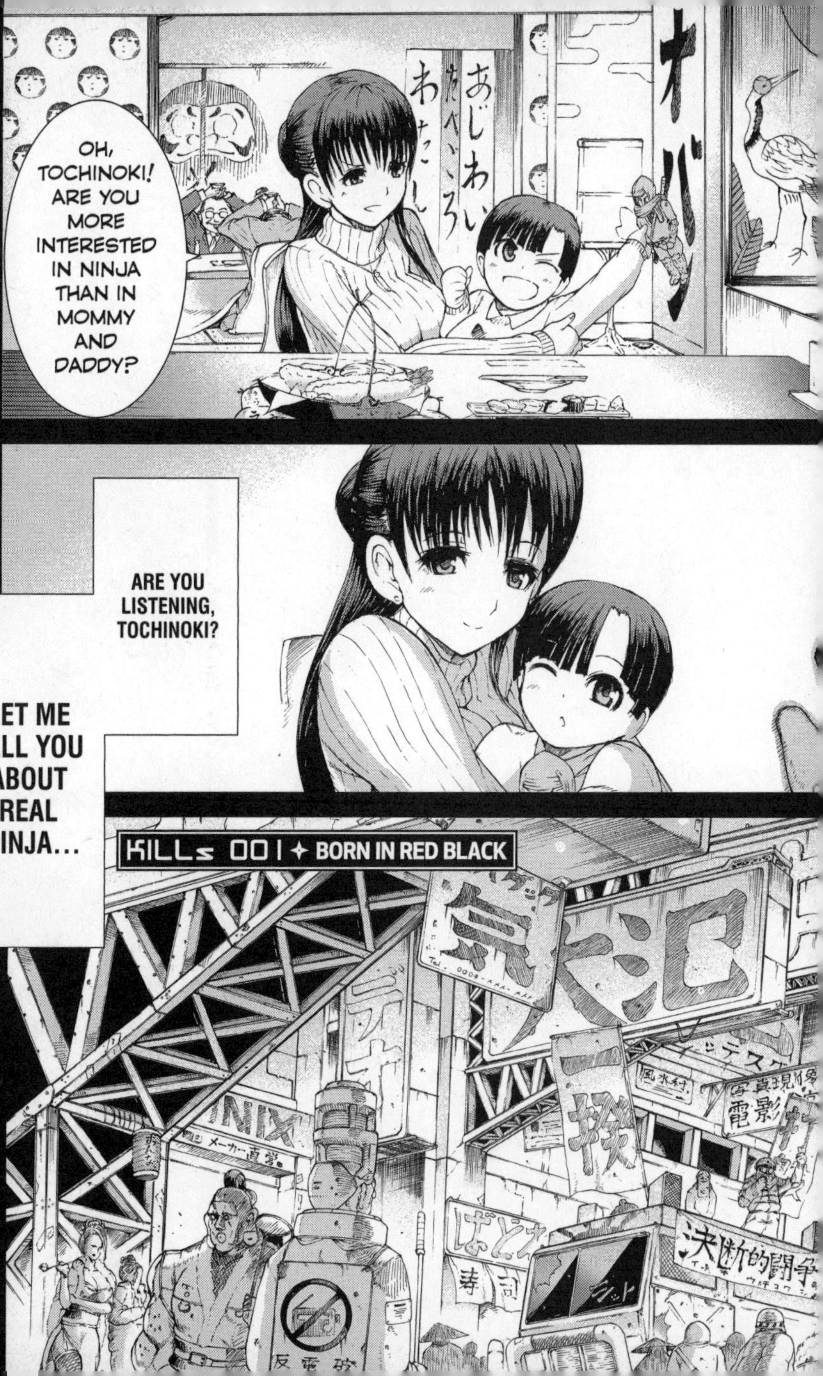
OH, TOCHINOKI! ARE YOU MORE INTERESTED IN NINJA THAN IN MOMMY AND DADDY?
ARE YOU LISTENING, TOCHINOKI?
LET ME TELL YOU ABOUT REAL NINJA…
KILLs 001 ✦ BORN IN RED BLACK
あじわい
風水村
電影
寿司
決断的闘争
メーカー直営

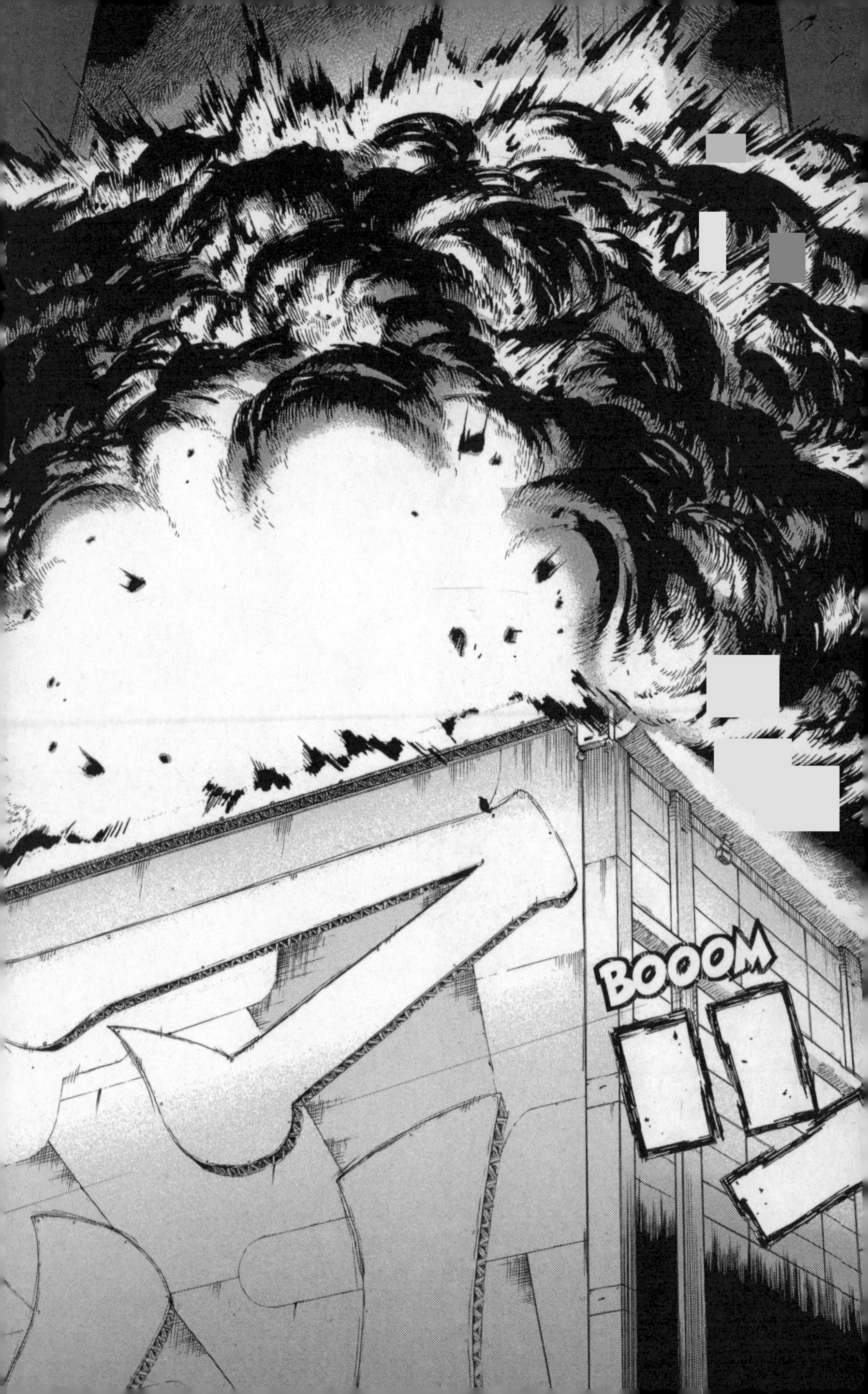
BOOOM

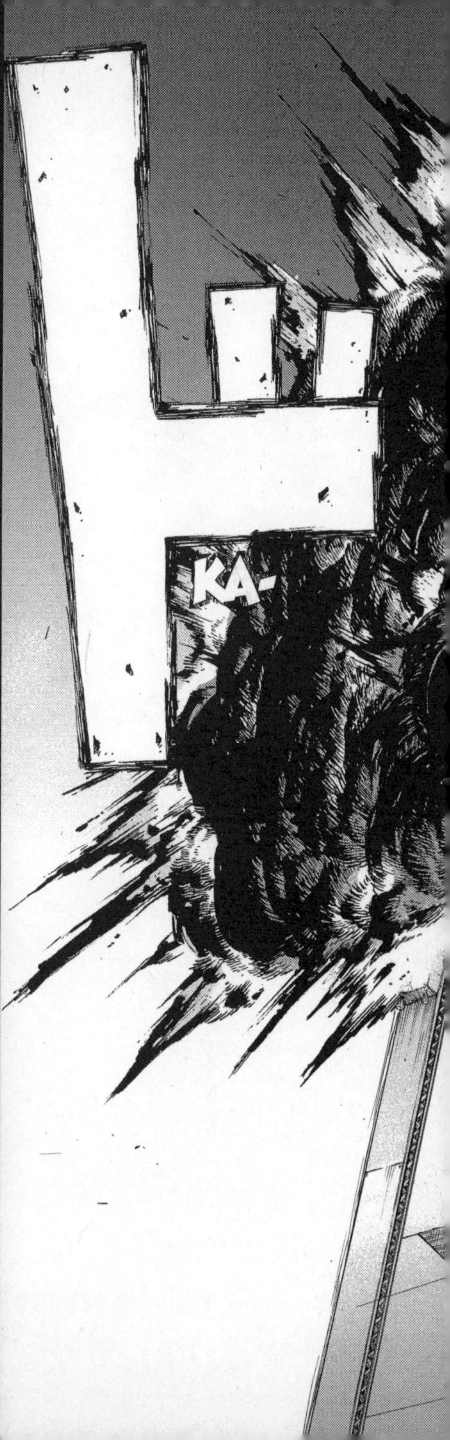
KA-
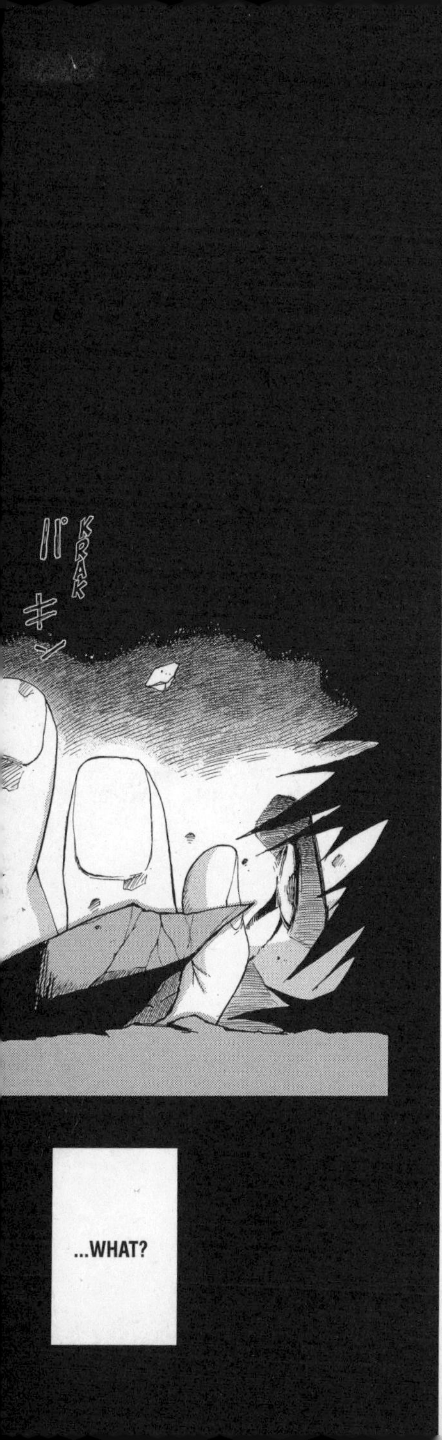
KRAK
パキン
...WHAT?

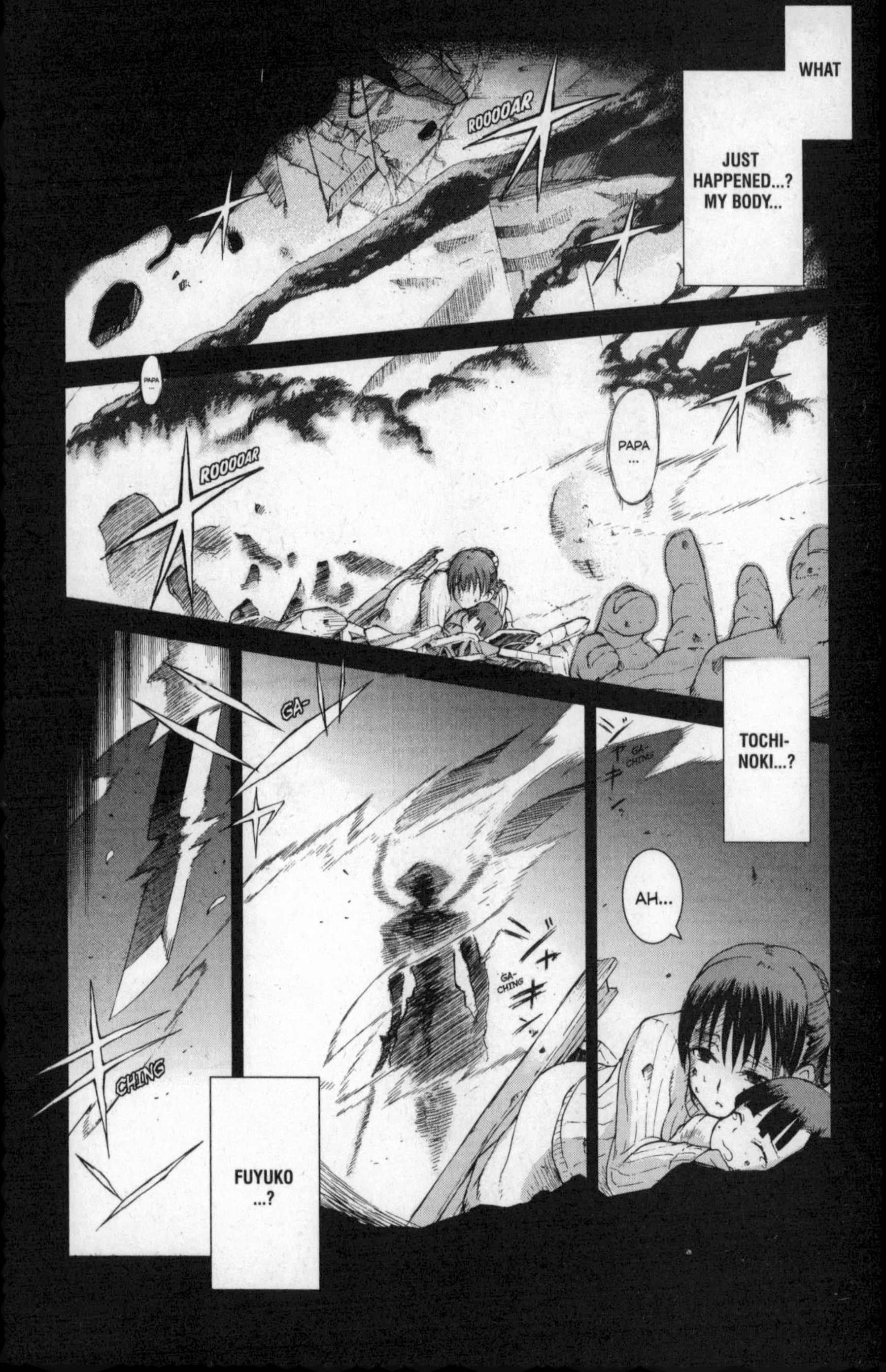
WHAT
JUST HAPPENED...? MY BODY...
ROOOOAR
PAPA ...
PAPA ...
ROOOOAR
TOCHI-NOKI...?
GA-CHING
AH...
GA-CHING
GA-
CHING
FUYUKO ...?

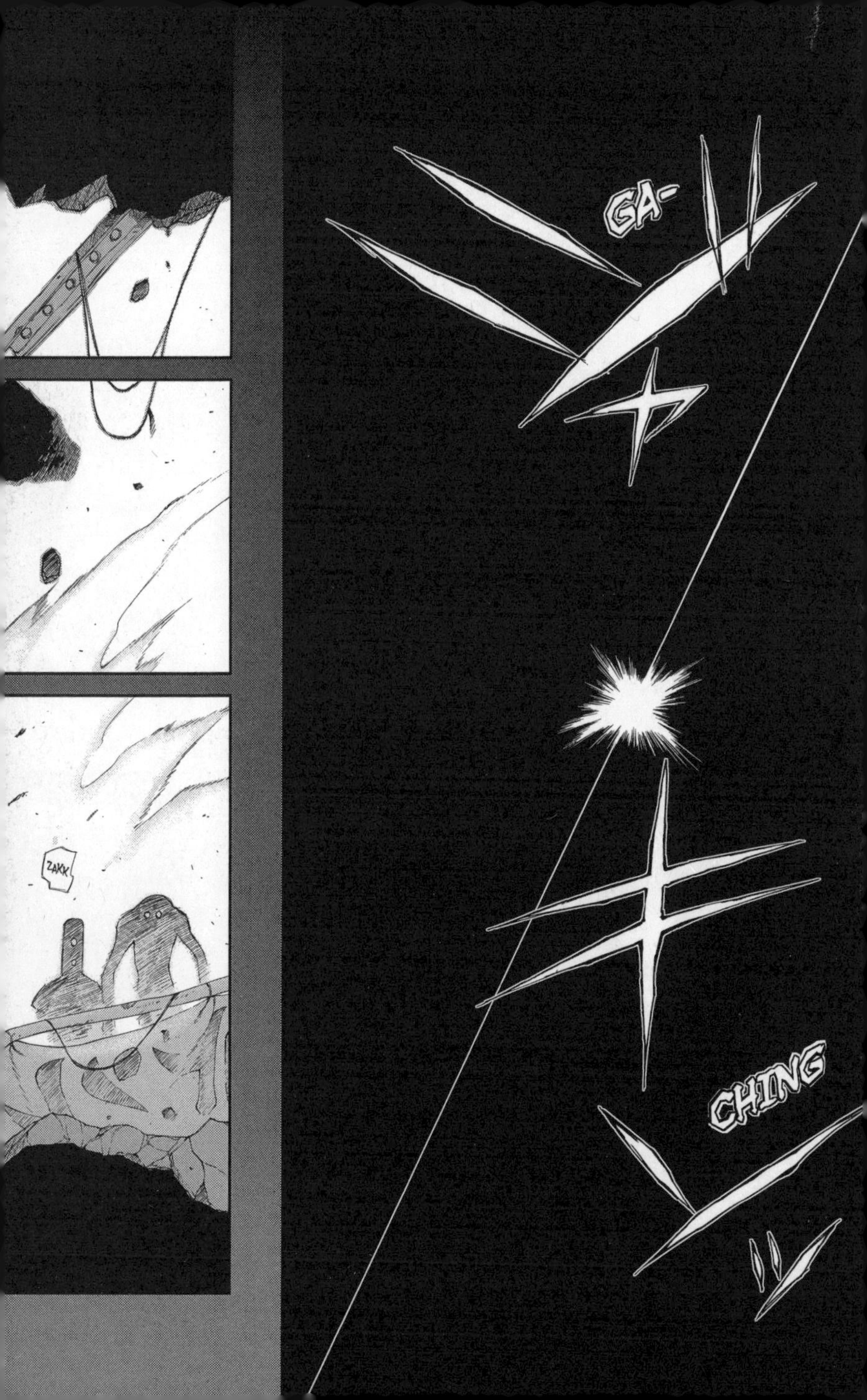
GA-
CHING
ZAKK

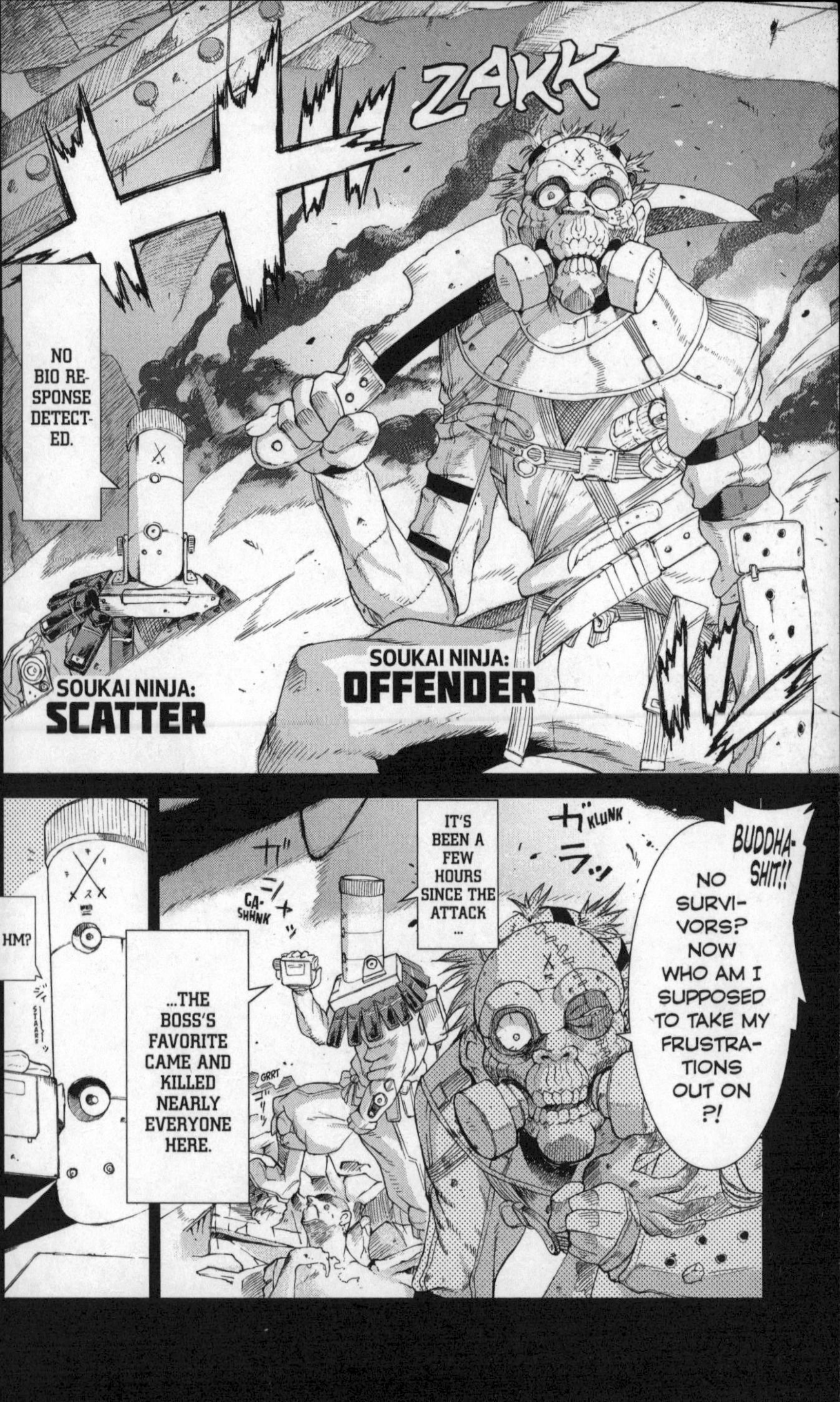
ZAKK
NO BIO RE-SPONSE DETECT-ED.
SOUKAI NINJA: OFFENDER
SOUKAI NINJA: SCATTER
BUDDHA-SHIT!!
NO SURVI-VORS? NOW WHO AM I SUPPOSED TO TAKE MY FRUSTRA-TIONS OUT ON ?!
KLUNK
IT'S BEEN A FEW HOURS SINCE THE ATTACK ...
GA-SHHNK
GRRT
...THE BOSS'S FAVORITE CAME AND KILLED NEARLY EVERYONE HERE.
HM?
STARE

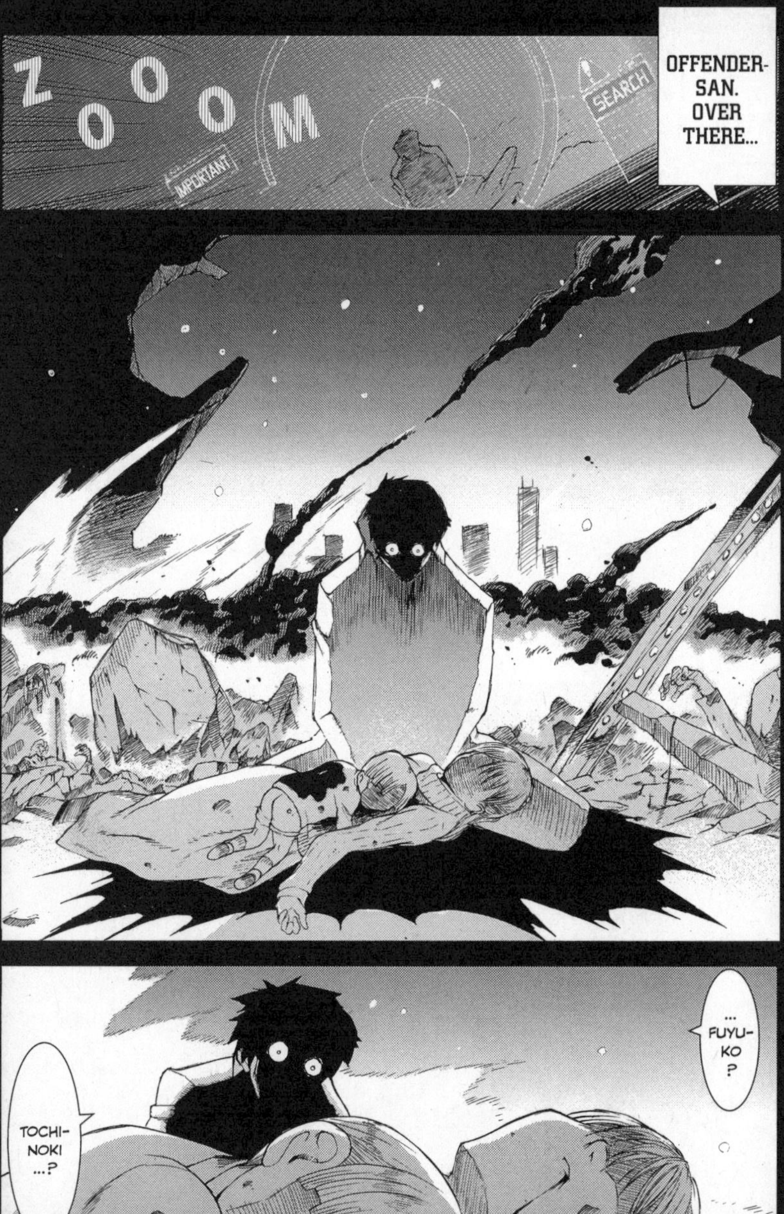
OFFENDER-SAN. OVER THERE...
SEARCH
ZOOOM
IMPORTANT
... FUYUKO?
TOCHINOKI ...?

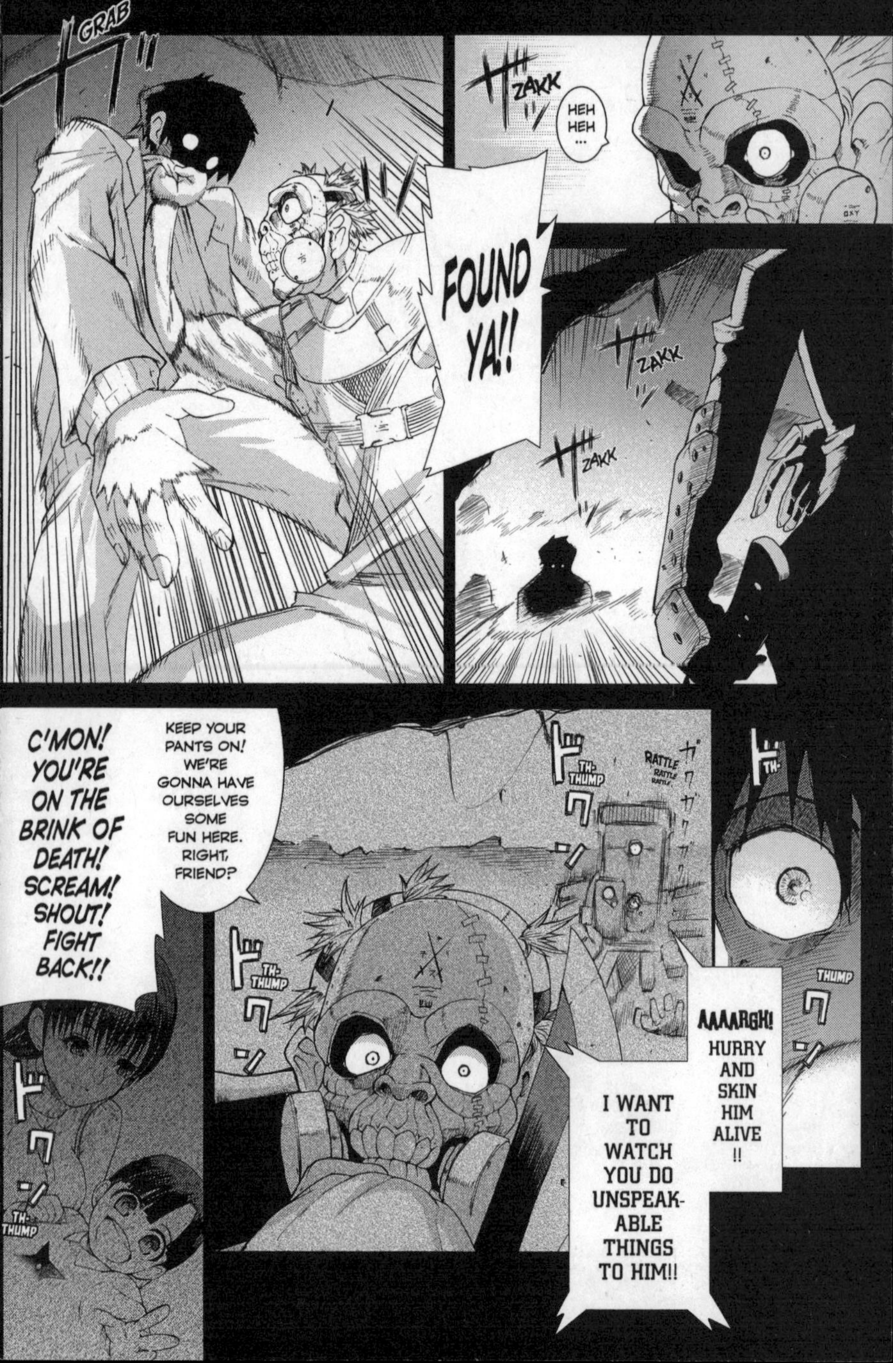

ZAKK
HEH HEH ...
ZAKK
ZAKK
GRAB
FOUND YA!!
TH-
THUMP
RATTLE RATTLE RATTLE
TH-THUMP
KEEP YOUR PANTS ON! WE'RE GONNA HAVE OURSELVES SOME FUN HERE. RIGHT, FRIEND?
AAAARGH! HURRY AND SKIN HIM ALIVE !!
I WANT TO WATCH YOU DO UNSPEAK-ABLE THINGS TO HIM!!
TH-THUMP
C'MON! YOU'RE ON THE BRINK OF DEATH! SCREAM! SHOUT! FIGHT BACK!!
TH-THUMP

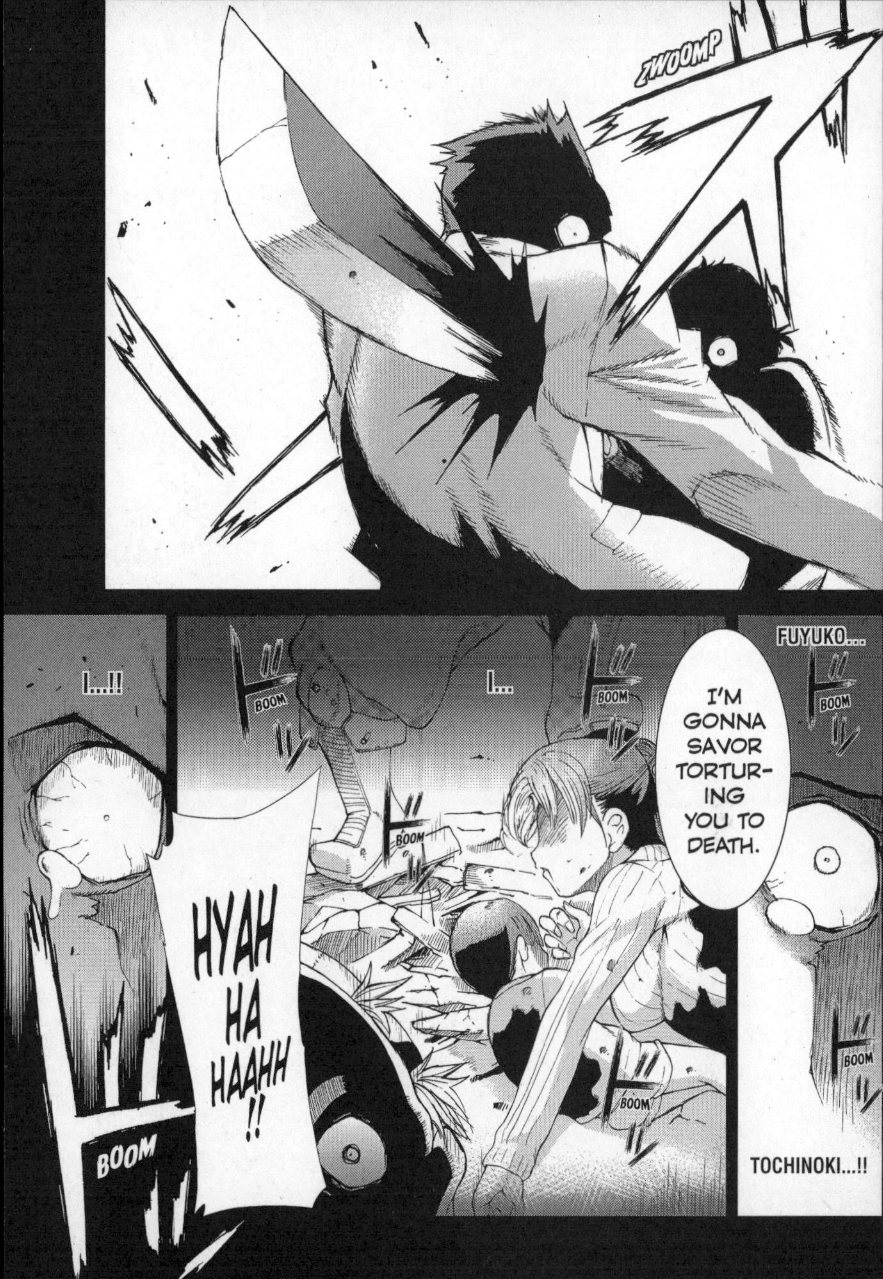
ZWOOMP
FUYUKO...
BOOM
I'M GONNA SAVOR TORTURING YOU TO DEATH.
BOOM
I...
BOOM
I...!!
BOOM
BOOM
TOCHINOKI...!!
BOOM
HYAH HA HAAHH!!
BOOM

DO YOU FEEL HATE IN YOUR HEART?

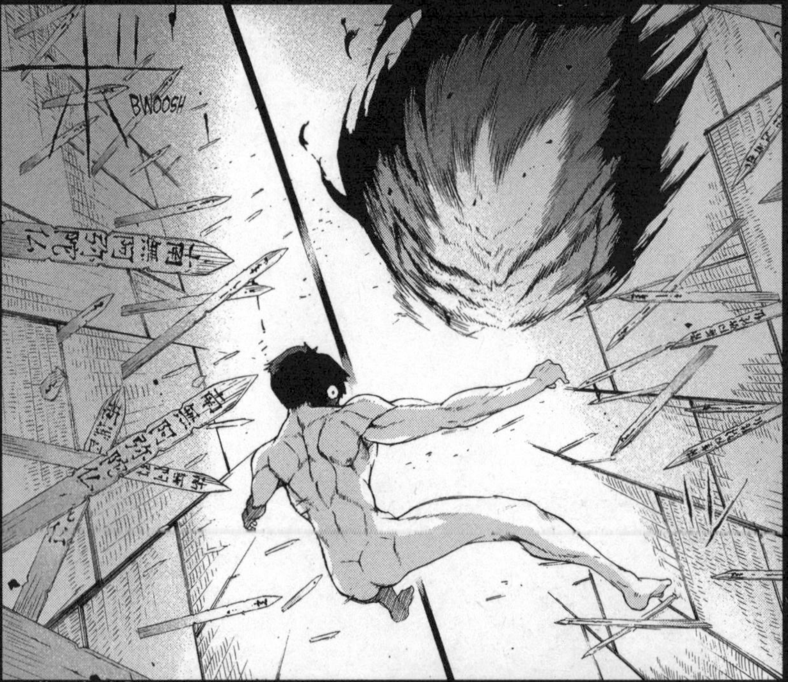
BWOOSH

SIGNS: Namu-Amida-Butsu

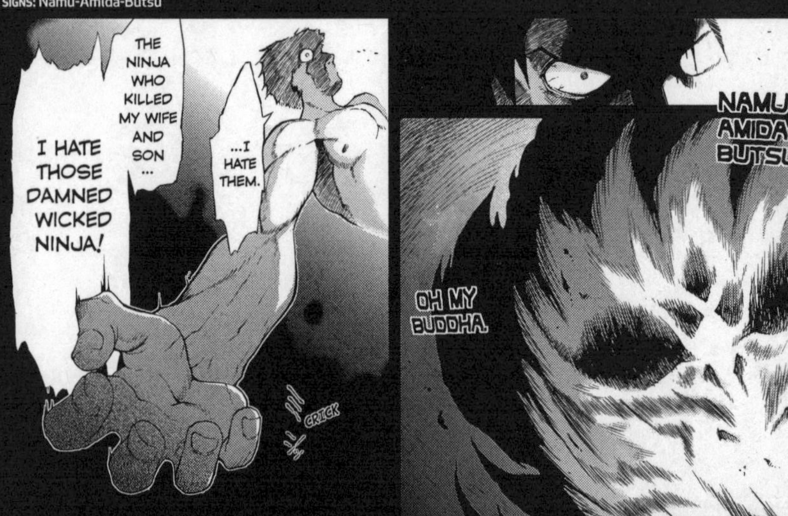
THE NINJA WHO KILLED MY WIFE AND SON ...
...I HATE THEM.
I HATE THOSE DAMNED WICKED NINJA!
CRICK
NAMU-AMIDA-BUTSU.
OH MY BUDDHA.

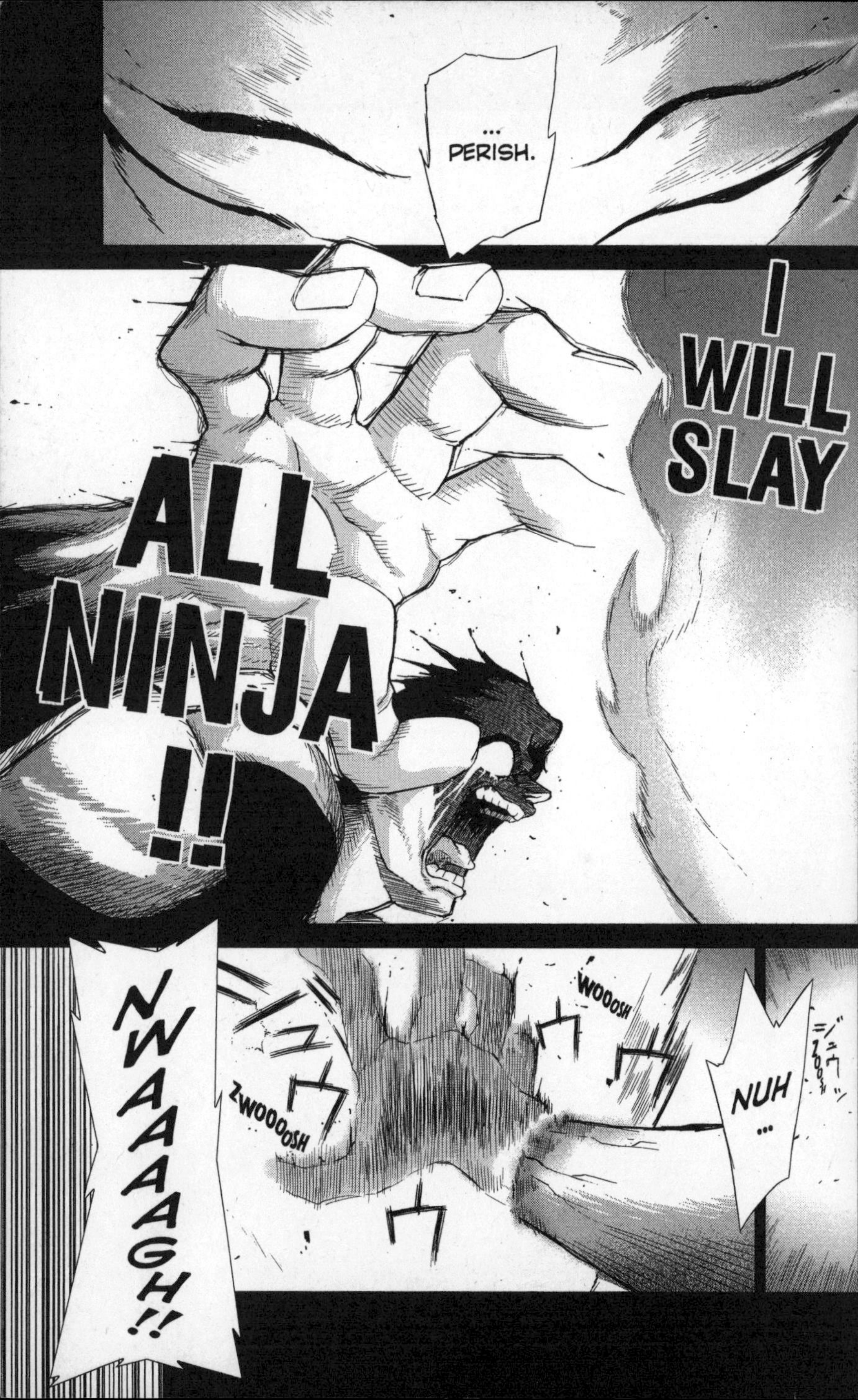
...
PERISH.
I WILL SLAY
ALL NINJA!!
NUH...
WOOOSH
ZWOOOOSH
NWAAAAAGH!!

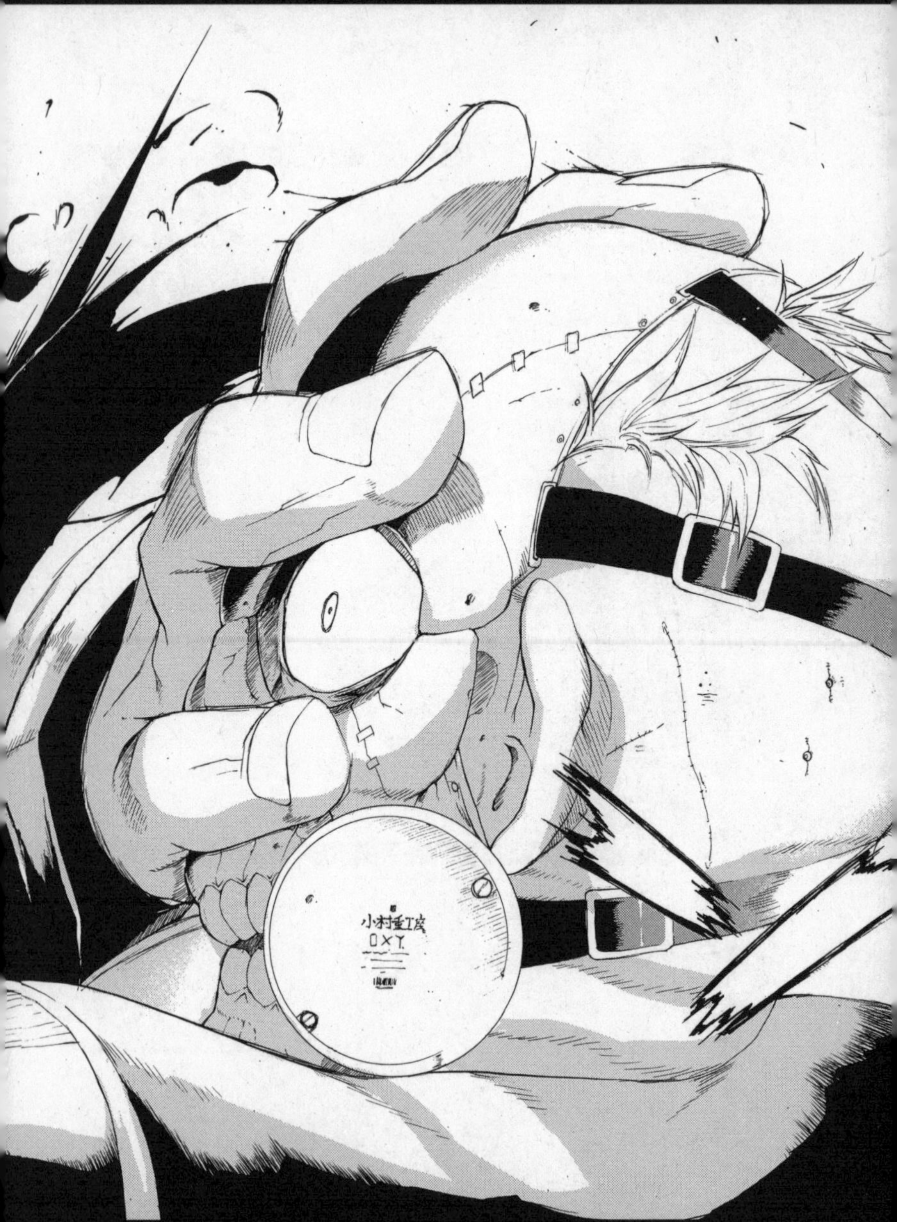
OXY.

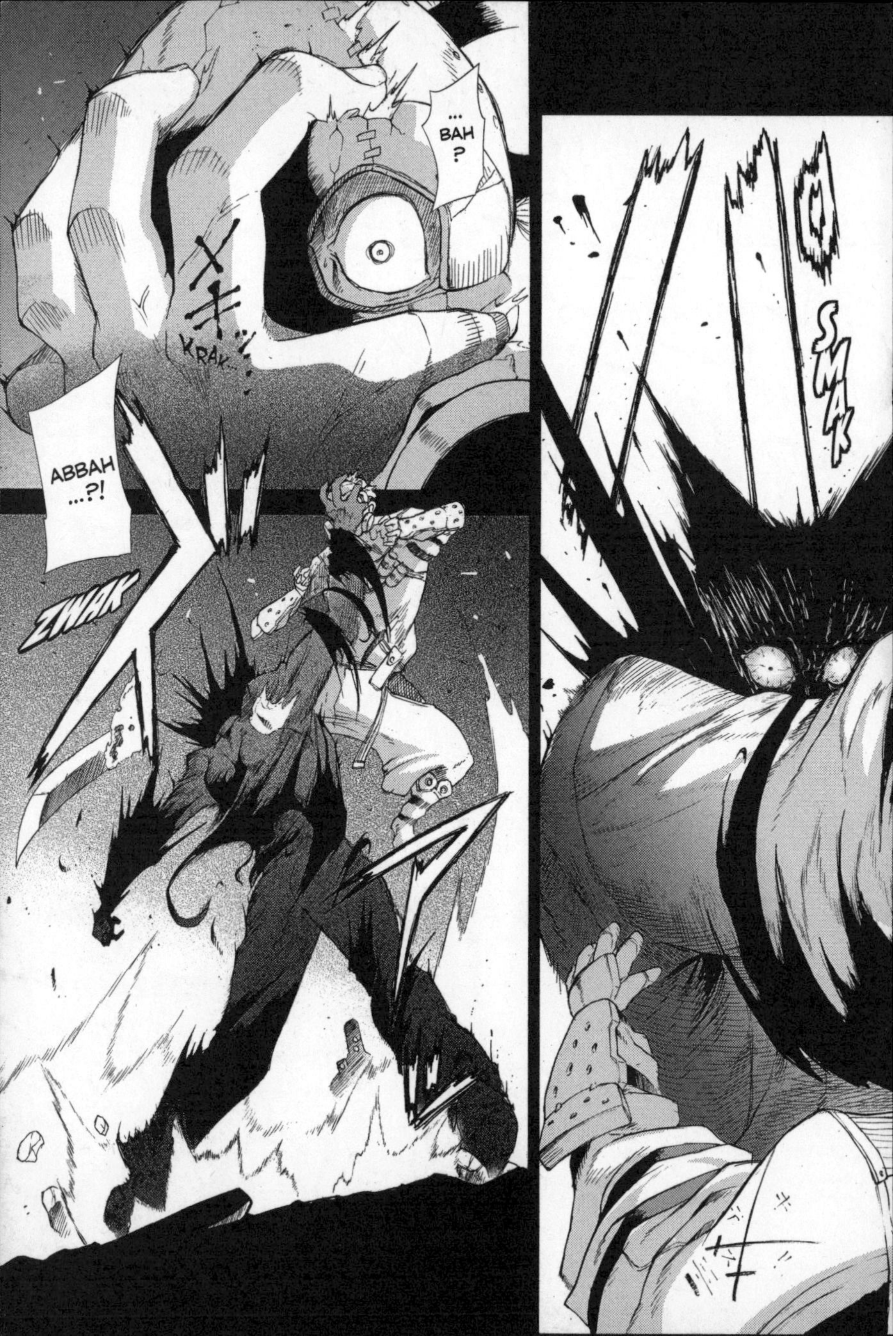
...BAH?
KRAK...
ABBAH...?!
ZWAK
SMAK

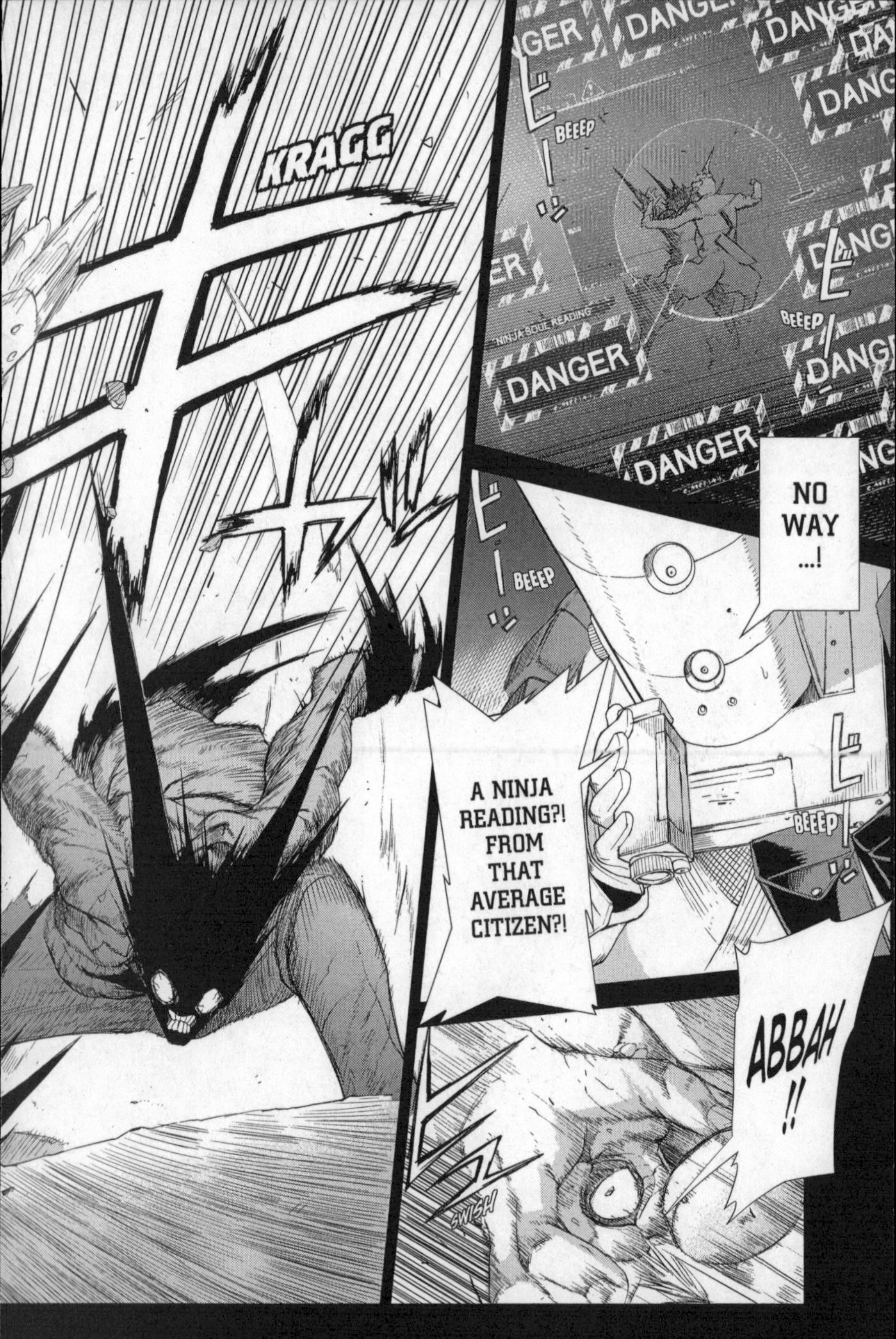
DANGER
DANGER
DANGER
BEEEP
NINJA SOUL READING
DANGER
BEEEP
DANGER
DANGER
BEEEP
NO WAY ...!
A NINJA READING?! FROM THAT AVERAGE CITIZEN?!
BEEEP
ABBAH!!
SWISH
KRAGG

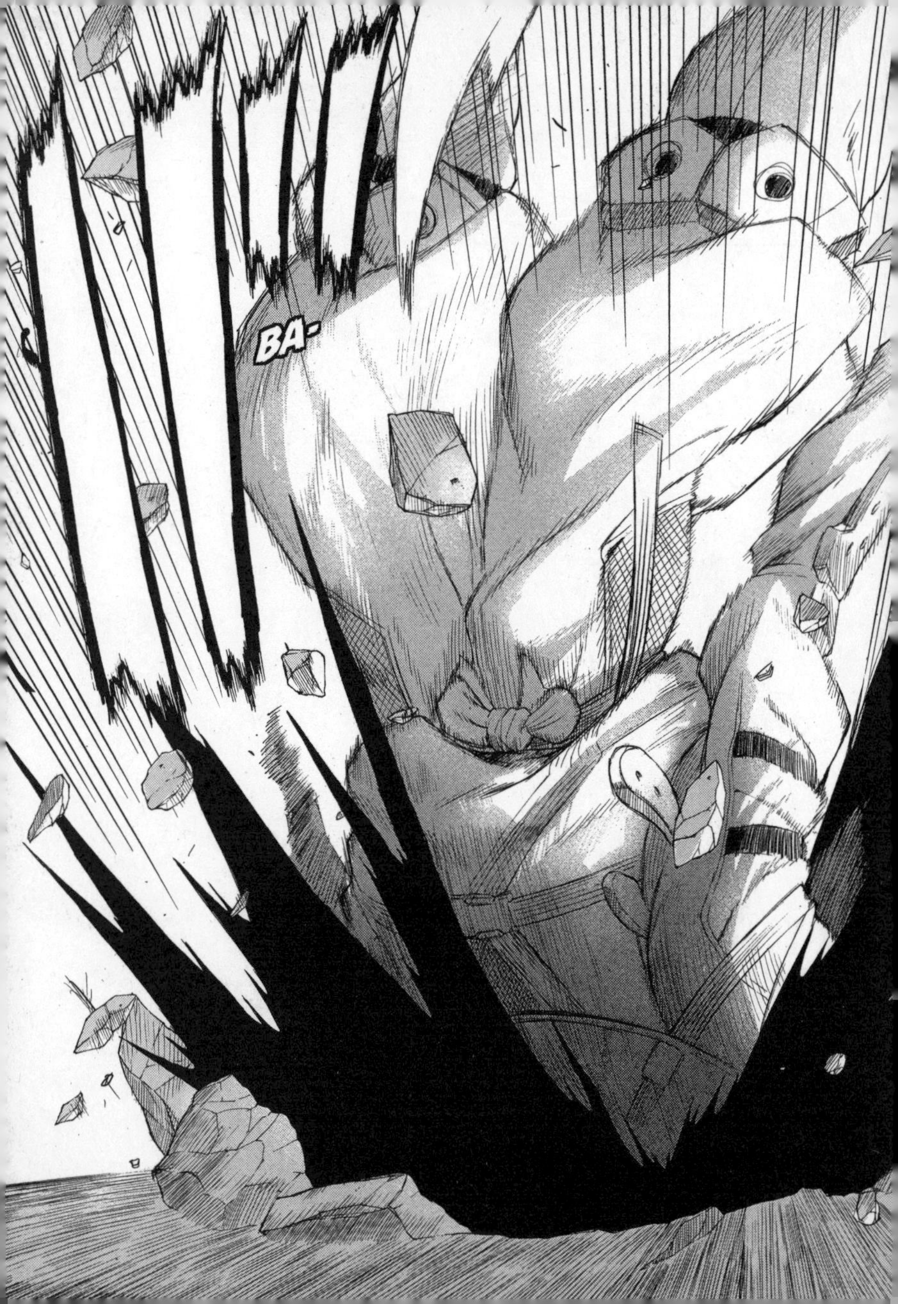
BA-

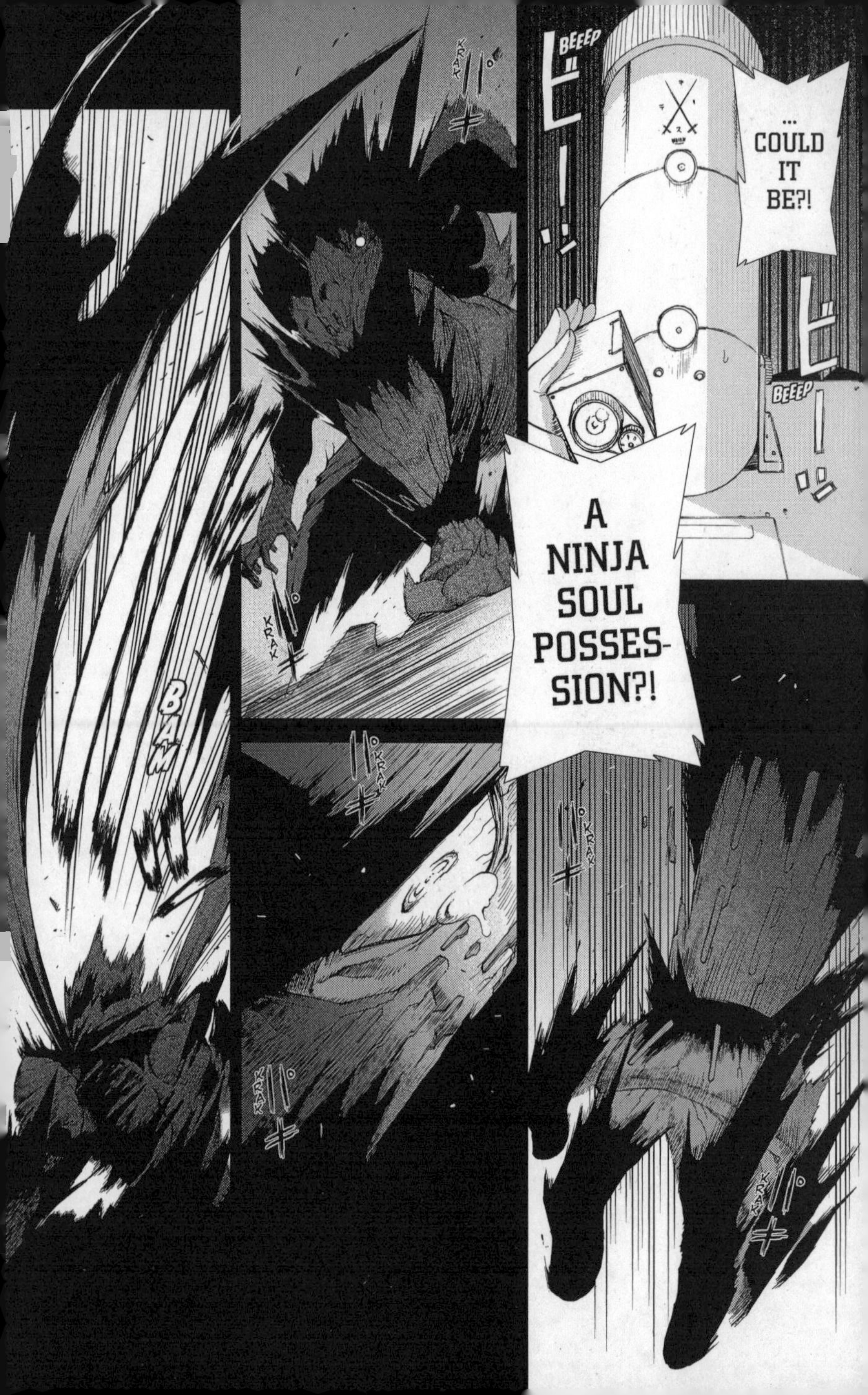
BEEEP
... COULD IT BE?!
BEEEP
A NINJA SOUL POSSESSION?!
KRAK
KRAK
KRAK
KRAK
KRAK
KRAK
BAM

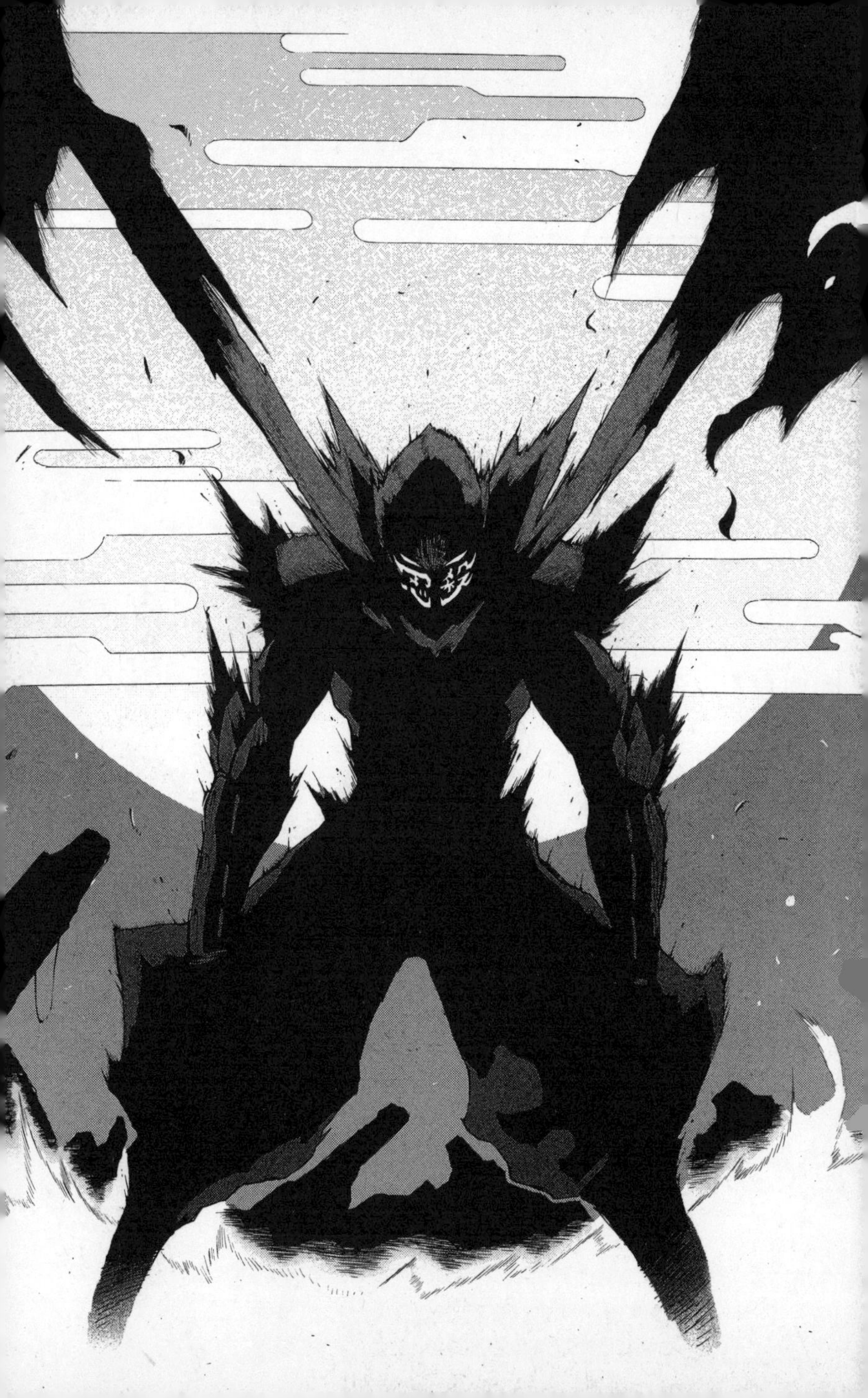
忍殺

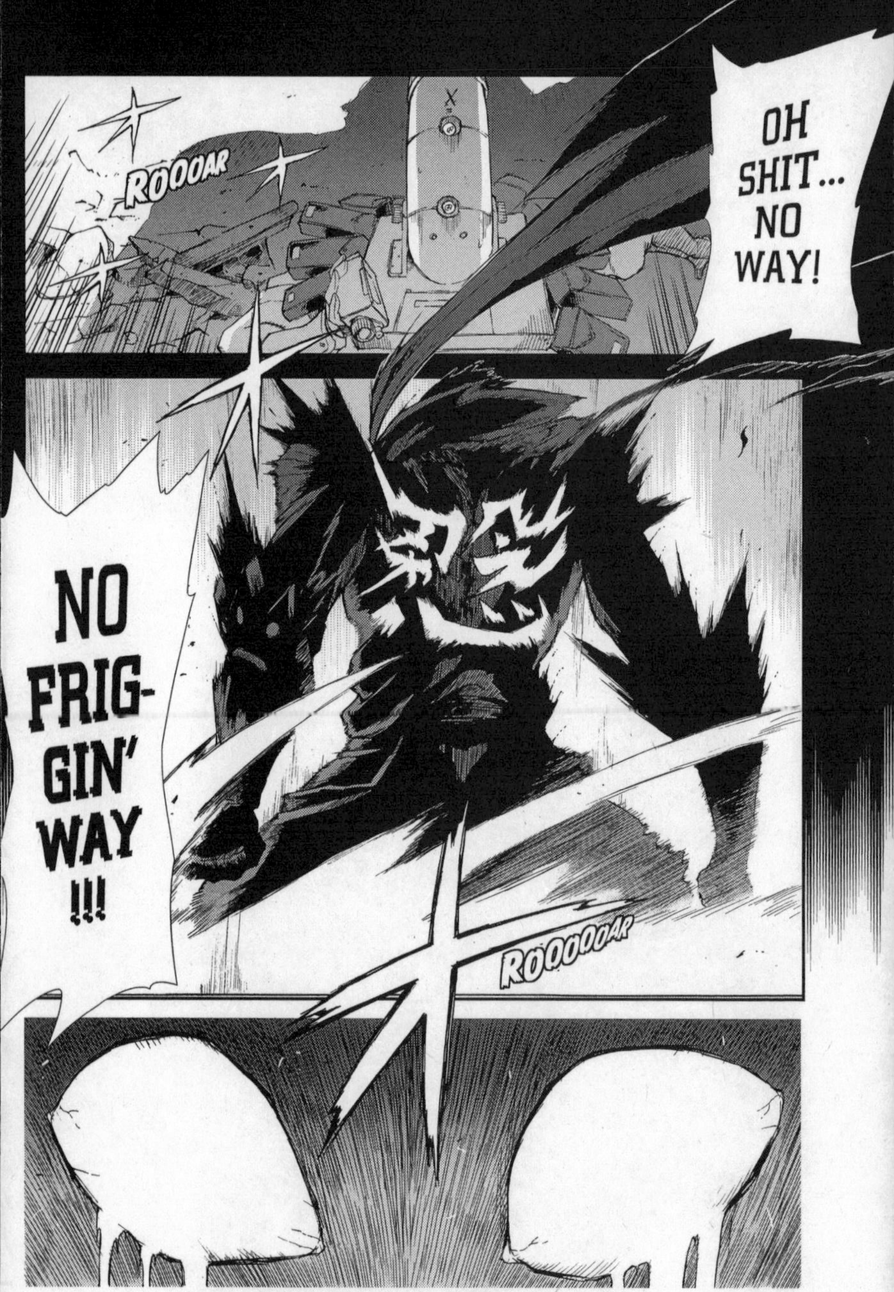
OH SHIT... NO WAY!
ROOOAR
NO FRIG-GIN' WAY!!!
ROOOOOAR

[BORN IN RED BLACK] • END

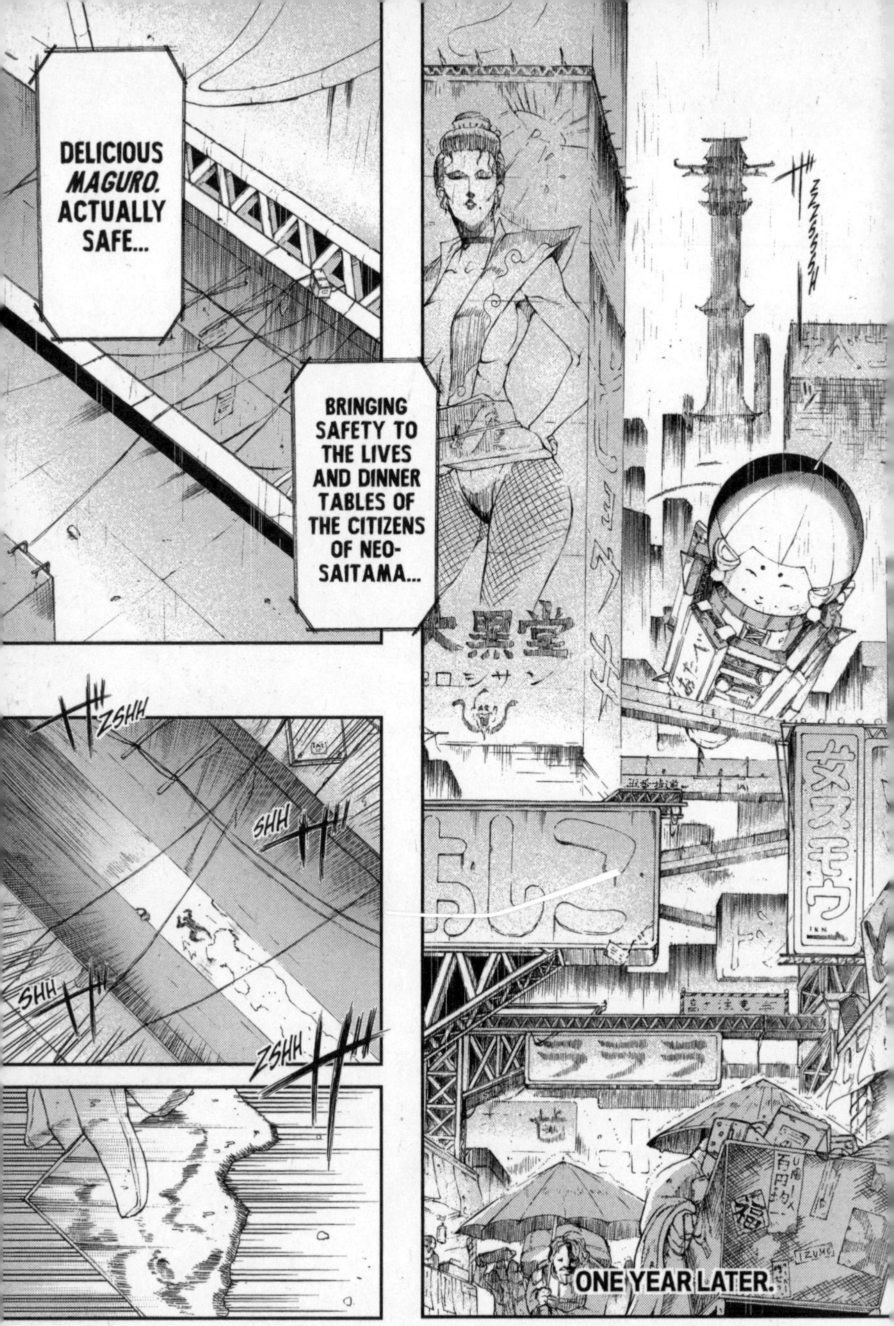
ONE YEAR LATER.
DELICIOUS *MAGURO.* ACTUALLY SAFE...
BRINGING SAFETY TO THE LIVES AND DINNER TABLES OF THE CITIZENS OF NEO-SAITAMA...
ZSHH
SHH
SHH
ZSHH

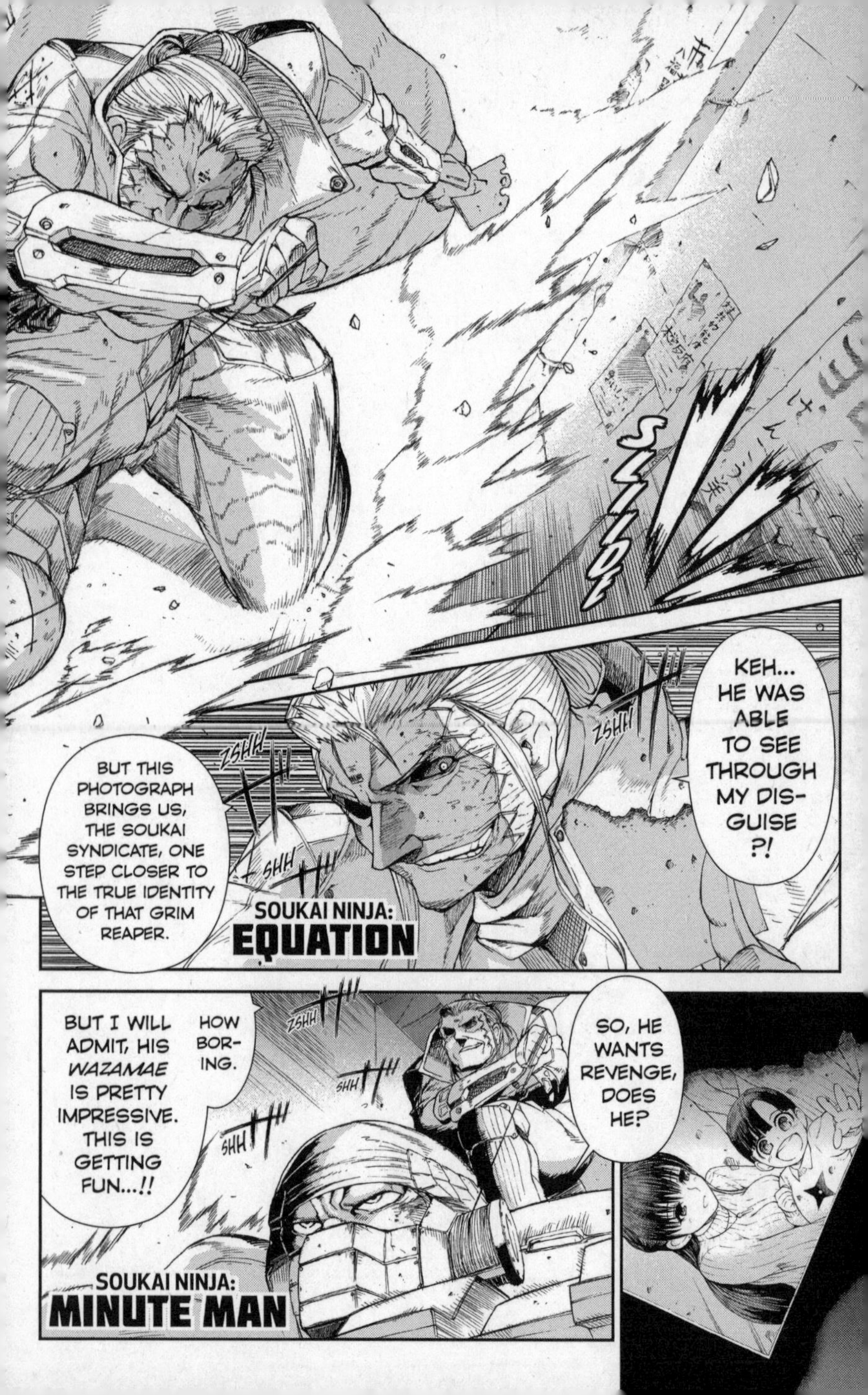
KEH... HE WAS ABLE TO SEE THROUGH MY DIS-GUISE ?!
ZSHH
BUT THIS PHOTOGRAPH BRINGS US, THE SOUKAI SYNDICATE, ONE STEP CLOSER TO THE TRUE IDENTITY OF THAT GRIM REAPER.
ZSHH
SHH
SOUKAI NINJA: EQUATION
SO, HE WANTS REVENGE, DOES HE?
ZSHH
SHH
HOW BOR-ING.
BUT I WILL ADMIT, HIS *WAZAMAE* IS PRETTY IMPRESSIVE. THIS IS GETTING FUN...!!
SHH
SOUKAI NINJA: MINUTE MAN

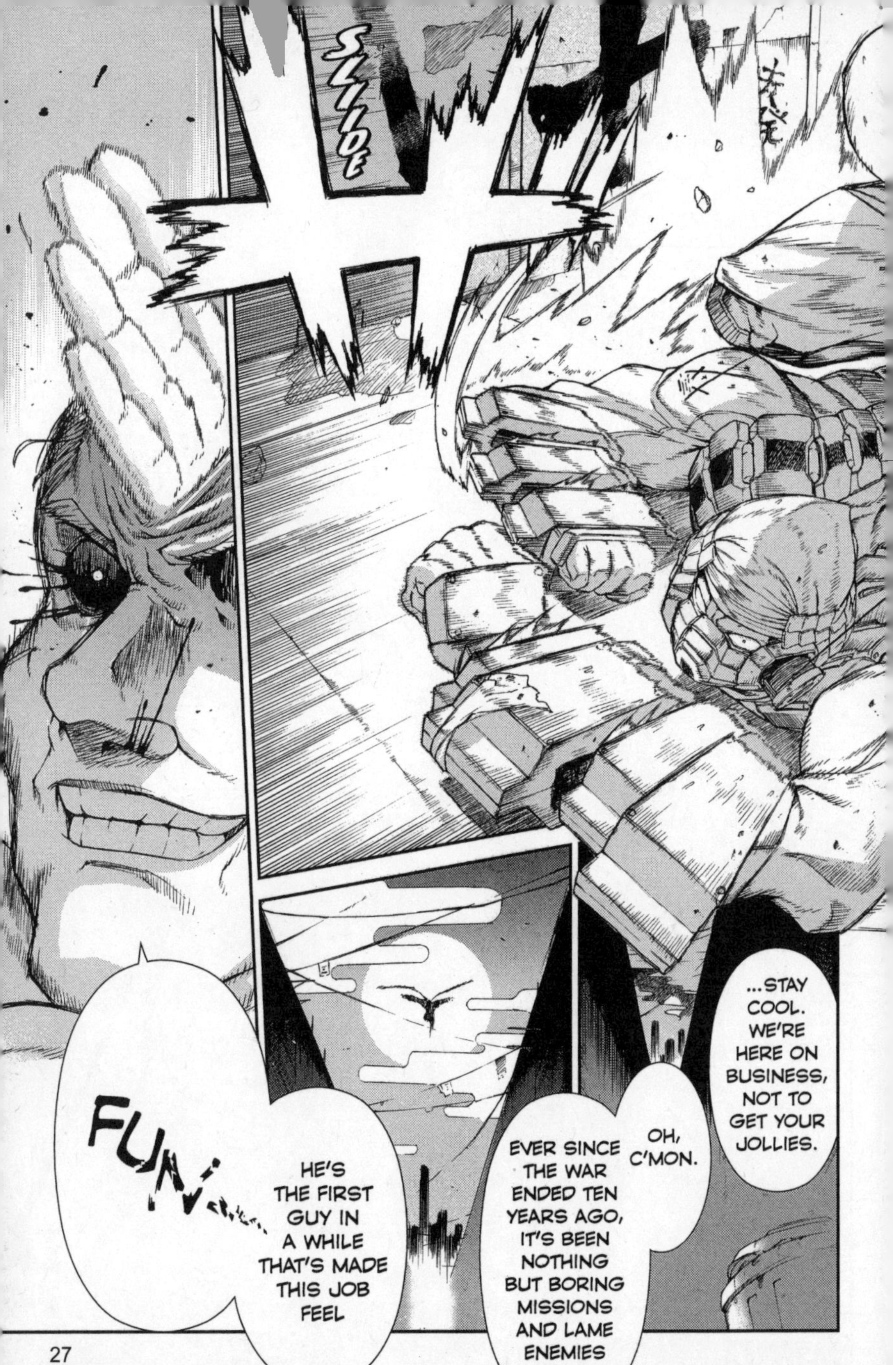
SLIIDE
...STAY COOL. WE'RE HERE ON BUSINESS, NOT TO GET YOUR JOLLIES.
OH, C'MON.
EVER SINCE THE WAR ENDED TEN YEARS AGO, IT'S BEEN NOTHING BUT BORING MISSIONS AND LAME ENEMIES ...
HE'S THE FIRST GUY IN A WHILE THAT'S MADE THIS JOB FEEL
FUN...

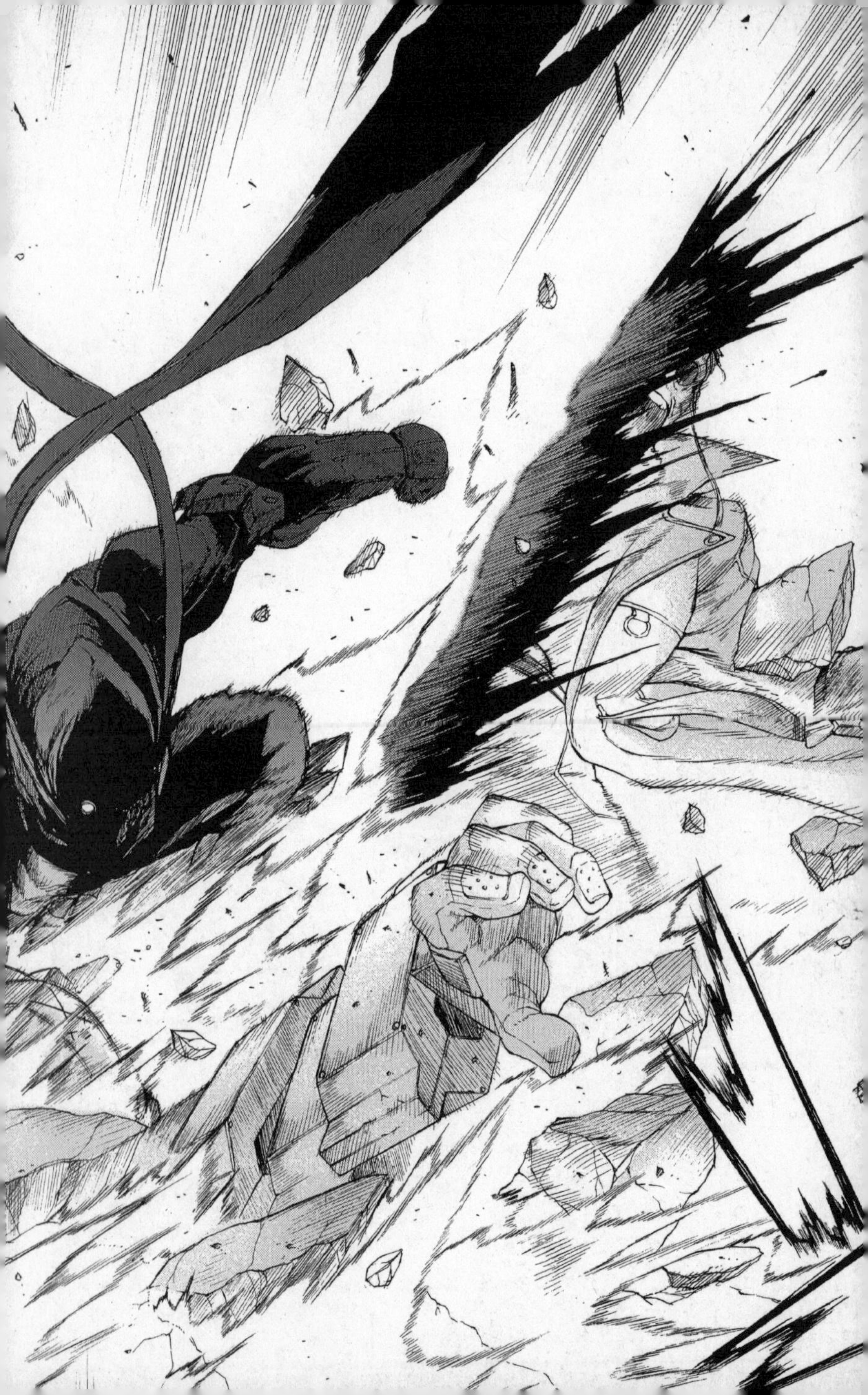

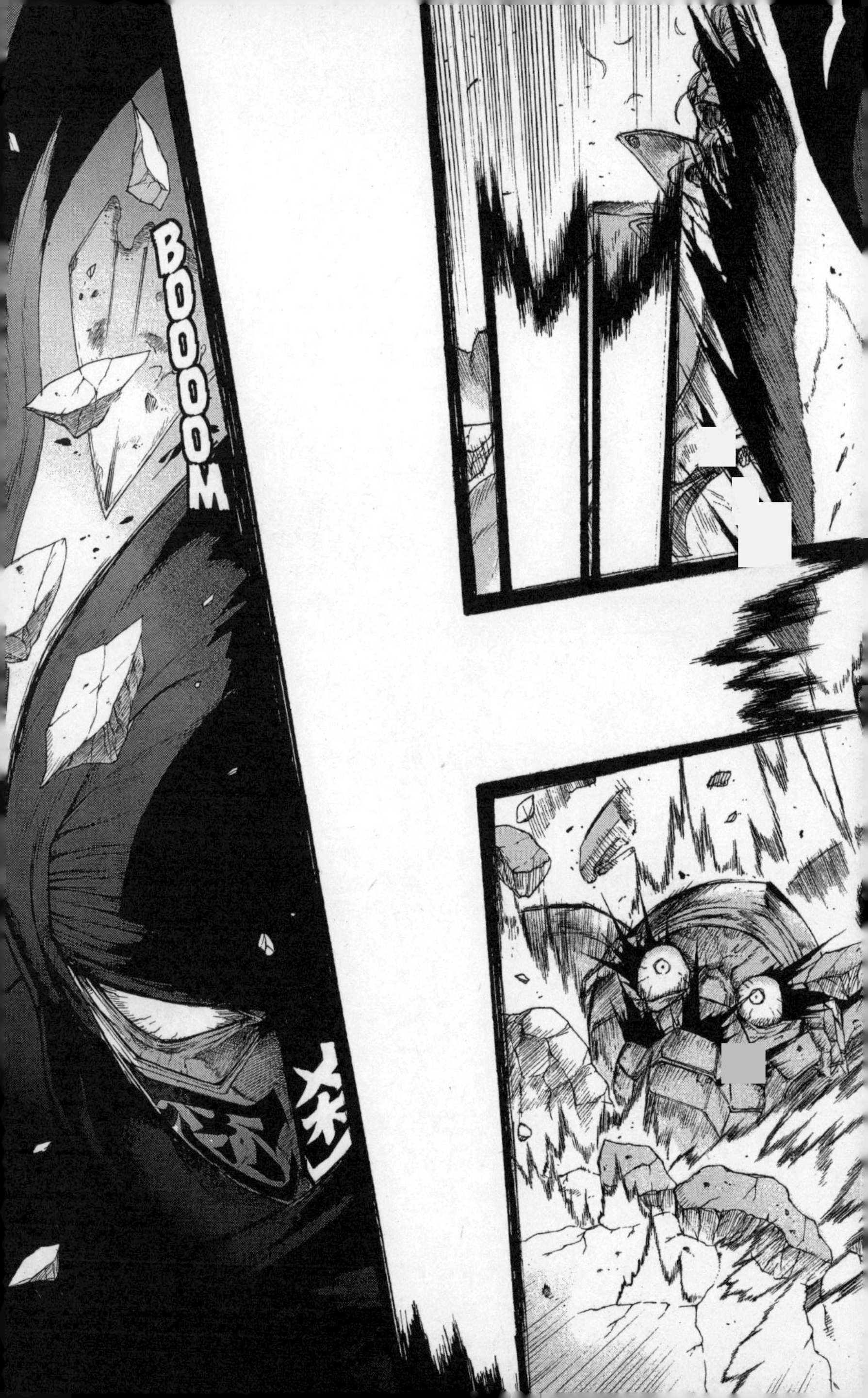
BOOOOM

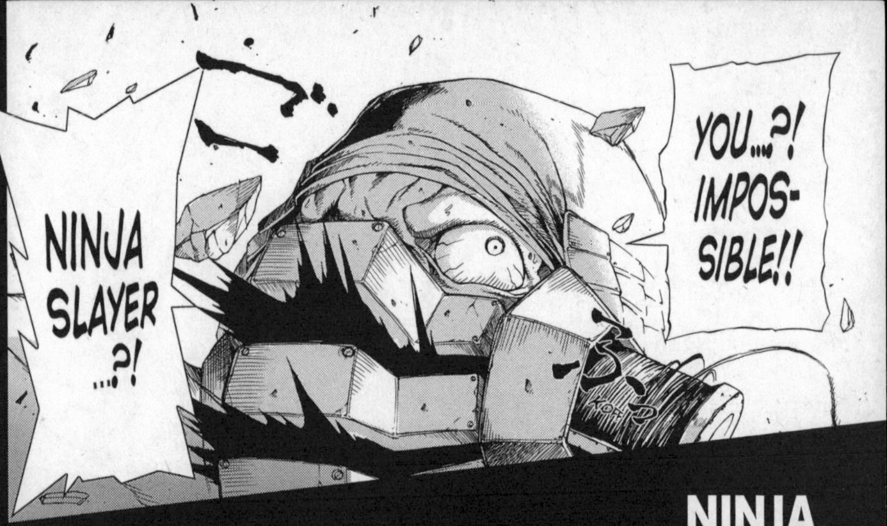
YOU...?! IMPOS-SIBLE!!
NINJA SLAYER ...?!

NINJA.

DEMIGOD-LIKE BEINGS WHO ONCE RULED JAPAN IN ITS HEIAN PERIOD. THEY ERASED THEMSELVES FROM HISTORY AFTER PERFORMING THE MYSTERIOUS HARA-KIRI RITES IN THE GOLDEN KINKAKU TEMPLE.

HOWEVER...

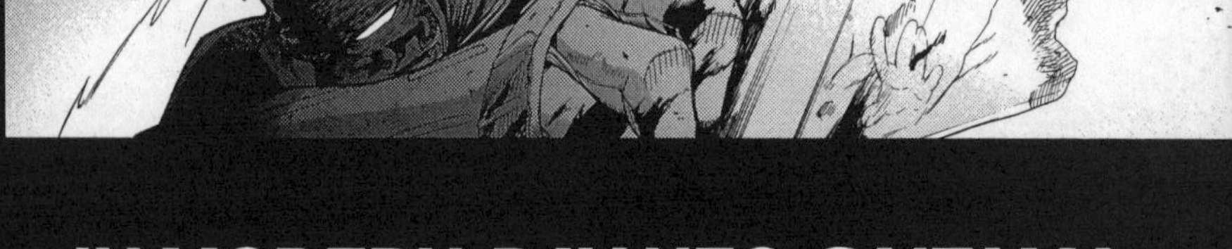

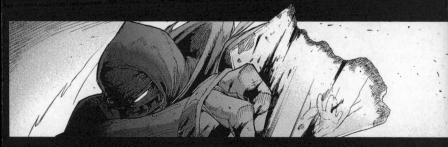

IN MODERN-DAY NEO-SAITAMA, NINJA HAVE BEEN RESURRECTED.

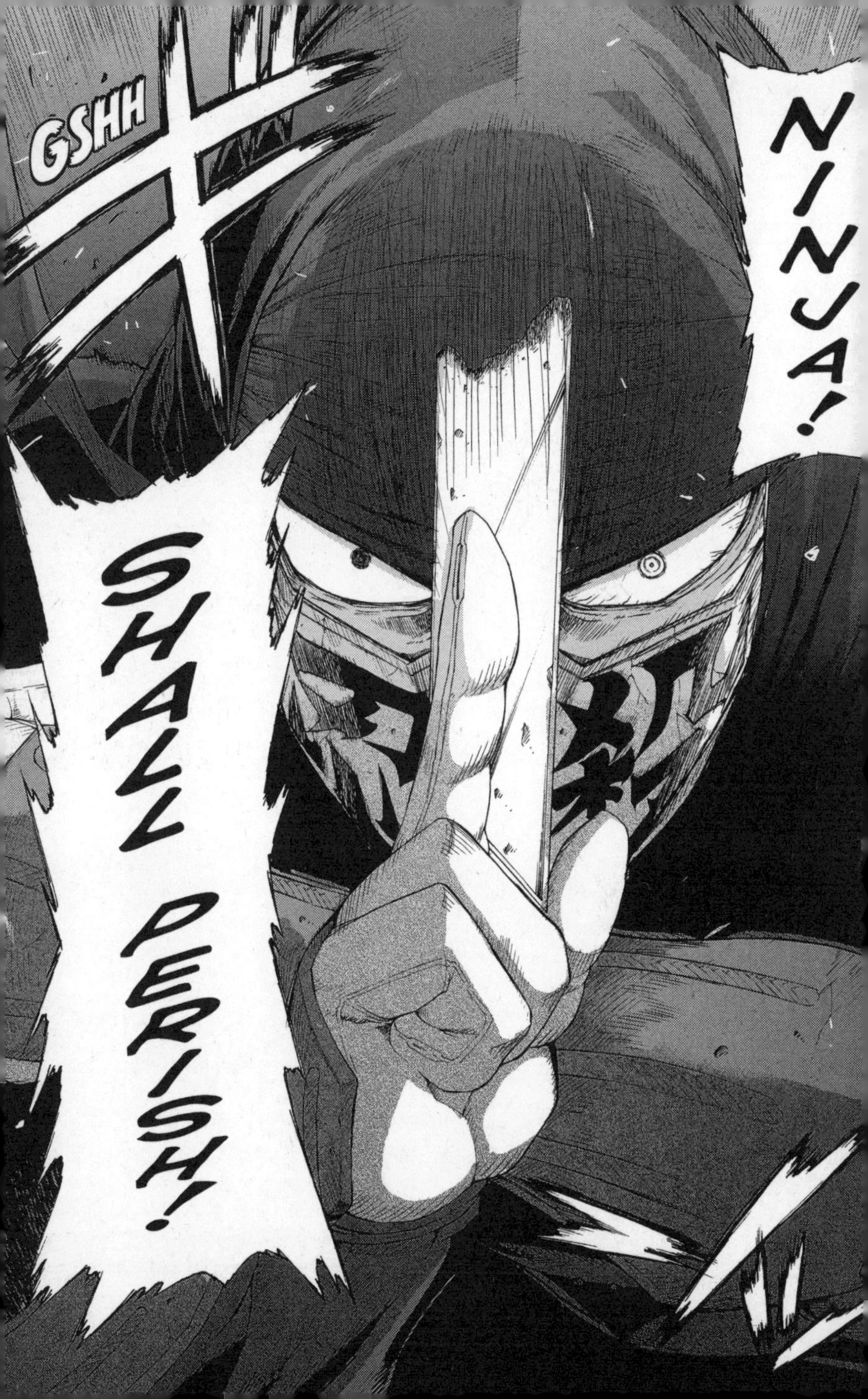
NINJA!
SHALL PERISH!
GSHH

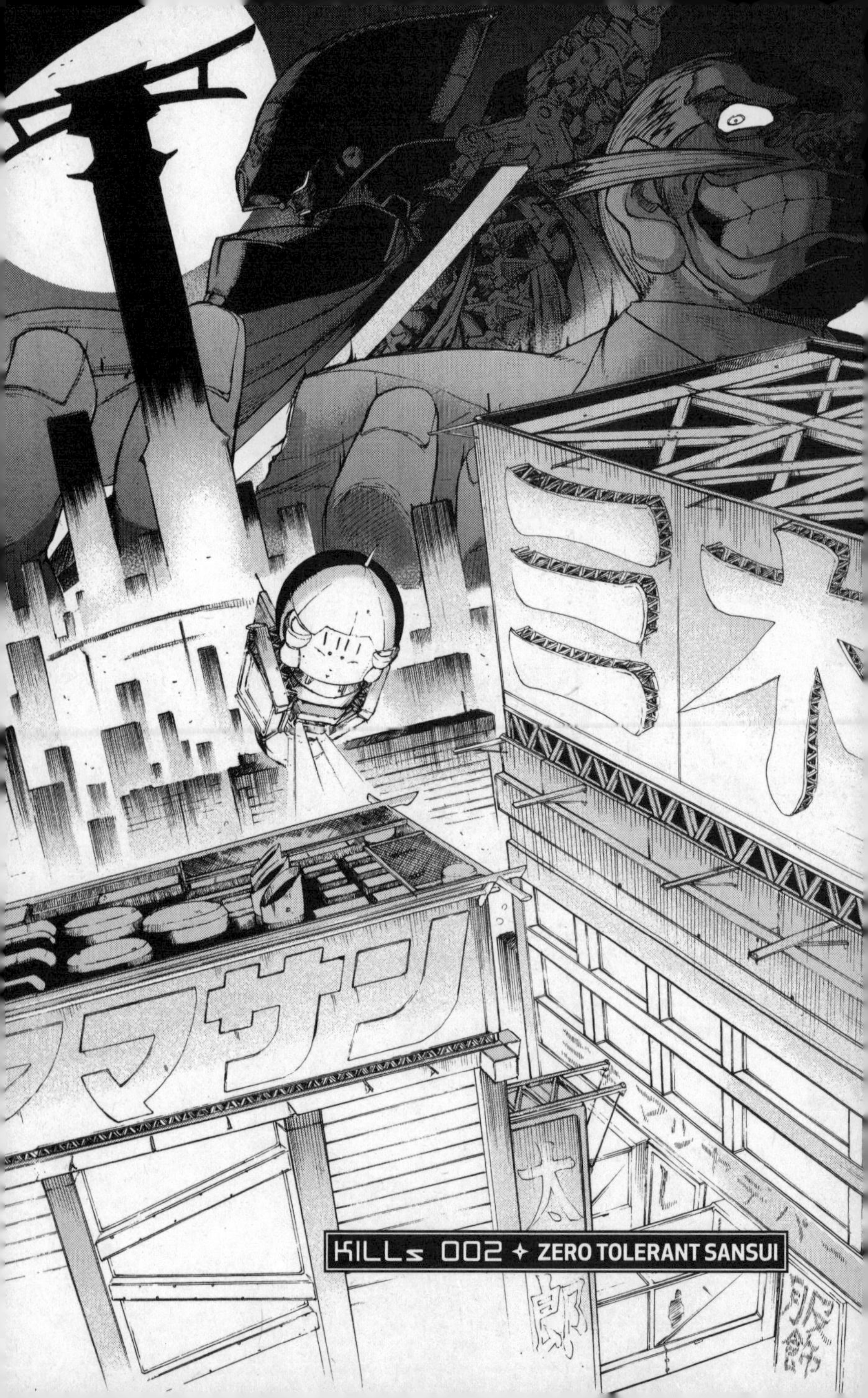
KILLs 002 ✦ ZERO TOLERANT SANSUI

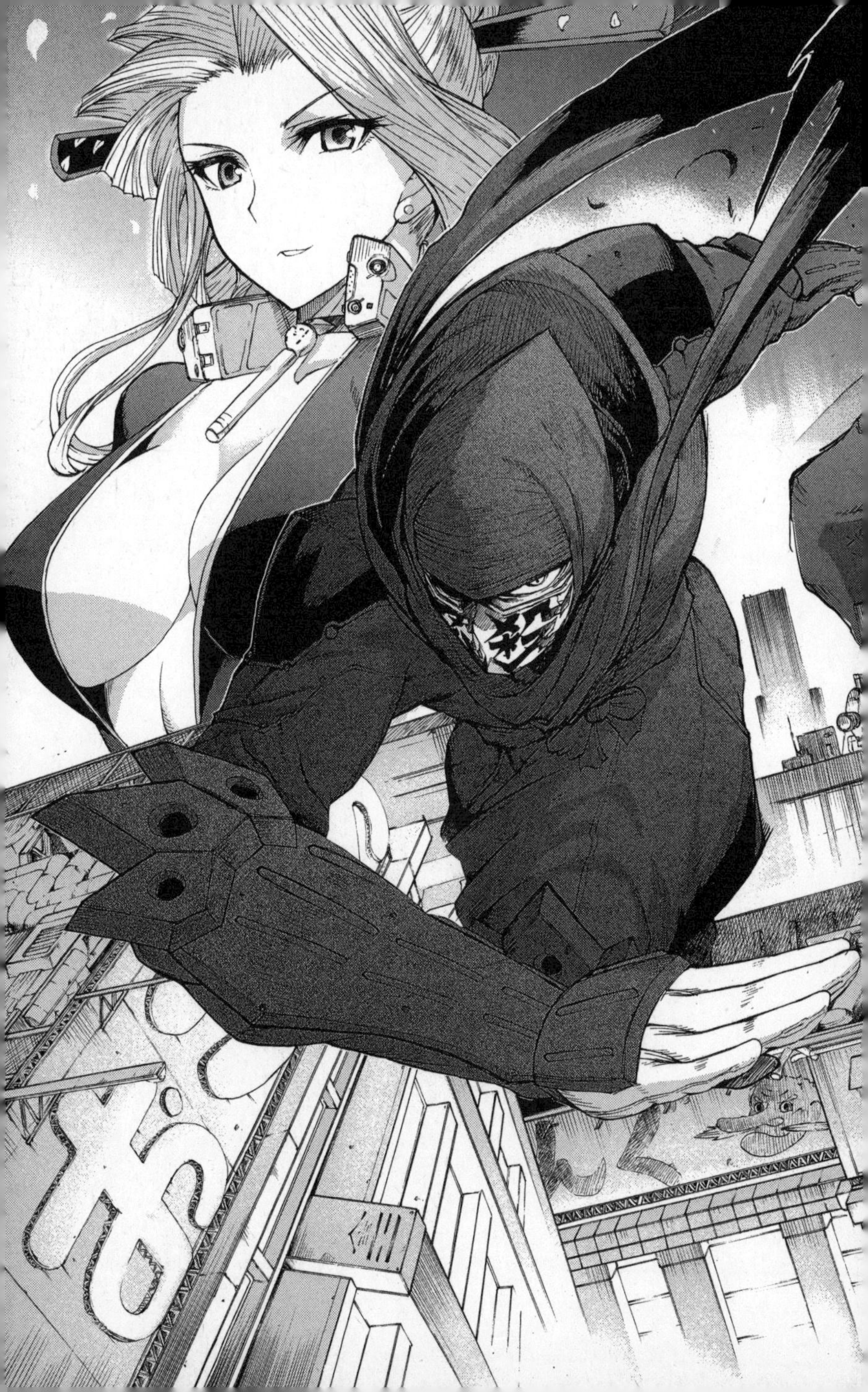

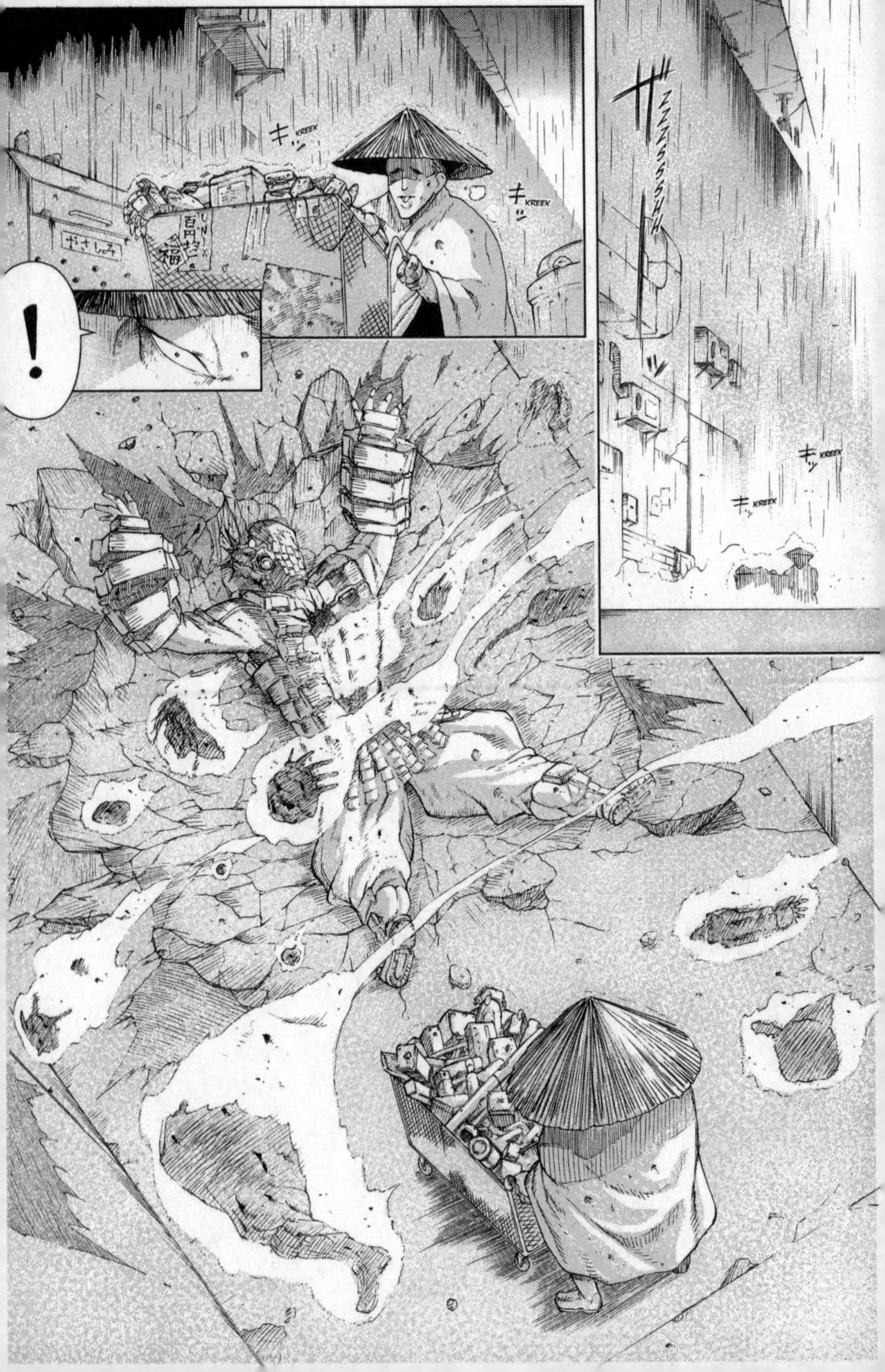
ザ ZZZSSSHH
ッ
キッ KREEK
キッ KREEK
キッ KREEK
キッ KREEK
百円均一
福
!

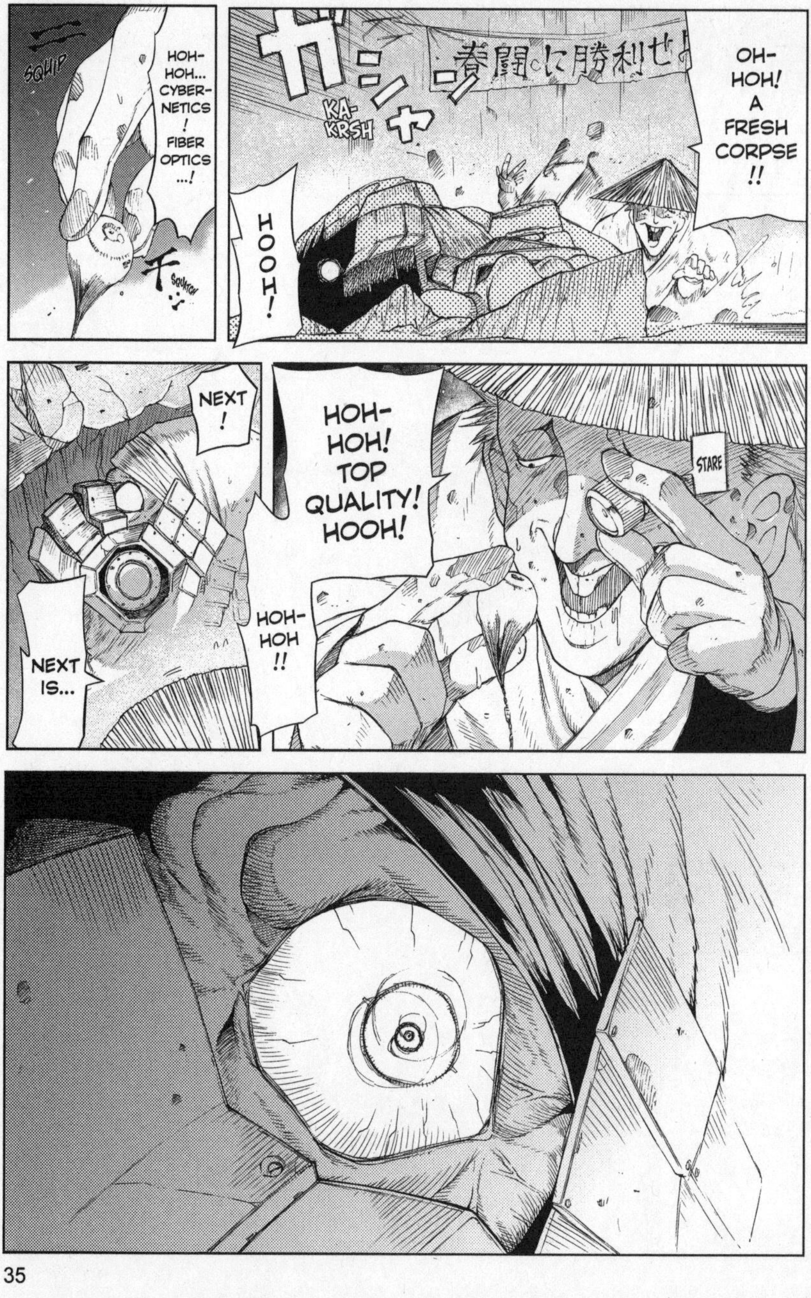
ガシャ
KA-KRSH
春闘に勝利せよ
OH-HOH! A FRESH CORPSE !!
HOOH!
HOH-HOH... CYBER-NETICS ! FIBER OPTICS ...!
SQUIP
SQUATCH
STARE
HOH-HOH! TOP QUALITY! HOOH!
HOH-HOH !!
NEXT !
NEXT IS...

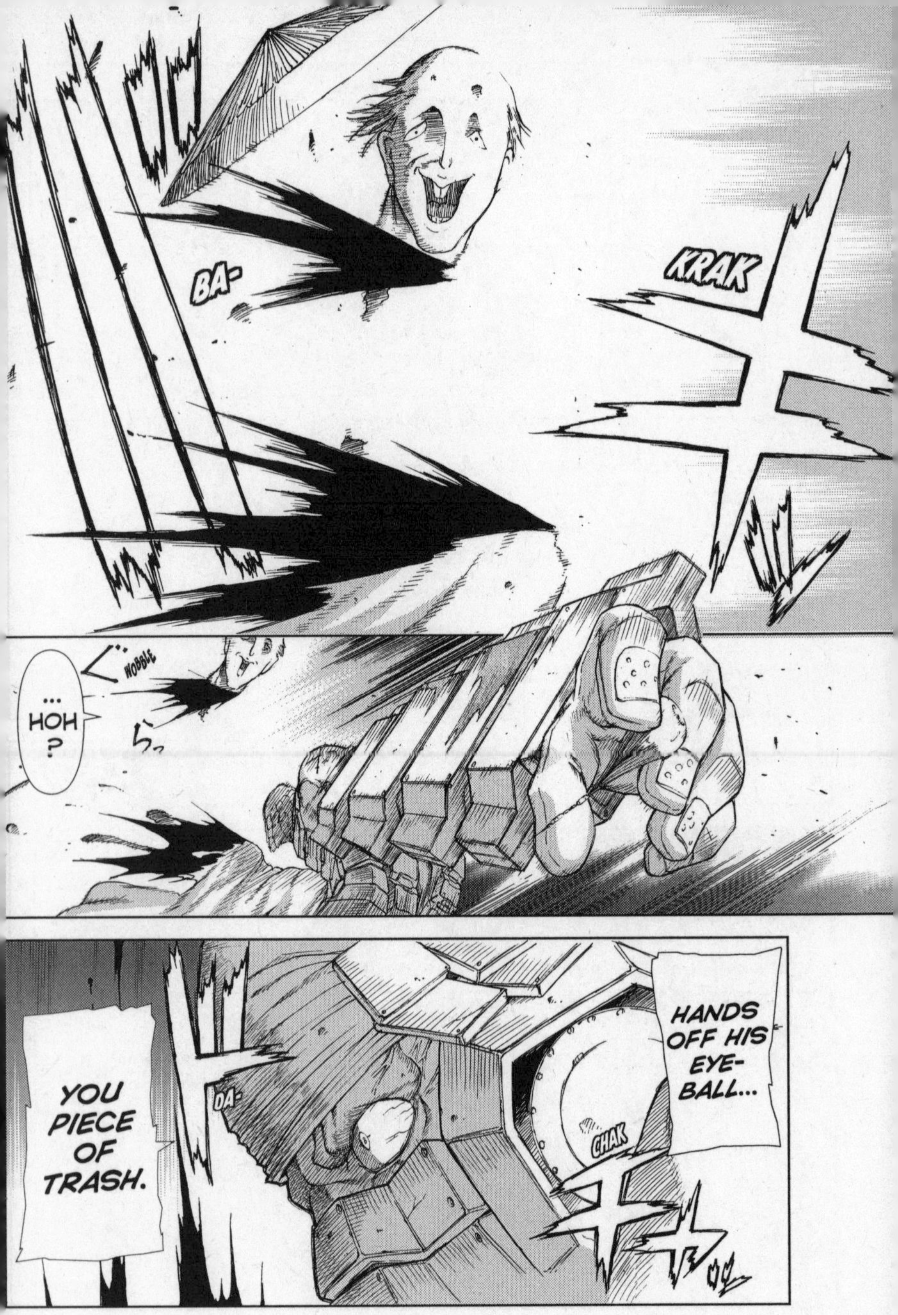
KRAK
BA-
WOBBLE
...HOH?
HANDS OFF HIS EYE-BALL...
CHAK
DA-
YOU PIECE OF TRASH.

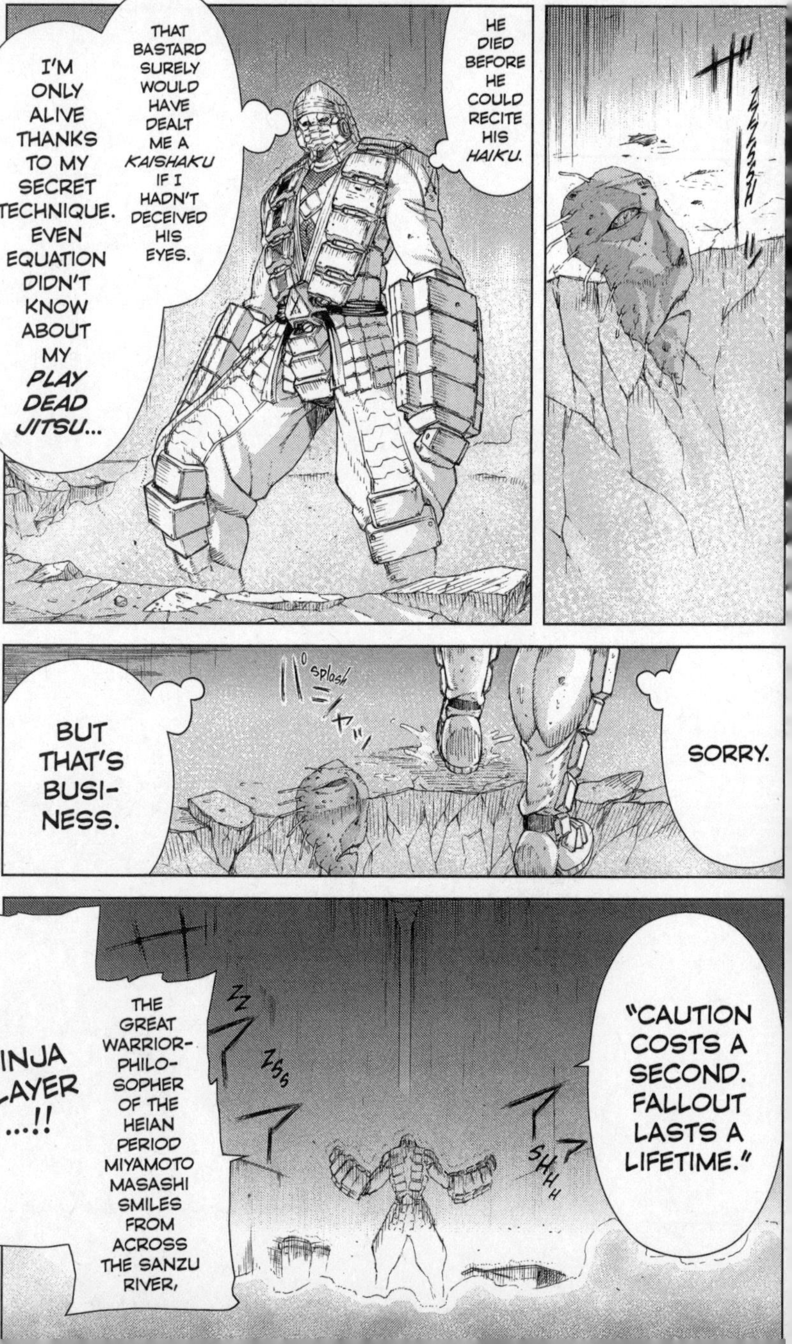
HE DIED BEFORE HE COULD RECITE HIS *HAIKU*.
THAT BASTARD SURELY WOULD HAVE DEALT ME A *KAISHAKU* IF I HADN'T DECEIVED HIS EYES.
I'M ONLY ALIVE THANKS TO MY SECRET TECHNIQUE. EVEN EQUATION DIDN'T KNOW ABOUT MY ***PLAY DEAD JITSU***...
SORRY.
splash
BUT THAT'S BUSI- NESS.
"CAUTION COSTS A SECOND. FALLOUT LASTS A LIFETIME."
THE GREAT WARRIOR-PHILO- SOPHER OF THE HEIAN PERIOD MIYAMOTO MASASHI SMILES FROM ACROSS THE SANZU RIVER,
SHHH
ZSS
NINJA SLAYER ...!!

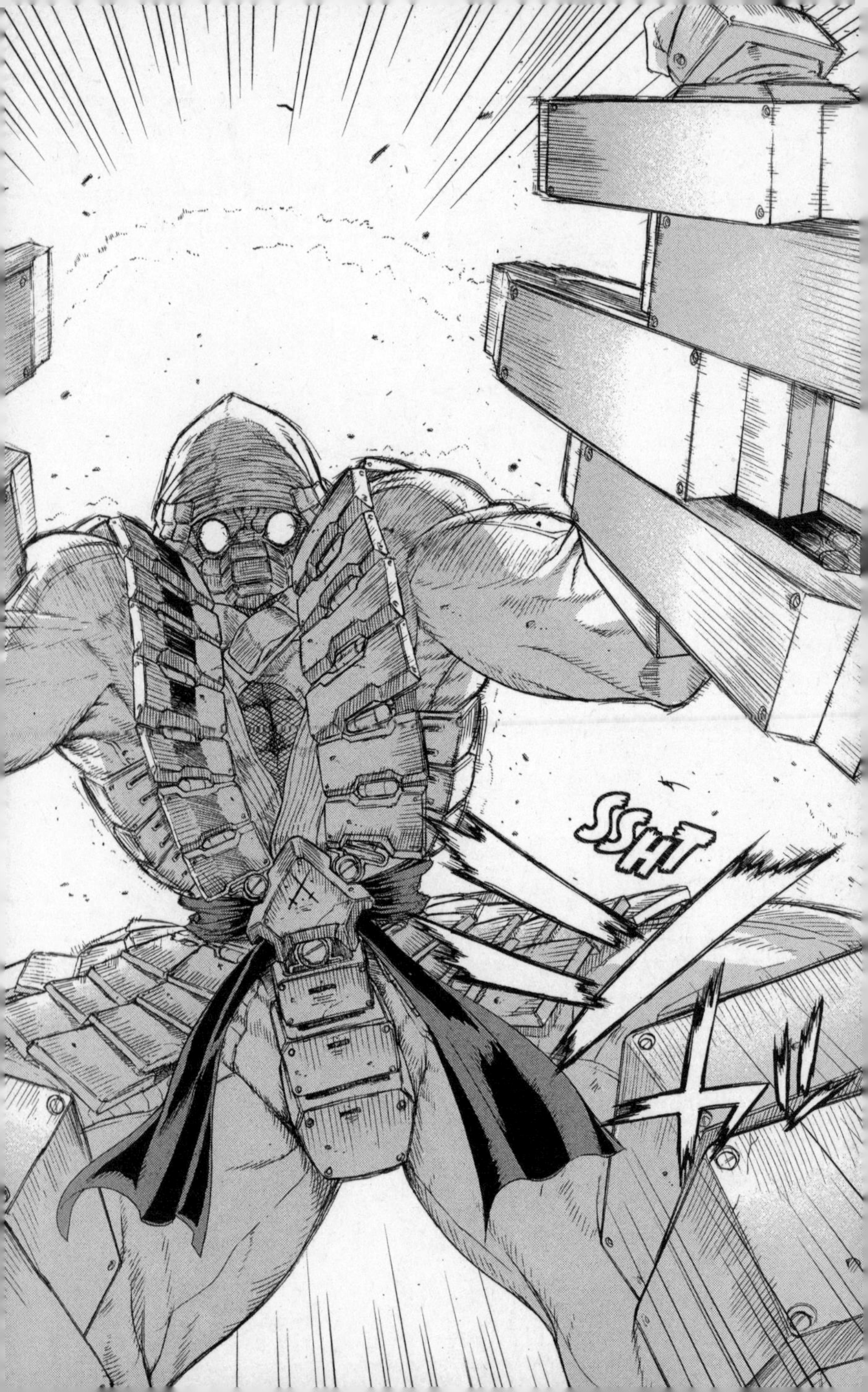
SSHT

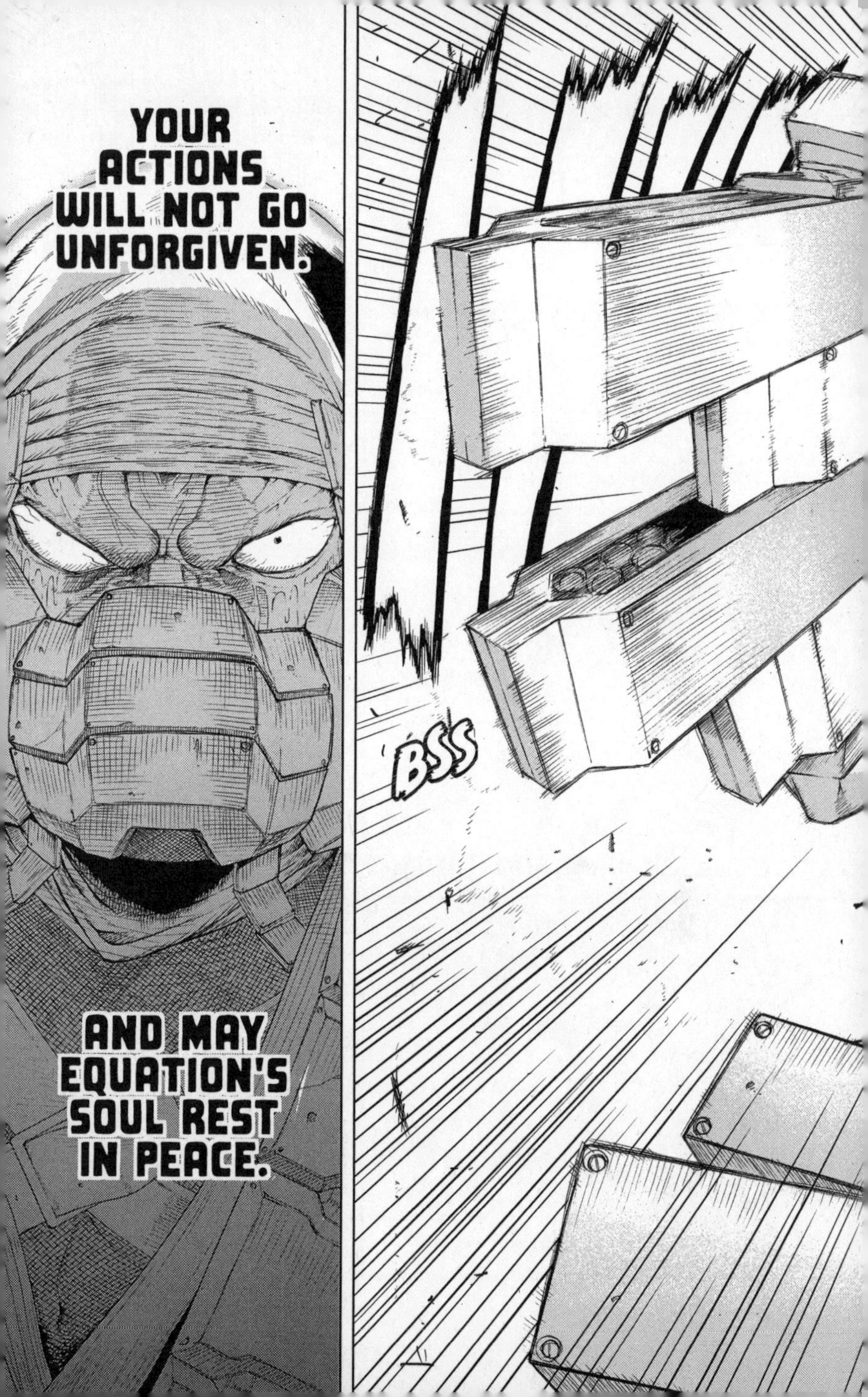
BSS
YOUR ACTIONS WILL NOT GO UNFORGIVEN.
AND MAY EQUATION'S SOUL REST IN PEACE.

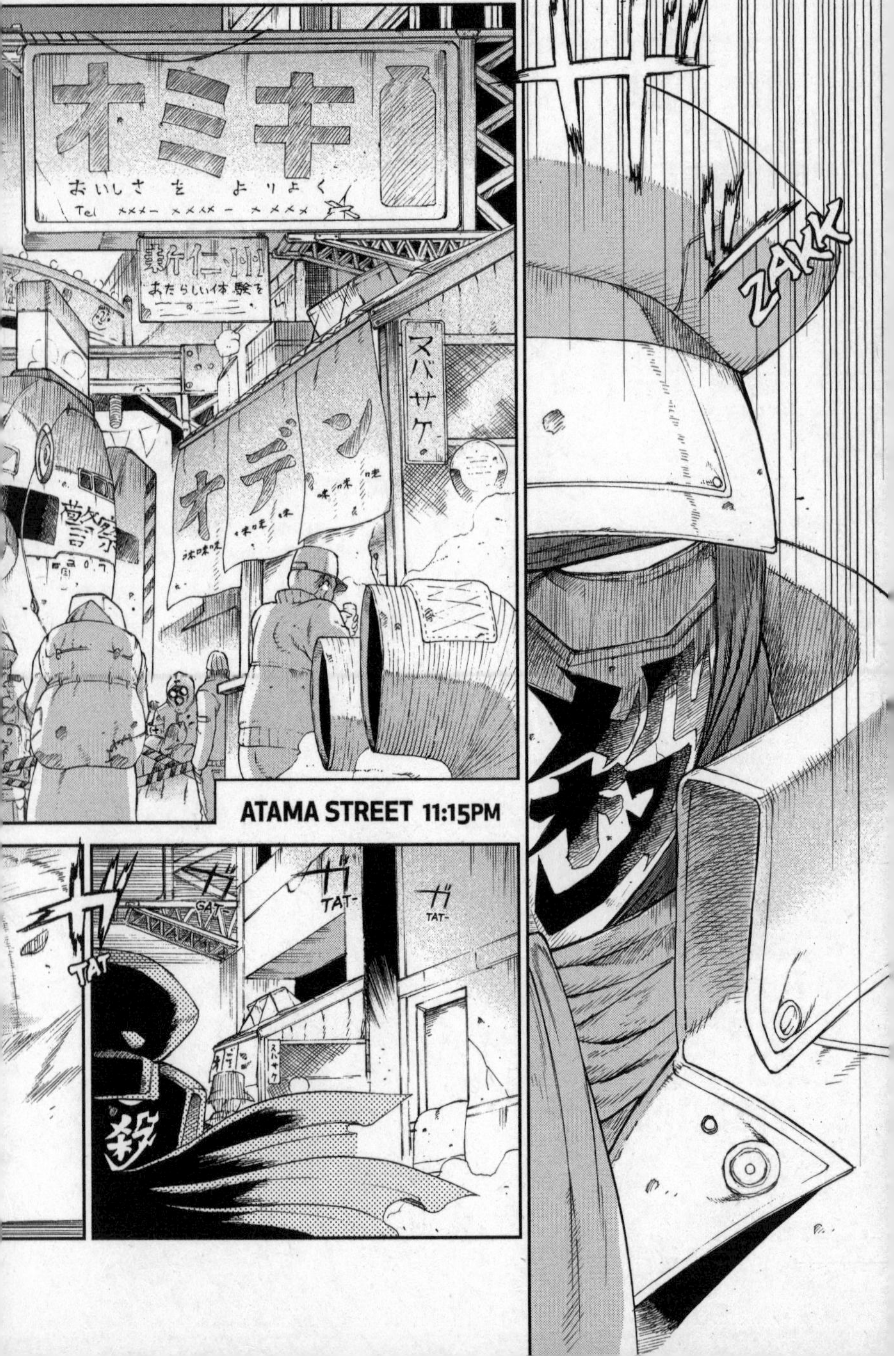
ZAKK
オミキ
おいしさを よりよく
あたらしい体験を
スバサケ
オデン
警察
ATAMA STREET 11:15PM
ガ
TAT-
ガ
TAT-
ガ
GAT
TAT

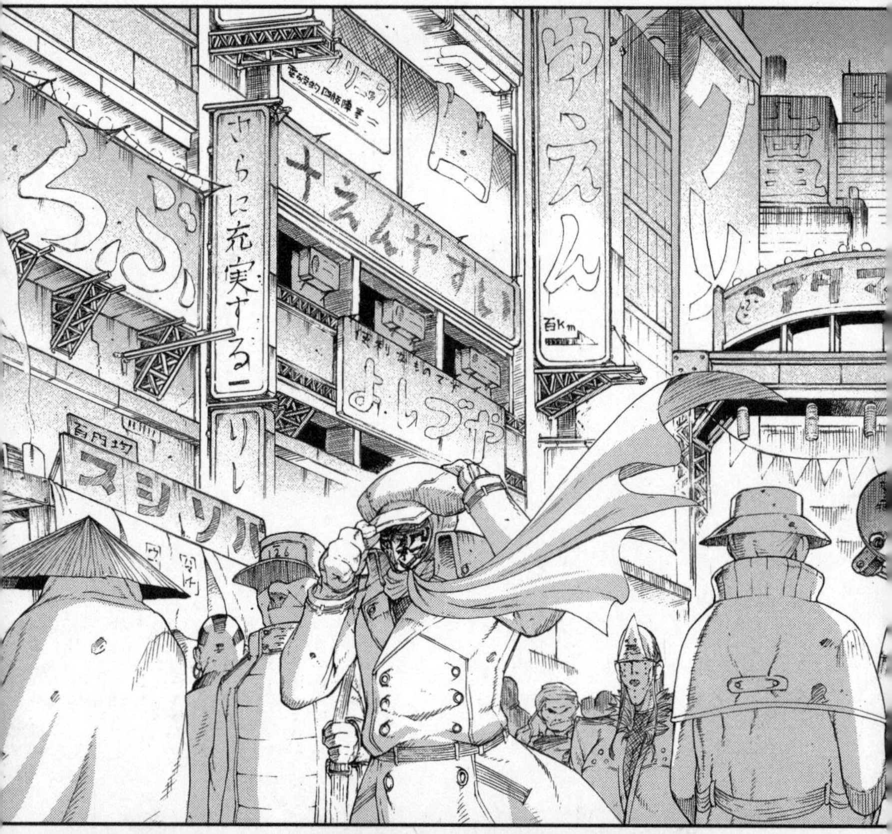
さらに充実する
十えんやすい
よしづや
ゆうえん
百Km
スシツバ
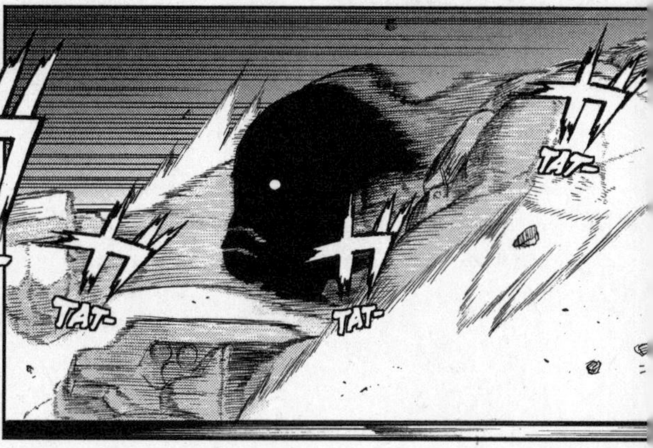
TAT-
TAT-
TAT-
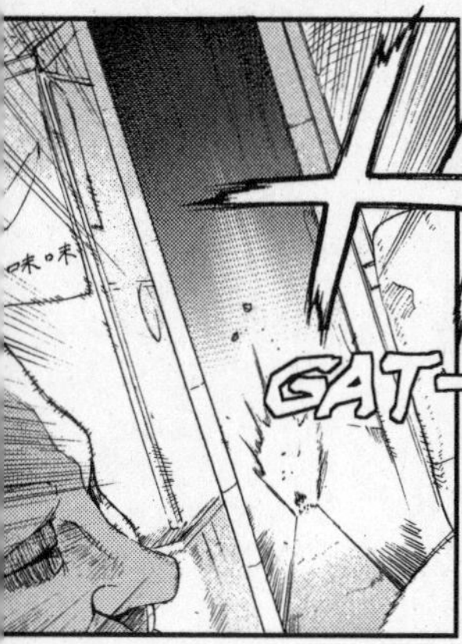
GAT-

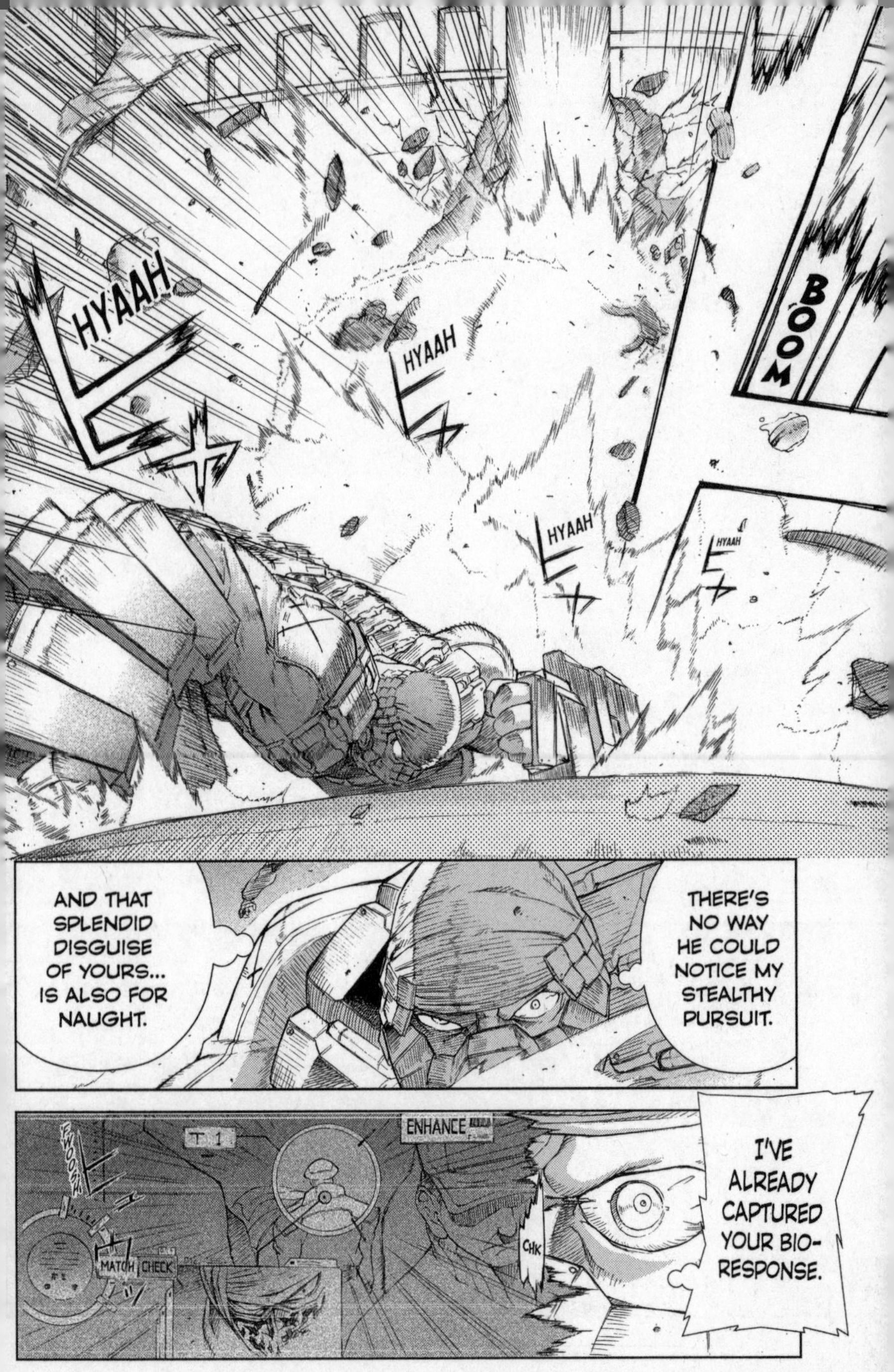
BOOM
HYAAH
HYAAH
HYAAH
HYAAH
THERE'S NO WAY HE COULD NOTICE MY STEALTHY PURSUIT.
AND THAT SPLENDID DISGUISE OF YOURS... IS ALSO FOR NAUGHT.
I'VE ALREADY CAPTURED YOUR BIO-RESPONSE.
CHK
ENHANCE
MATCH CHECK

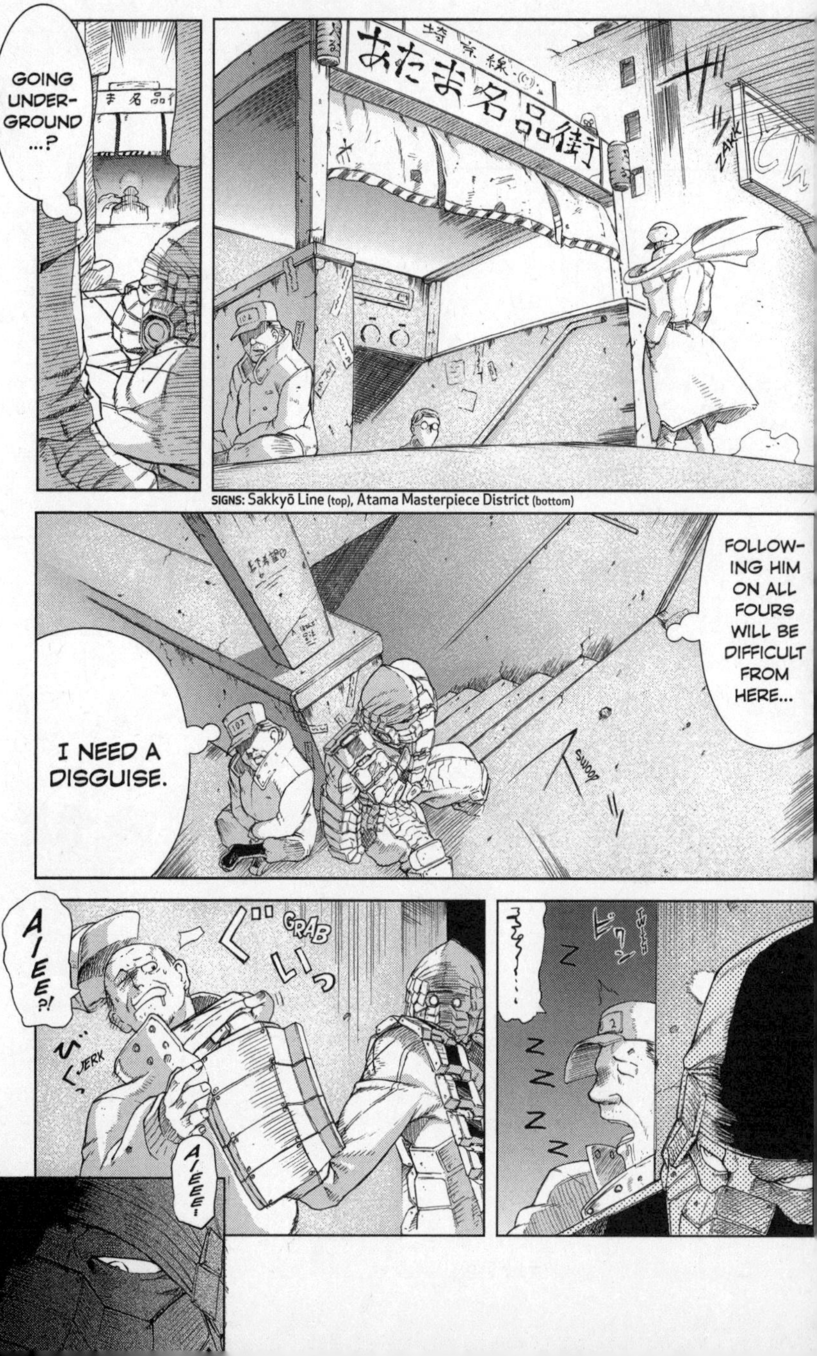
ZAKK
GOING UNDER-GROUND ...?
FOLLOWING HIM ON ALL FOURS WILL BE DIFFICULT FROM HERE...
I NEED A DISGUISE.
SWOOP
TWITCH
Z Z Z Z Z
Nn...
GRAB
AIEE?!
JERK
AIEEE...

SIGNS: Sakkyō Line (top), Atama Masterpiece District (bottom)

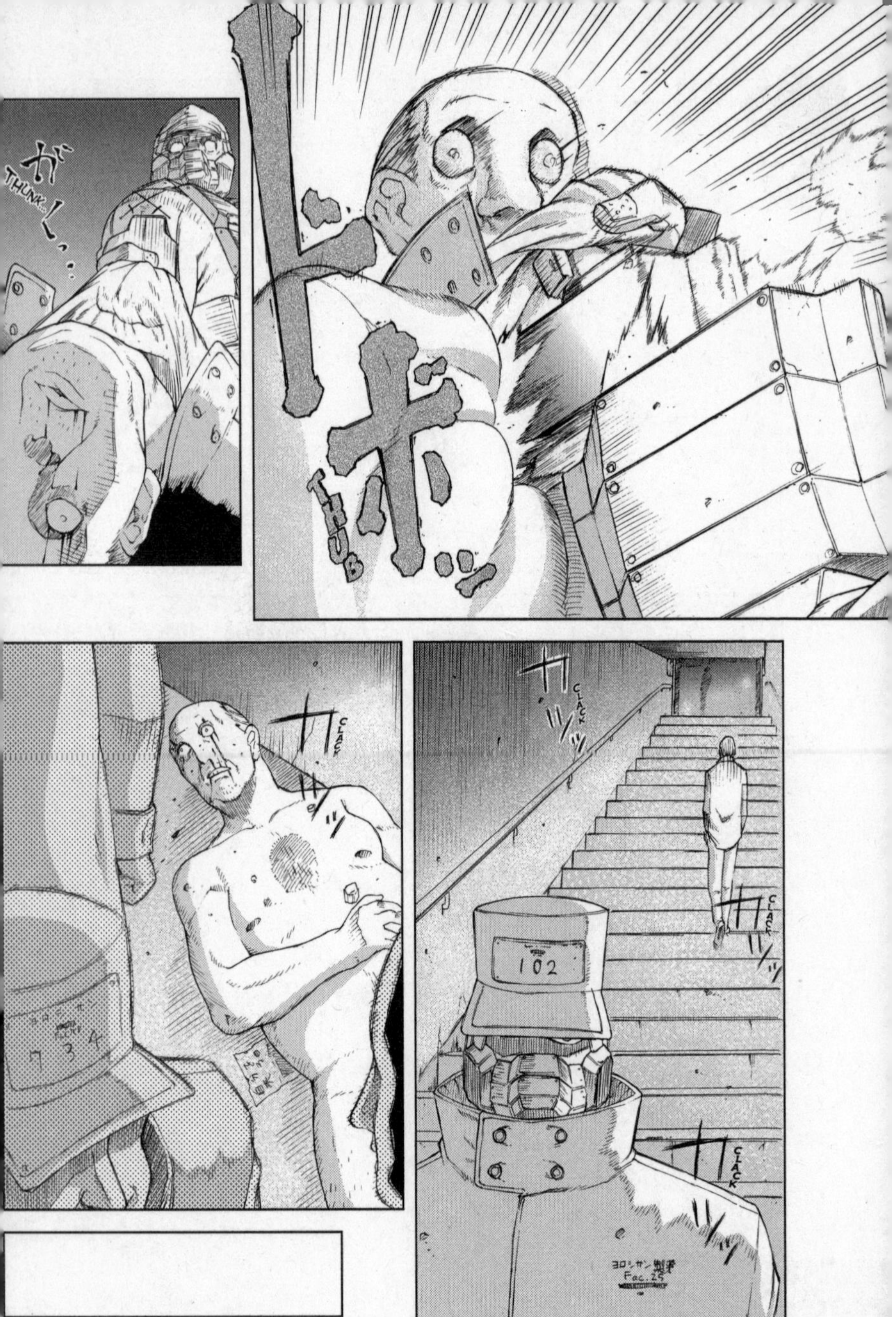
THUB
THUNK...
CLACK
102
ヨロシサン製薬
Fac.25
CLACK
CLACK
CLACK
734

CLOTHES (ABOVE), HAT (LEFT): Yoroshisan Pharmaceuticals

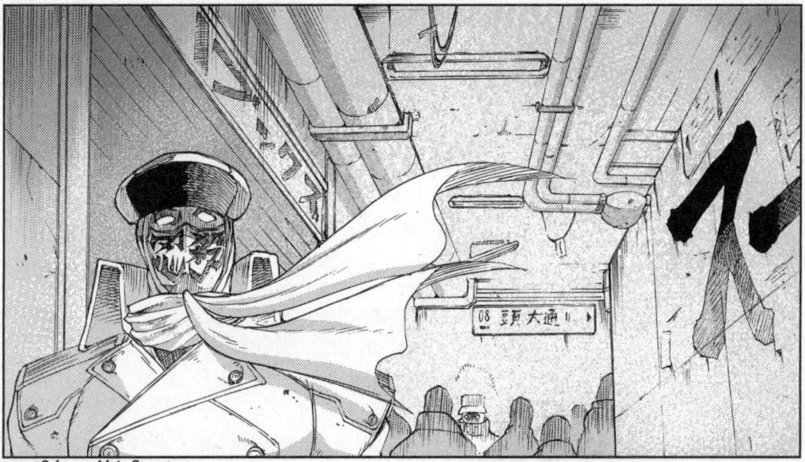
08 頭大通り

SIGN: 08 Atama Main Street

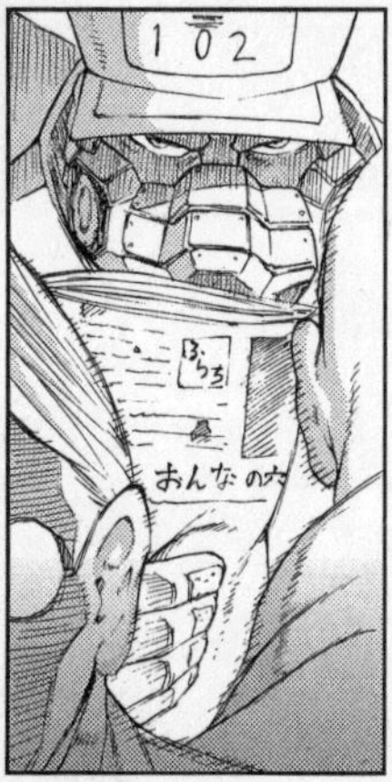
102

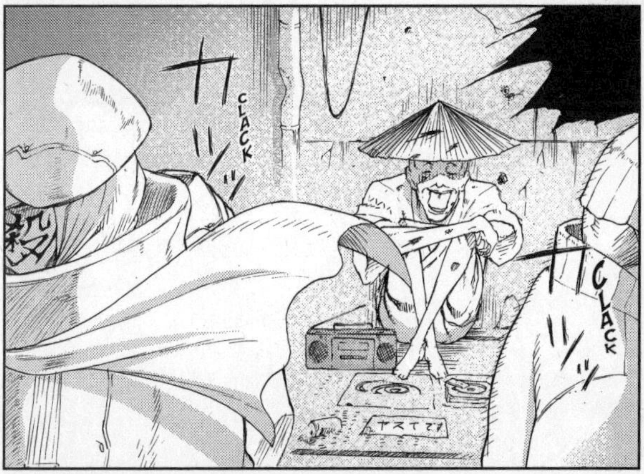
CLACK
CLACK

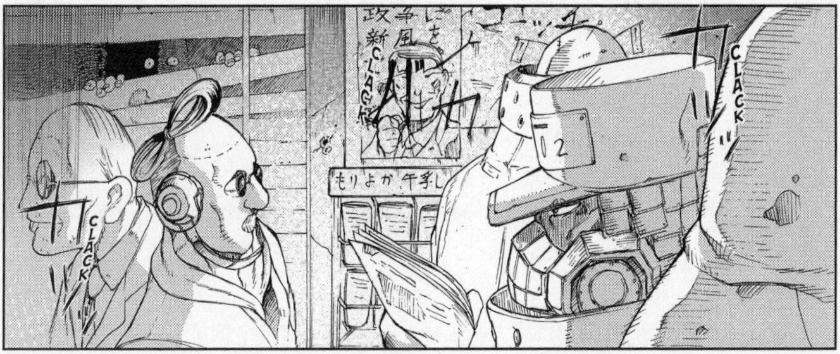
CLACK
CLACK

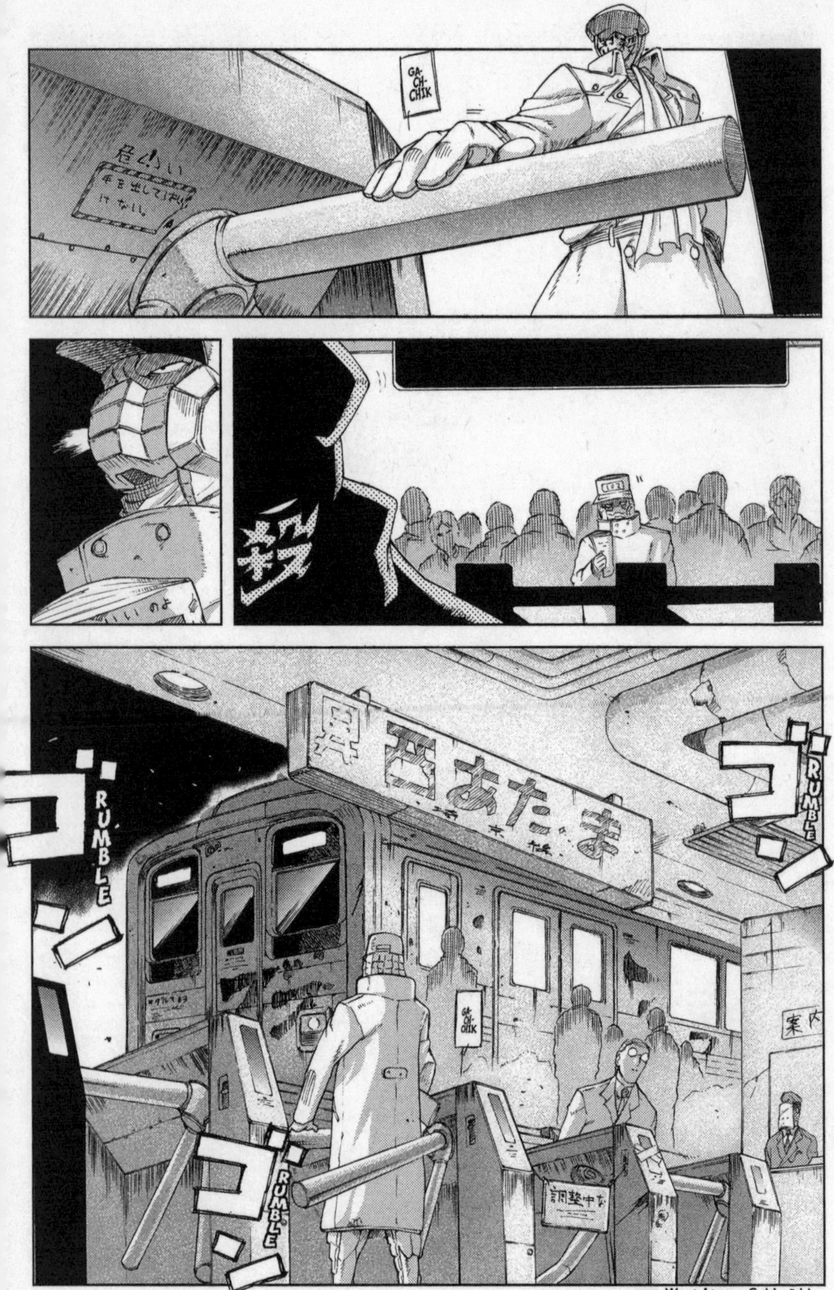
GA-CHI-CHIK
殺
西あたま
RUMBLE
RUMBLE
GA-CHIK
案内
調整中
RUMBLE

SIGN: West Atama Sakkyō Line

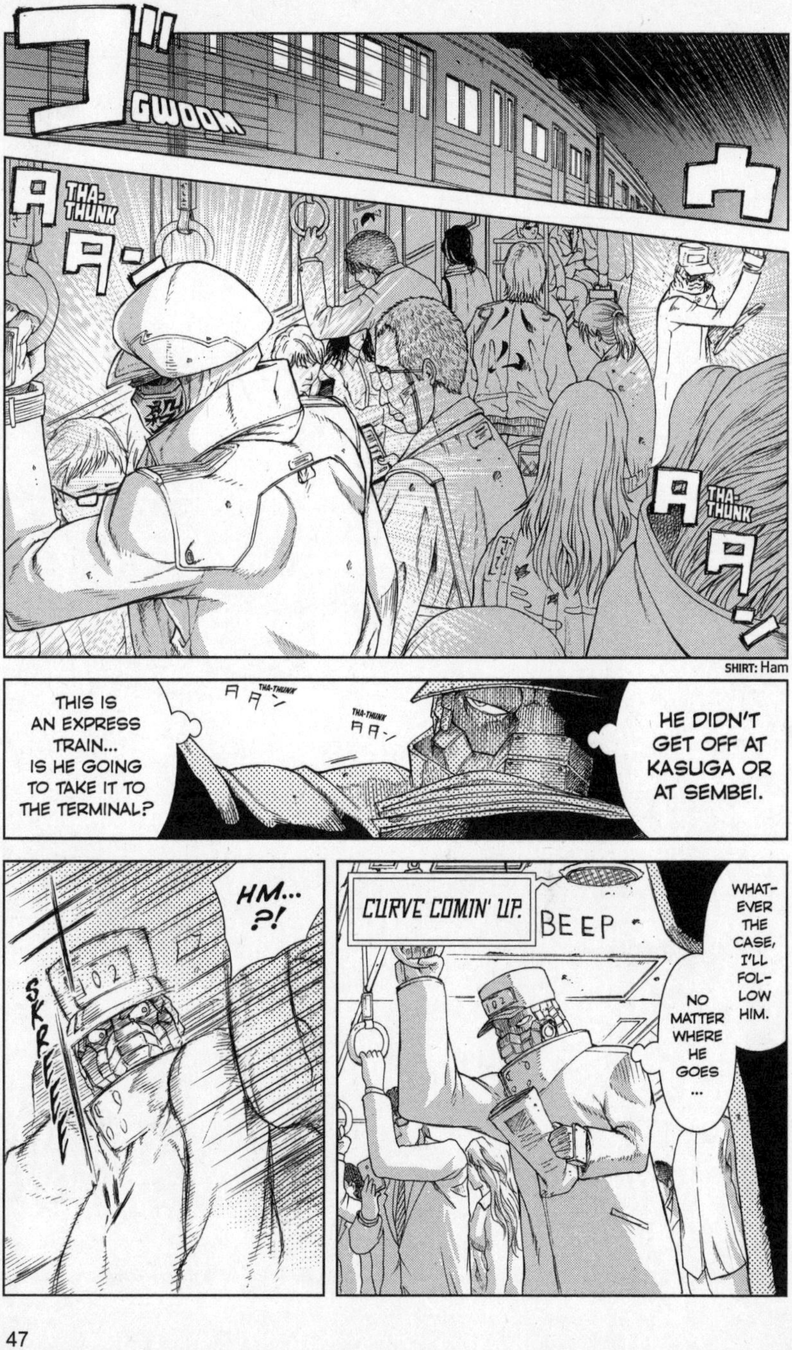
GWOOM
THA-THUNK
THA-THUNK
SHIRT: Ham
HE DIDN'T GET OFF AT KASUGA OR AT SEMBEI.
THA-THUNK
THA-THUNK
THIS IS AN EXPRESS TRAIN... IS HE GOING TO TAKE IT TO THE TERMINAL?
CURVE COMIN' UP.
BEEP
WHATEVER THE CASE, I'LL FOLLOW HIM.
NO MATTER WHERE HE GOES...
HM... ?!
SKREEEE

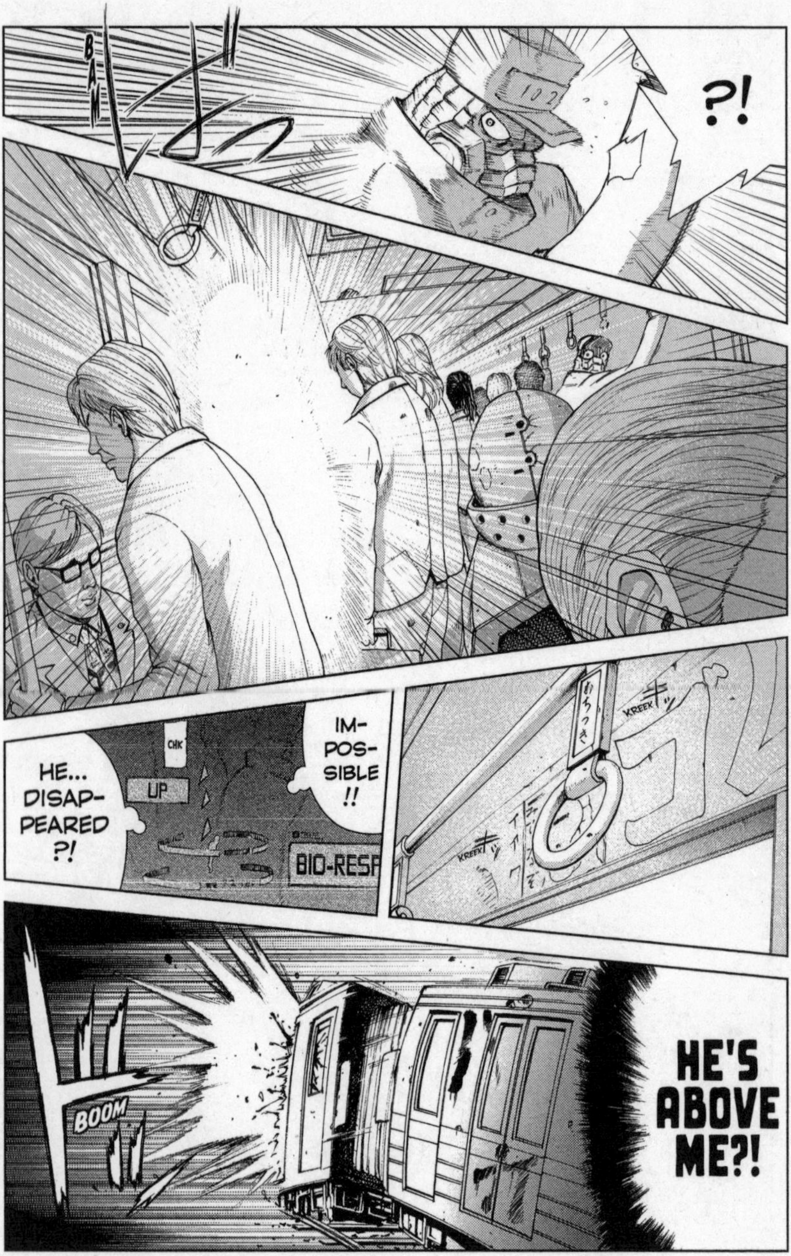
?!
BAM
KREEK
KREEK
IM-POSSIBLE!!
CHK
HE... DISAPPEARED?!
UP
BIO-RESP
HE'S ABOVE ME?!
BOOM

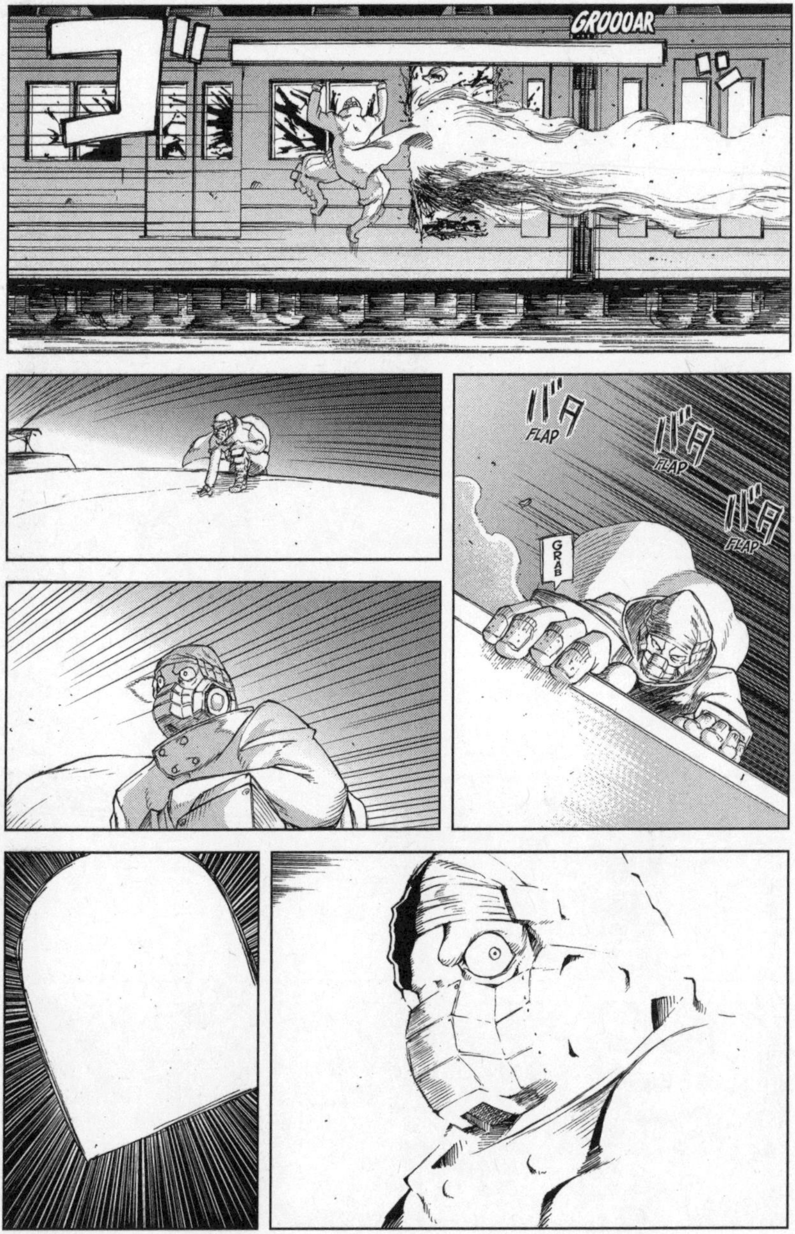
ゴ
GROOOAR
ゴ
バタ
FLAP
バタ
FLAP
バタ
FLAP
GRAB

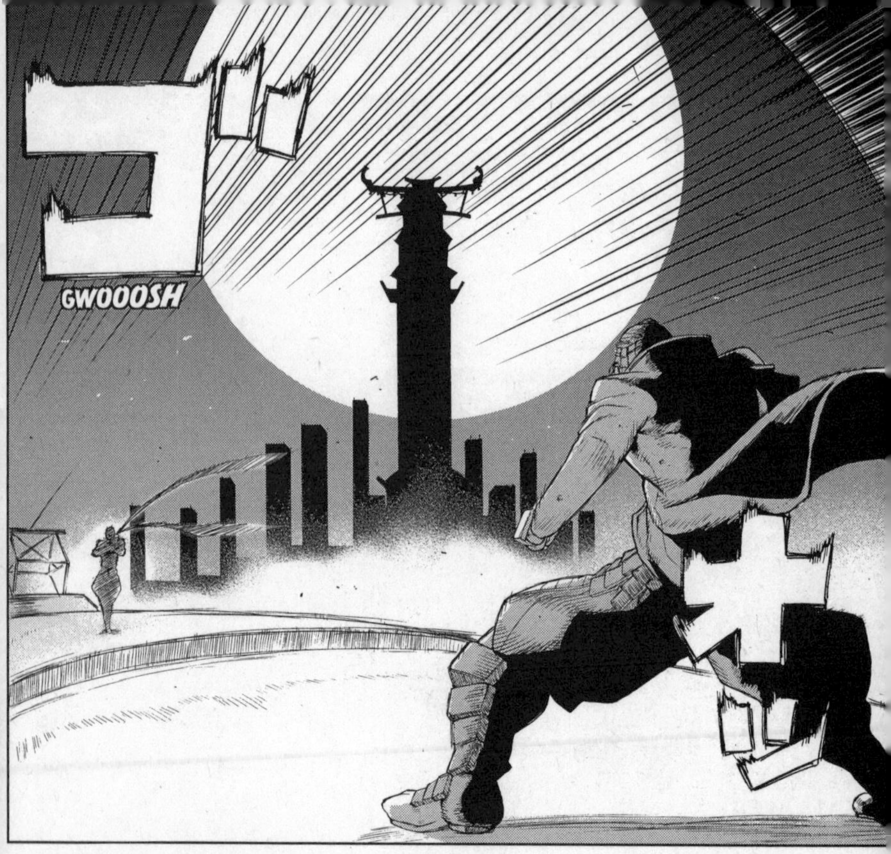
ゴゴ
GWOOOSH
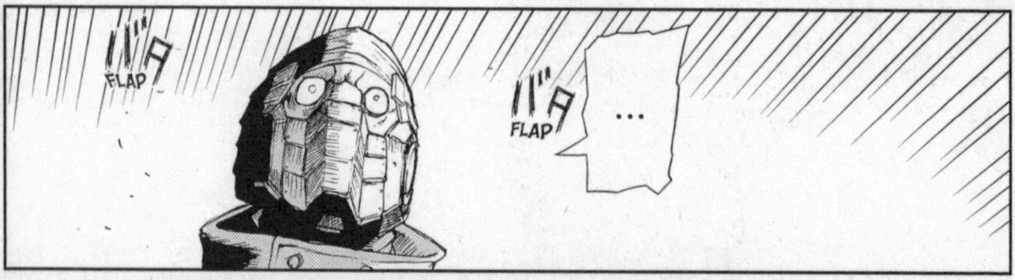
バ
FLAP
...
バ
FLAP
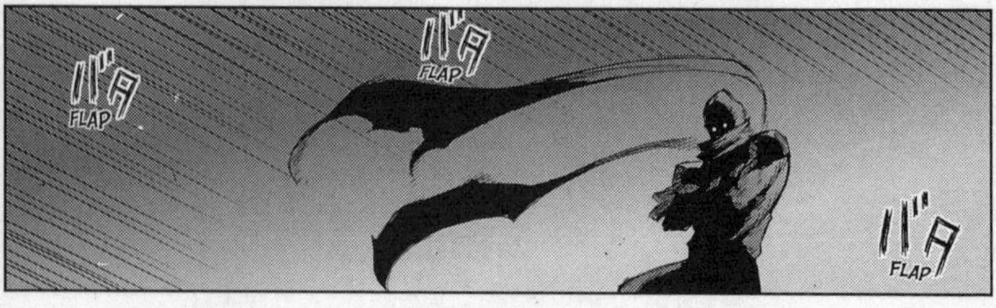
バ
FLAP
バ
FLAP
バ
FLAP

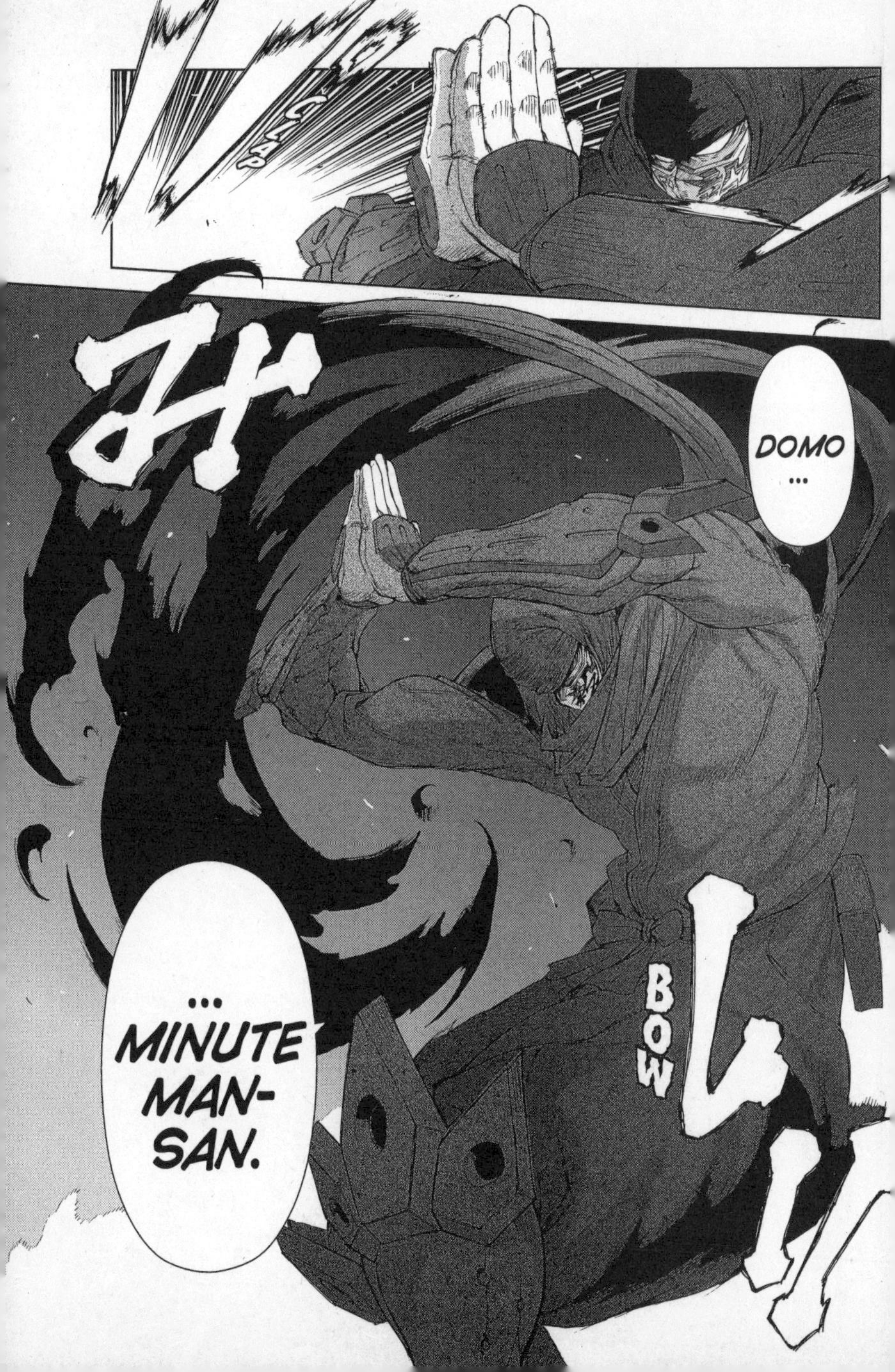
CLAP
DOMO ...
... MINUTE MAN-SAN.
BOW

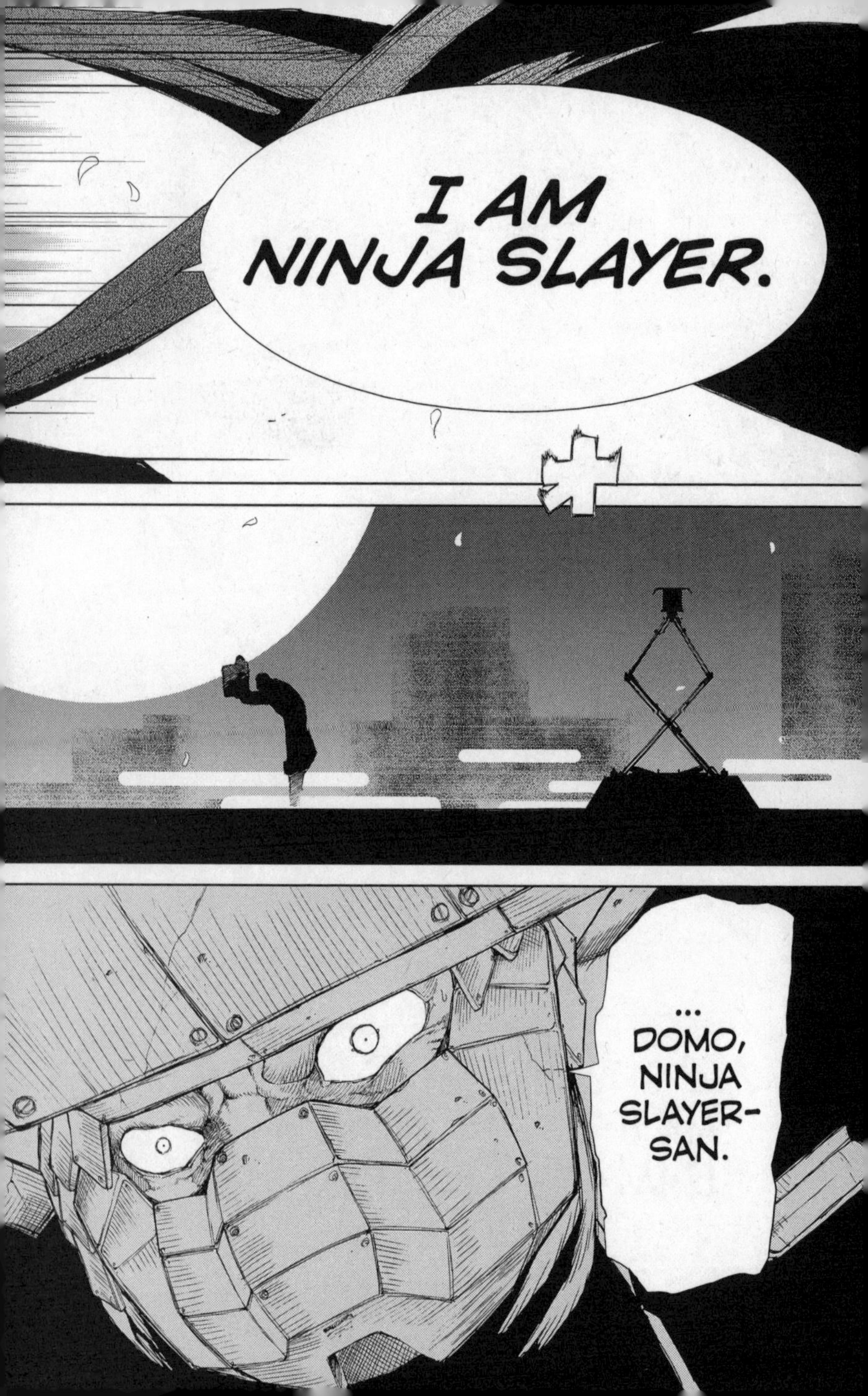
I AM NINJA SLAYER.
...DOMO, NINJA SLAYER-SAN.

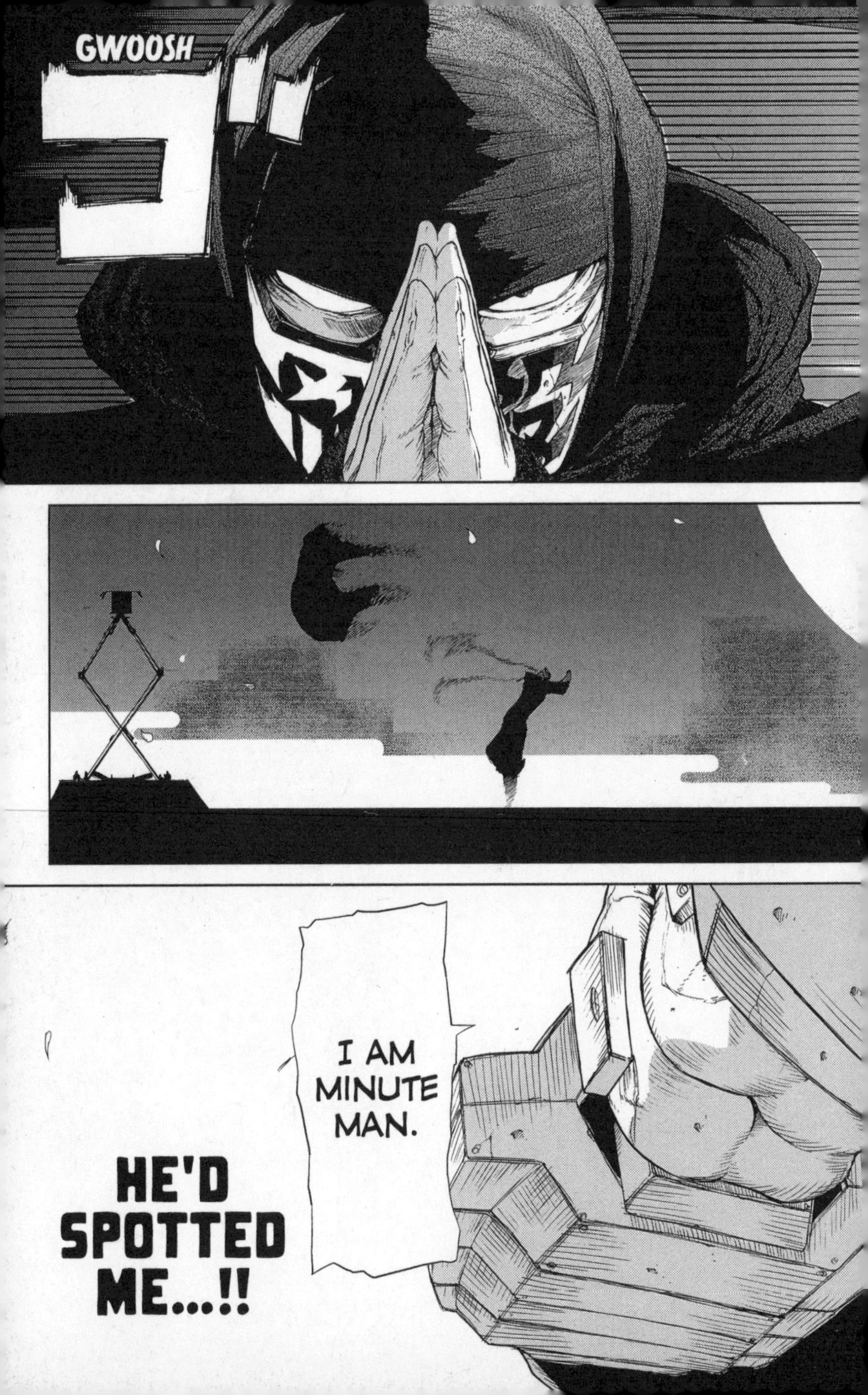
GWOOSH
I AM MINUTE MAN.
HE'D SPOTTED ME...!!

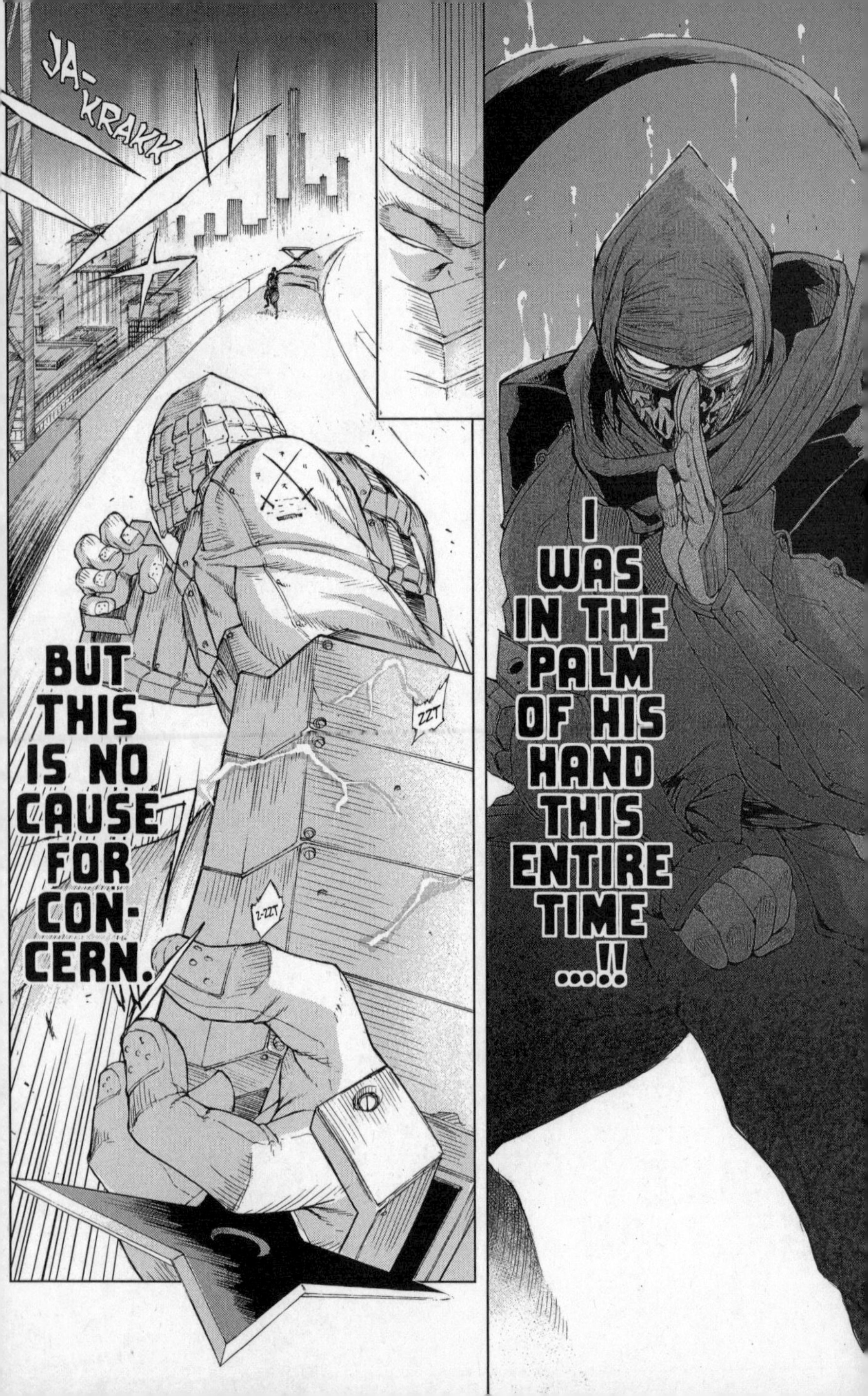
I WAS IN THE PALM OF HIS HAND THIS ENTIRE TIME ...!!
JA-KRAKK
ZZT
Z-ZZT
BUT THIS IS NO CAUSE FOR CON-CERN.

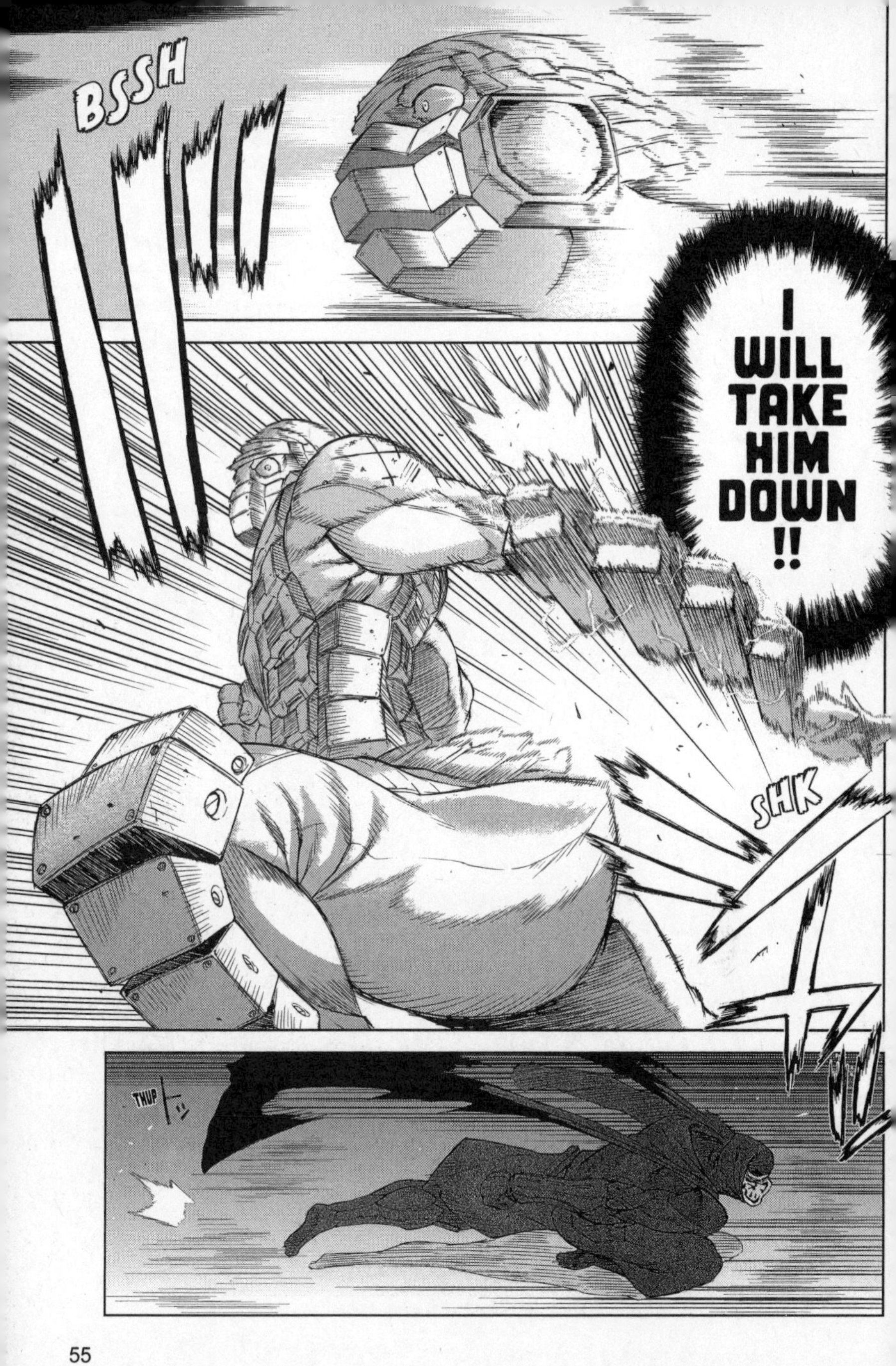
BSSH
I WILL TAKE HIM DOWN!!
SHK
THUP

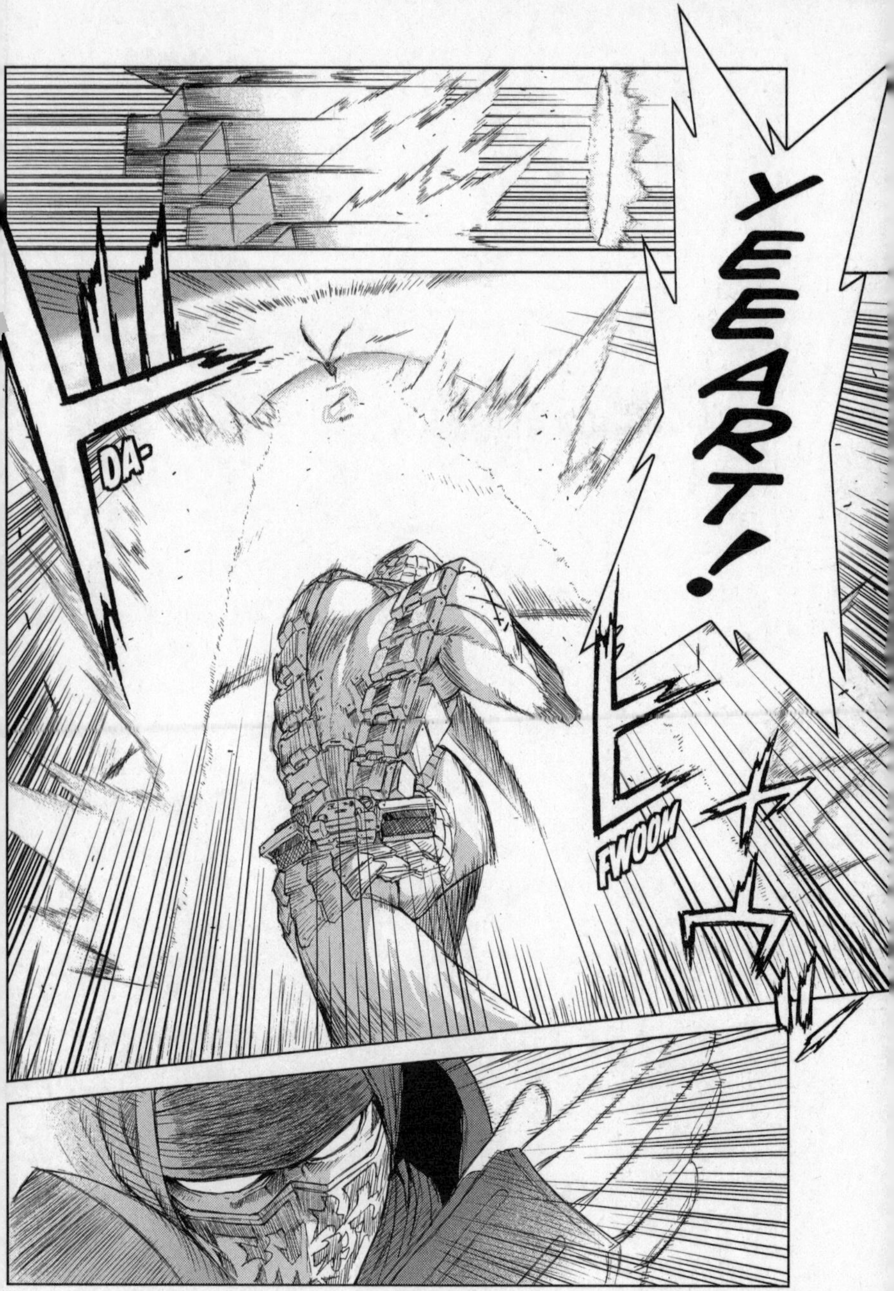
YEART!
DA-
FWOOM

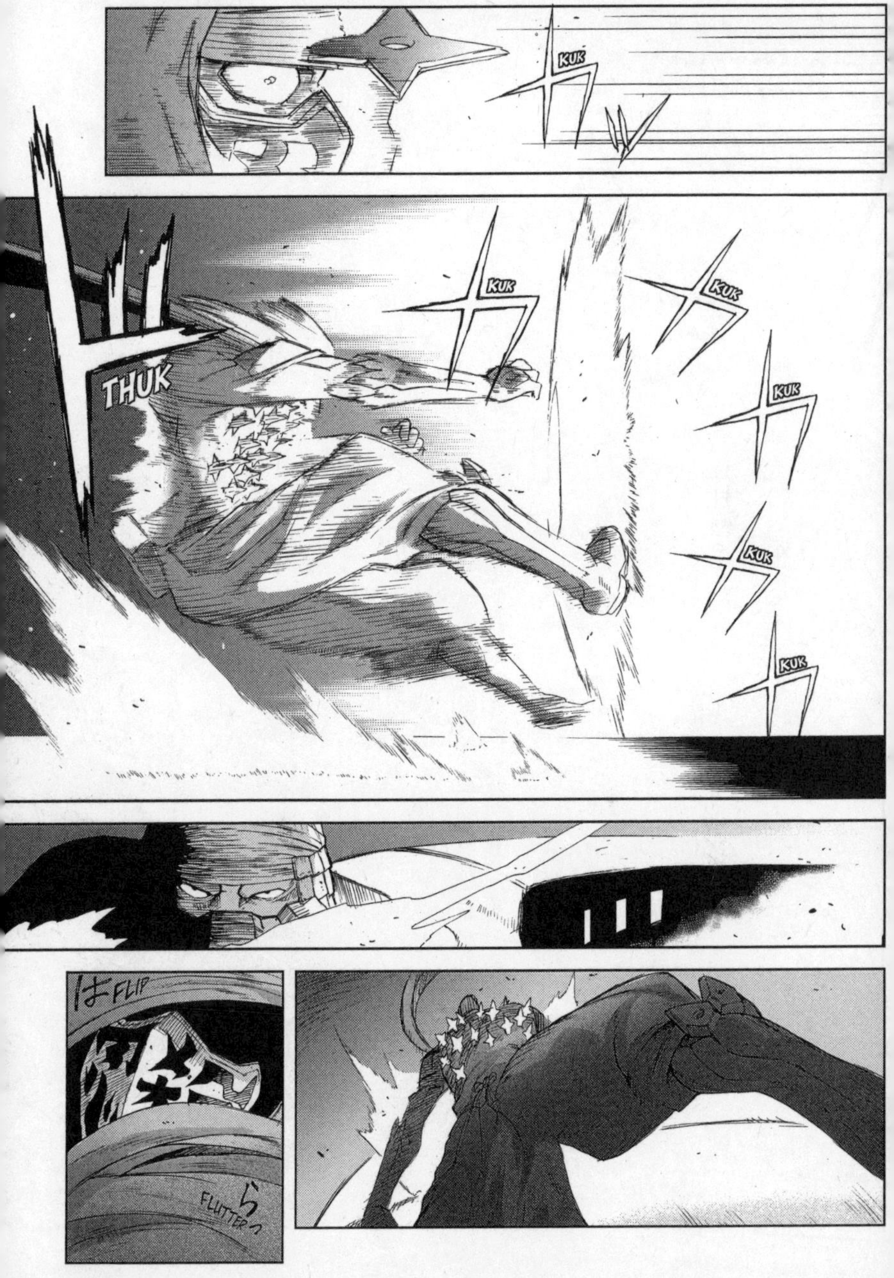
KUK
KUK
KUK
KUK
KUK
KUK
THUK
はFLIP
らFLUTTER

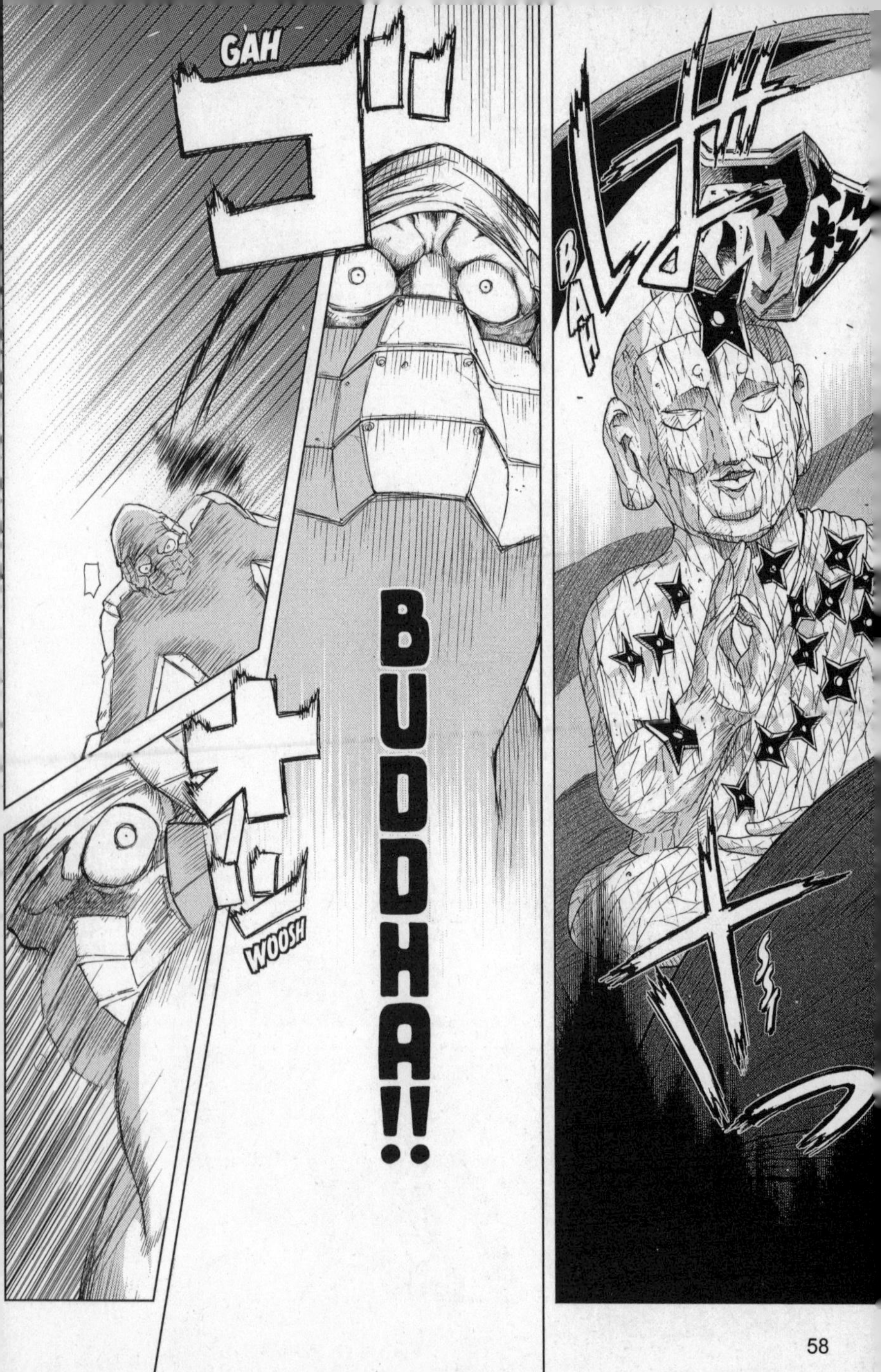
BAH
GAH
BUDDHA!!
WOOSH

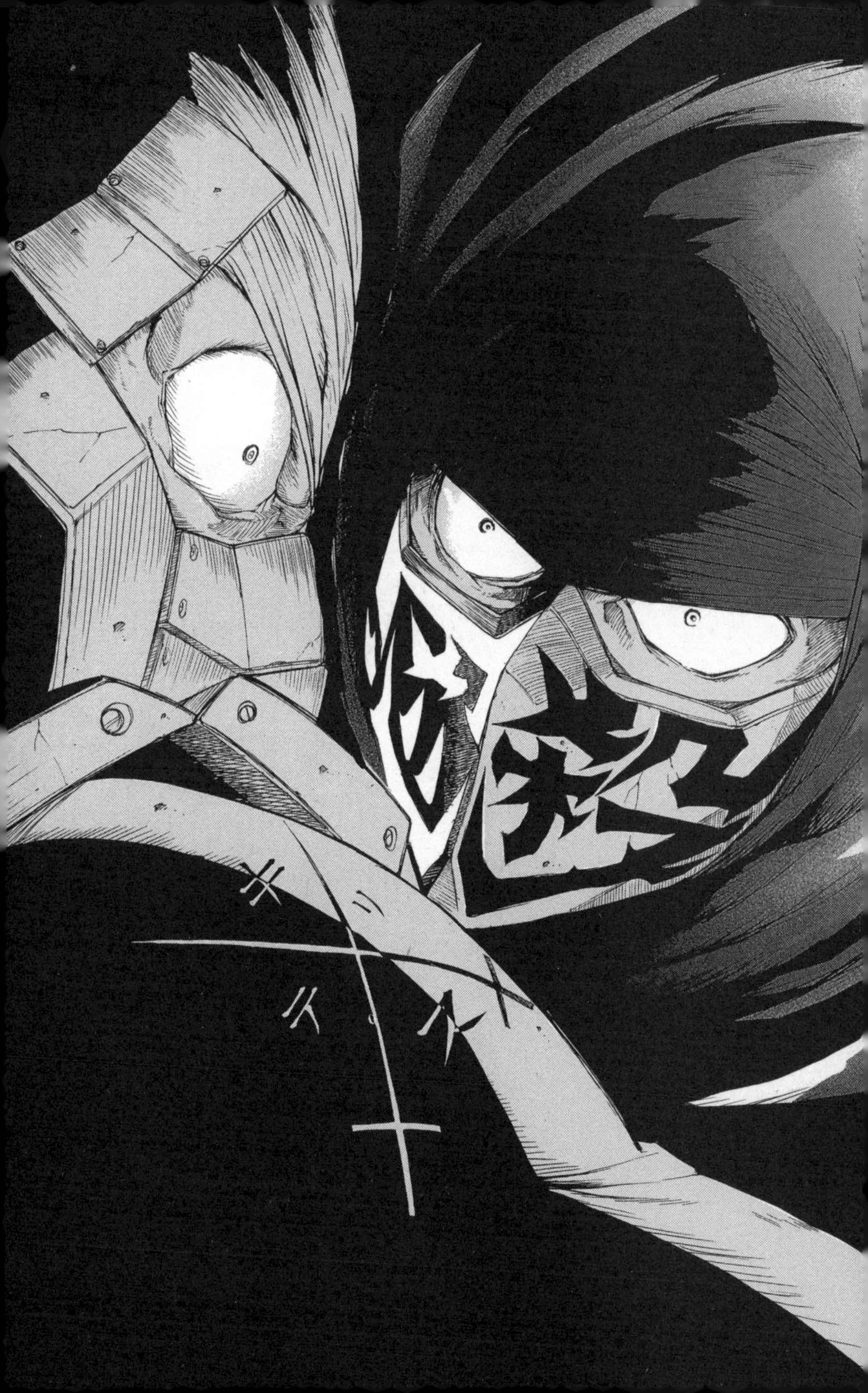

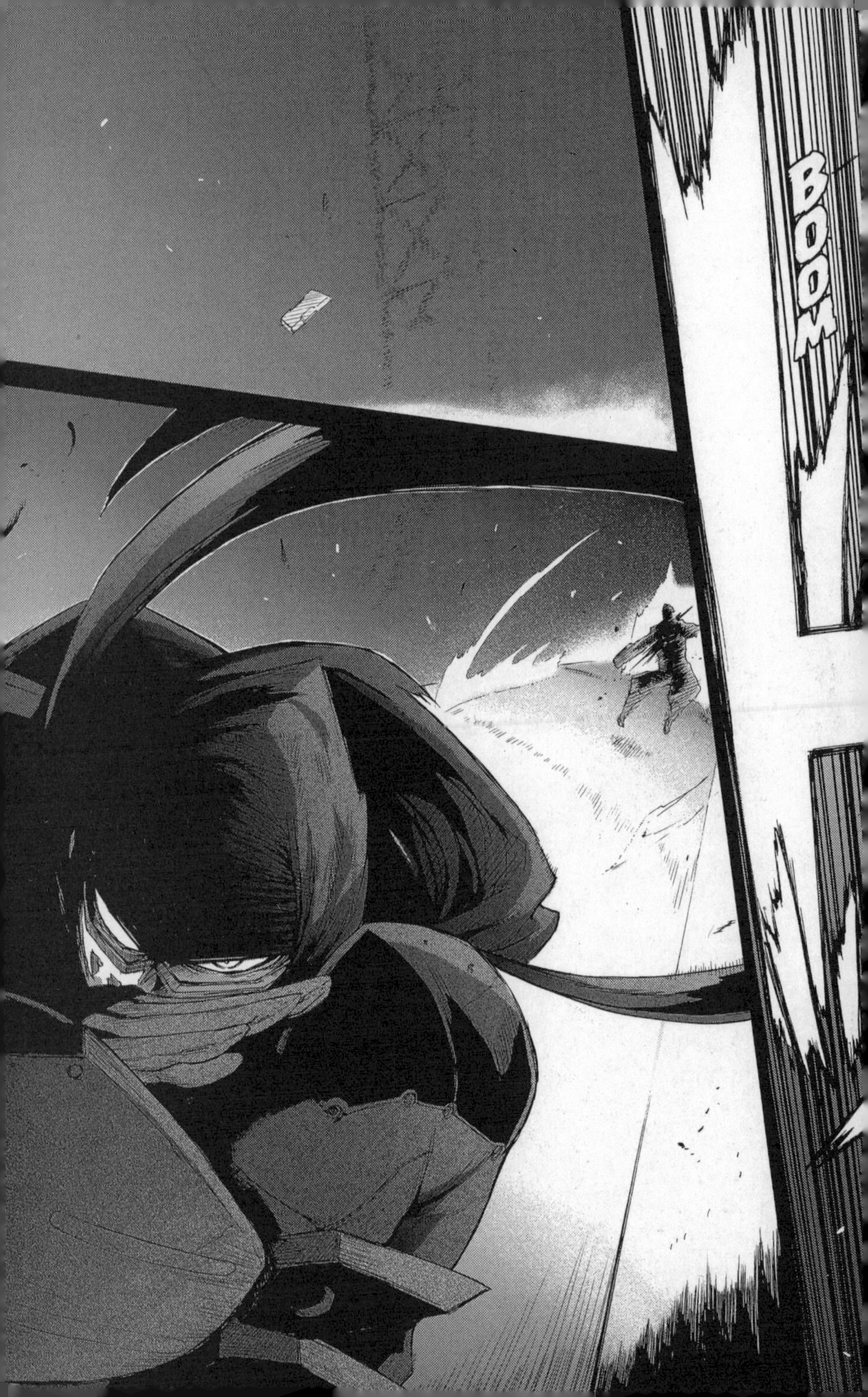
BOOM

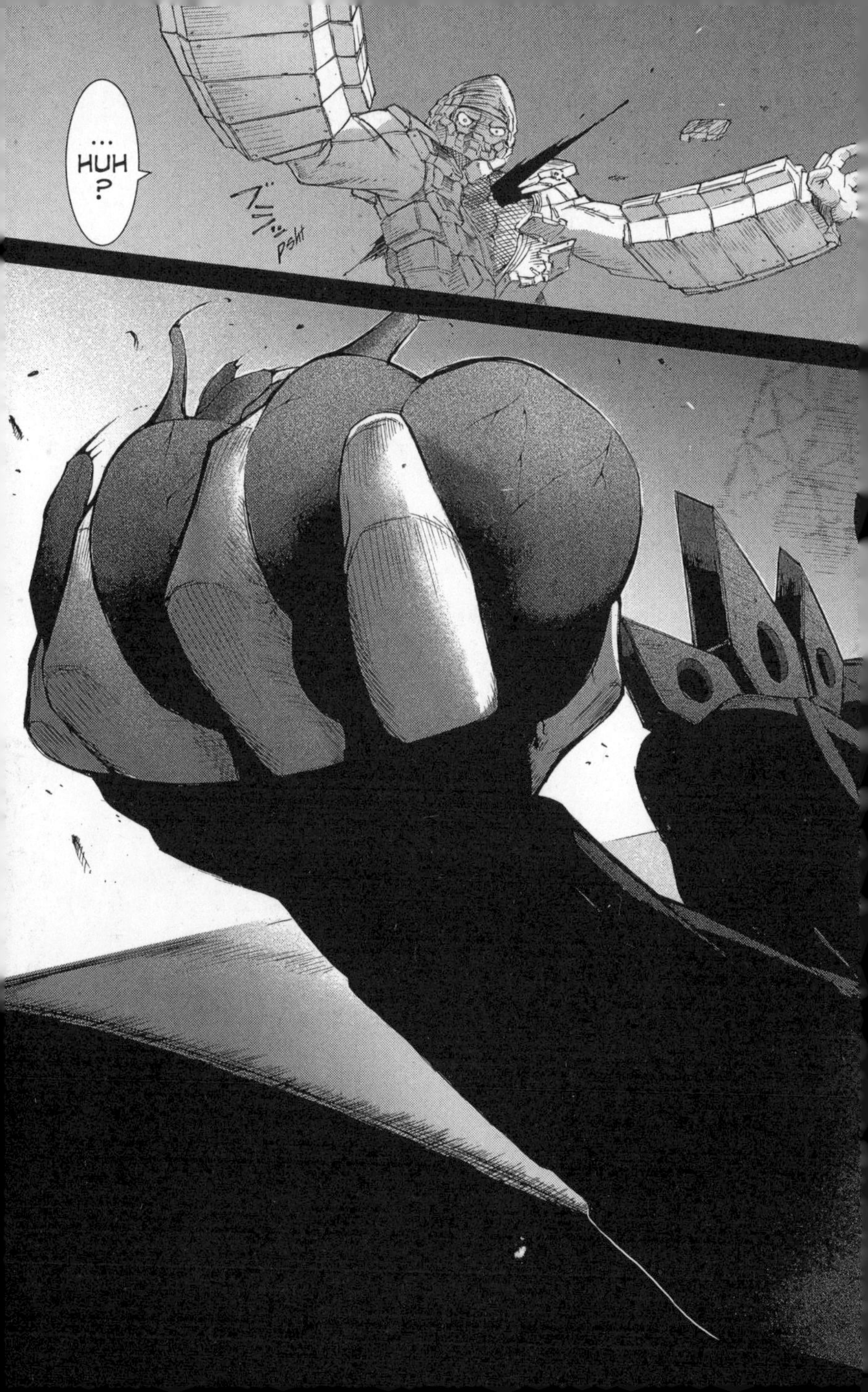
... HUH ?
psht

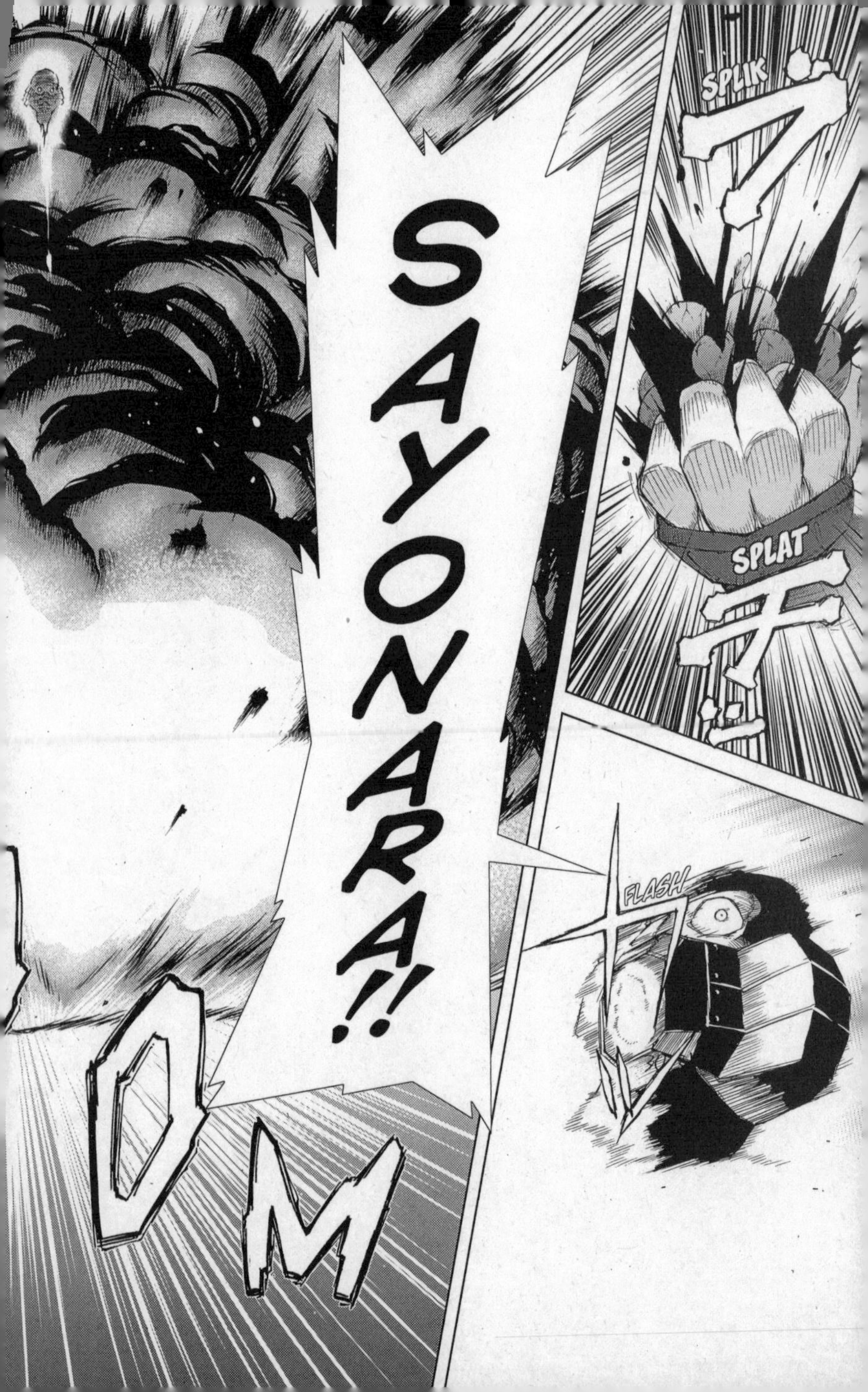
SPLIK
SPLAT
FLASH
SAYONARA!!
DOM

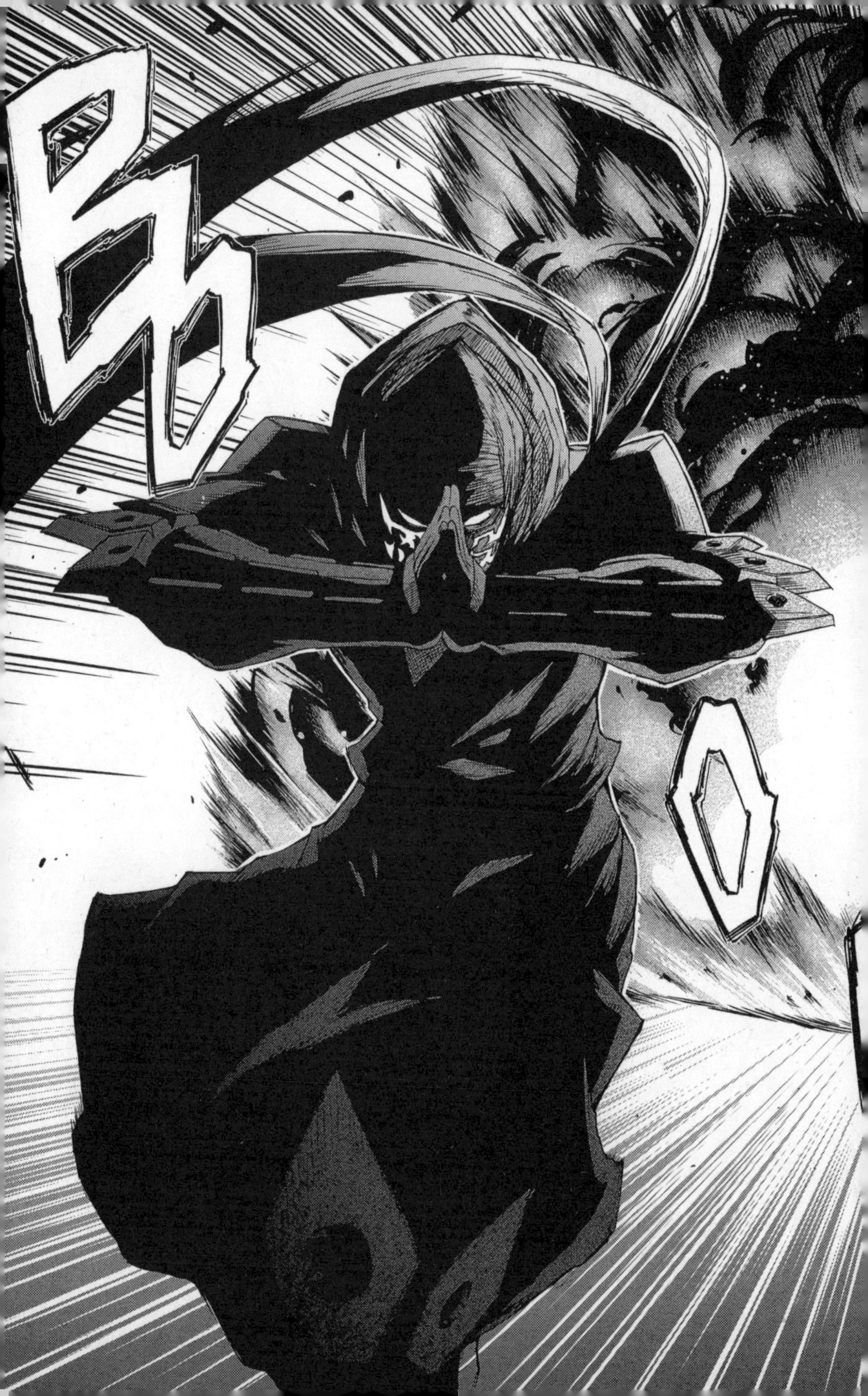

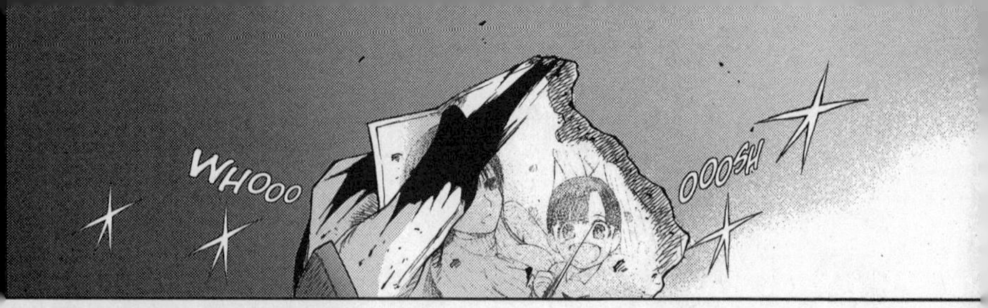
WHOOO
OOOSH
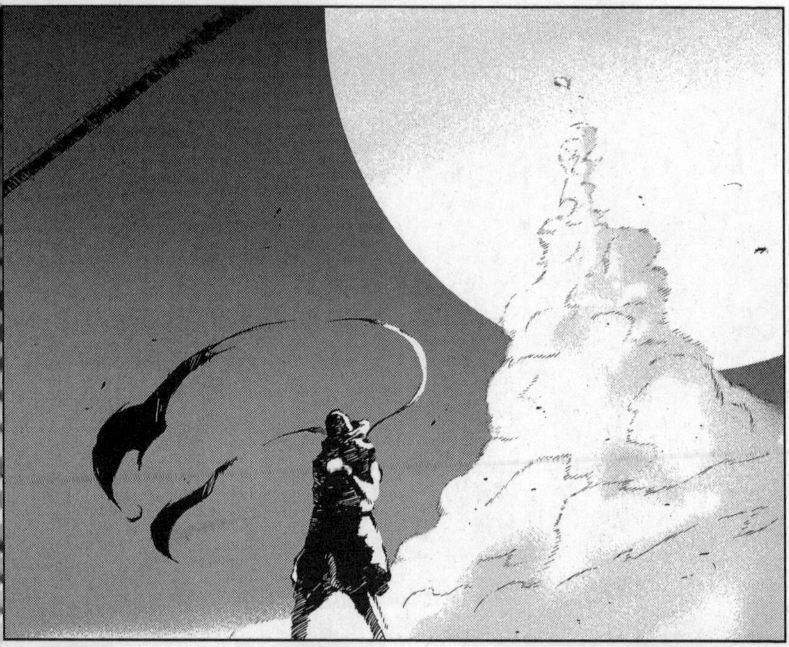
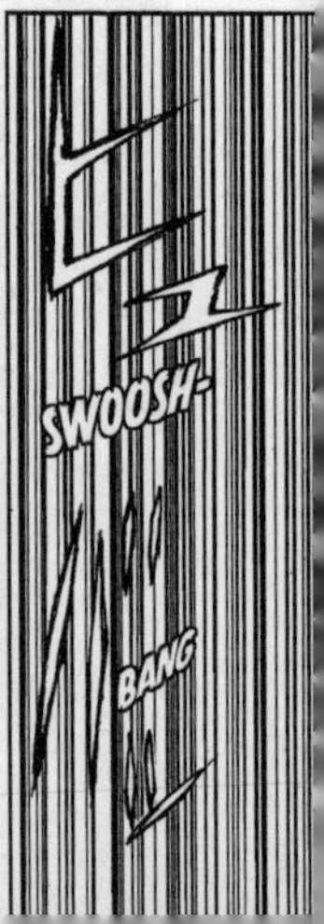
SWOOSH-
BANG
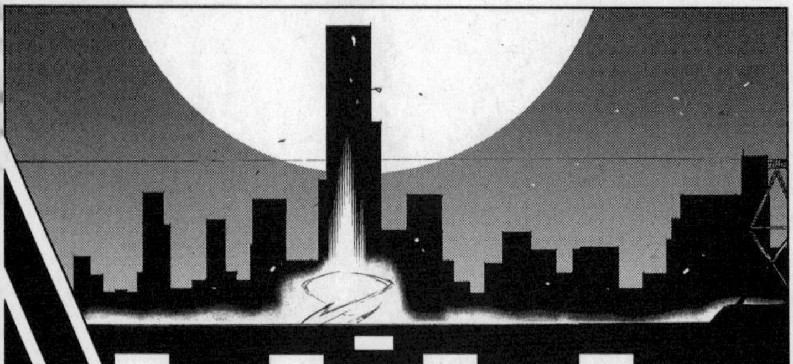

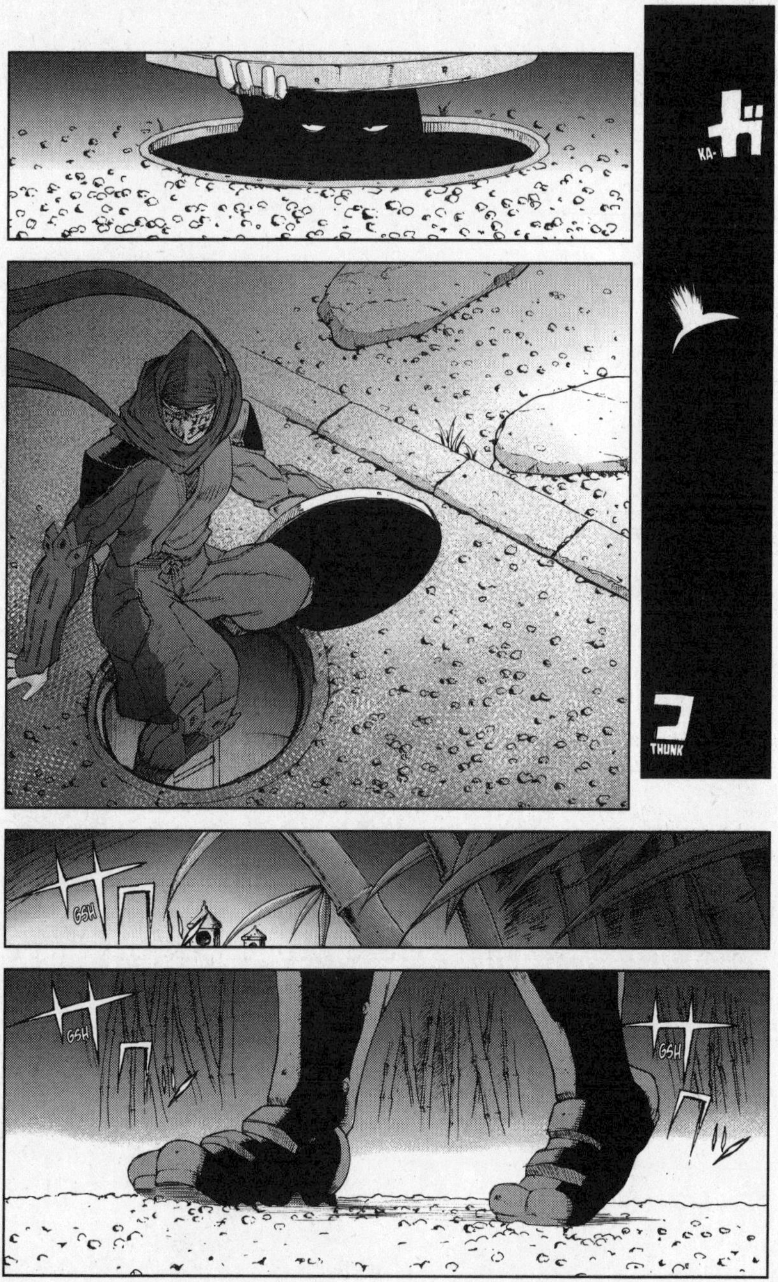

ガ
KA-
コ
THUNK
GSH
GSH
GSH

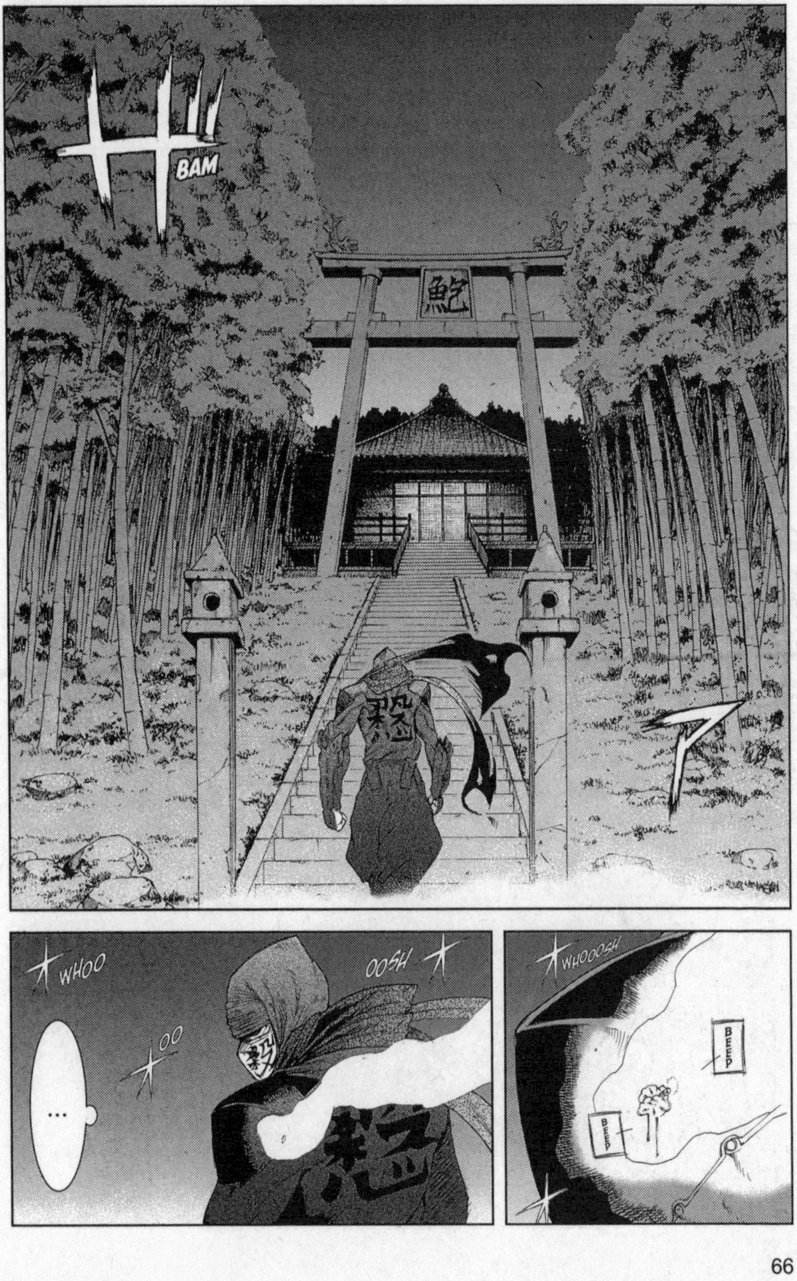
BAM
WHOOOSH
BEEP
BEEP
WHOO
OOSH
OO
...

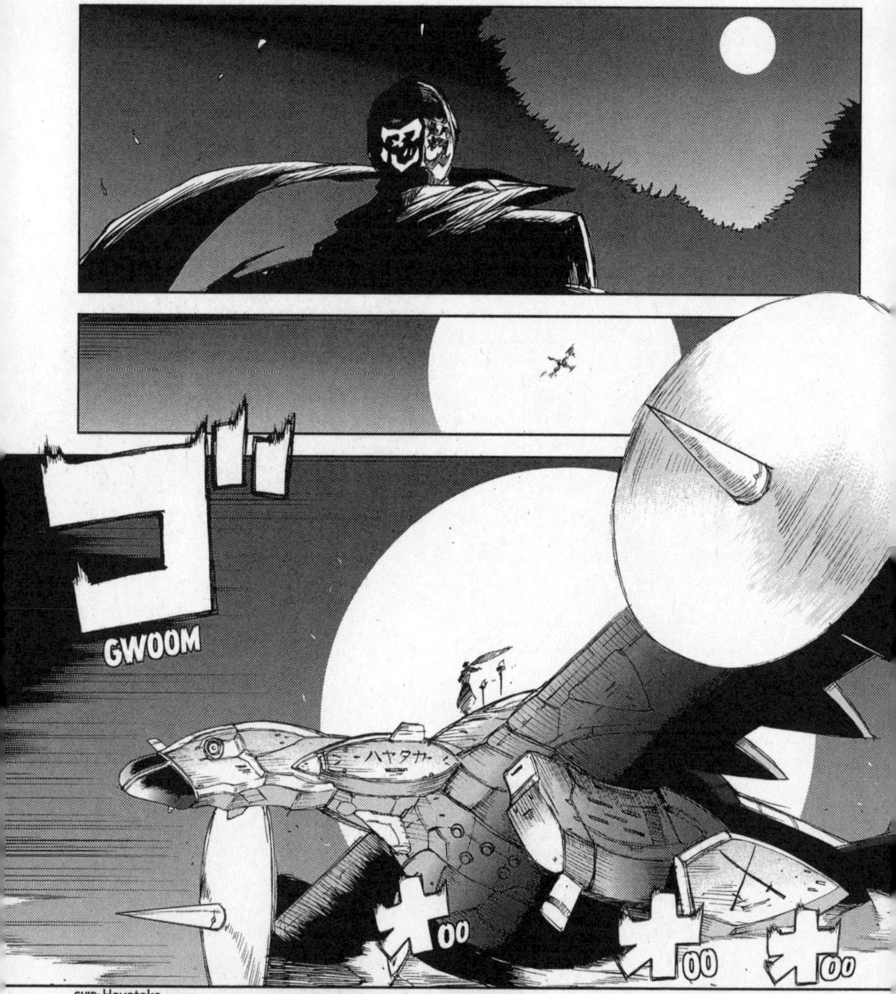
ゴ
GWOOM
ハヤタカ
オ OO
オ OO
オ OO

SHIP: Hayataka

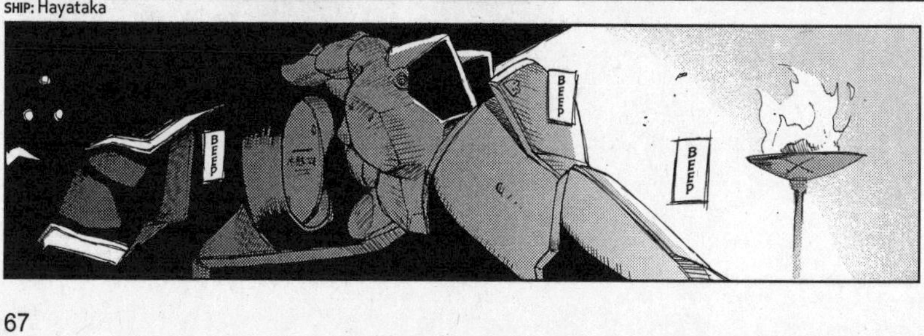
BEEP
BEEP
BEEP

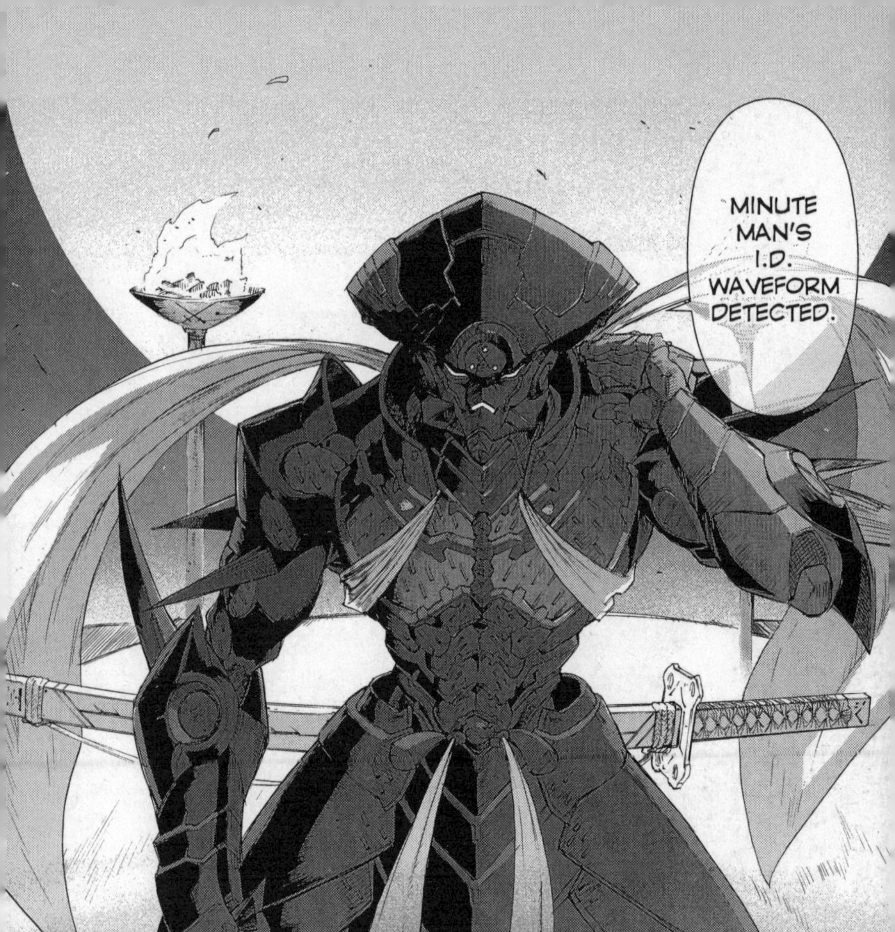
MINUTE MAN'S I.D. WAVEFORM DETECTED.
SOUKAI NINJA:
DARKNINJA
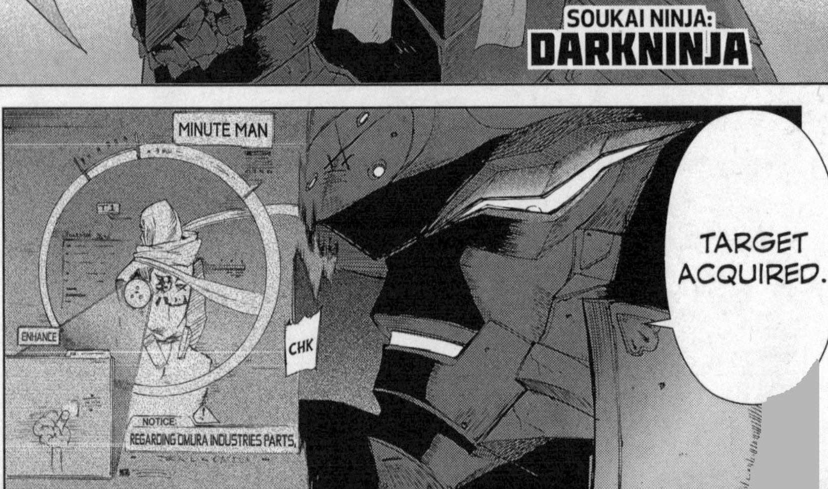
TARGET ACQUIRED.
CHK
MINUTE MAN
ENHANCE
NOTICE:
REGARDING OMURA INDUSTRIES PARTS,

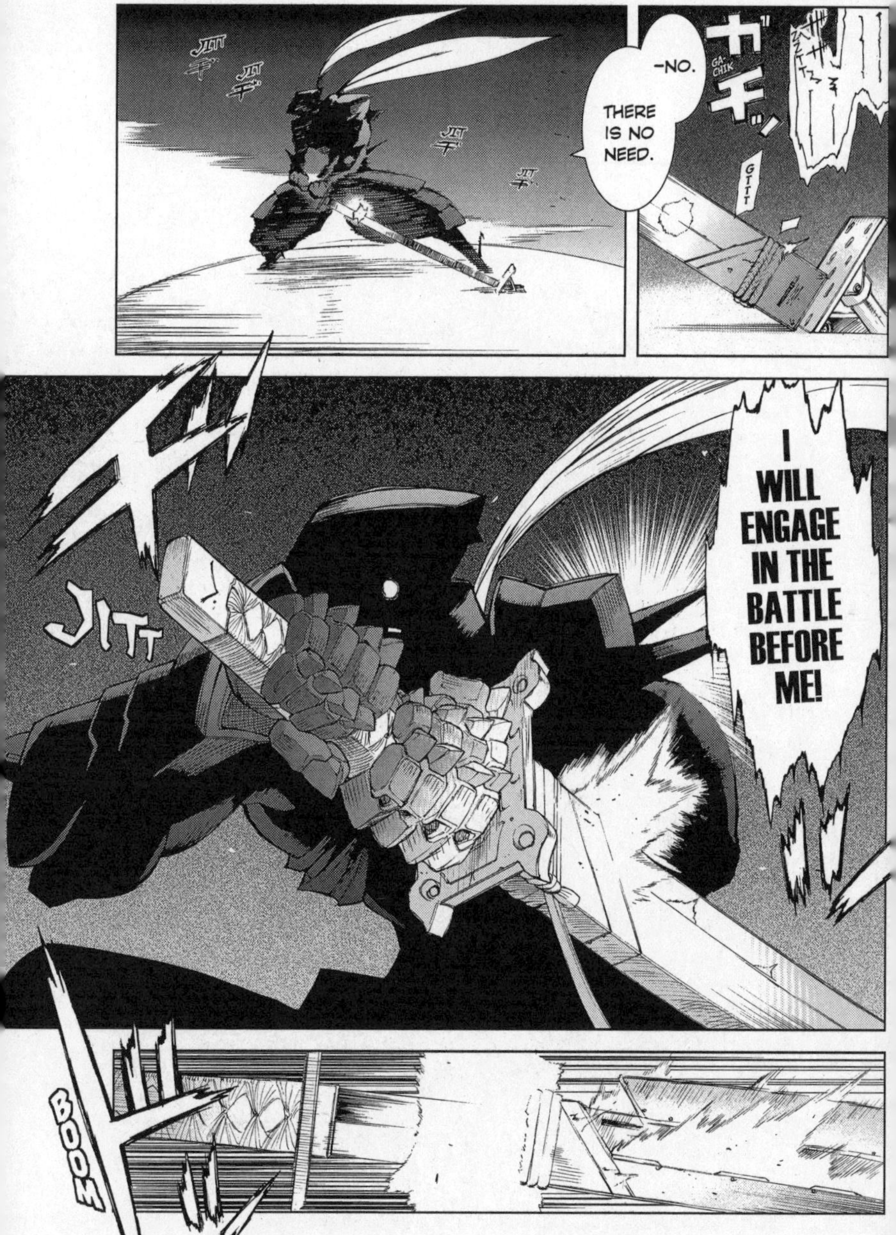
GA-CHIK
–NO.
THERE IS NO NEED.
GITT
JITT
I WILL ENGAGE IN THE BATTLE BEFORE ME!
JITT
BOOM

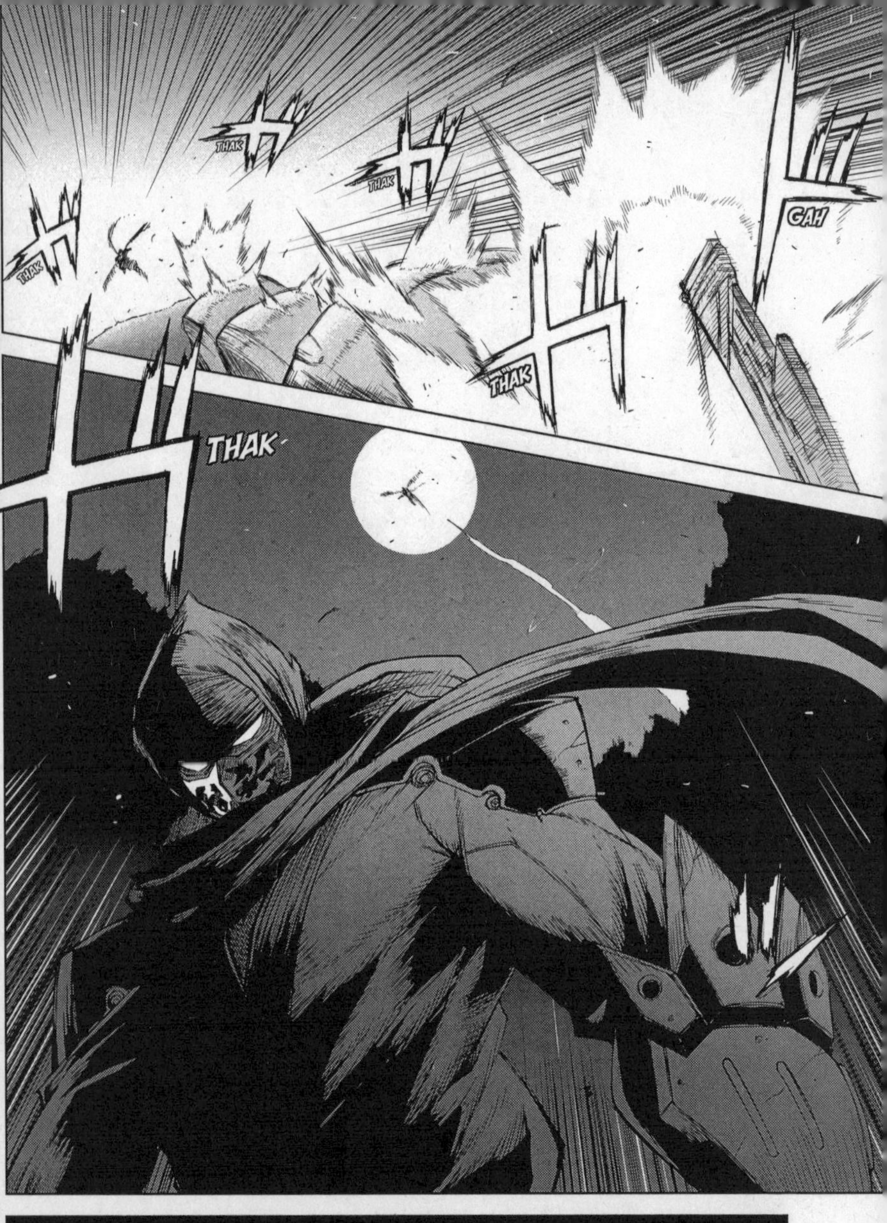
GAH
THAK
THAK
THAK
THAK
THAK

[ZERO TOLERANT SANSUI] • END

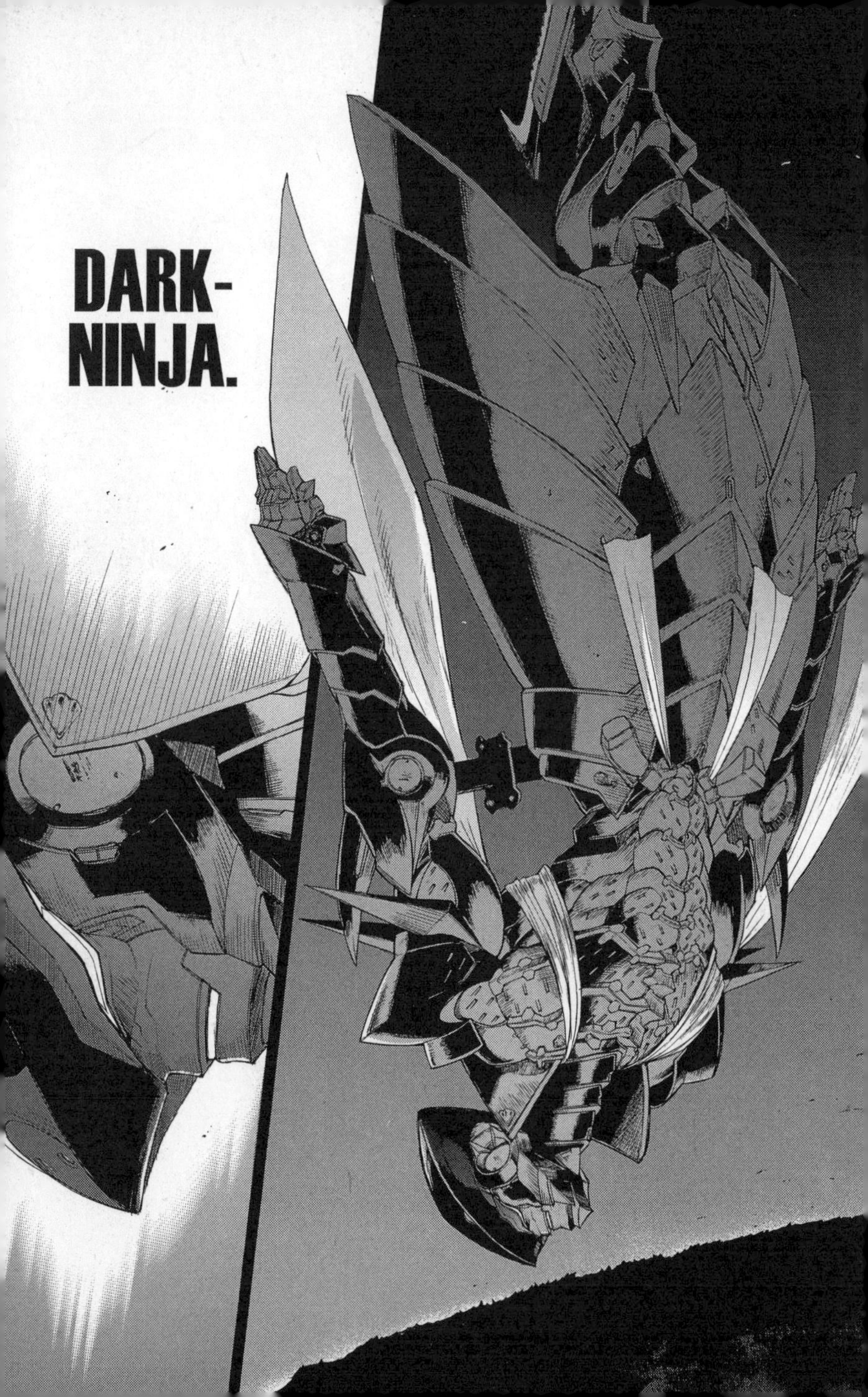
DARK-
NINJA.

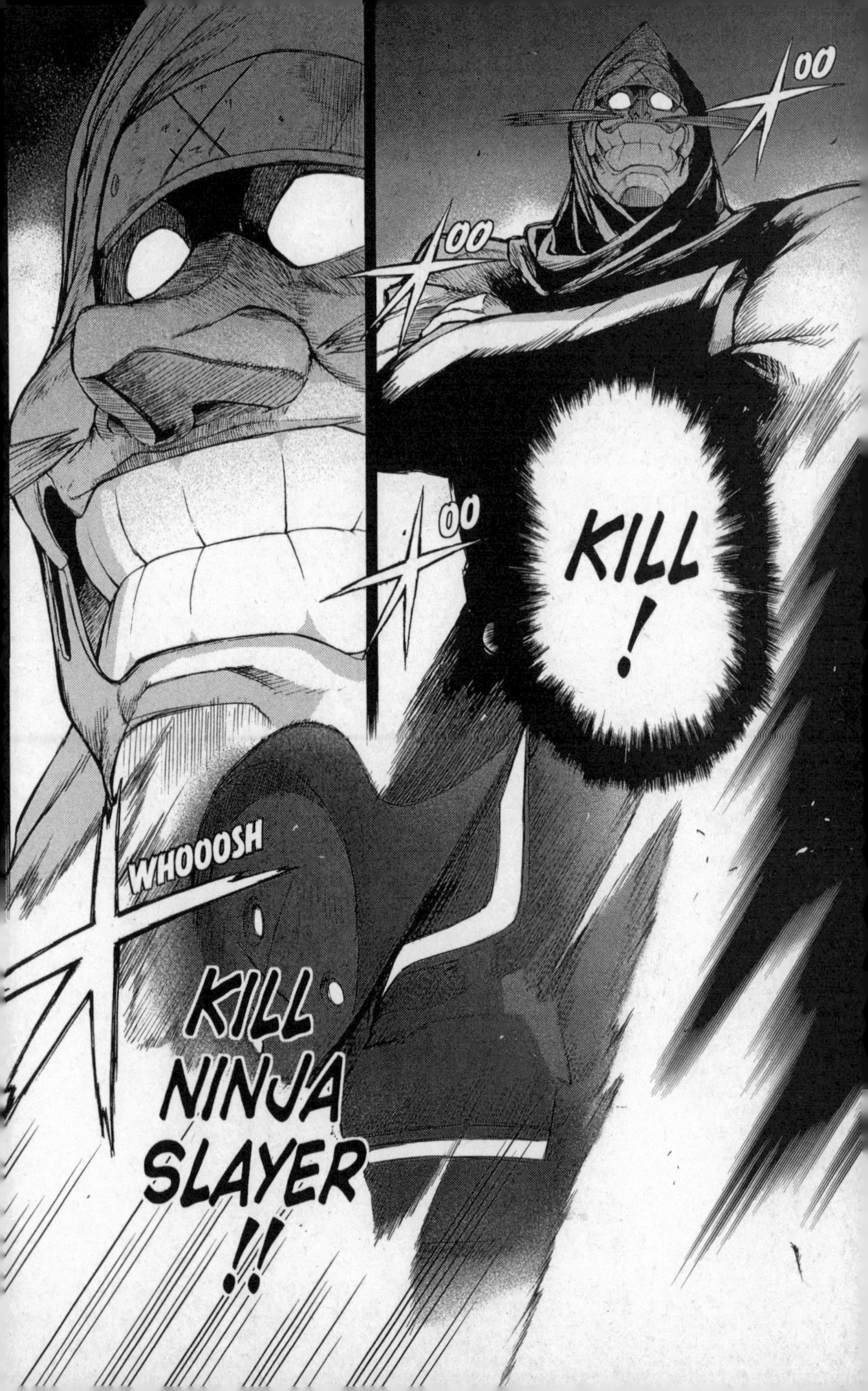
OO
OO
OO
KILL !
WHOOOSH
KILL NINJA SLAYER !!

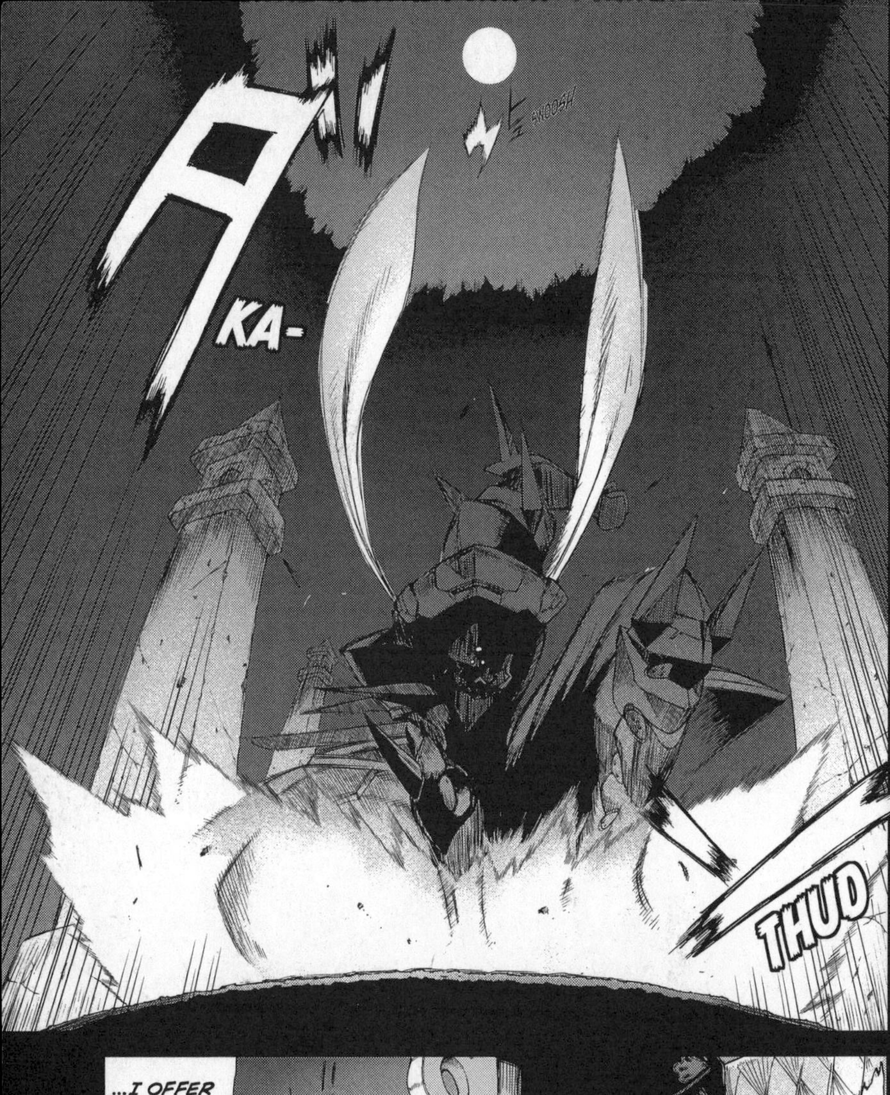
SWOOSH
KA-
THUD

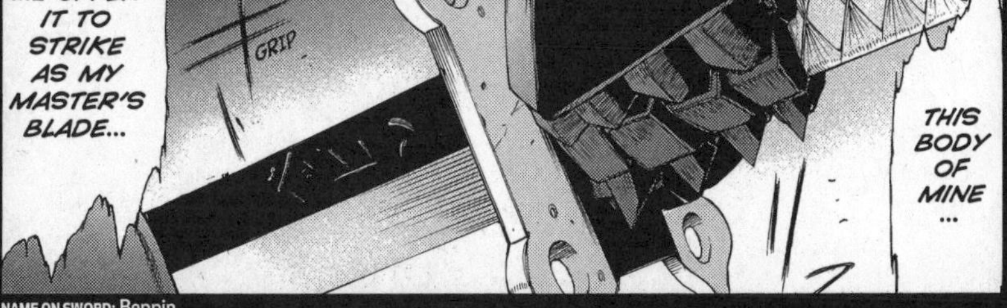
THIS BODY OF MINE...
GRIP
...I OFFER IT TO STRIKE AS MY MASTER'S BLADE...

NAME ON SWORD: Beppin

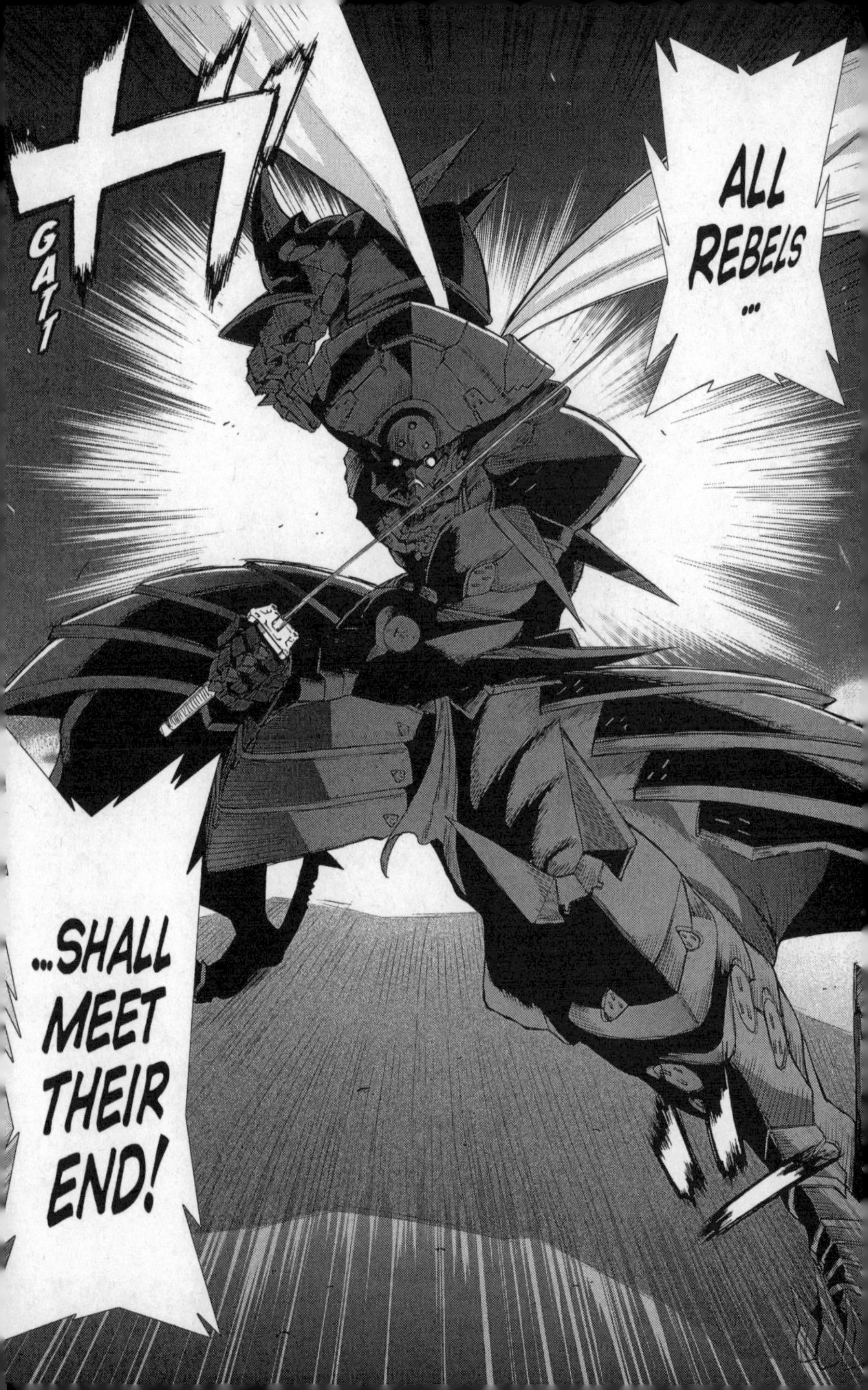
ALL REBELS ...
GATI
...SHALL MEET THEIR END!

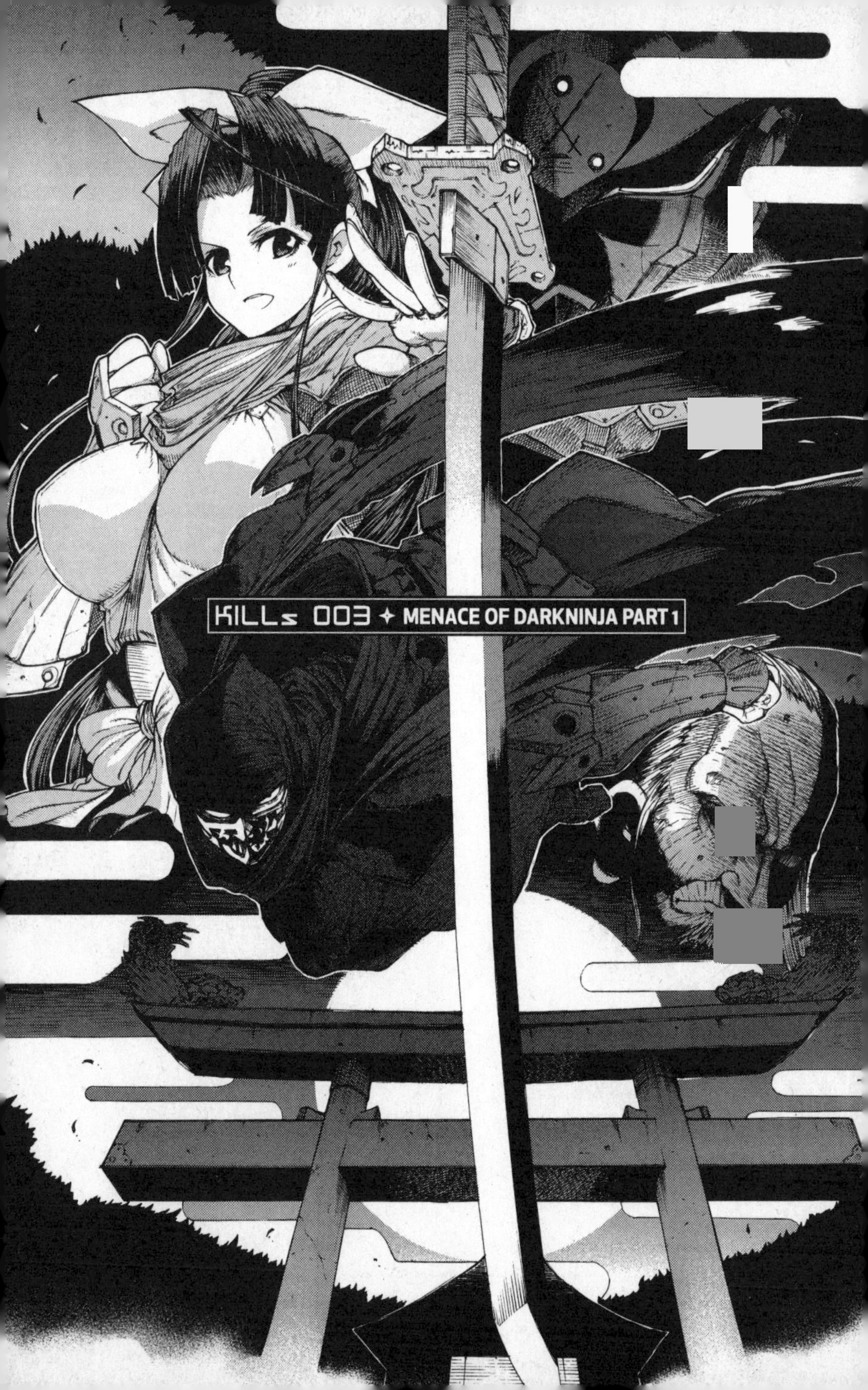
KILLs 003 ✦ MENACE OF DARKNINJA PART 1

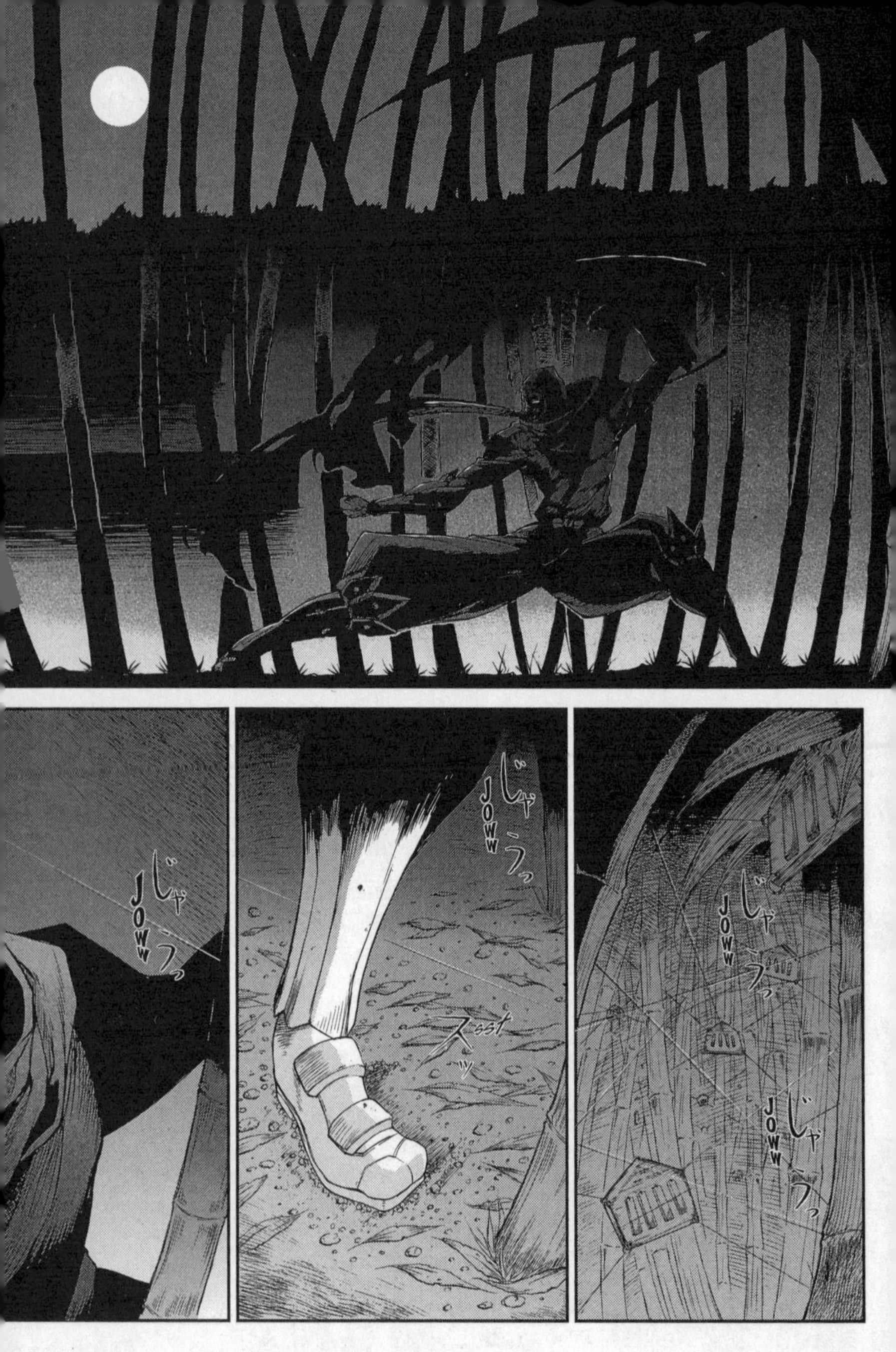
じゃ～フっ
JOWW
じゃ～フっ
JOWW
じゃ～フっ
JOWW
スッ
SSST
じゃフっ
JOWW

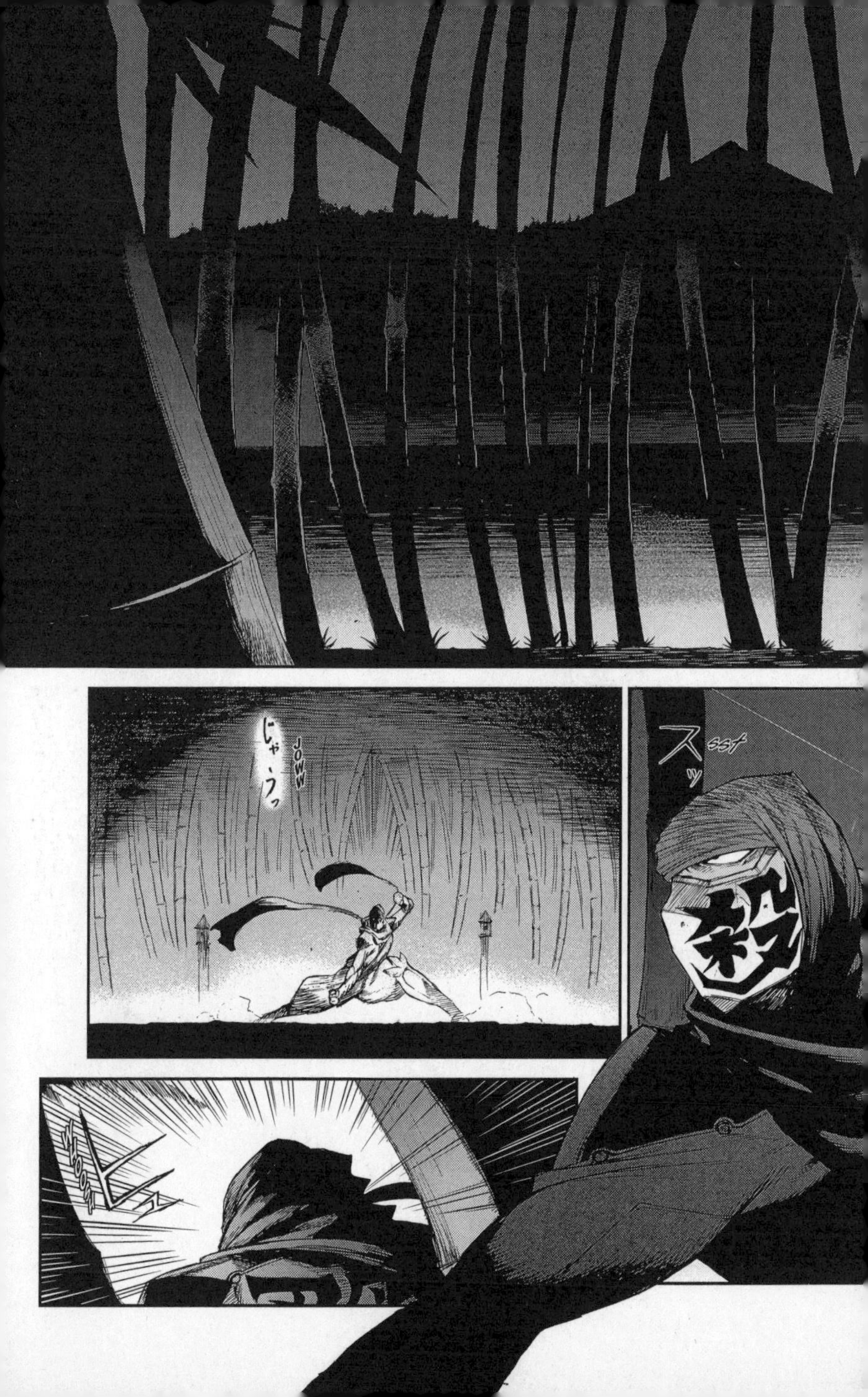
スッ
SST
じゃっ
JOWW
ビュ
WHOOSH!

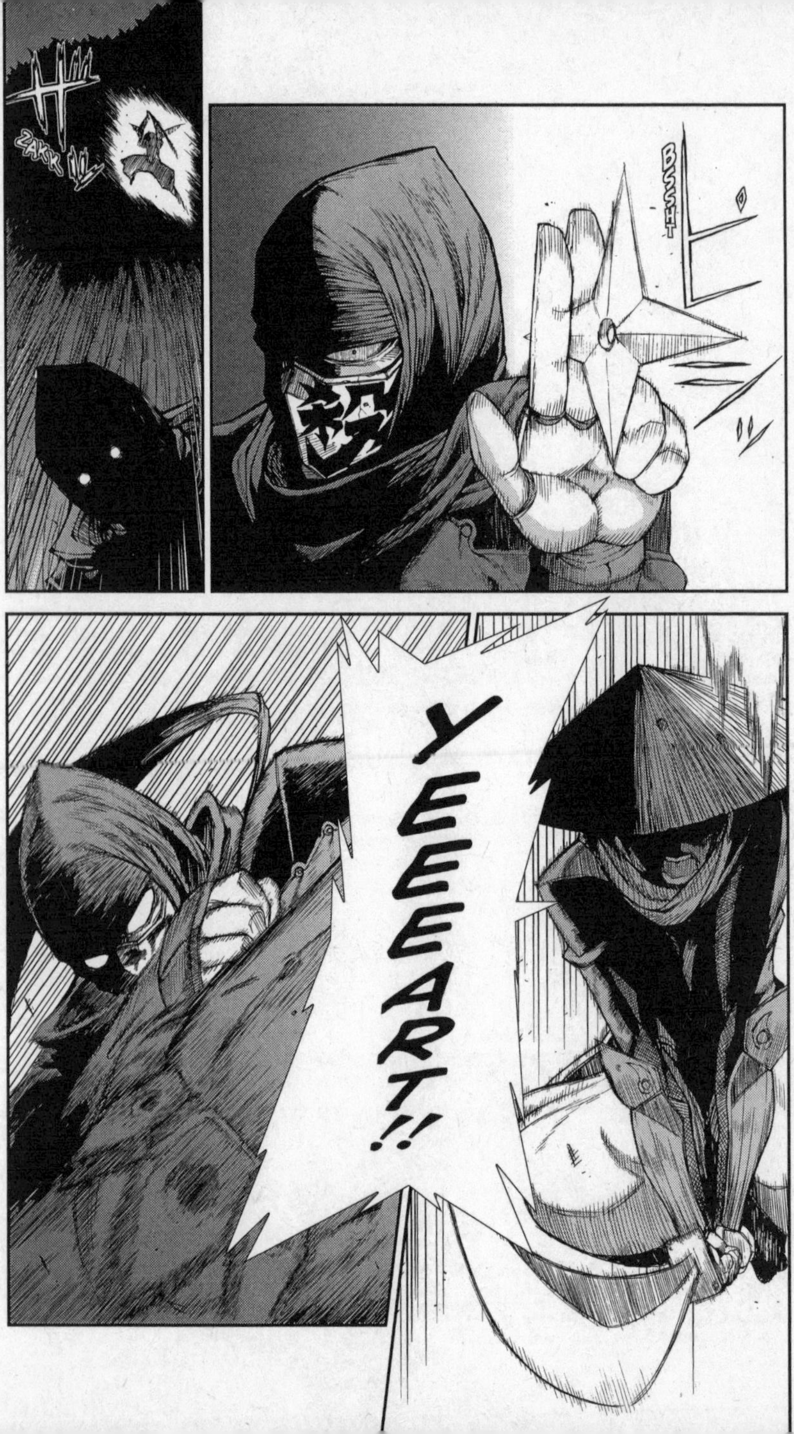
BSSHT
ZAKK
YEEEART!!

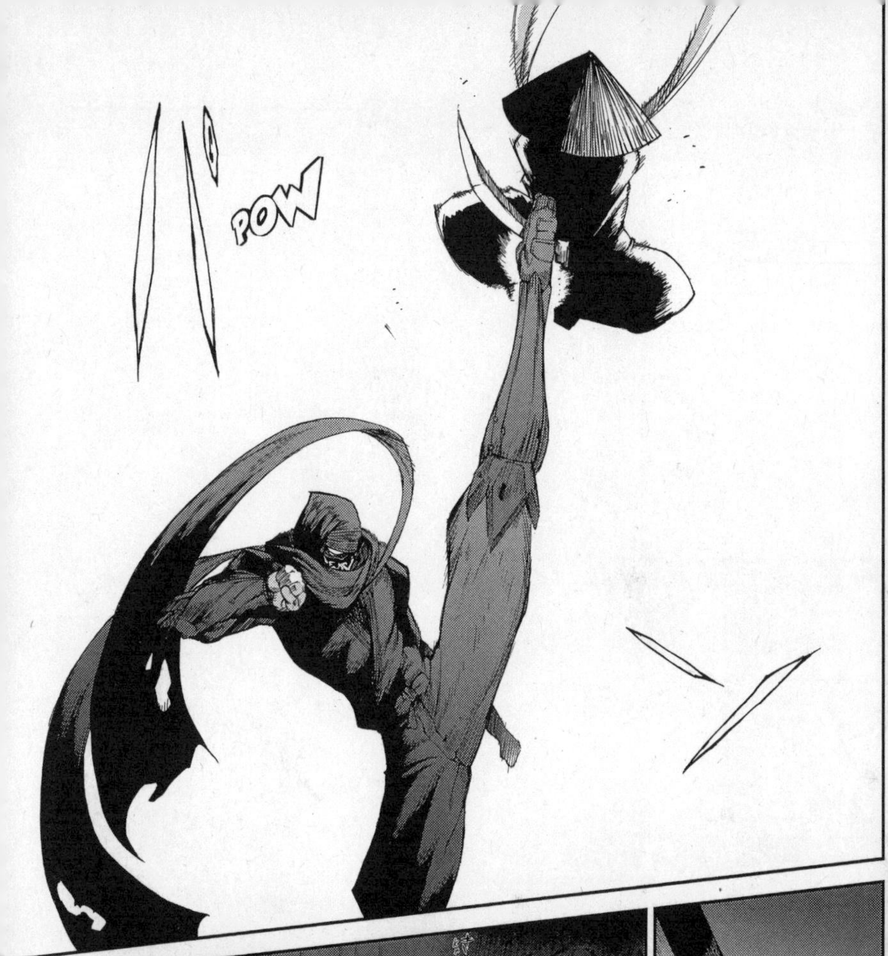
POW
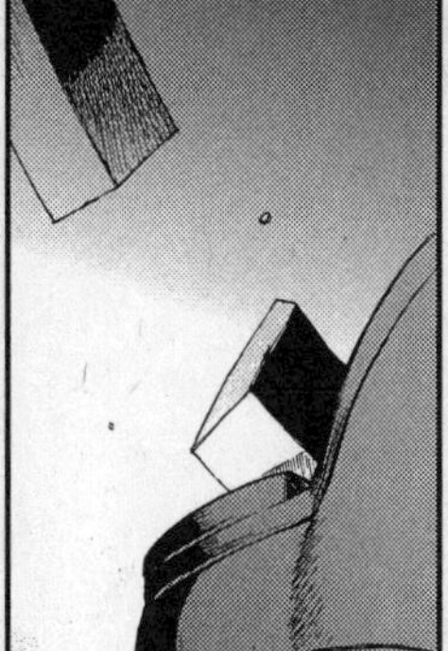
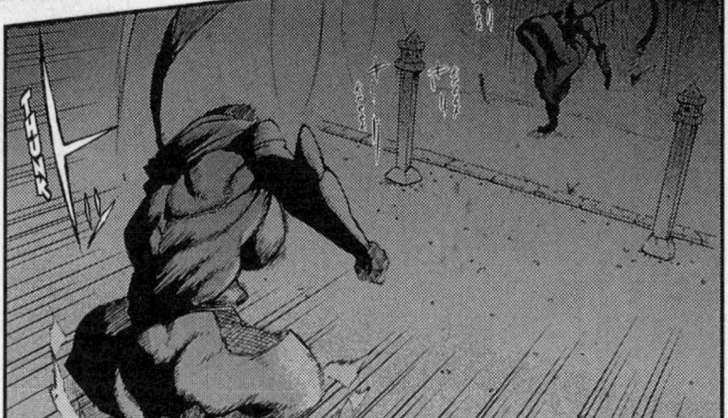
THUNK

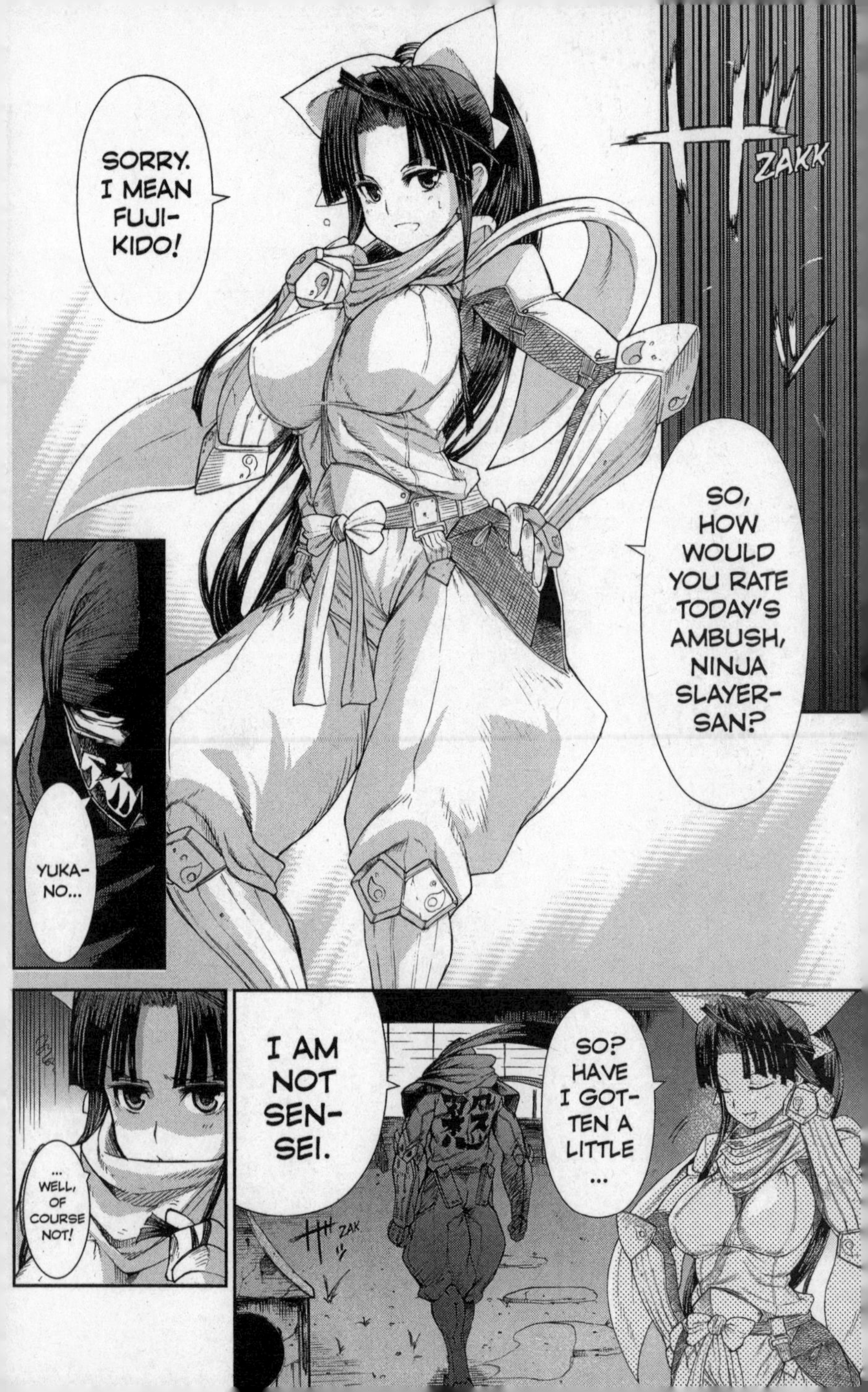
ZAKK
SO, HOW WOULD YOU RATE TODAY'S AMBUSH, NINJA SLAYER-SAN?
YUKA-NO...
SORRY. I MEAN FUJI-KIDO!
SO? HAVE I GOT-TEN A LITTLE ...
I AM NOT SEN-SEI.
ZAK
... WELL, OF COURSE NOT!

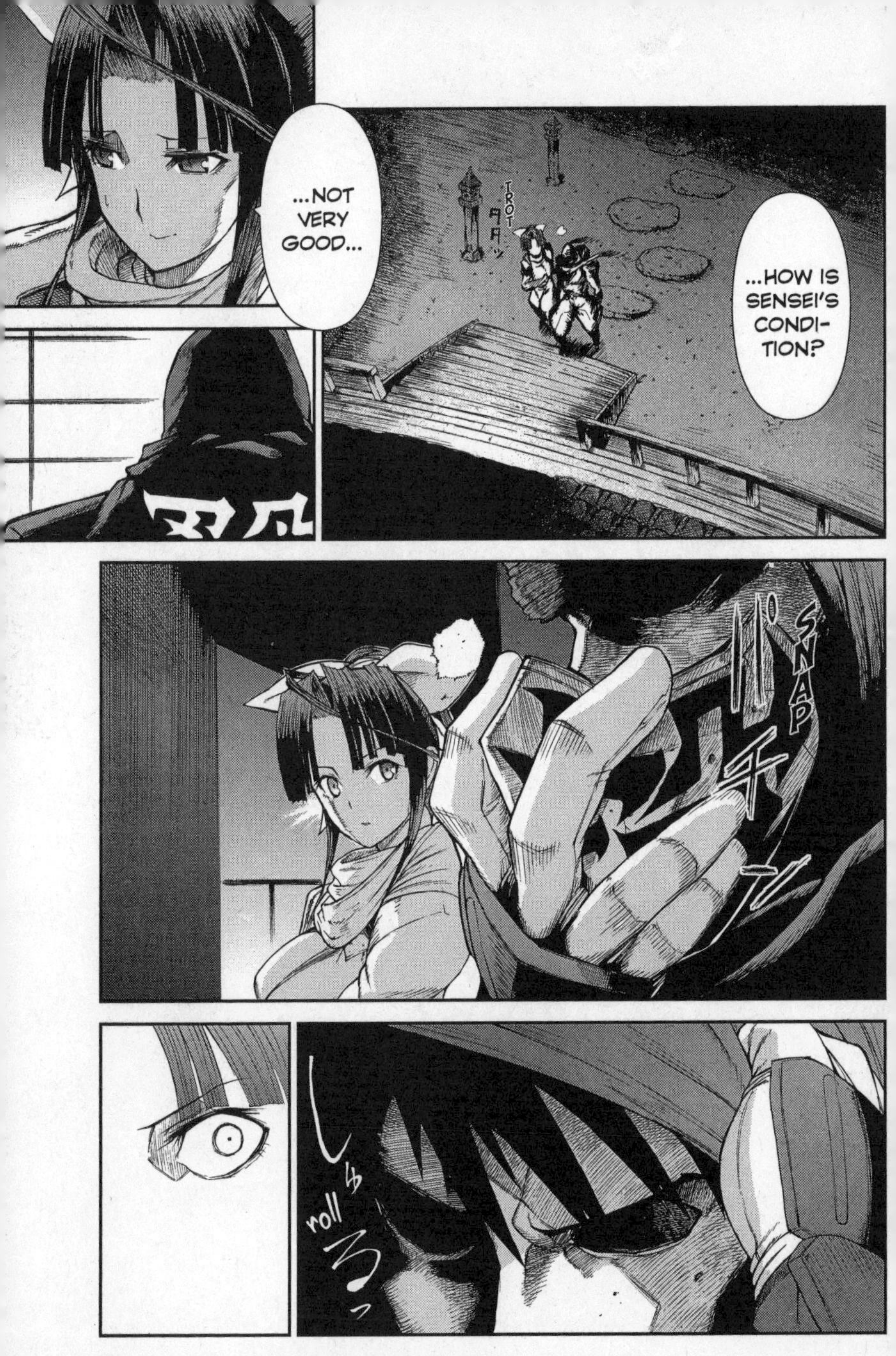
...HOW IS SENSEI'S CONDITION?
TROT
...NOT VERY GOOD...
SNAP
roll

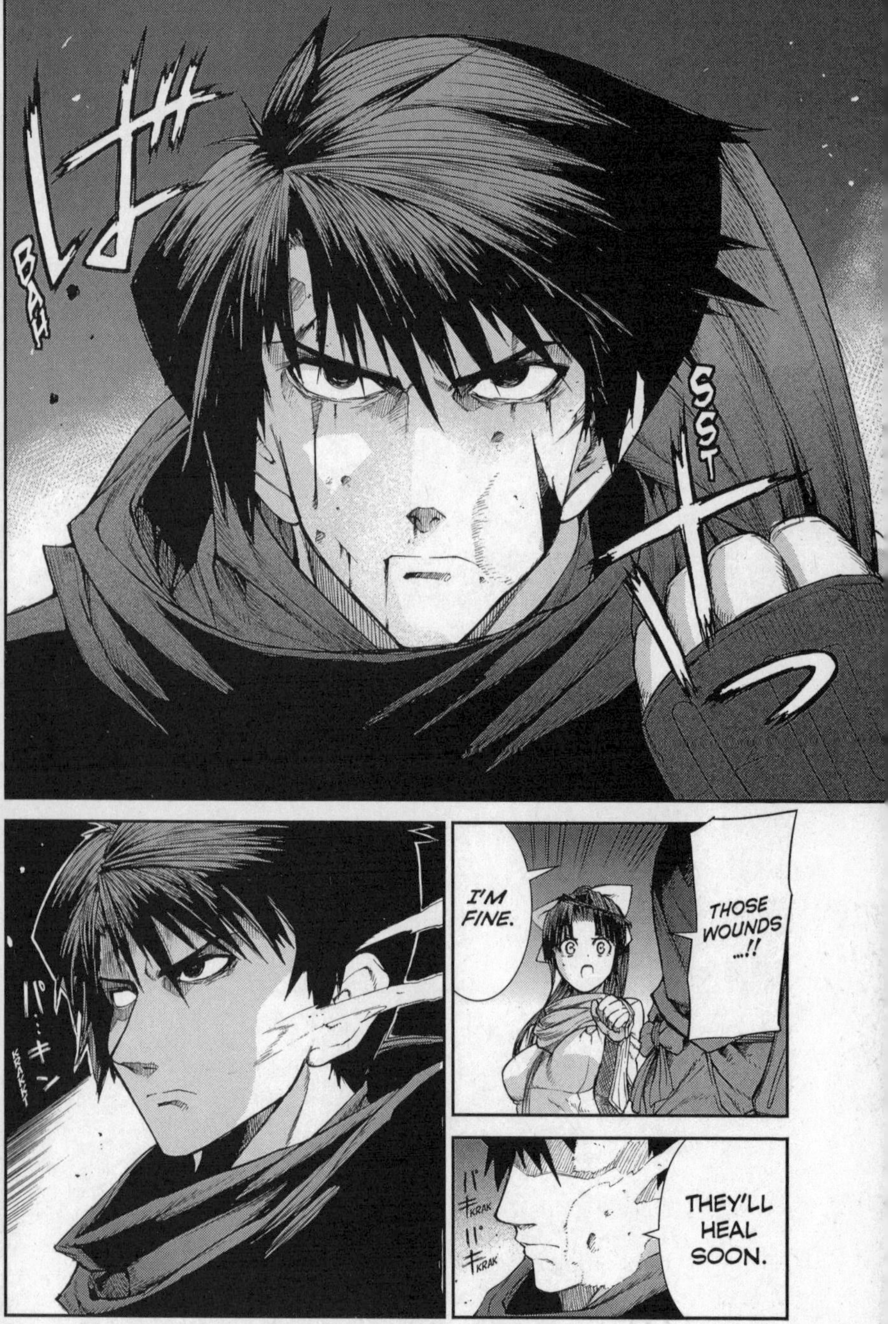
BAM
SSST
THOSE WOUNDS ...!!
I'M FINE.
KRAK
KRAK
THEY'LL HEAL SOON.
パ…キン

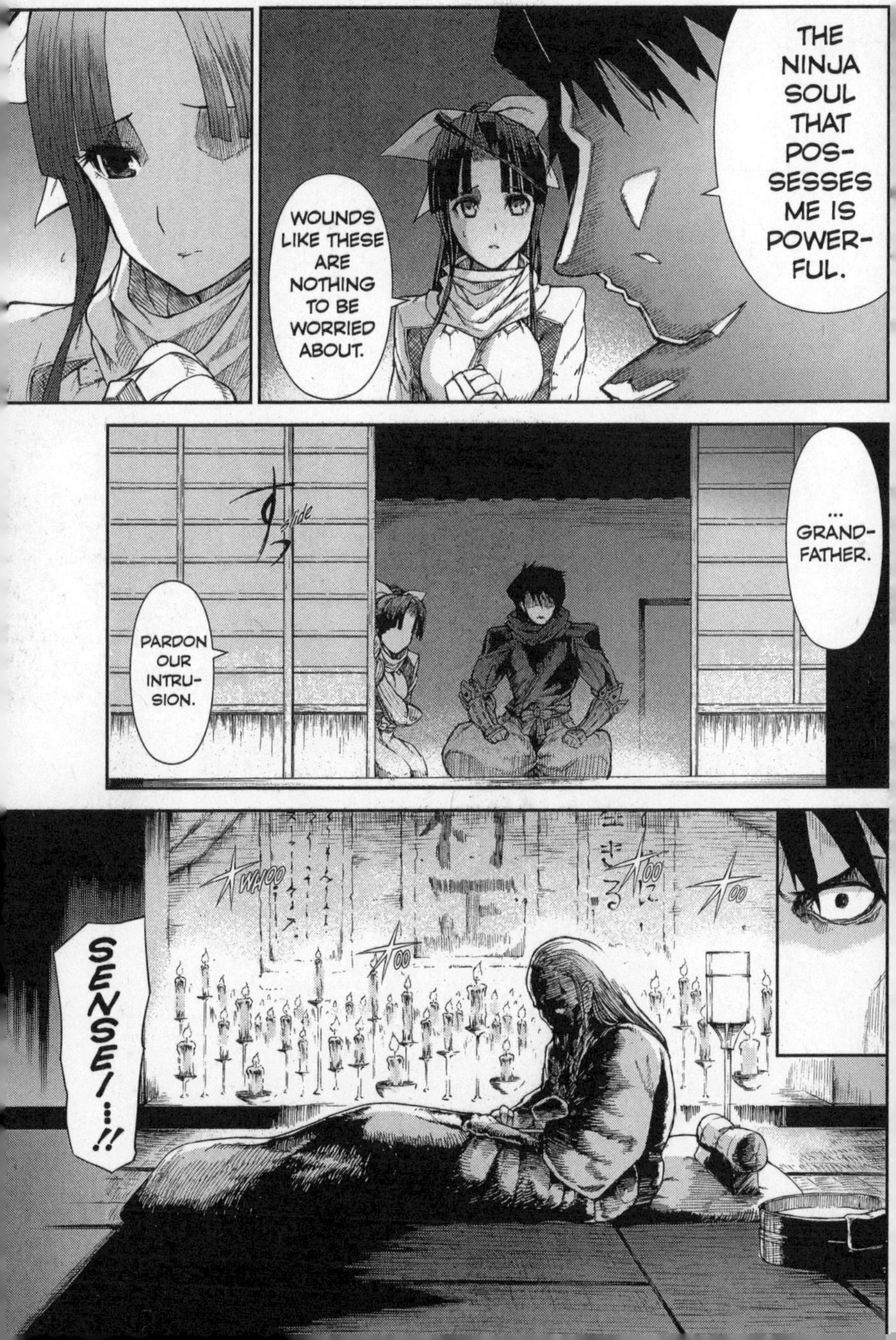
THE NINJA SOUL THAT POSSESSES ME IS POWERFUL.
WOUNDS LIKE THESE ARE NOTHING TO BE WORRIED ABOUT.
... GRANDFATHER.
slide
PARDON OUR INTRUSION.
OO
OO
WHOO
OO
SENSEI...!!

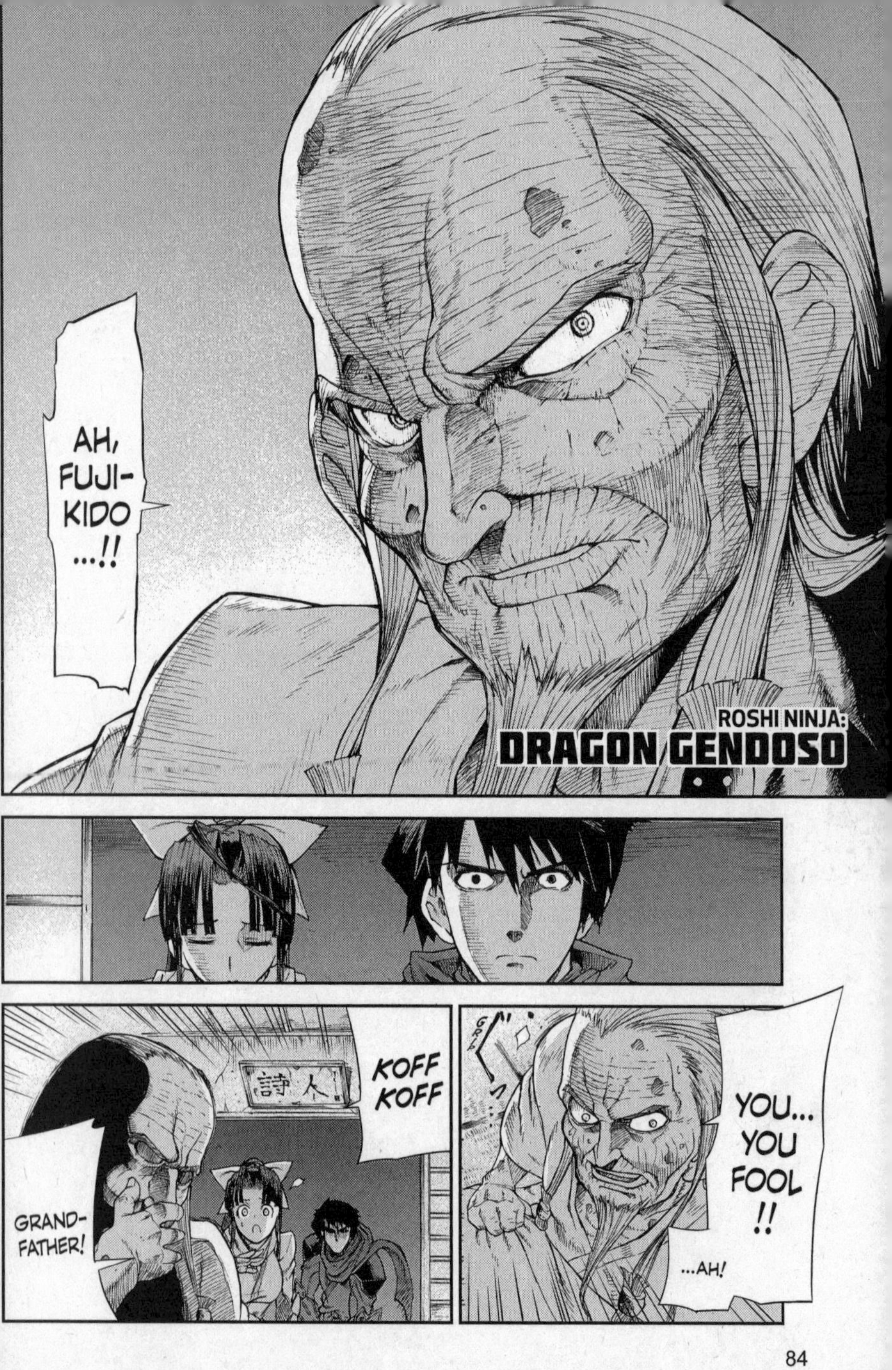
AH, FUJI-KIDO ...!!
ROSHI NINJA:
DRAGON GENDOSO
GRIP
YOU... YOU FOOL !!
...AH!
KOFF KOFF
詩人
GRAND-FATHER!

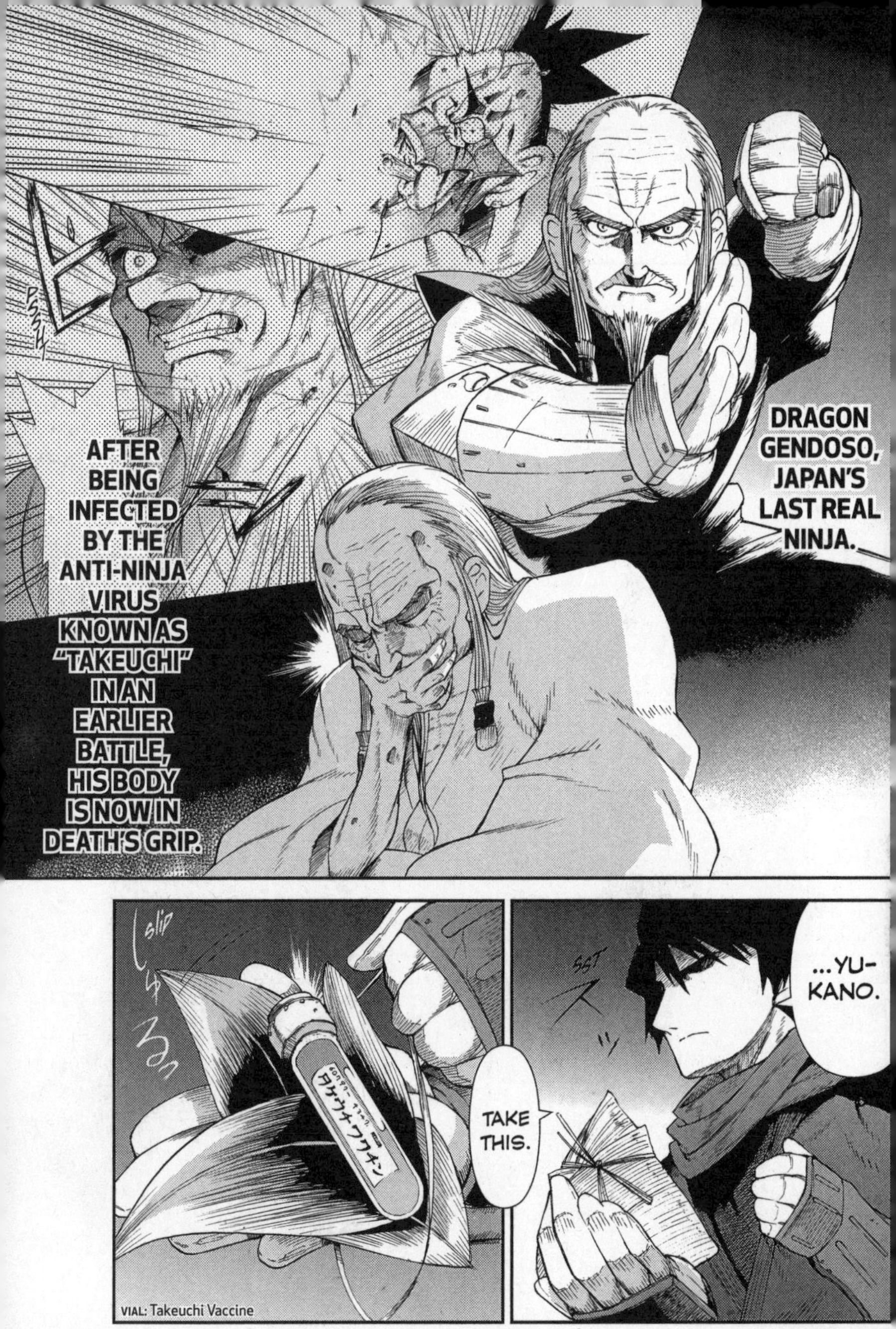
DRAGON GENDOSO, JAPAN'S LAST REAL NINJA.
AFTER BEING INFECTED BY THE ANTI-NINJA VIRUS KNOWN AS "TAKEUCHI" IN AN EARLIER BATTLE, HIS BODY IS NOW IN DEATH'S GRIP.
PSSH
SST
...YU-KANO.
TAKE THIS.
slip
VIAL: Takeuchi Vaccine

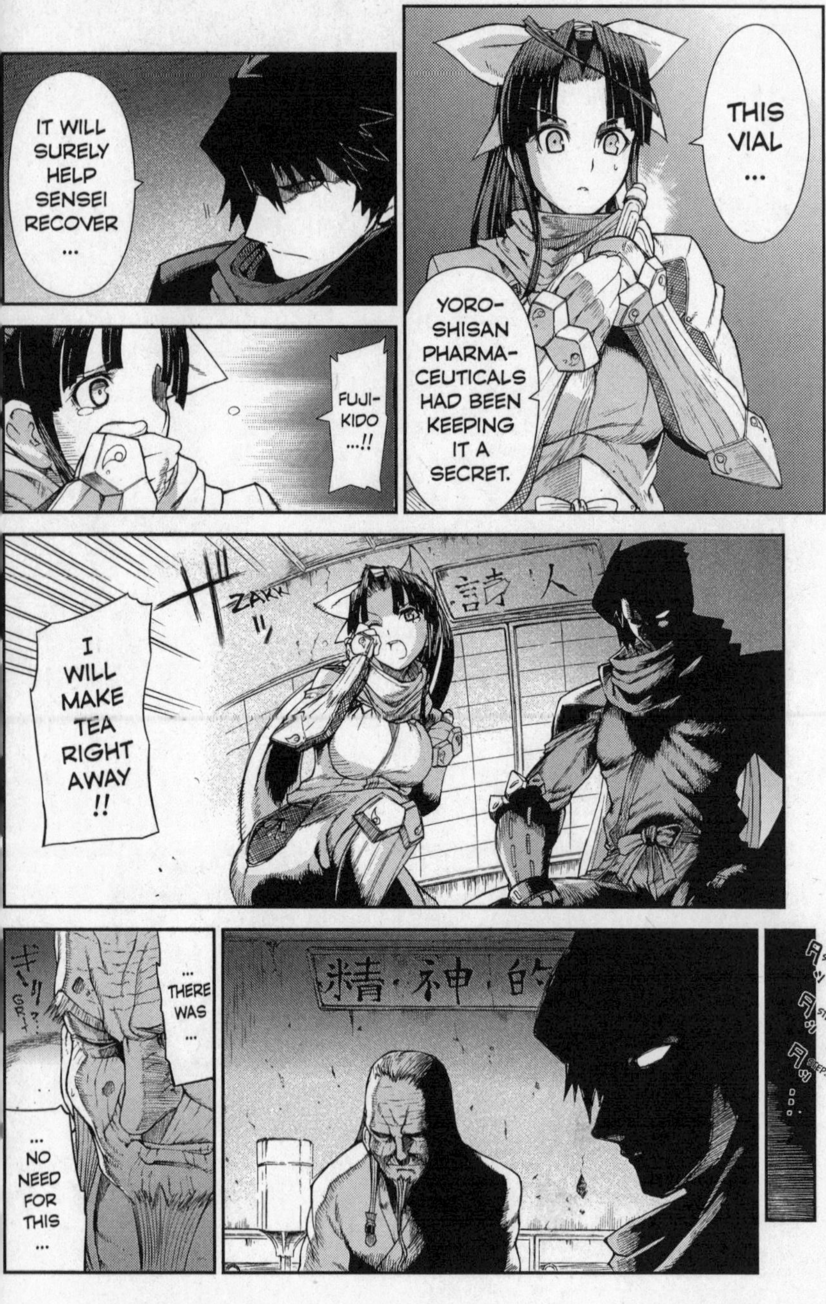
THIS VIAL ...
YORO-SHISAN PHARMA-CEUTICALS HAD BEEN KEEPING IT A SECRET.
IT WILL SURELY HELP SENSEI RECOVER ...
FUJI-KIDO ...!!
ZAKK
I WILL MAKE TEA RIGHT AWAY !!
STEP
STEP
STEP...
精神的
... THERE WAS ...
... NO NEED FOR THIS ...
GRIT

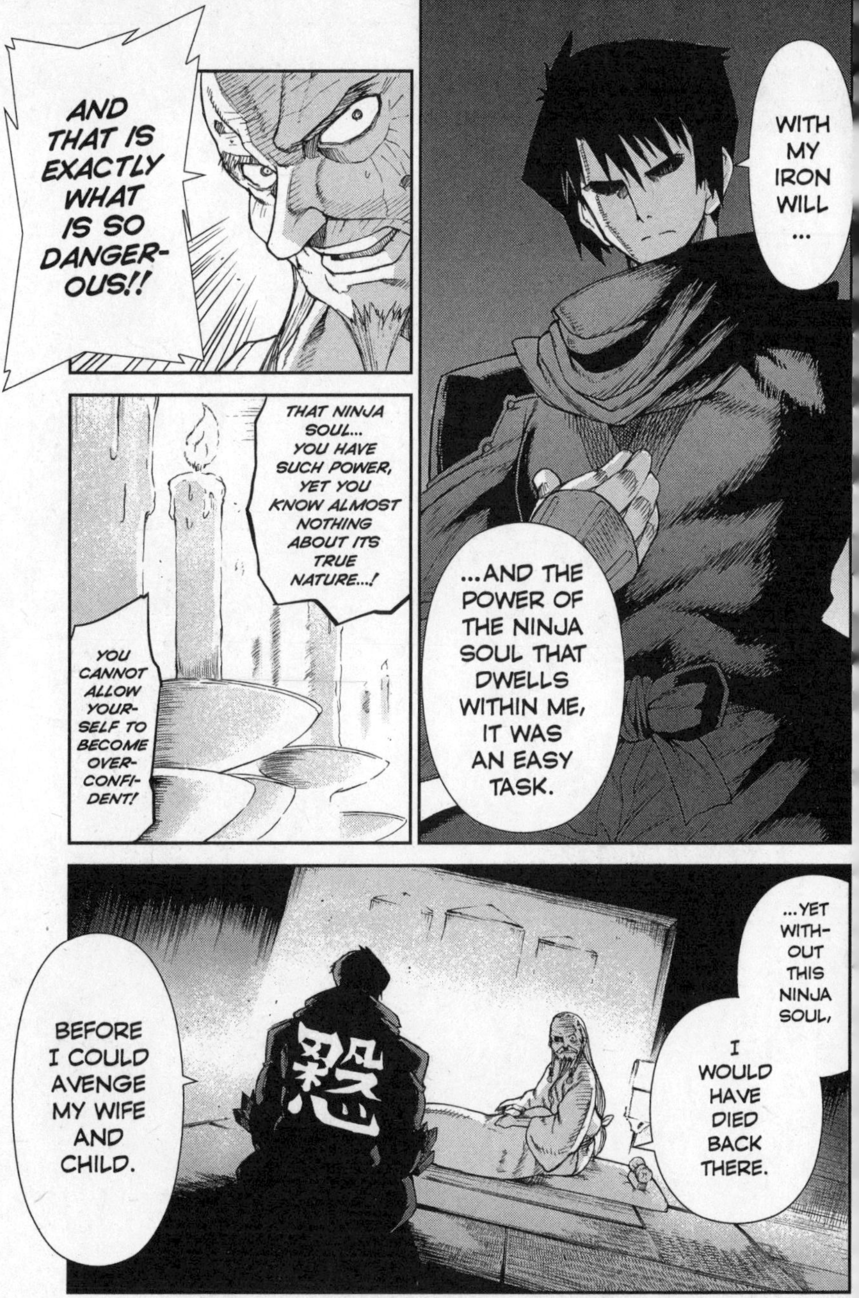
WITH MY IRON WILL...
...AND THE POWER OF THE NINJA SOUL THAT DWELLS WITHIN ME, IT WAS AN EASY TASK.
AND THAT IS EXACTLY WHAT IS SO DANGER-OUS!!
THAT NINJA SOUL... YOU HAVE SUCH POWER, YET YOU KNOW ALMOST NOTHING ABOUT ITS TRUE NATURE...!
YOU CANNOT ALLOW YOUR-SELF TO BECOME OVER-CONFI-DENT!
...YET WITH-OUT THIS NINJA SOUL,
I WOULD HAVE DIED BACK THERE.
BEFORE I COULD AVENGE MY WIFE AND CHILD.

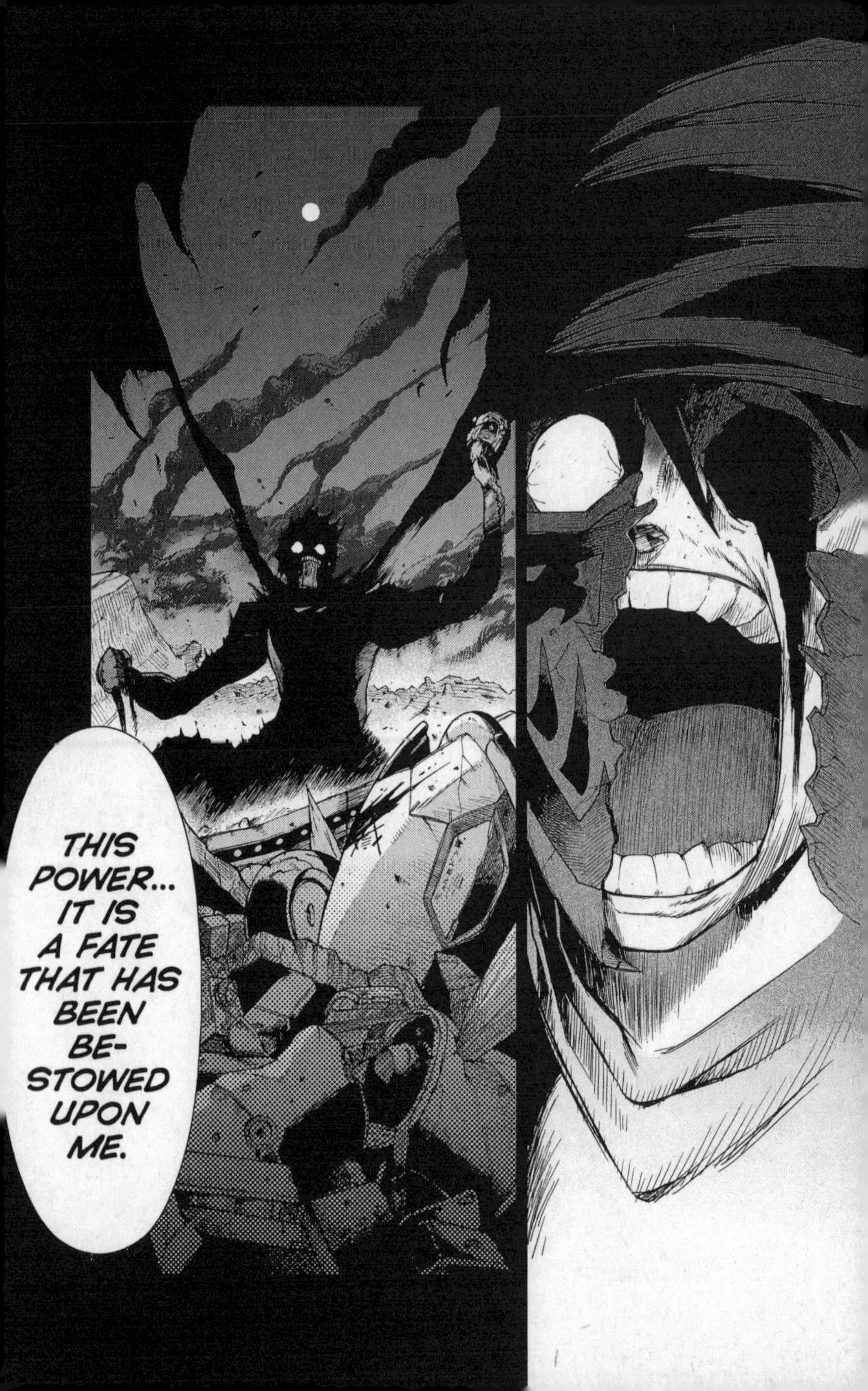
THIS POWER... IT IS A FATE THAT HAS BEEN BE-STOWED UPON ME.

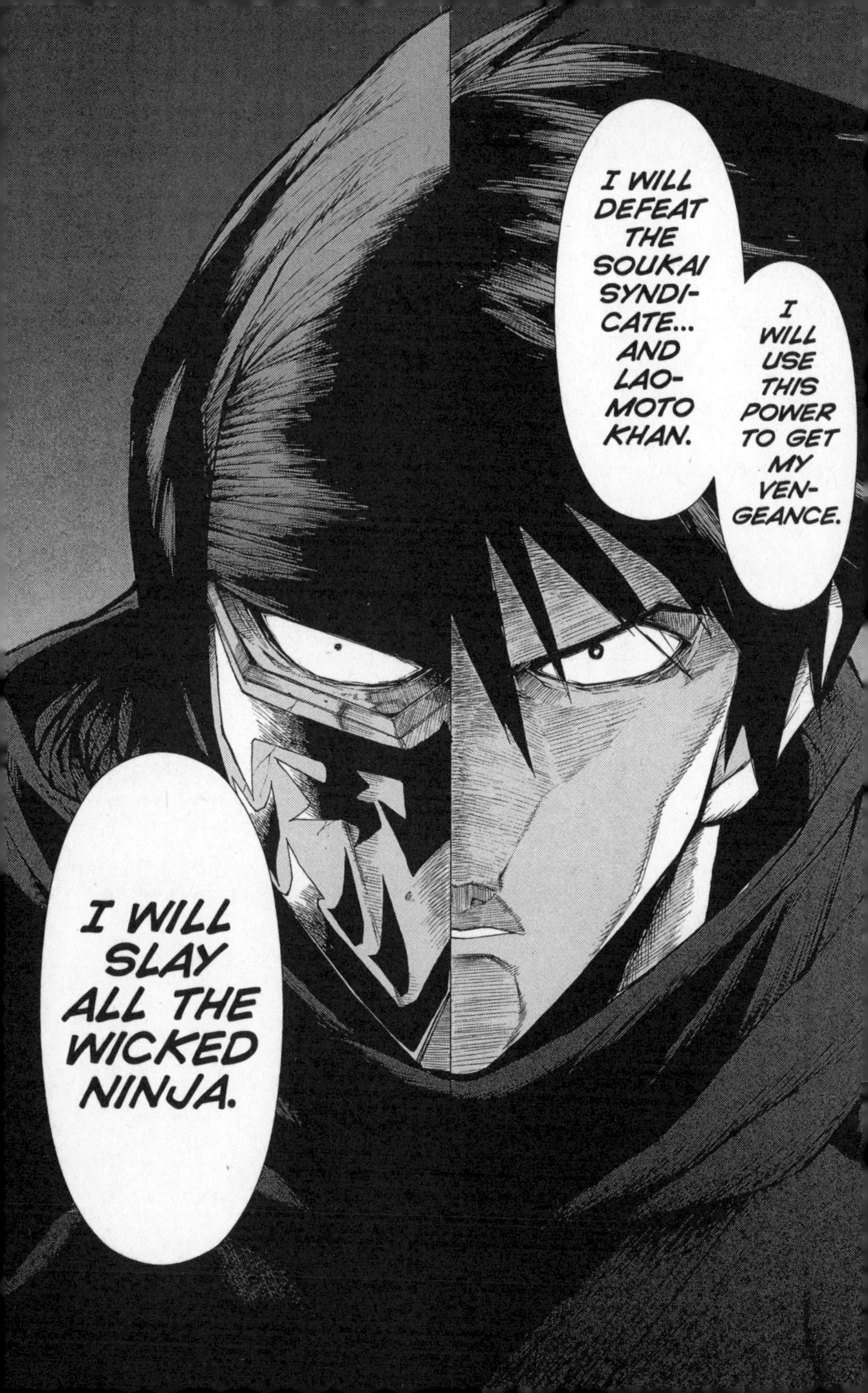
I WILL USE THIS POWER TO GET MY VEN-GEANCE.
I WILL DEFEAT THE SOUKAI SYNDI-CATE... AND LAO-MOTO KHAN.
I WILL SLAY ALL THE WICKED NINJA.

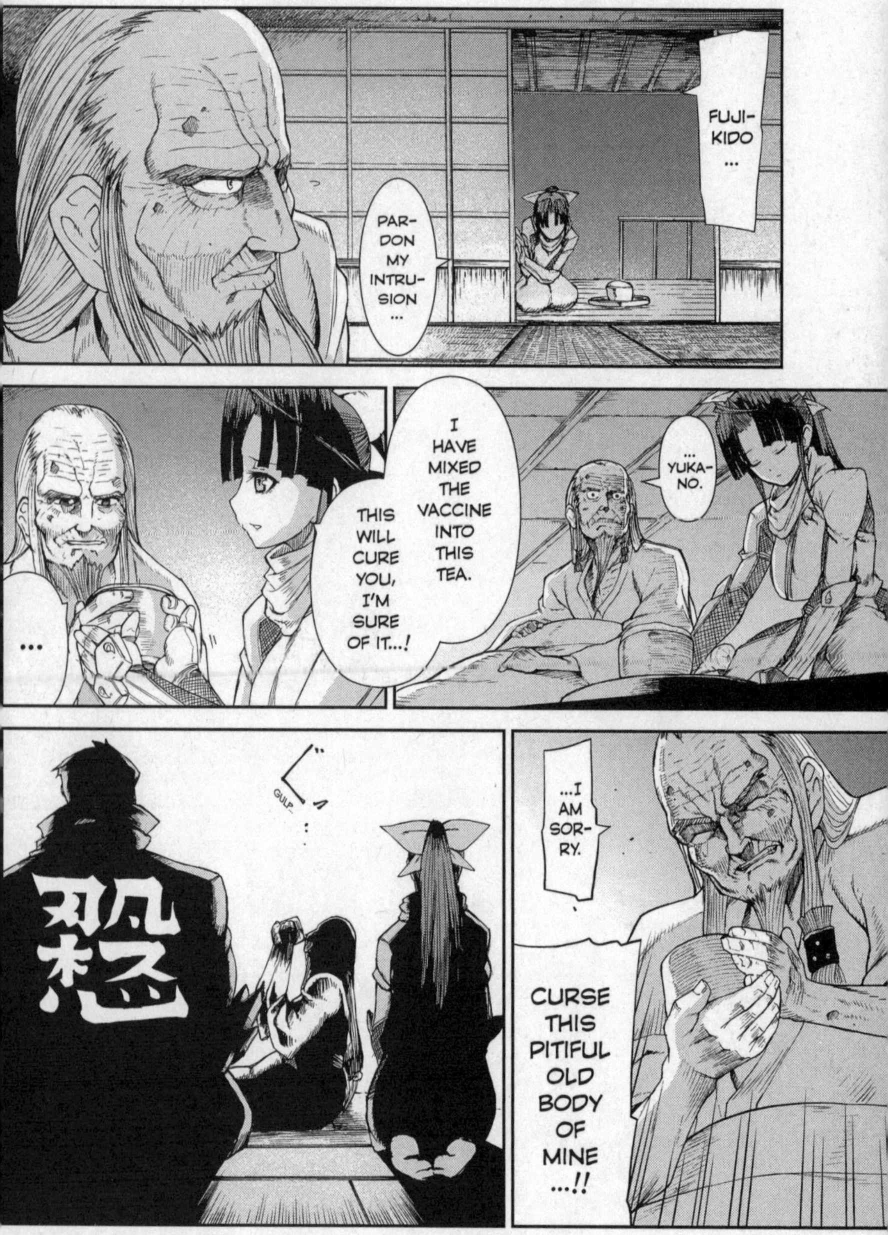
FUJI-KIDO...
PARDON MY INTRUSION...
...YUKANO.
I HAVE MIXED THE VACCINE INTO THIS TEA.
THIS WILL CURE YOU, I'M SURE OF IT...!
...
...I AM SORRY.
CURSE THIS PITIFUL OLD BODY OF MINE...!!
GULP...

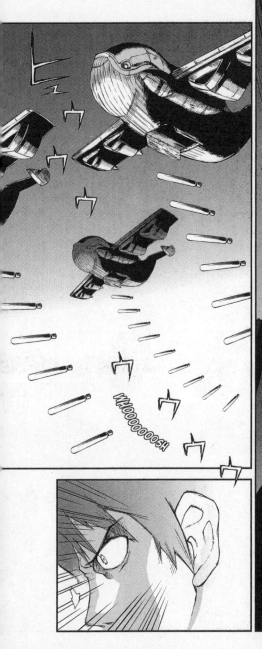

COM-
MENCE
THE
BOM-
BARD-
MENT!

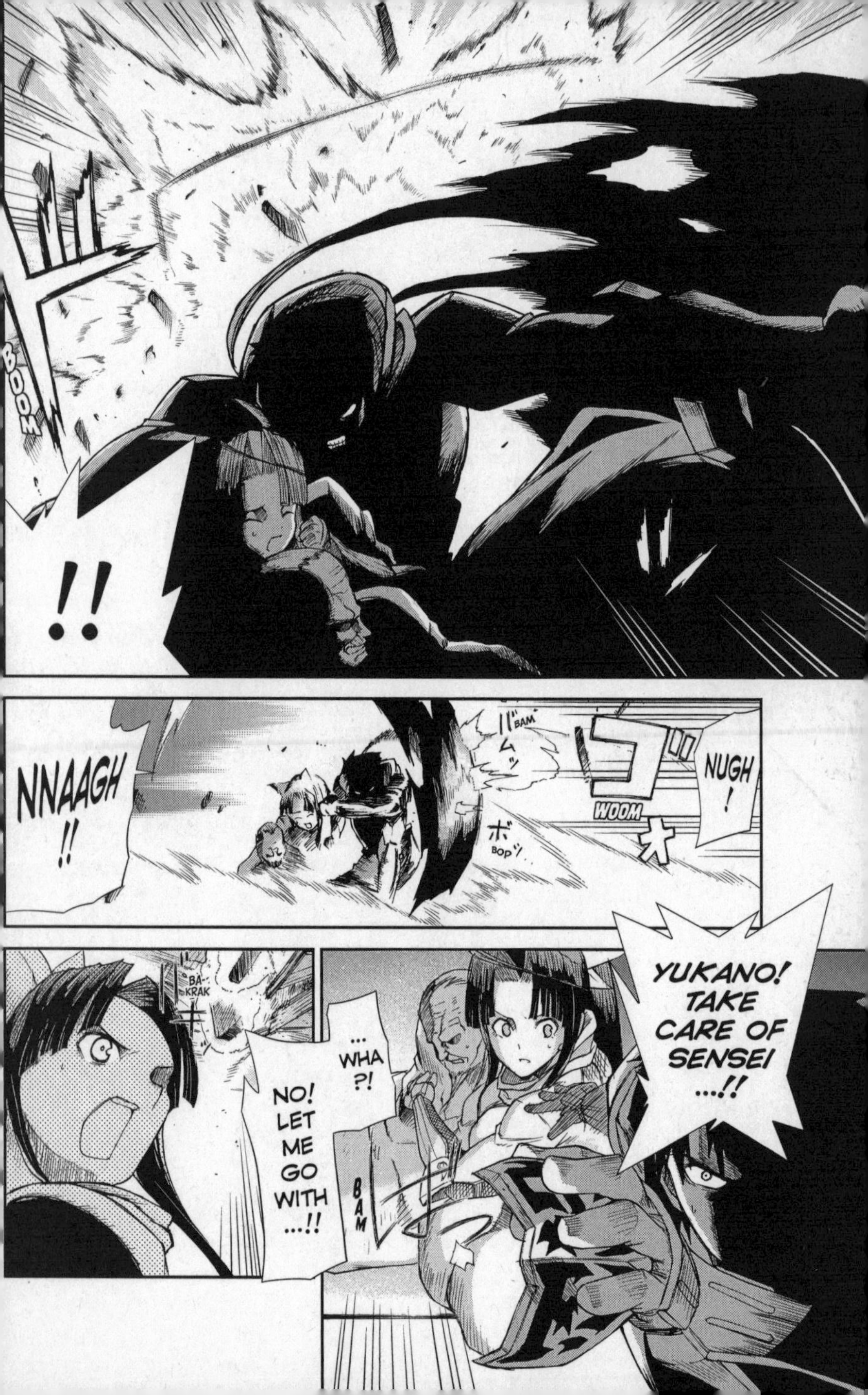
BOOM
!!
NUGH!
WOOM
BAM
BOP
NNAAGH!!
YUKANO! TAKE CARE OF SENSEI ...!!
BAM
... WHA?!
BA-KRAK
NO! LET ME GO WITH ...!!

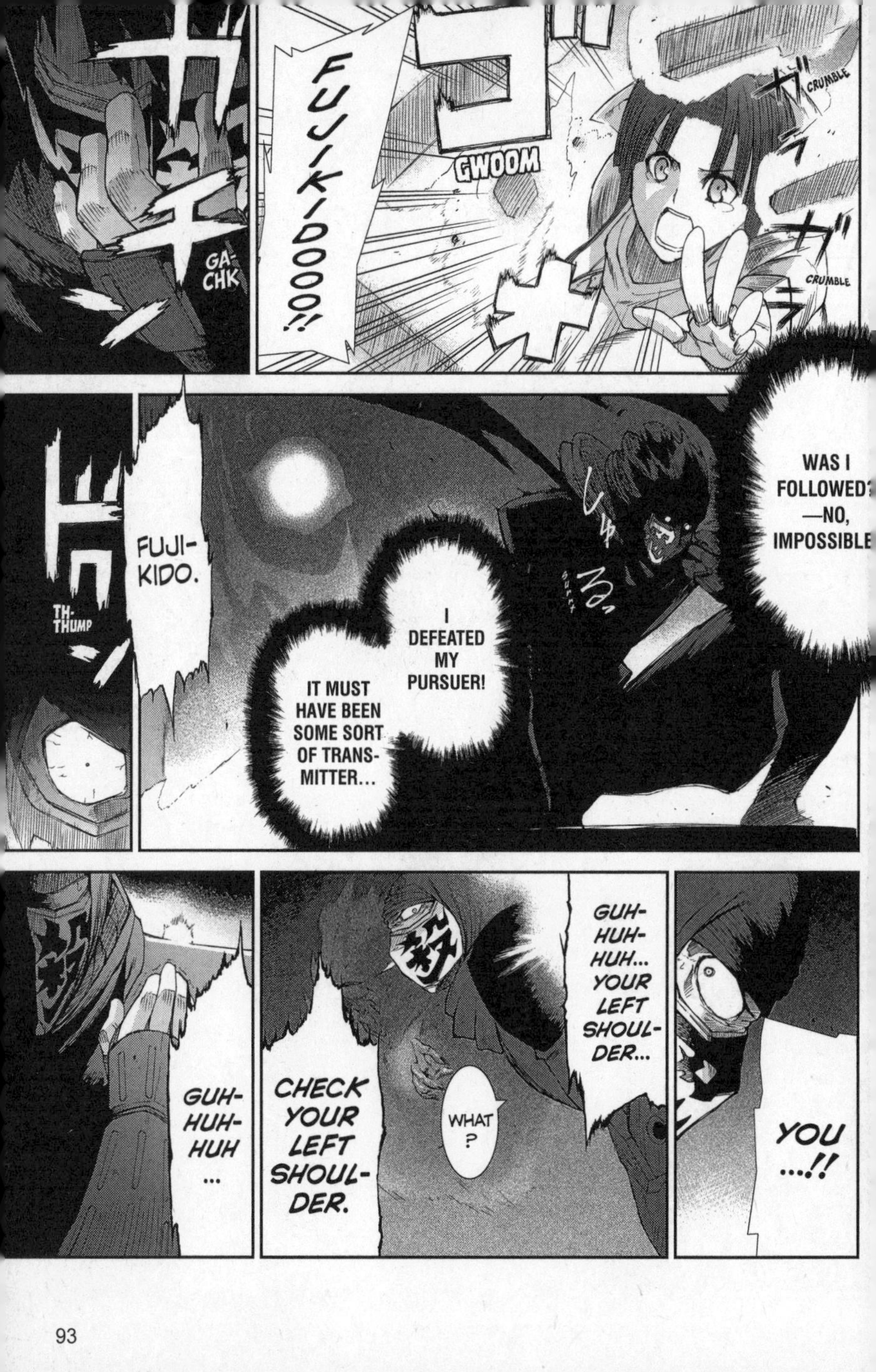
CRUMBLE
CRUMBLE
GWOOM
FUJIKIDOOOO!!
GA-CHK
WAS I FOLLOWED? —NO, IMPOSSIBLE
I DEFEATED MY PURSUER!
IT MUST HAVE BEEN SOME SORT OF TRANS-MITTER…
FUJI-KIDO.
TH-THUMP
YOU ...!!
GUH-HUH-HUH... YOUR LEFT SHOUL-DER...
WHAT?
CHECK YOUR LEFT SHOUL-DER.
GUH-HUH-HUH ...

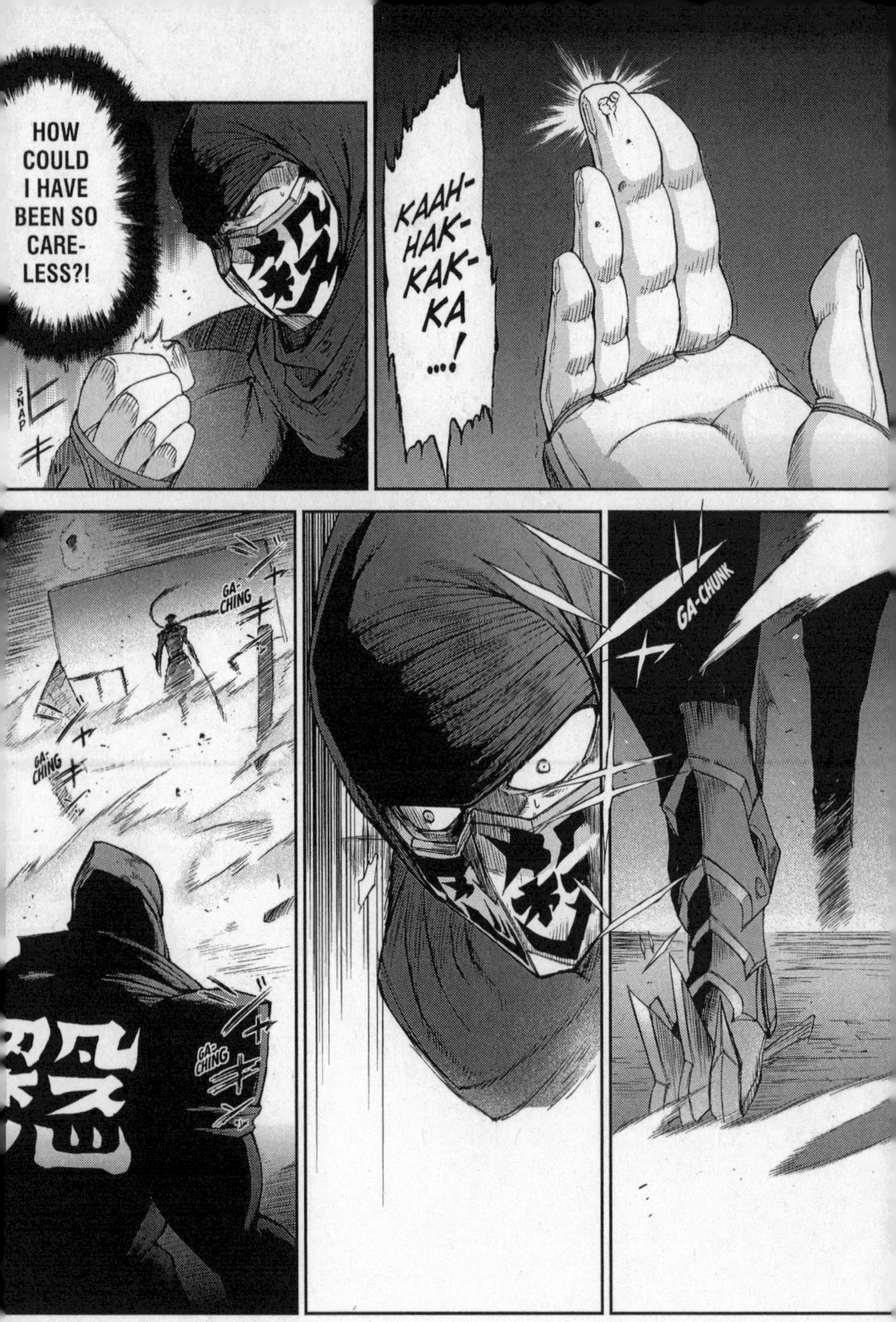
KAAH-HAK-KAK-KA ...!
HOW COULD I HAVE BEEN SO CARE-LESS?!
SNAP
GA-CHUNK
GA-CHING
GA-CHING
GA-CHING

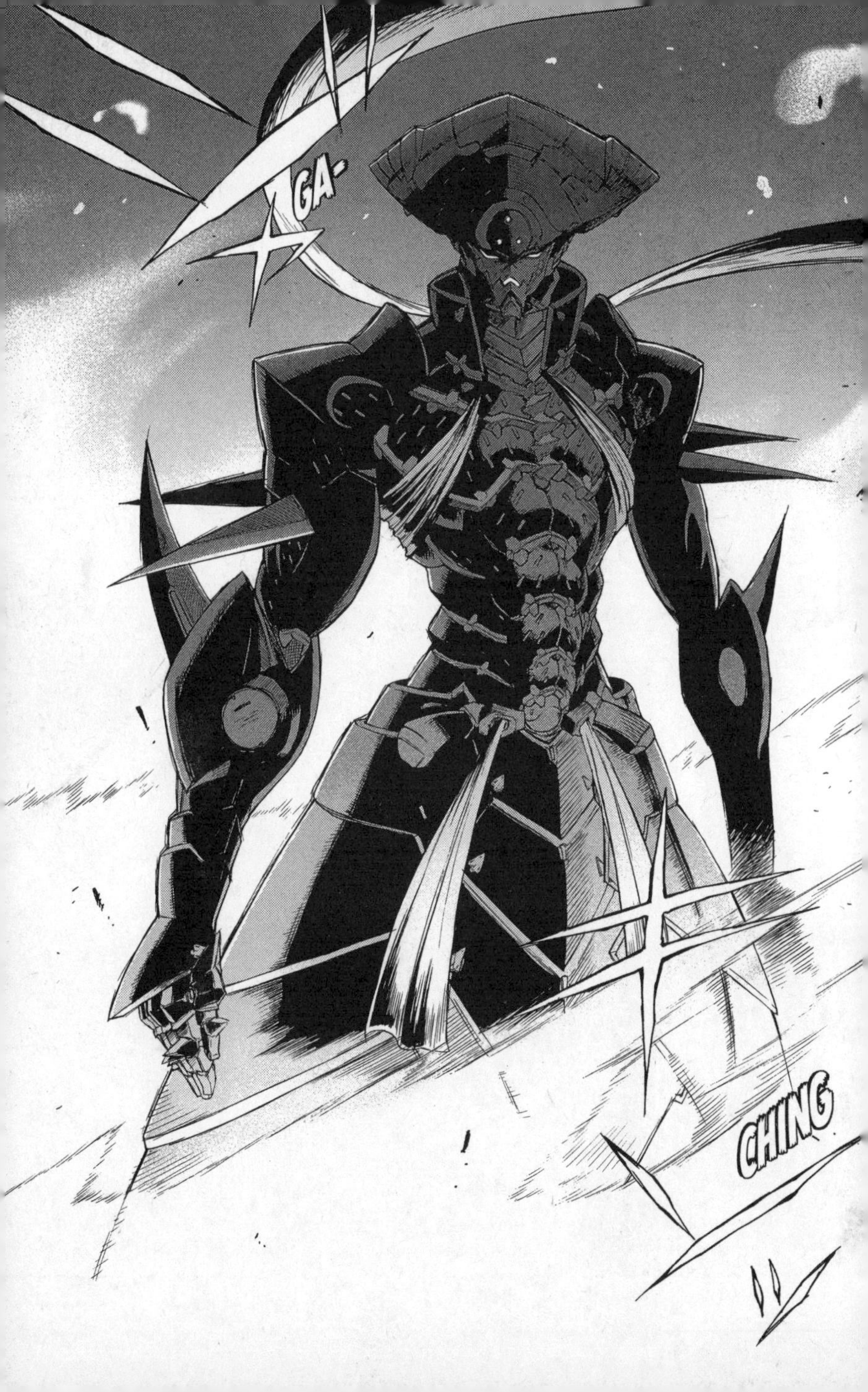
GA-
CHING

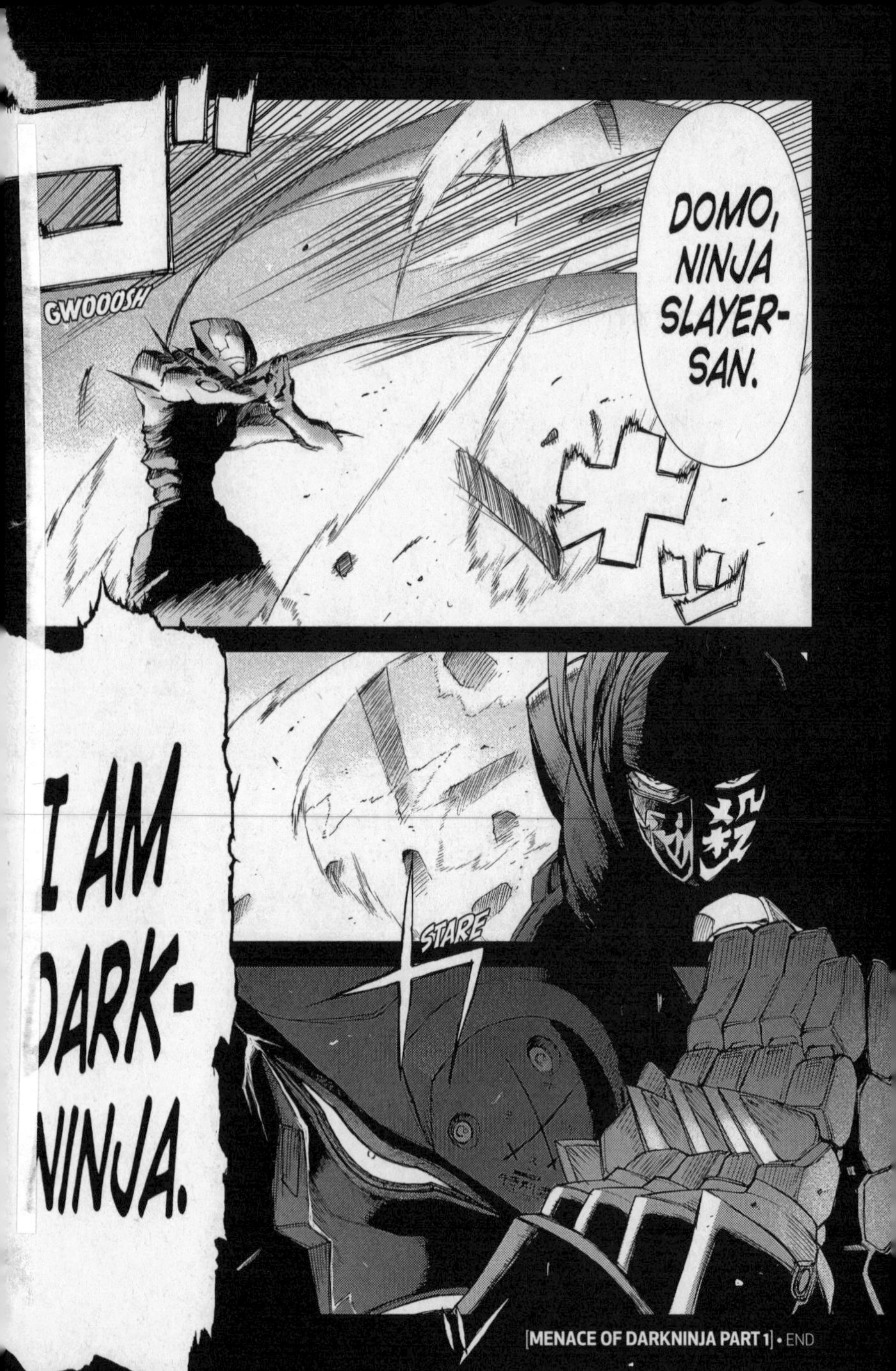
DOMO, NINJA SLAYER-SAN.
GWOOOSH
STARE
I AM DARK-NINJA.

[MENACE OF DARKNINJA PART 1] • END

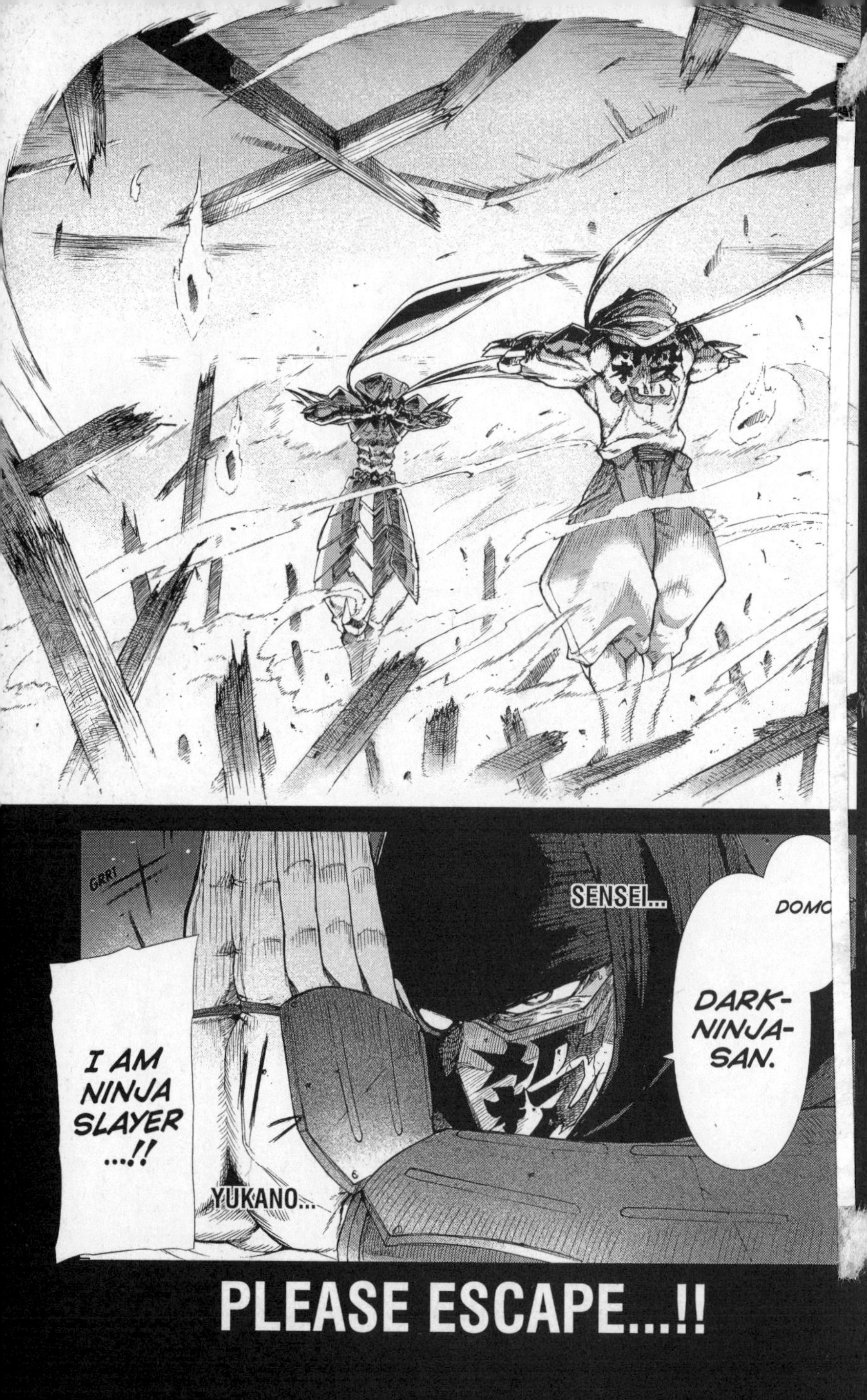
DOMO
DARK-NINJA-SAN.
SENSEI...
GRR!
I AM NINJA SLAYER ...!!
YUKANO...
PLEASE ESCAPE...!!

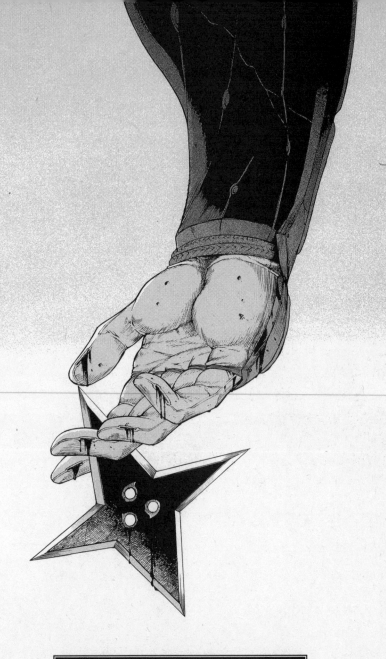

KILLs 004 ✦ MENACE OF DARKNINJA PART 2

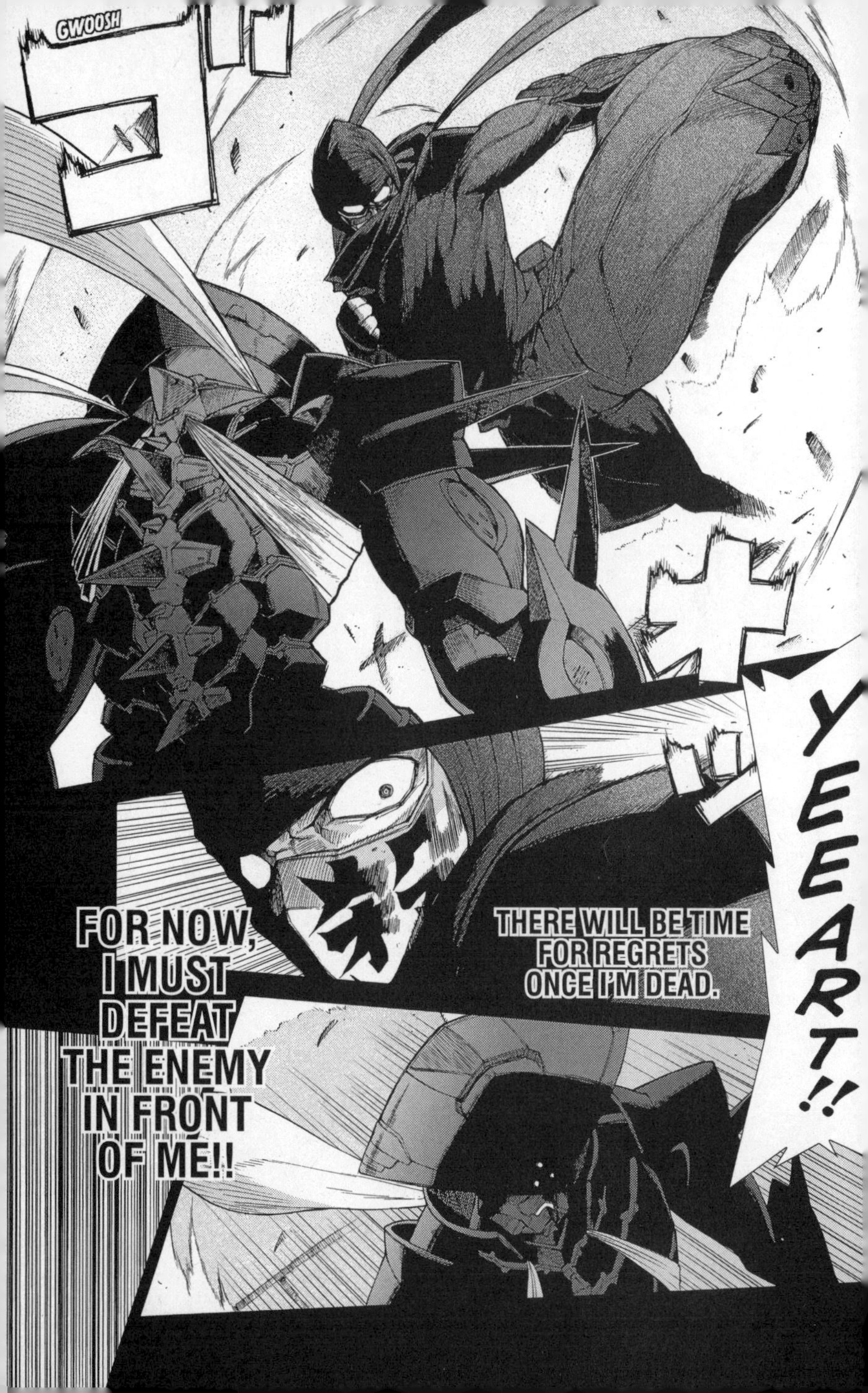
GWOOSH
YEEART!!
THERE WILL BE TIME FOR REGRETS ONCE I'M DEAD.
FOR NOW, I MUST DEFEAT THE ENEMY IN FRONT OF ME!!

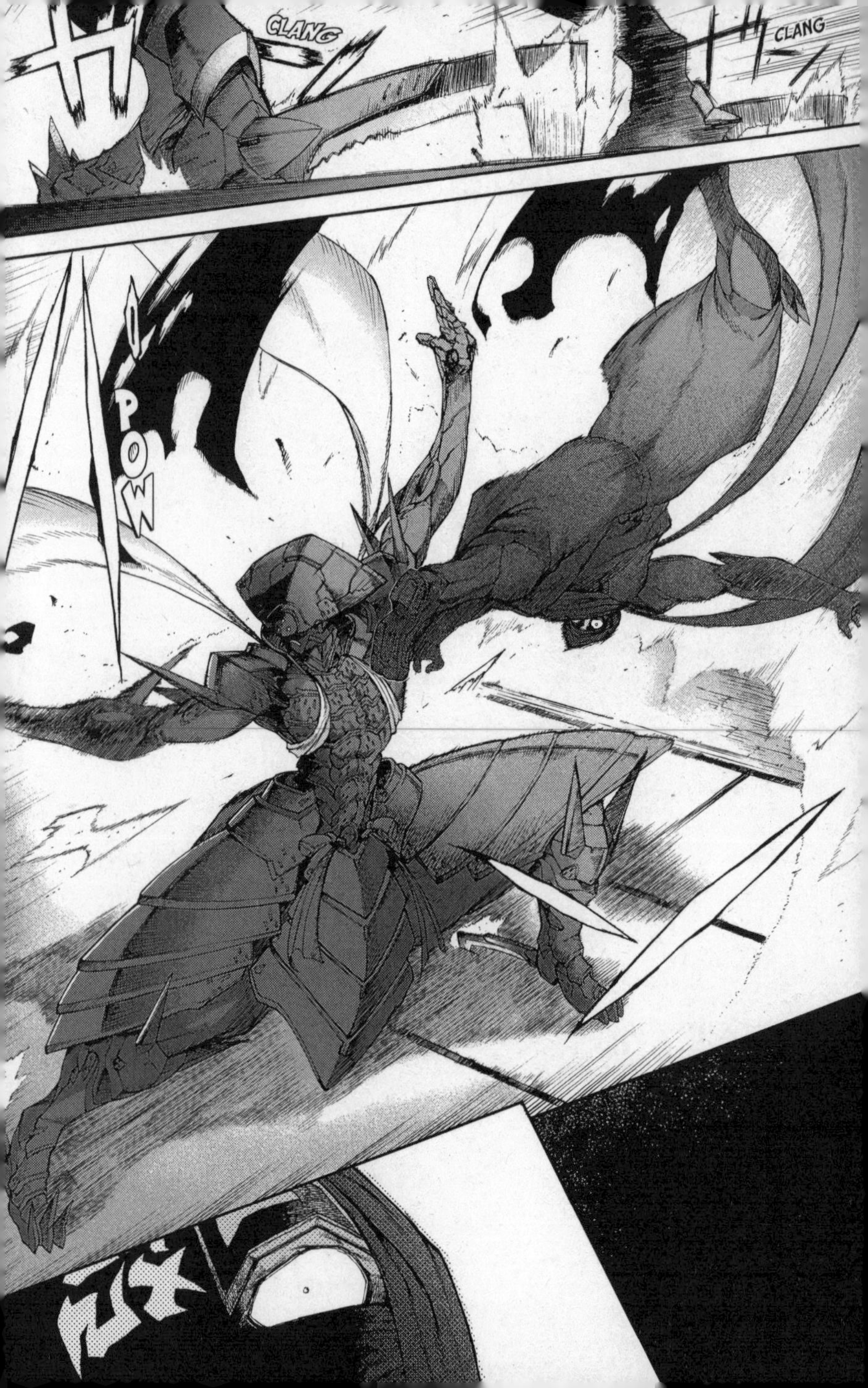

CLANG
CLANG
POW

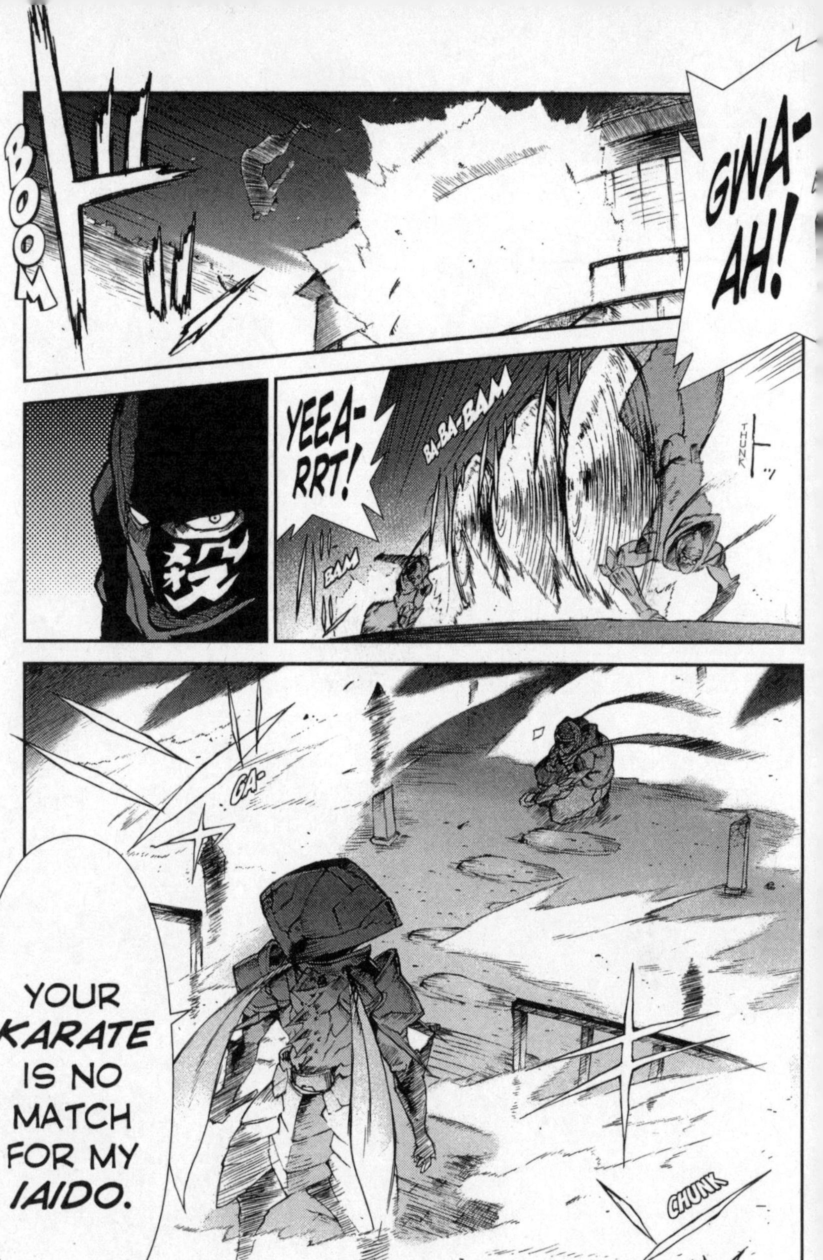
GWA-AH!
BOOM
THUNK
BA-BA-BAM
YEEA-RRT!
BAM
GA-
CHUNK
YOUR KARATE IS NO MATCH FOR MY IAIDO.

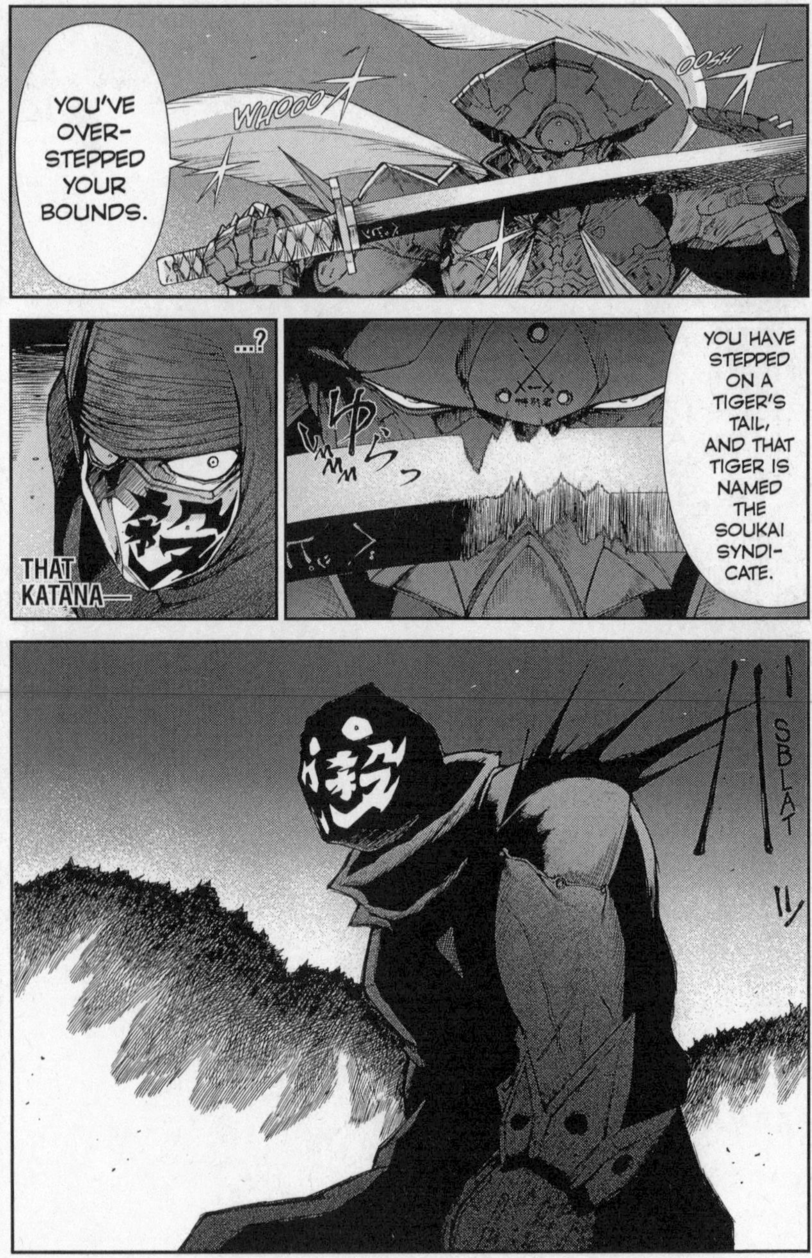
WHOOO
OOSH
YOU'VE OVER-STEPPED YOUR BOUNDS.
YOU HAVE STEPPED ON A TIGER'S TAIL, AND THAT TIGER IS NAMED THE SOUKAI SYNDI-CATE.
ゆらっ
...?
THAT KATANA—
SBLAT

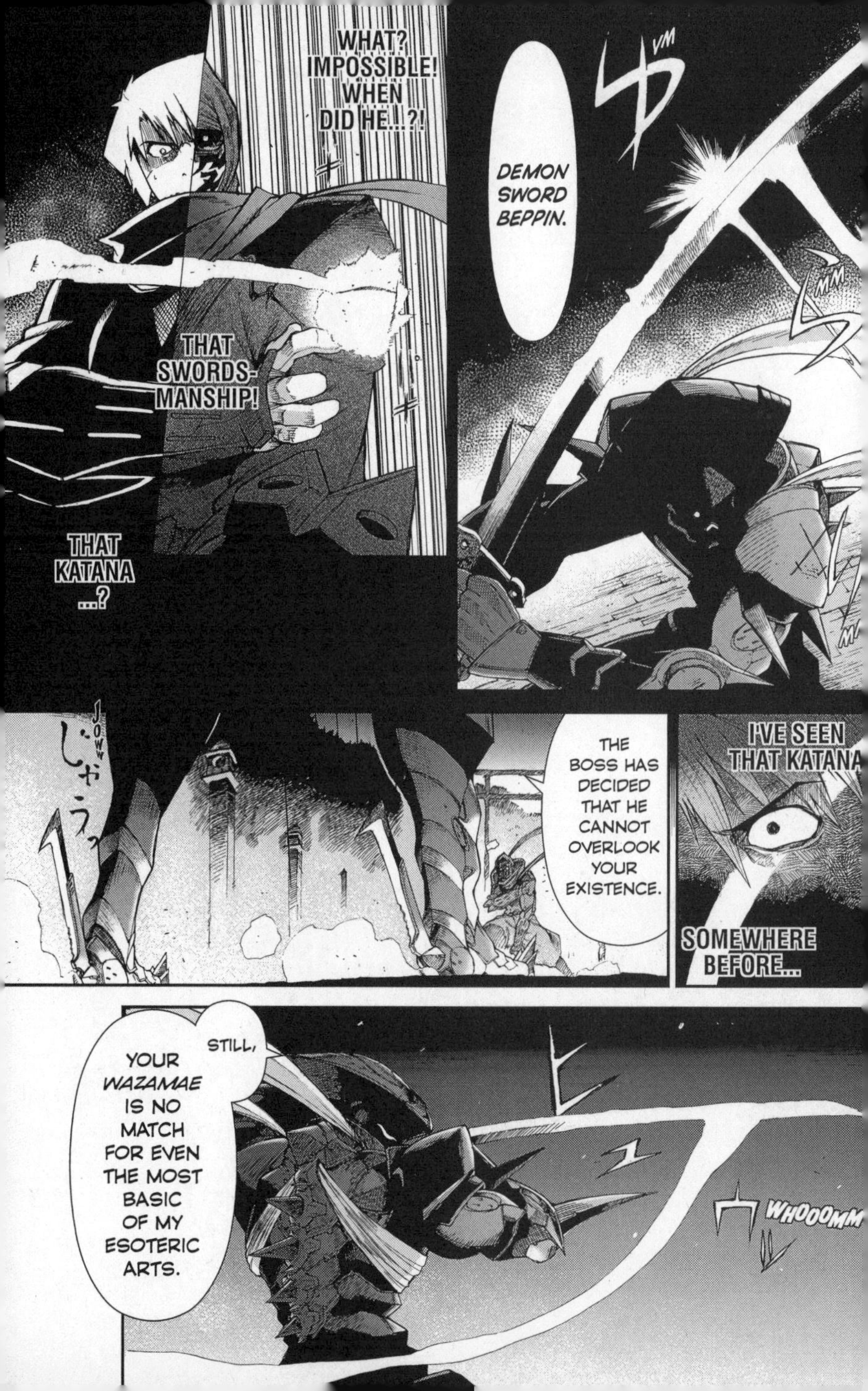
VM
DEMON SWORD BEPPIN.
MM
WHAT? IMPOSSIBLE! WHEN DID HE...?!
THAT SWORDS-MANSHIP!
THAT KATANA ...?
I'VE SEEN THAT KATANA
SOMEWHERE BEFORE...
THE BOSS HAS DECIDED THAT HE CANNOT OVERLOOK YOUR EXISTENCE.
JOWW
STILL, YOUR WAZAMAE IS NO MATCH FOR EVEN THE MOST BASIC OF MY ESOTERIC ARTS.
WHOOOMM

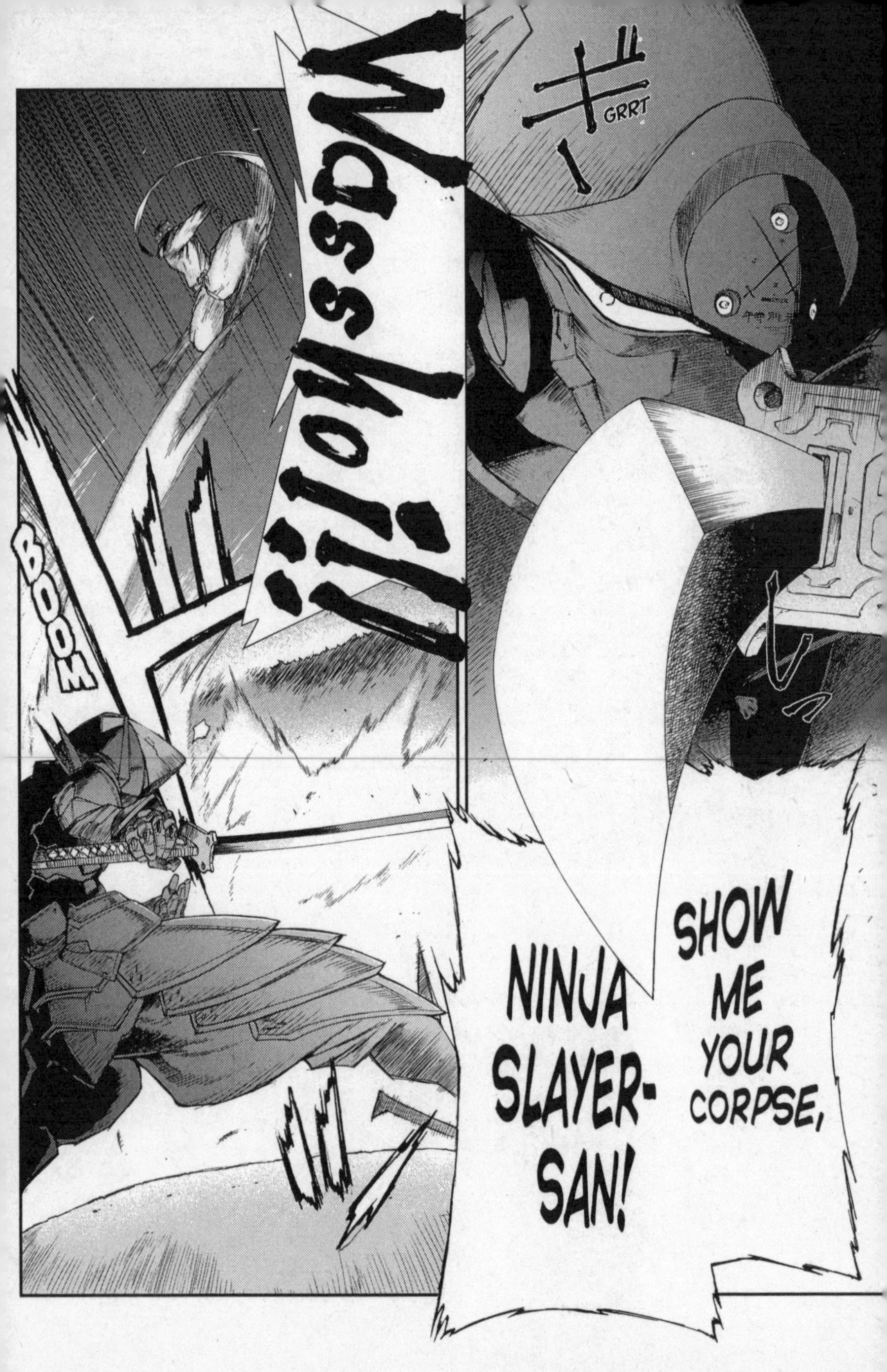
GRRT
SHOW ME YOUR CORPSE, NINJA SLAYER-SAN!
Wasshoi!!
BOOM

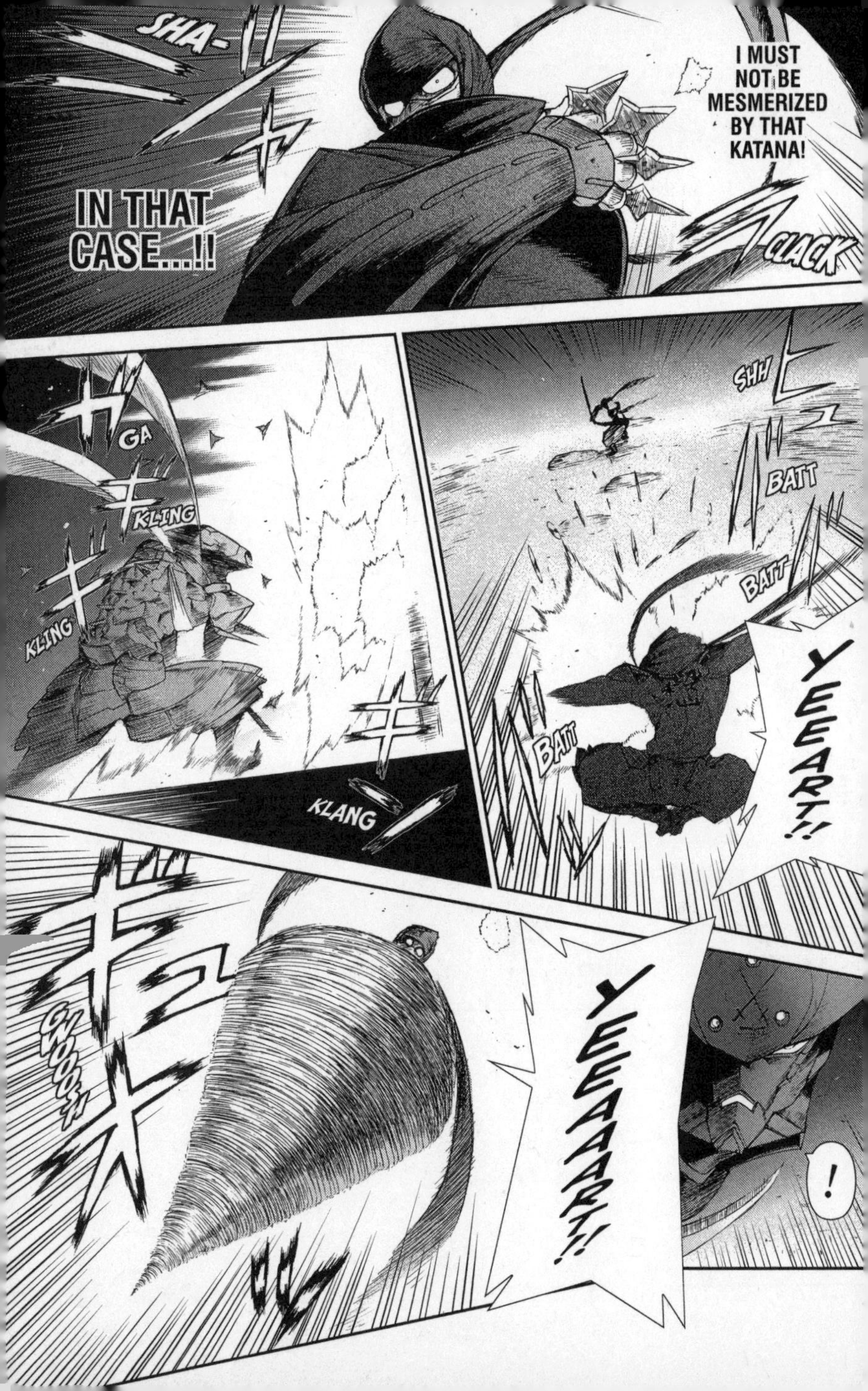
I MUST NOT BE MESMERIZED BY THAT KATANA!
CLACK
SHA-
IN THAT CASE...!!
SHH
BATT
BATT
YEEEART!!
BATT
GA
KLING
KLING
KLANG
!
YEEAAAART!!
GWOOOH

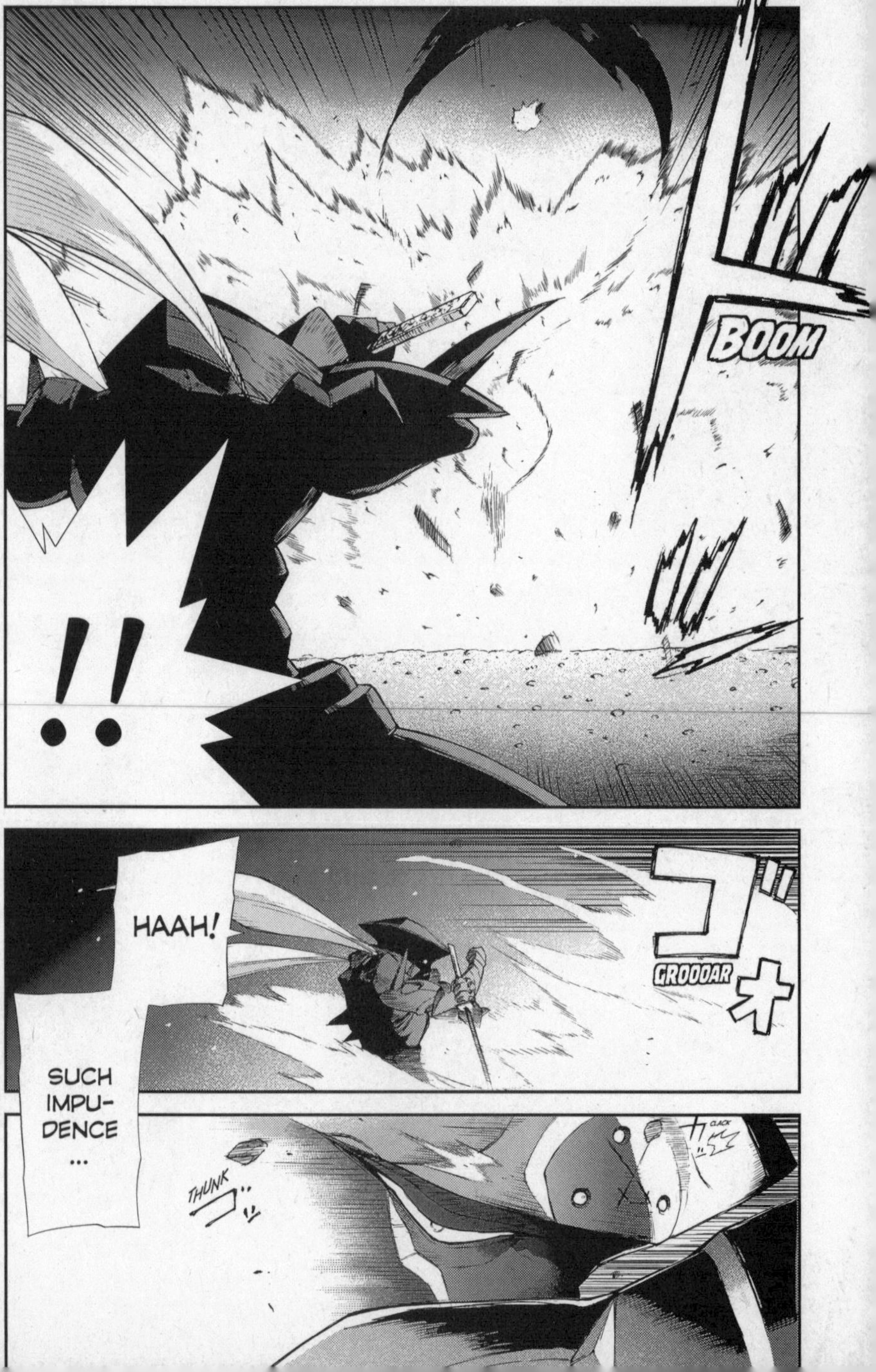
BOOM
!!
ゴオ
GROOOAR
HAAH!
CLACK
SUCH IMPU-DENCE ...
THUNK

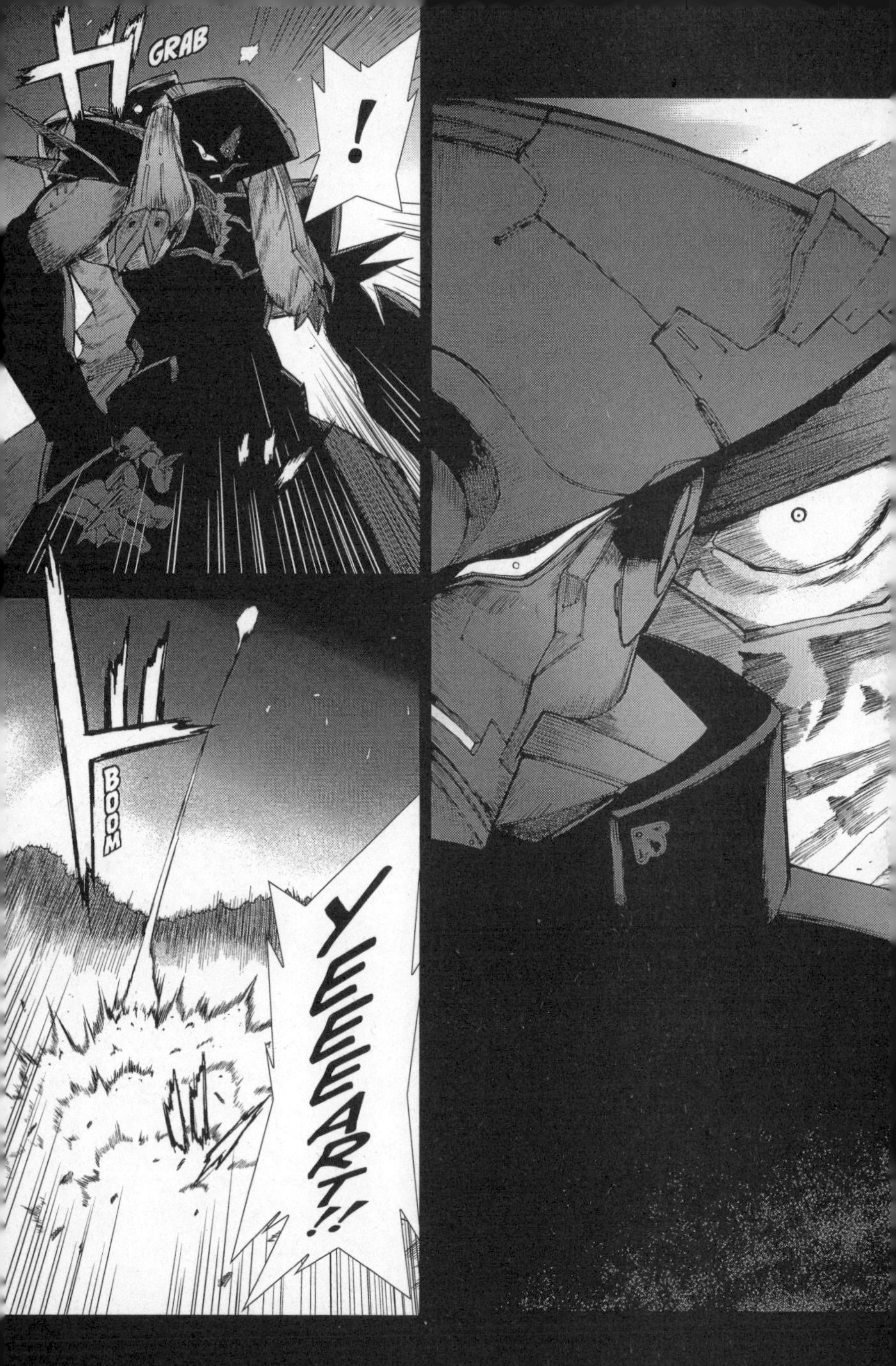
GRAB
!
BOOM
YEEEART!!

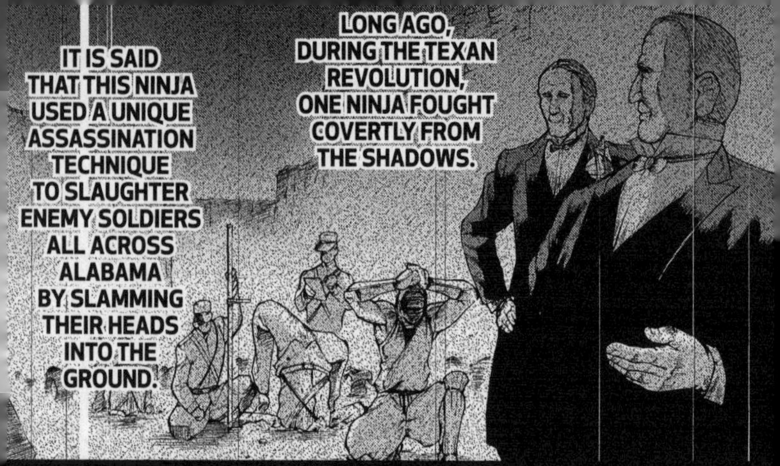
LONG AGO, DURING THE TEXAN REVOLUTION, ONE NINJA FOUGHT COVERTLY FROM THE SHADOWS.
IT IS SAID THAT THIS NINJA USED A UNIQUE ASSASSINATION TECHNIQUE TO SLAUGHTER ENEMY SOLDIERS ALL ACROSS ALABAMA BY SLAMMING THEIR HEADS INTO THE GROUND.

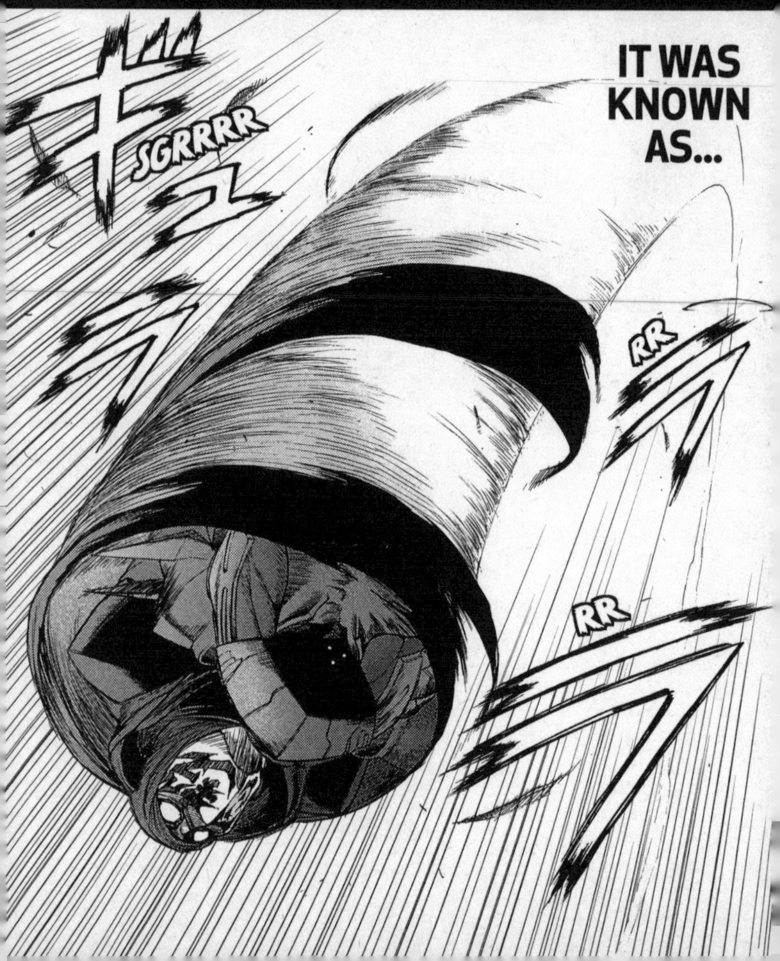
IT WAS KNOWN AS...
SGRRRR
RR
RR

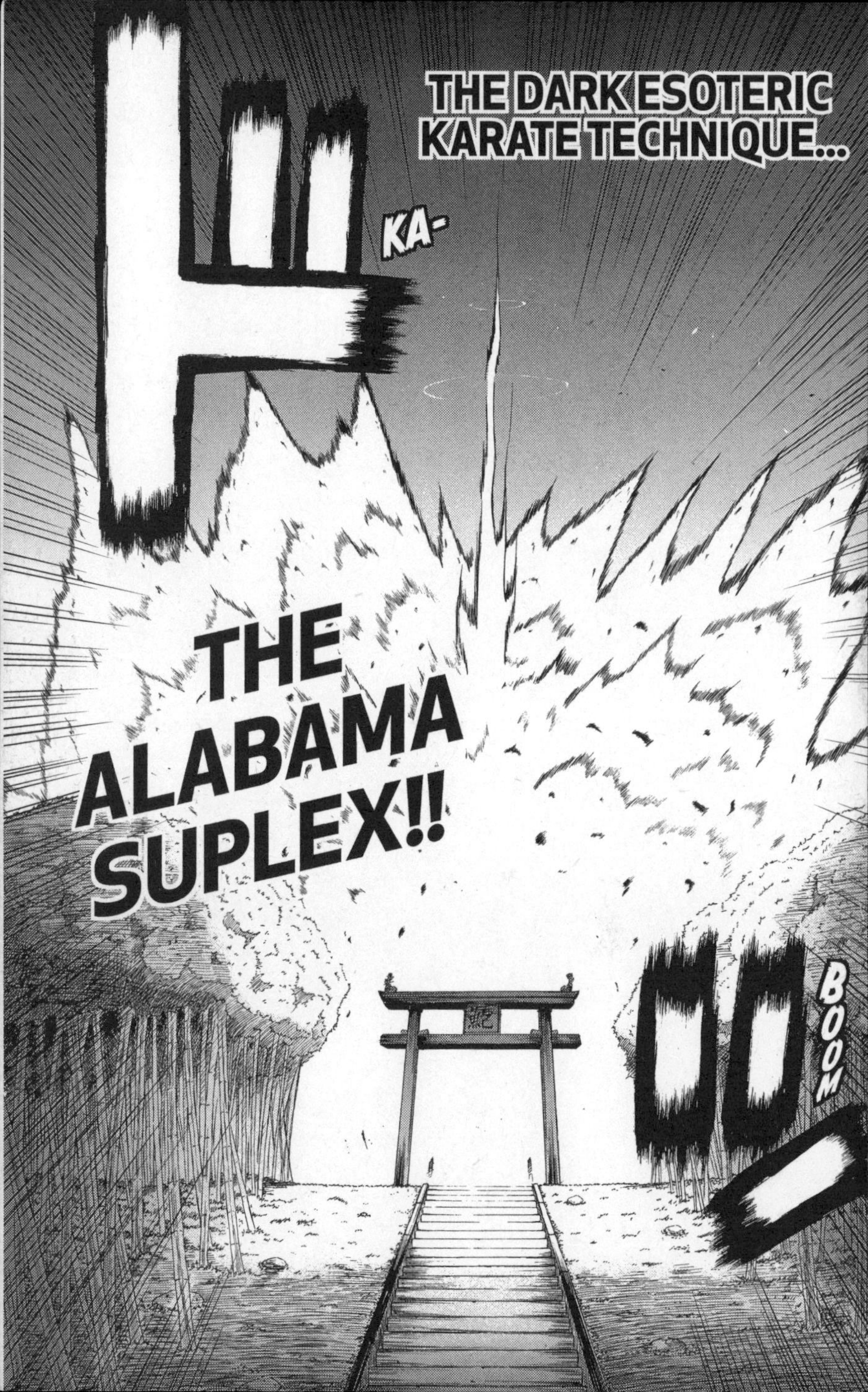
THE DARK ESOTERIC KARATE TECHNIQUE...
KA-
THE ALABAMA SUPLEX!!
BOOM

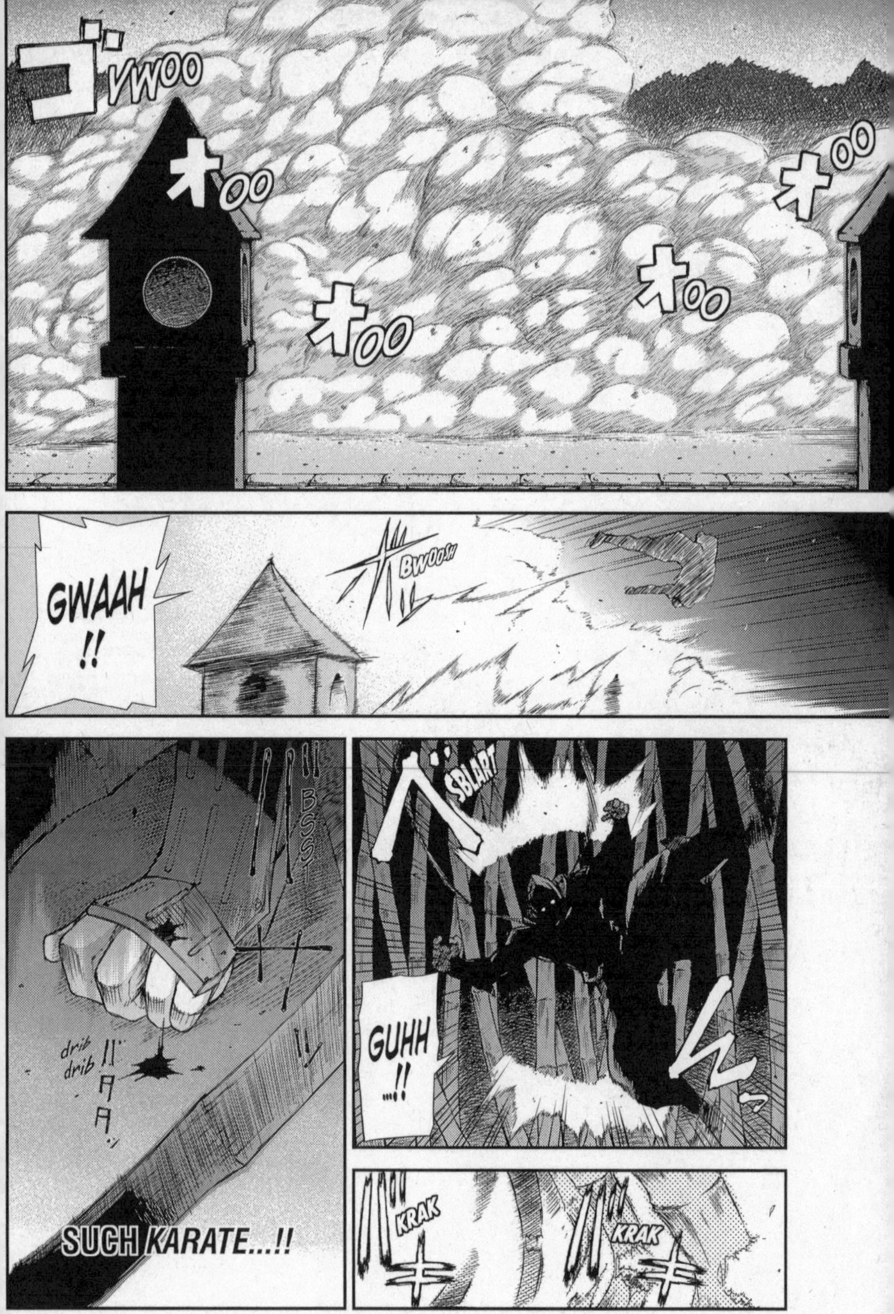
ゴ VWOO
オ OO
オ OO
オ OO
オ OO
GWAAH !!
BWOOSH
SBLART
GUHH ...!!
BSST
drib drib
SUCH KARATE...!!
KRAK
KRAK

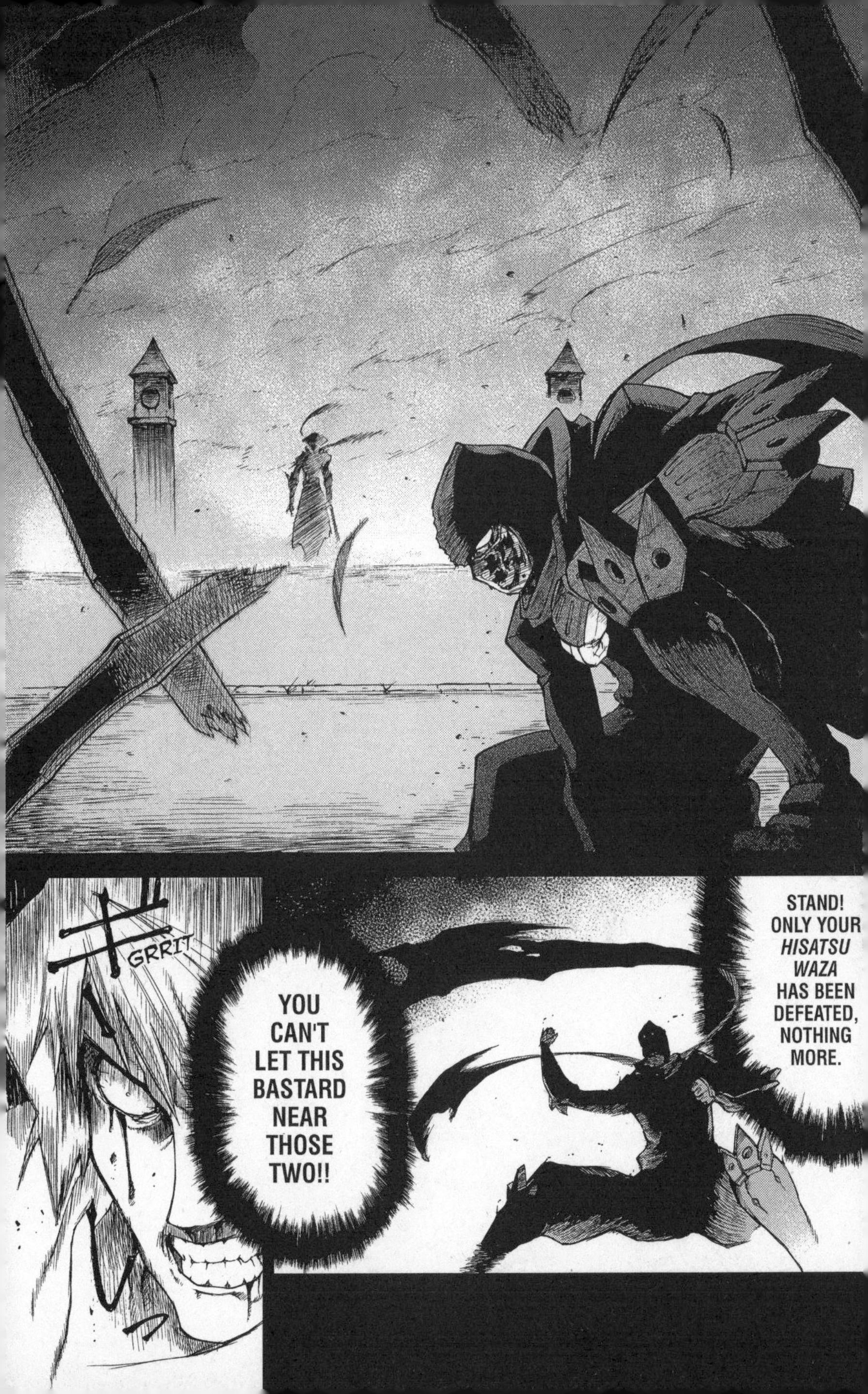
STAND! ONLY YOUR *HISATSU WAZA* HAS BEEN DEFEATED, NOTHING MORE.
YOU CAN'T LET THIS BASTARD NEAR THOSE TWO!!
GRRIT

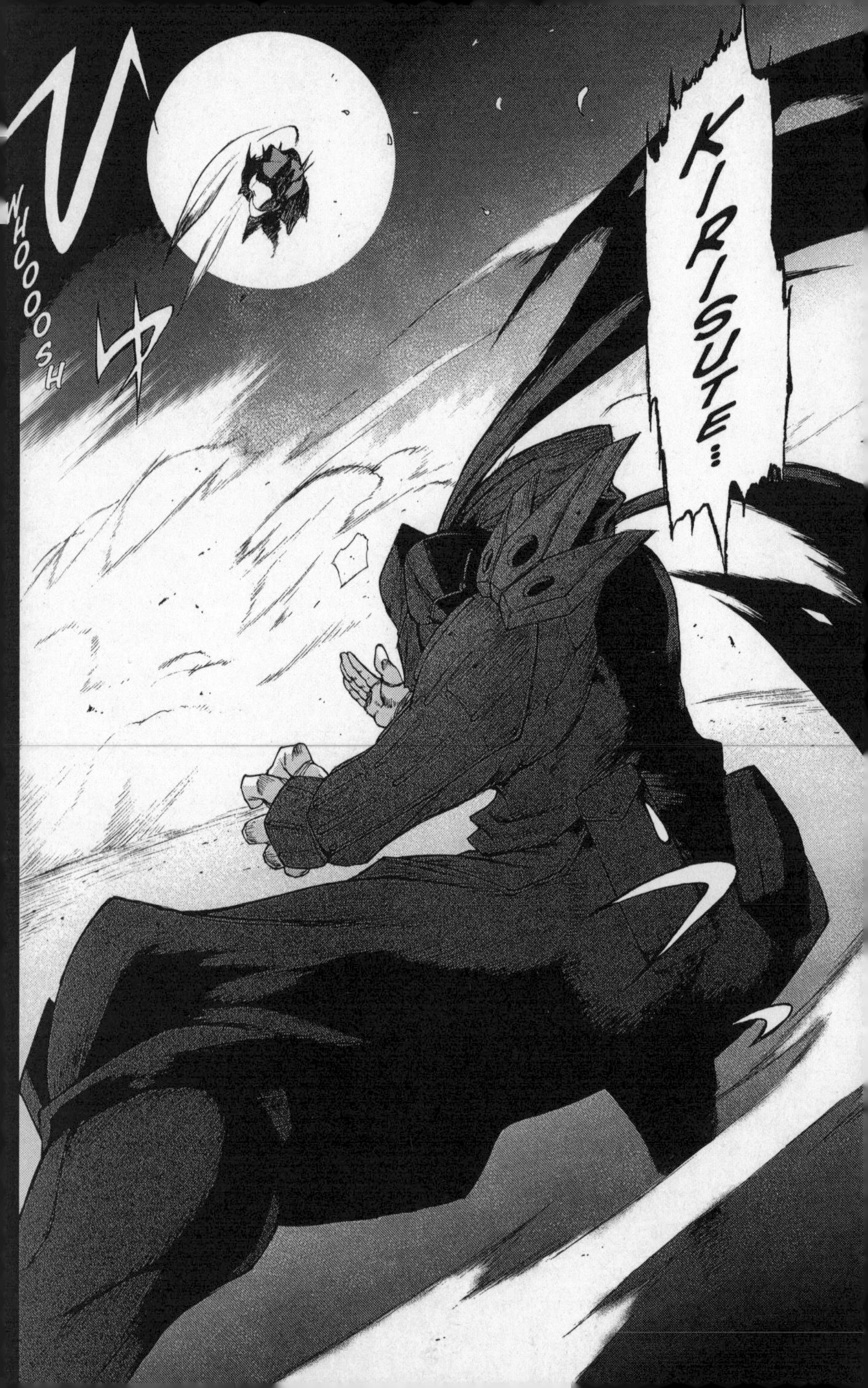
KIRISUTE...
WHOOOOOSH

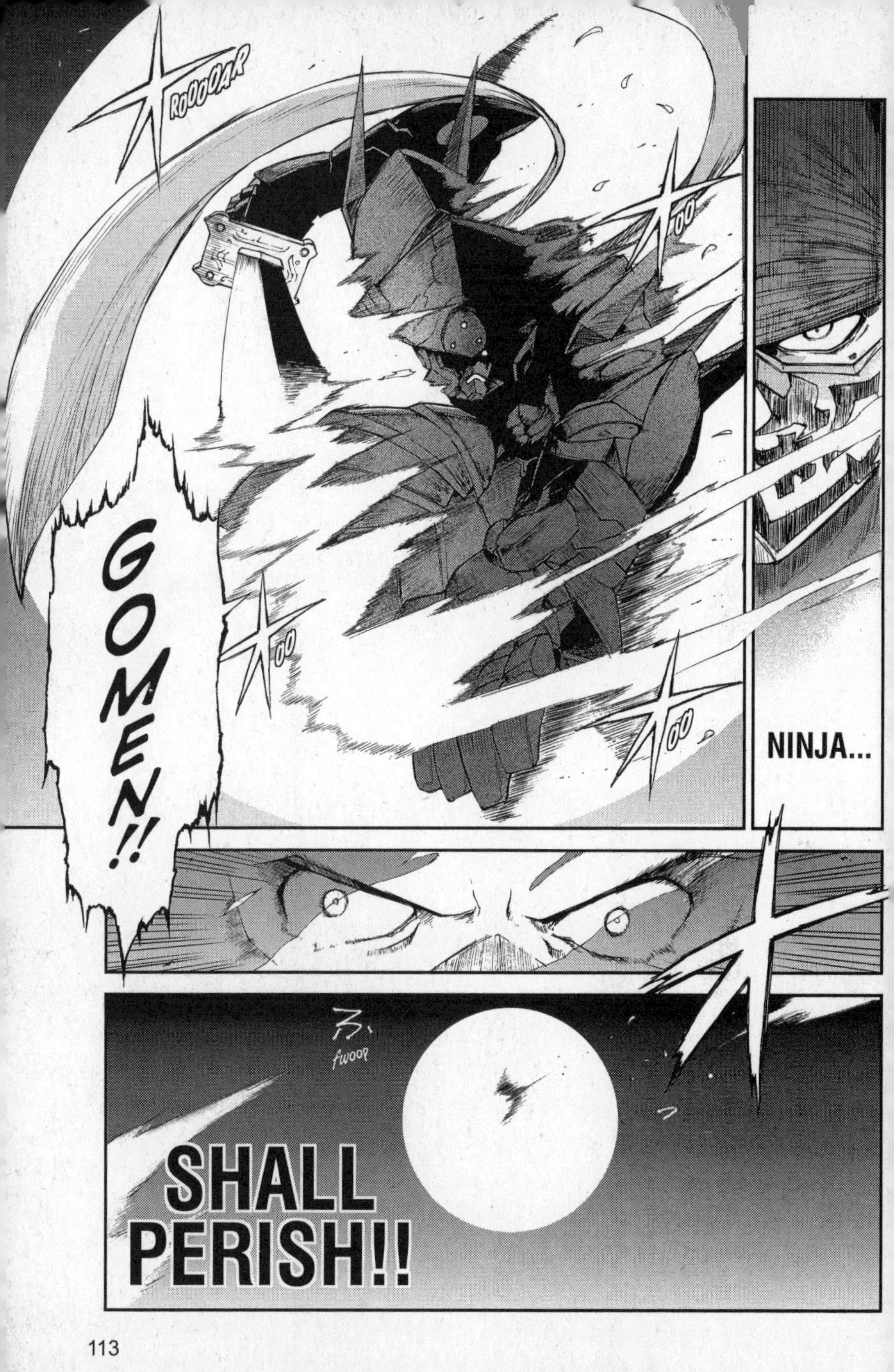
NINJA...
ROOOOAR
OO
OO
OO
GOMEN!!
fwoop
SHALL PERISH!!

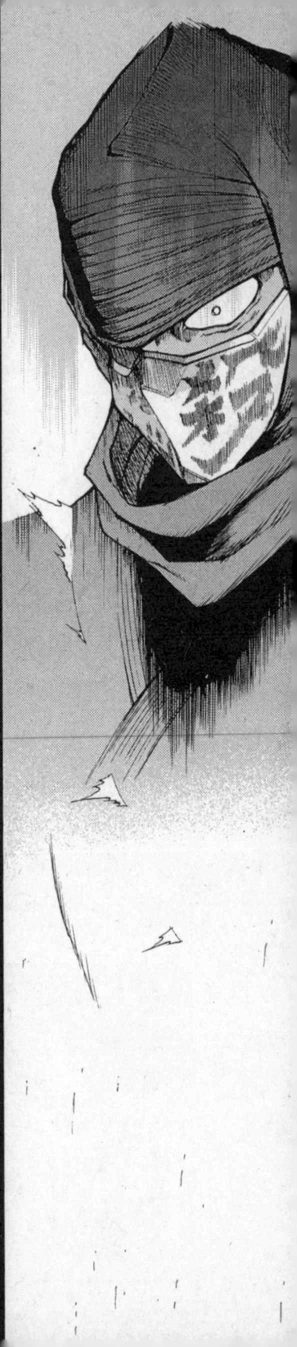

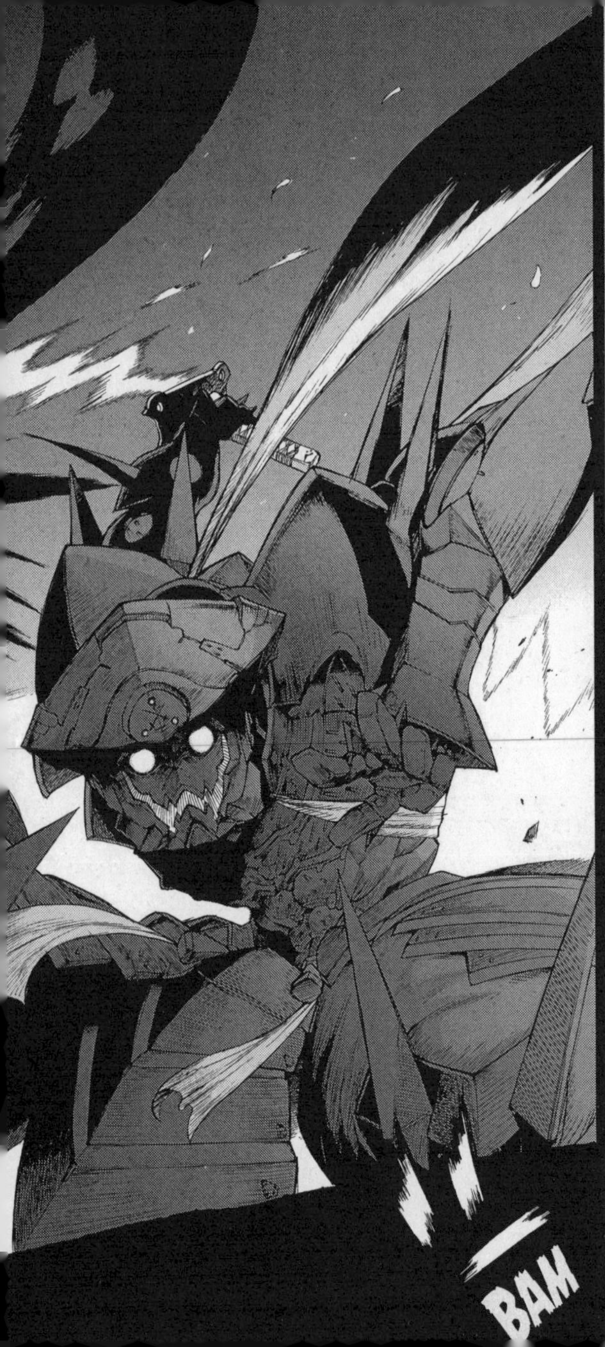
BAM

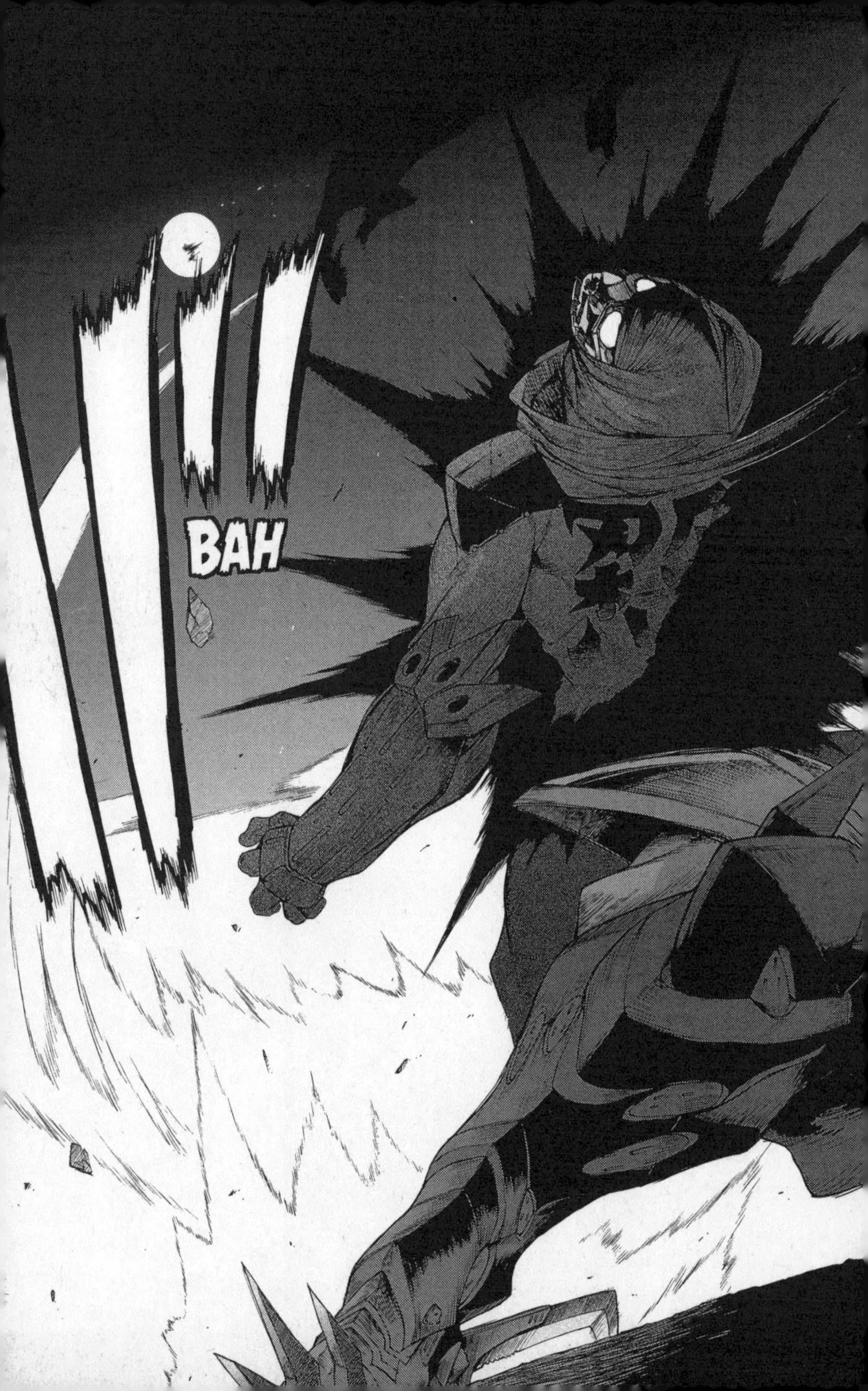
BAH

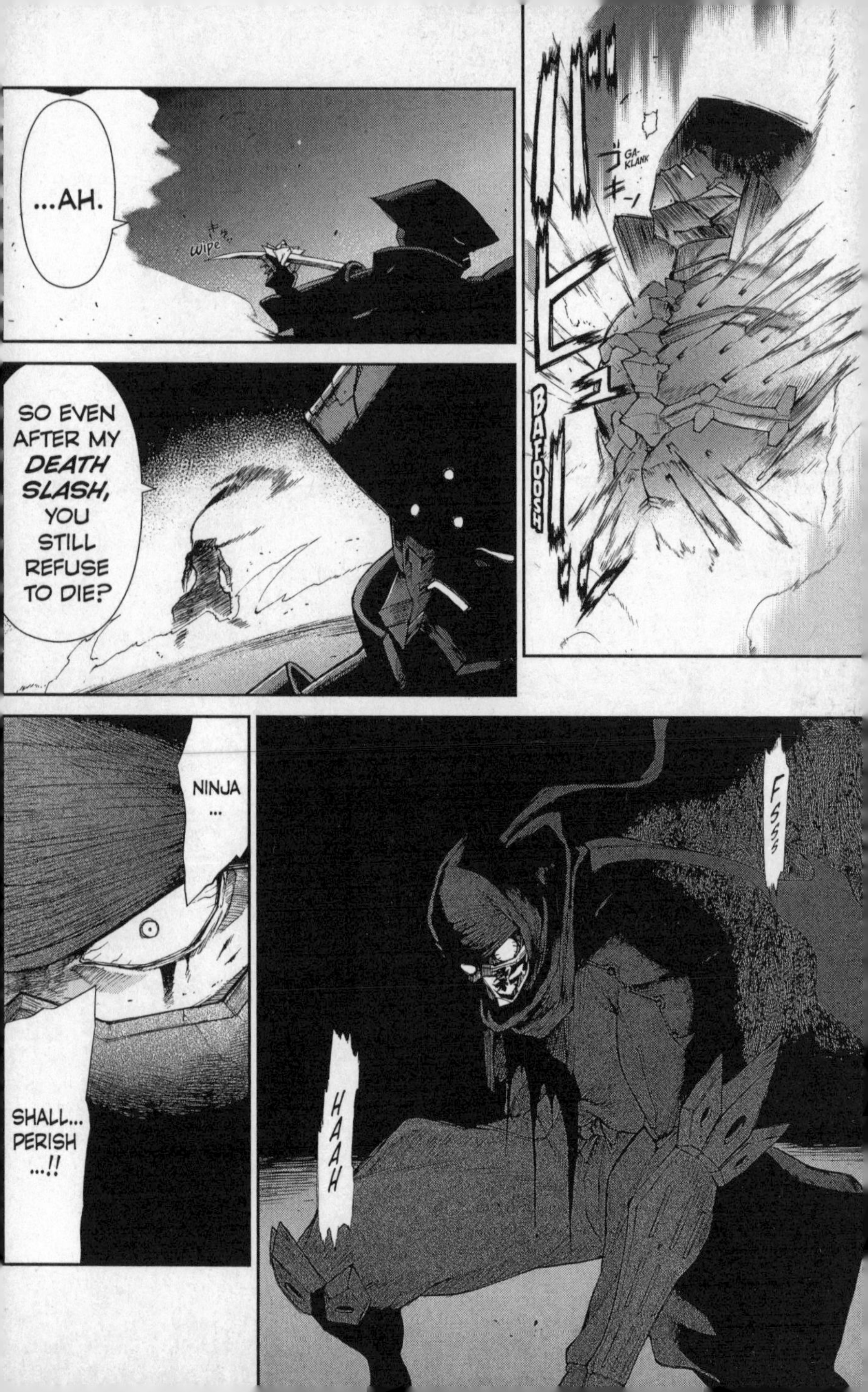
GA-KLANK
BAFOOSH
...AH.
wipe
SO EVEN AFTER MY *DEATH SLASH,* YOU STILL REFUSE TO DIE?
FSSS
HAAH
NINJA...
SHALL... PERISH...!!

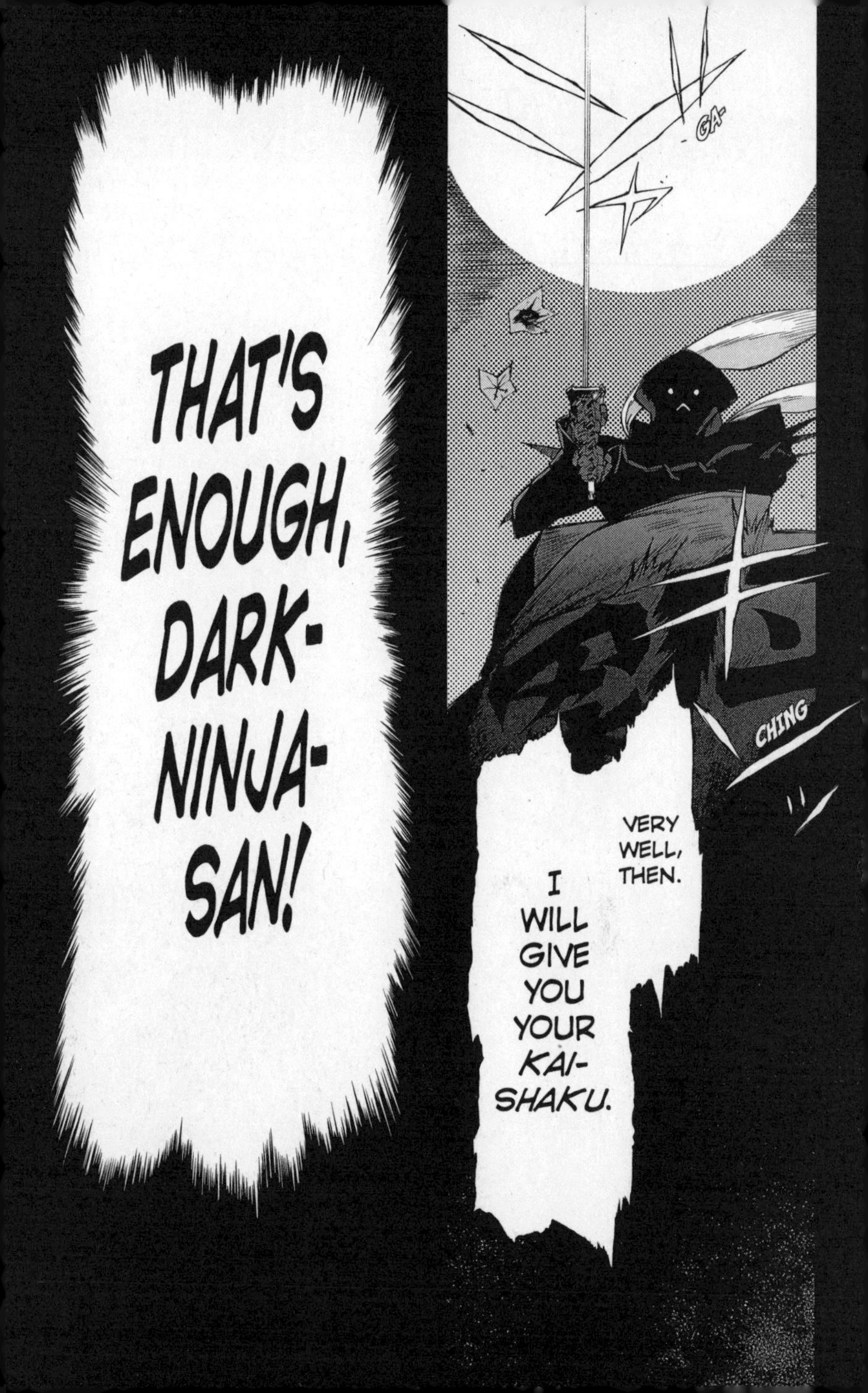
GA-
CHING
VERY WELL, THEN.
I WILL GIVE YOU YOUR *KAI-SHAKU.*
THAT'S ENOUGH, DARK-NINJA-SAN!

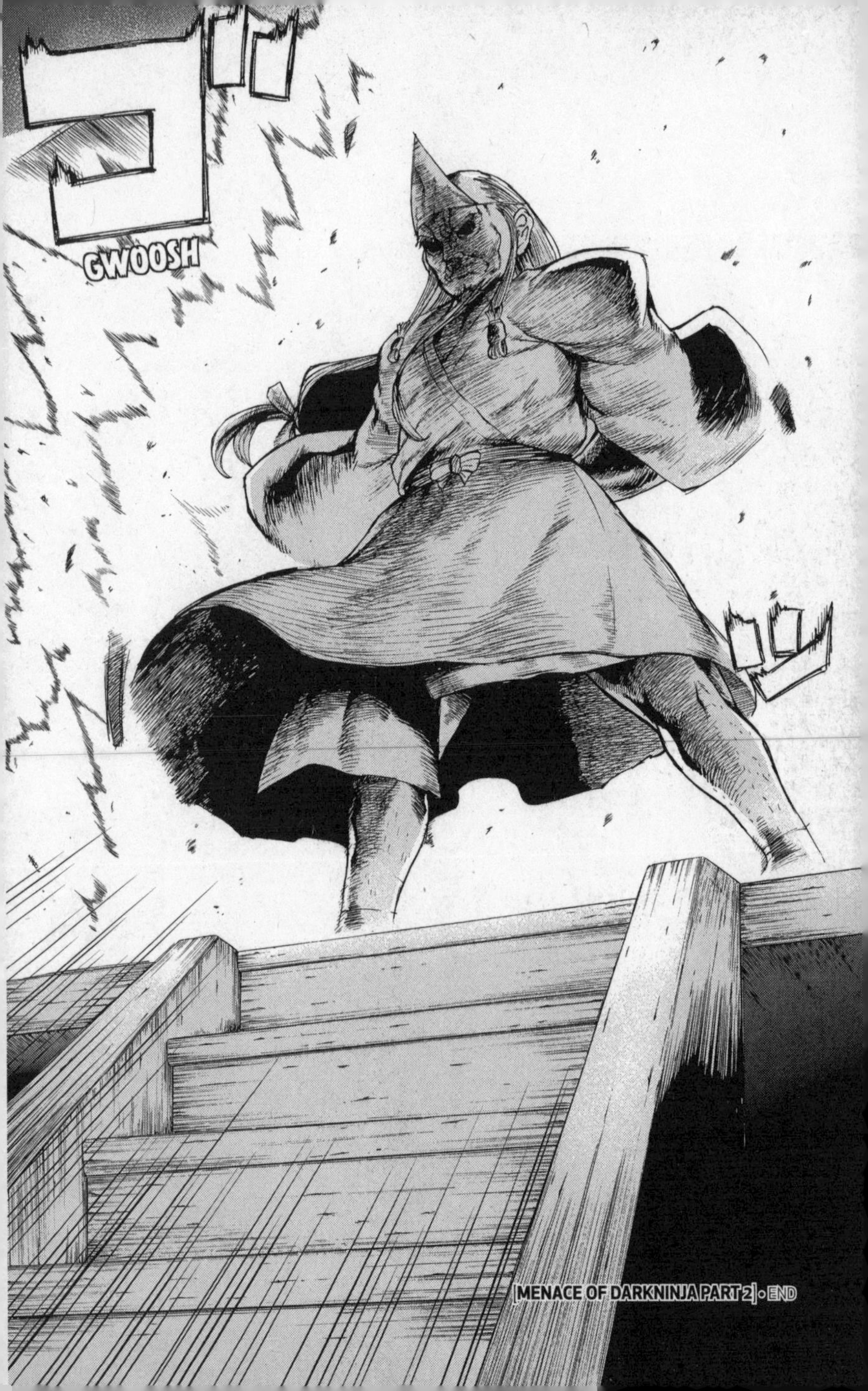
GWOOSH
[MENACE OF DARKNINJA PART 2] • END

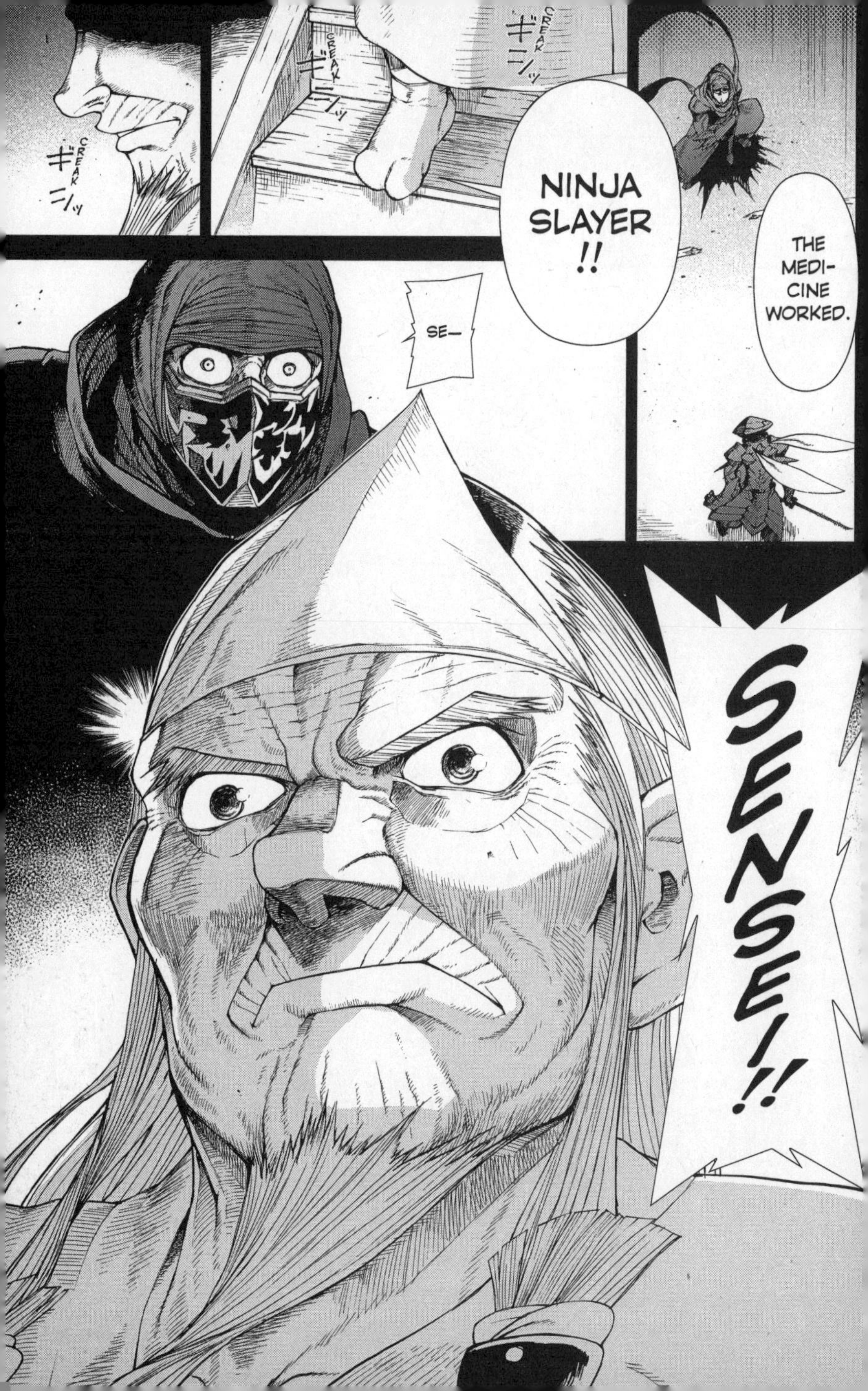

CREAK
CREAK
CREAK
NINJA SLAYER!!
THE MEDICINE WORKED.
SE—
SENSEI!!

KILLs 005 ✦ MENACE OF DARKNINJA PART 3

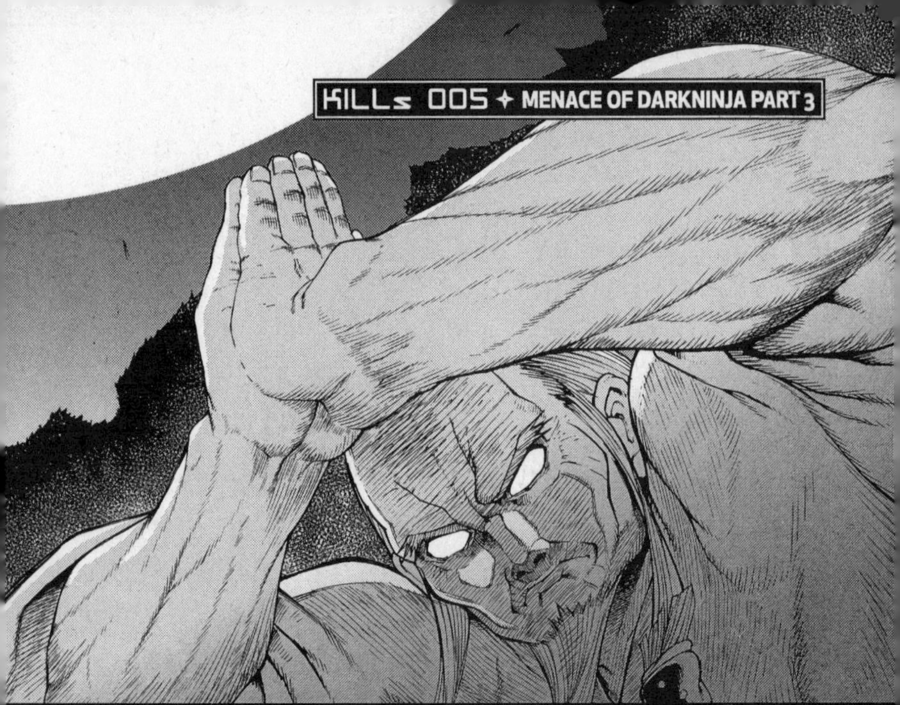

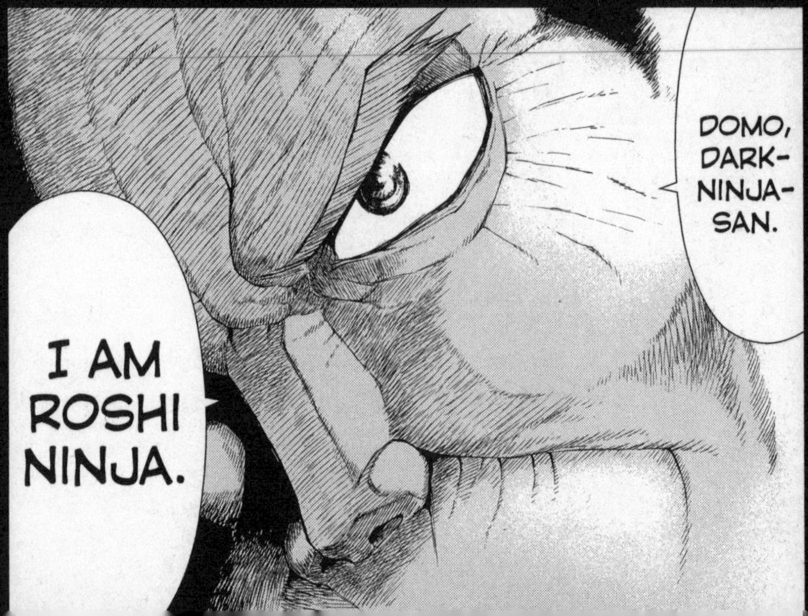
DOMO, DARK-NINJA-SAN.
I AM ROSHI NINJA.

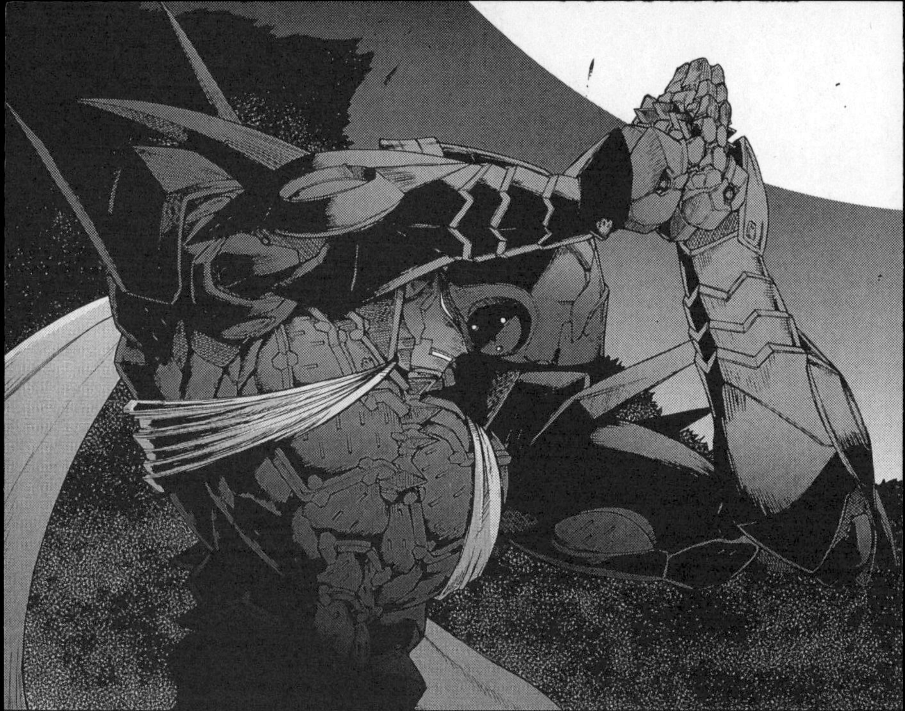

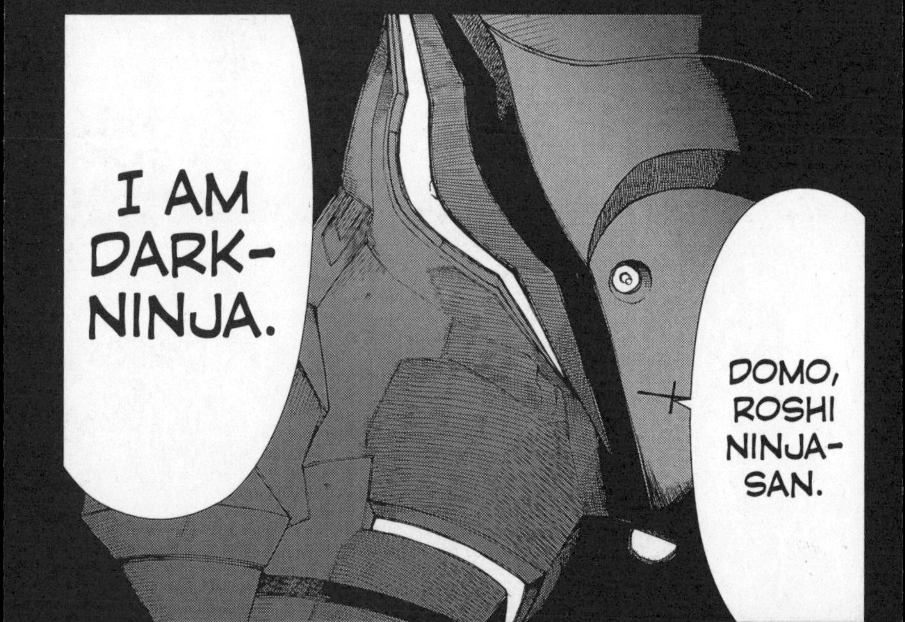
DOMO, ROSHI NINJA-SAN.
I AM DARK-NINJA.

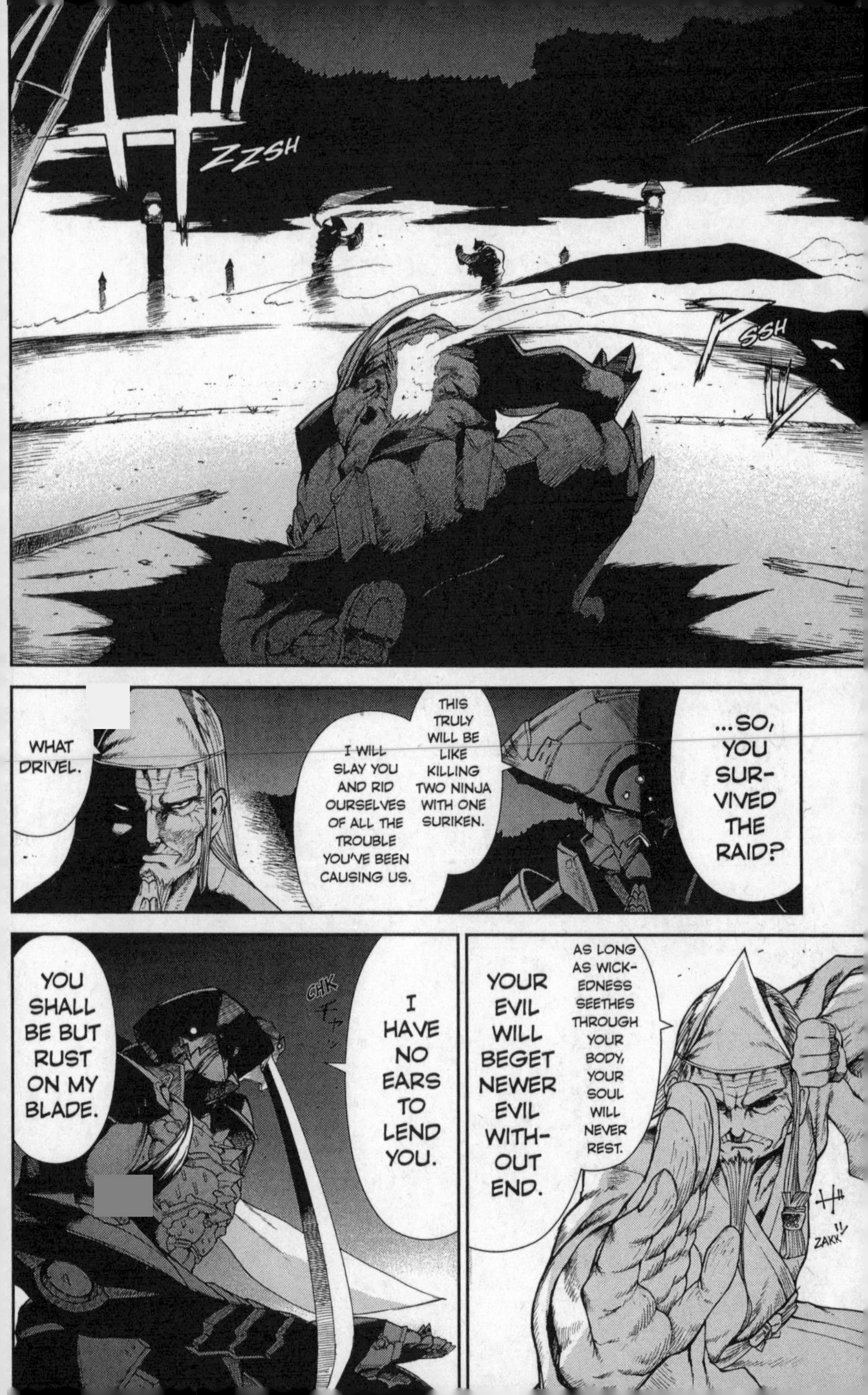
ZSSH
ZZSH
...SO, YOU SURVIVED THE RAID?
I WILL SLAY YOU AND RID OURSELVES OF ALL THE TROUBLE YOU'VE BEEN CAUSING US.
THIS TRULY WILL BE LIKE KILLING TWO NINJA WITH ONE SURIKEN.
WHAT DRIVEL.
AS LONG AS WICKEDNESS SEETHES THROUGH YOUR BODY, YOUR SOUL WILL NEVER REST.
YOUR EVIL WILL BEGET NEWER EVIL WITHOUT END.
ZAKK!!
I HAVE NO EARS TO LEND YOU.
CHK
YOU SHALL BE BUT RUST ON MY BLADE.

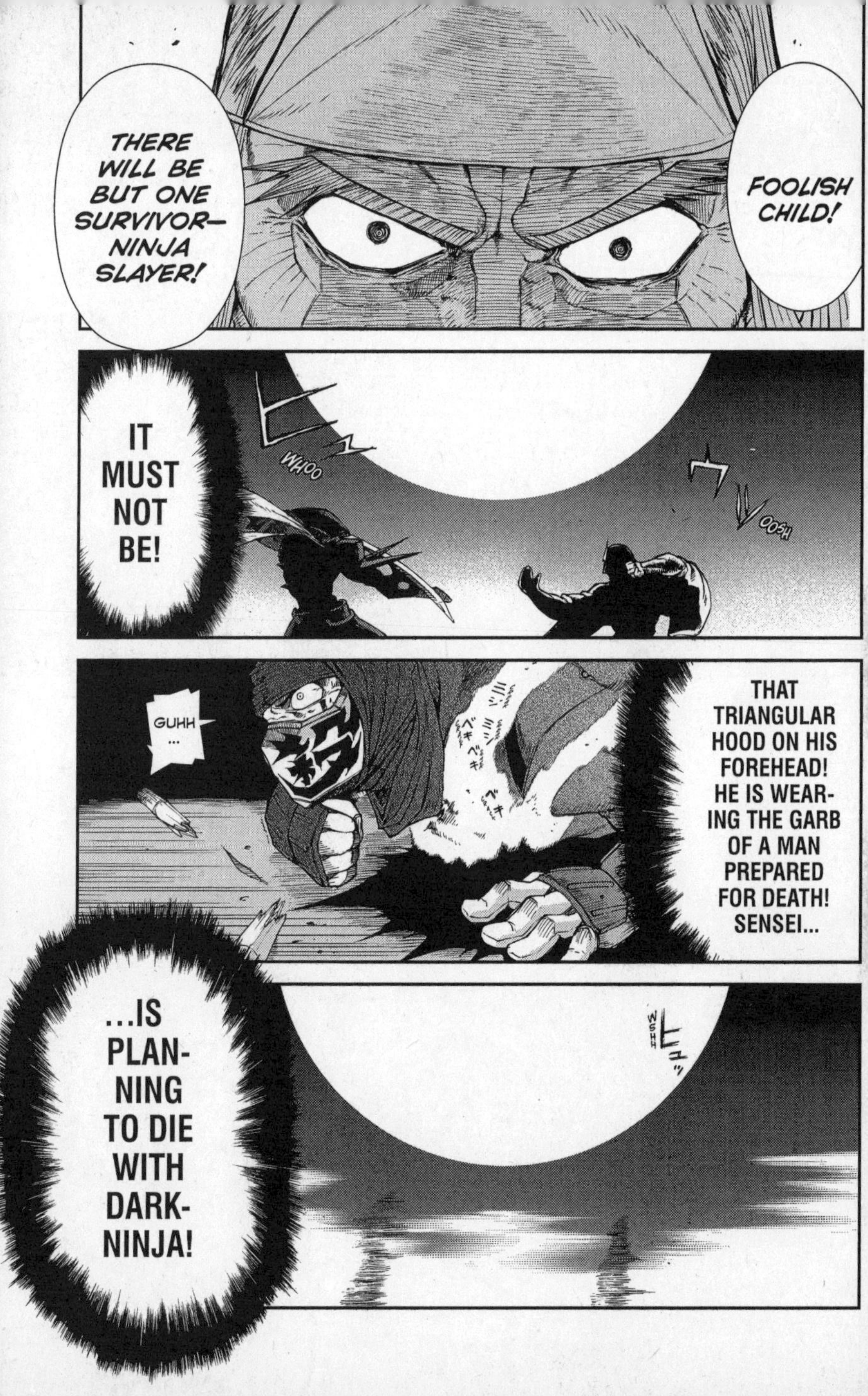
FOOLISH CHILD!
THERE WILL BE BUT ONE SURVIVOR—NINJA SLAYER!
WOOSH
WHOO
IT MUST NOT BE!
THAT TRIANGULAR HOOD ON HIS FOREHEAD! HE IS WEARING THE GARB OF A MAN PREPARED FOR DEATH! SENSEI...
GUHH...
WSHH
...IS PLANNING TO DIE WITH DARK-NINJA!

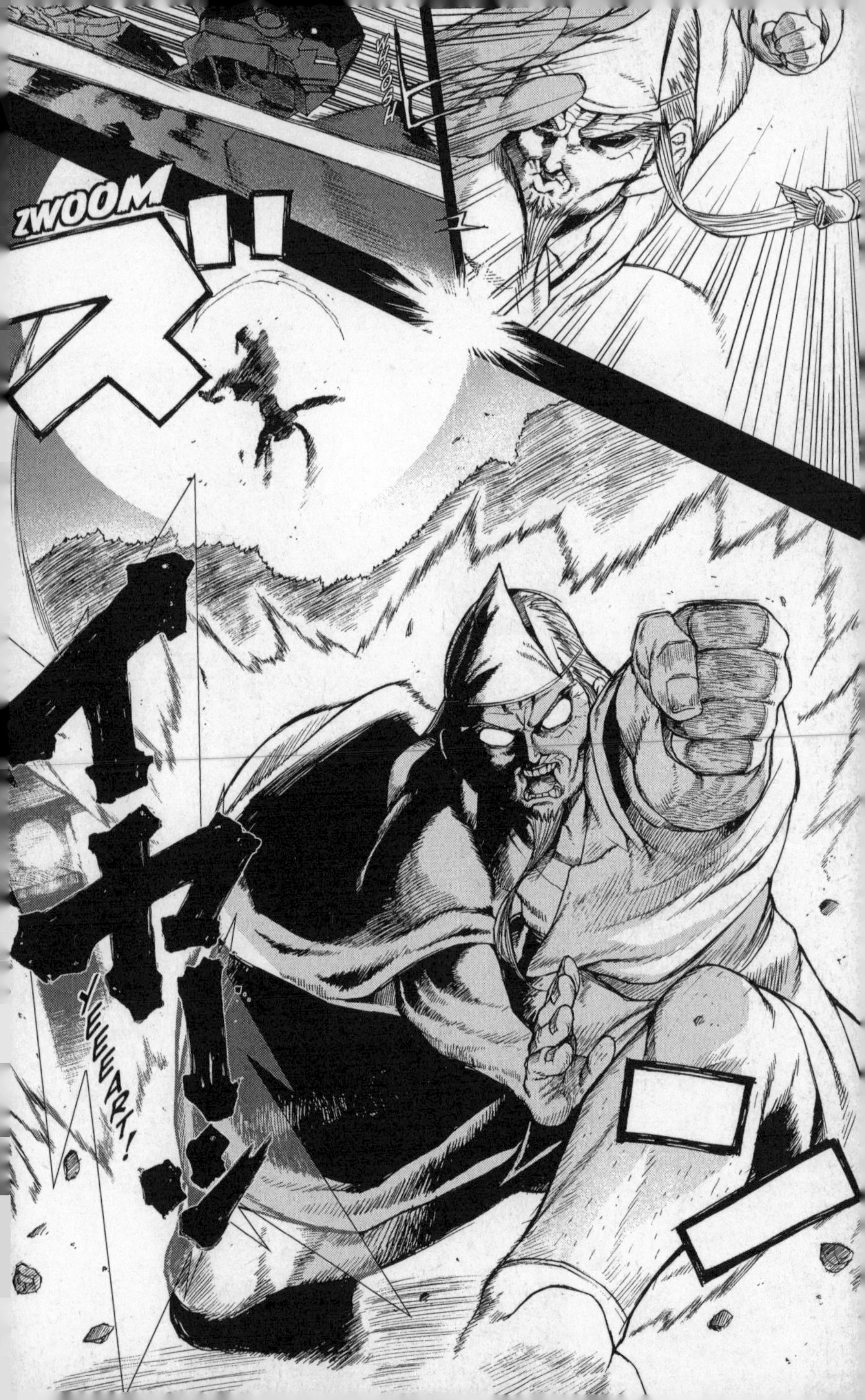
WHOOSH
ZWOOM
YEEEARK!

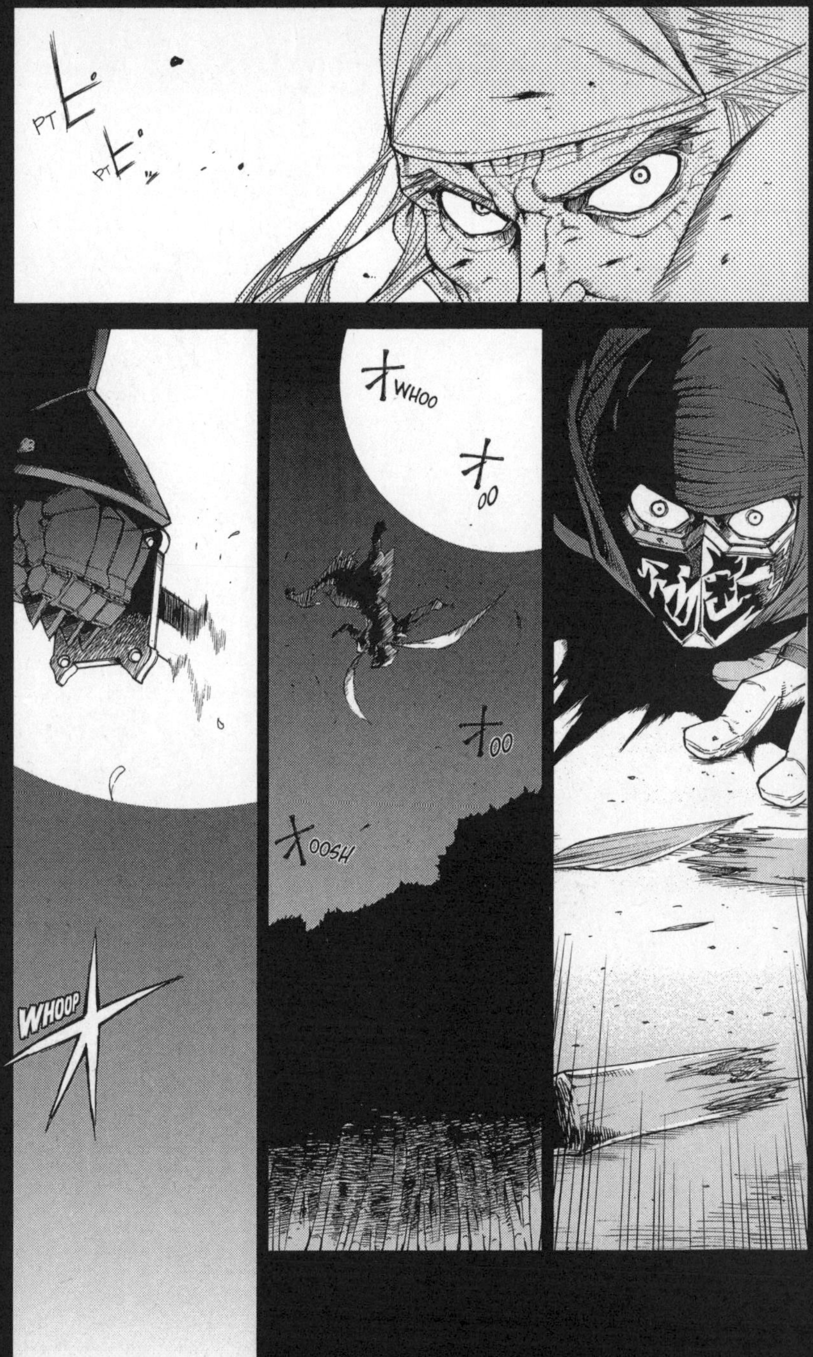
PT ピ
PT ピッ
オ WHOO
オ OO
オ OO
オ OOSH
WHOOP

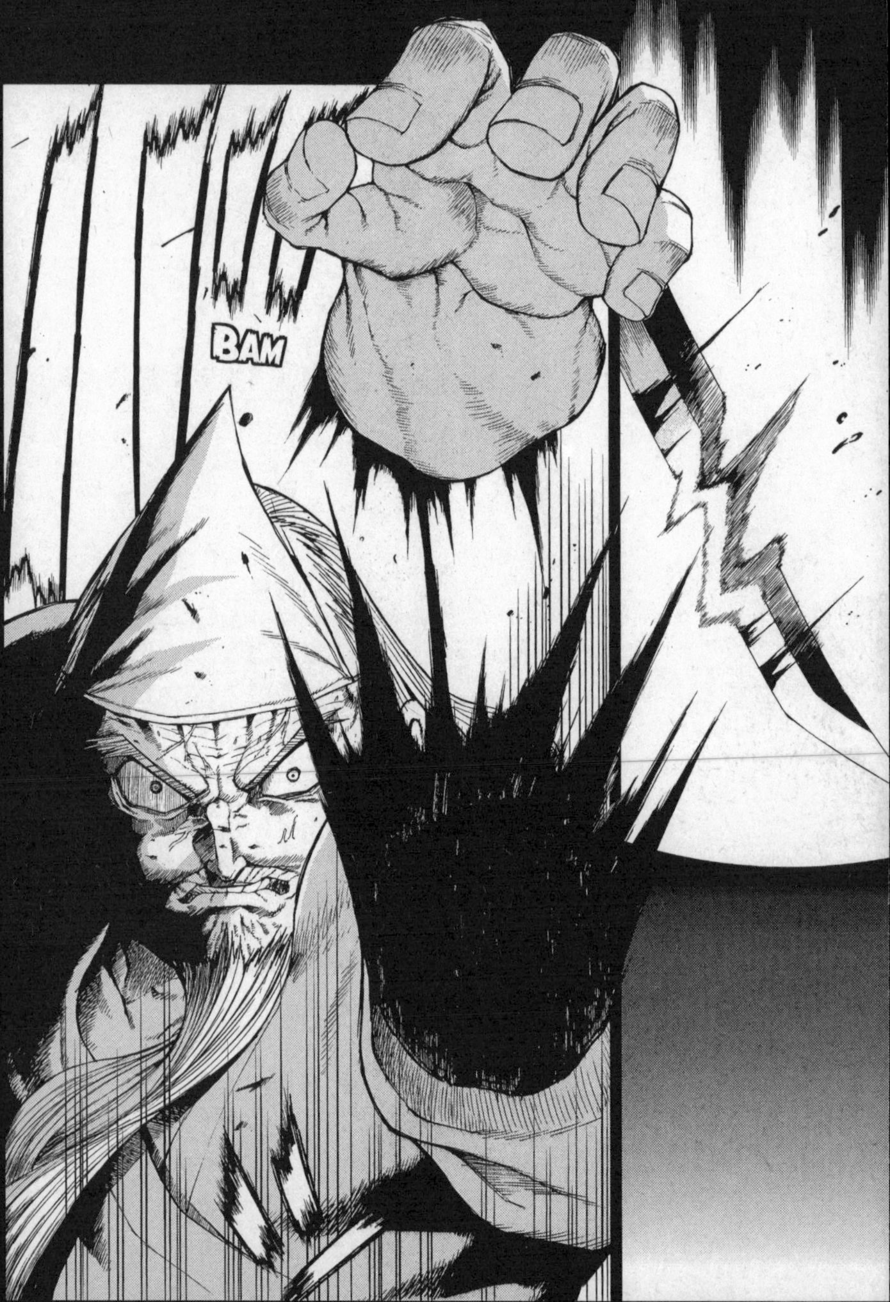
BAM

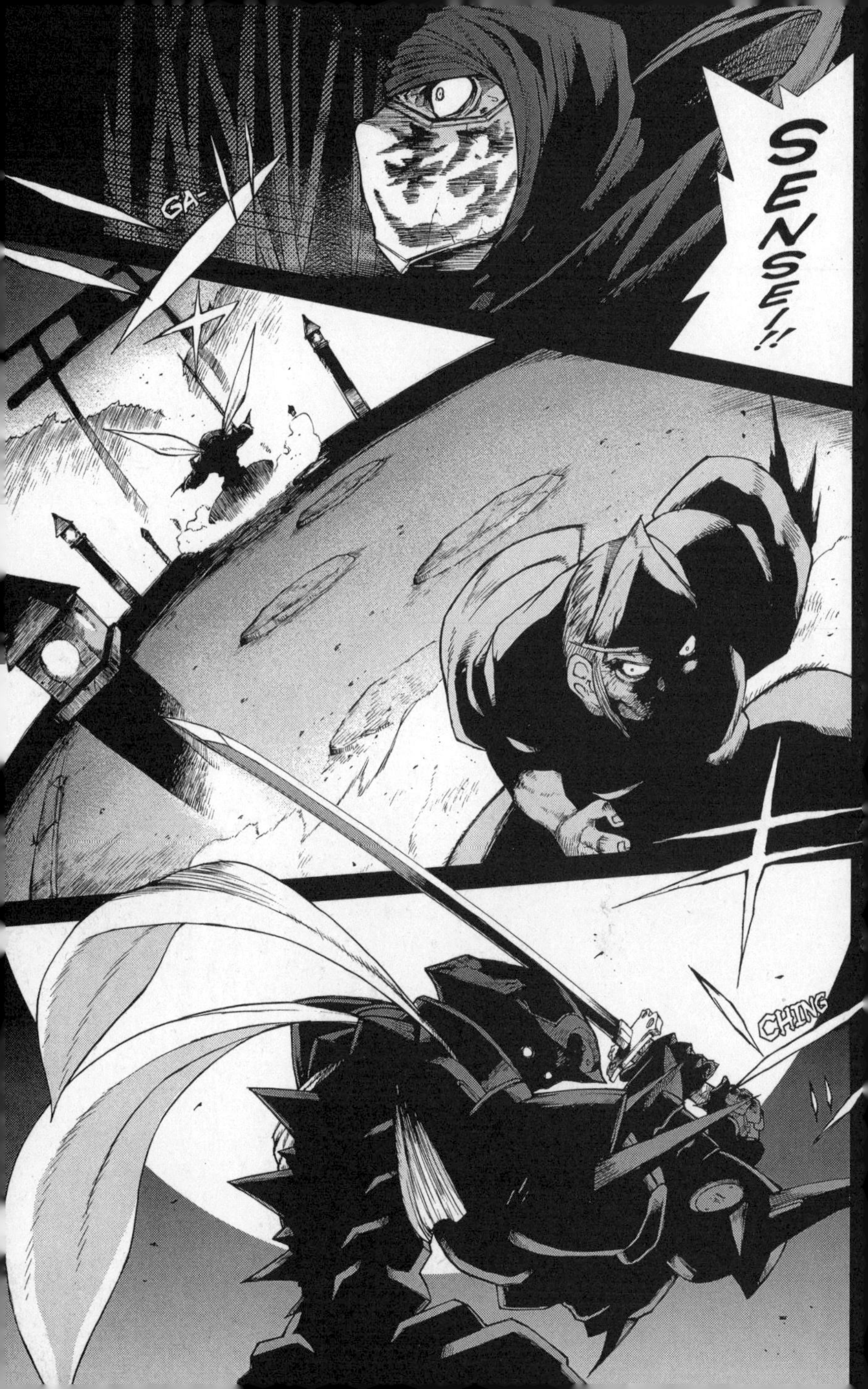
SENSEI!!
GA-
CHING

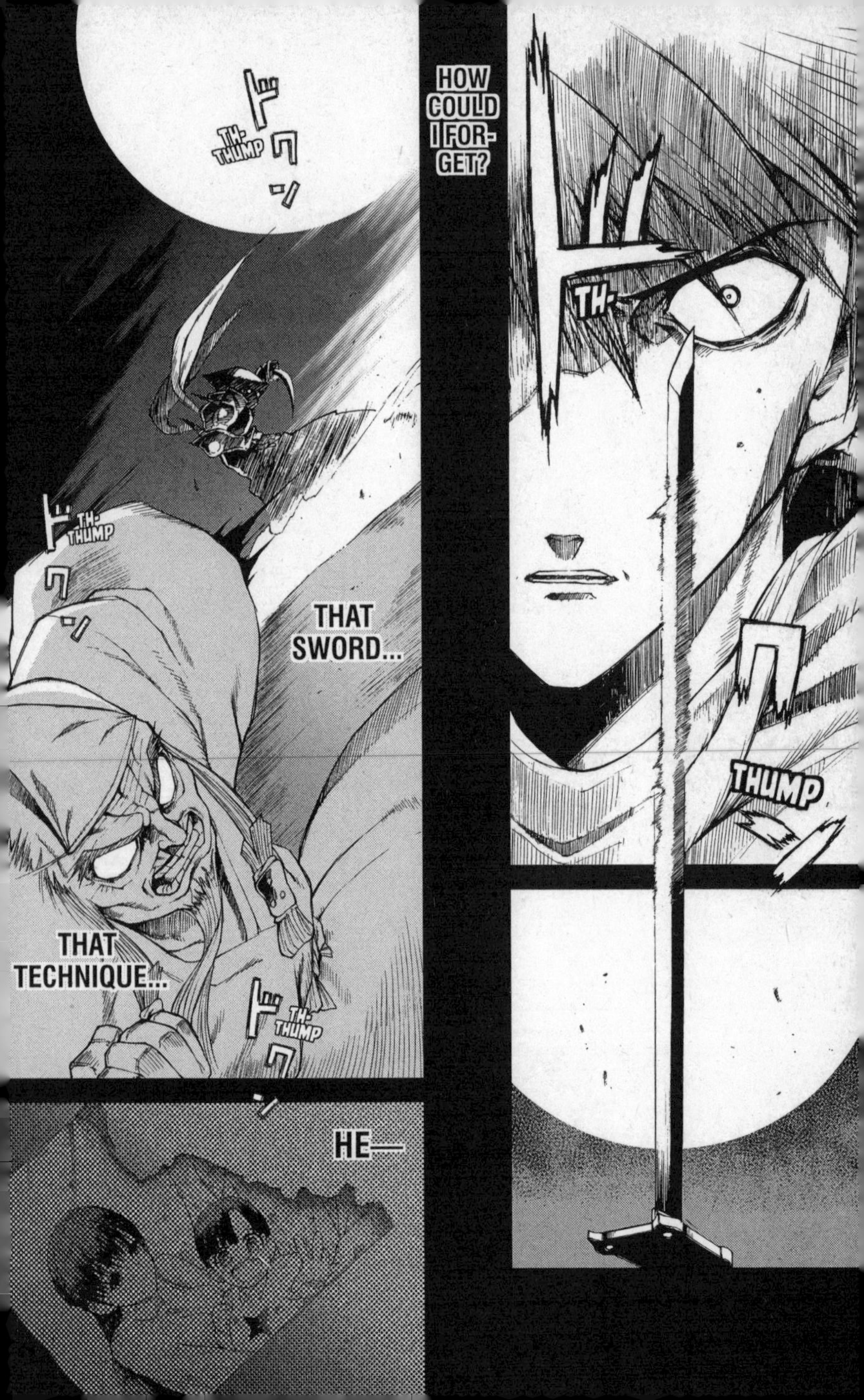
HOW COULD I FOR-GET?
TH-
THUMP
TH-THUMP
TH-THUMP
THAT SWORD...
THAT TECHNIQUE...
TH-THUMP
HE—

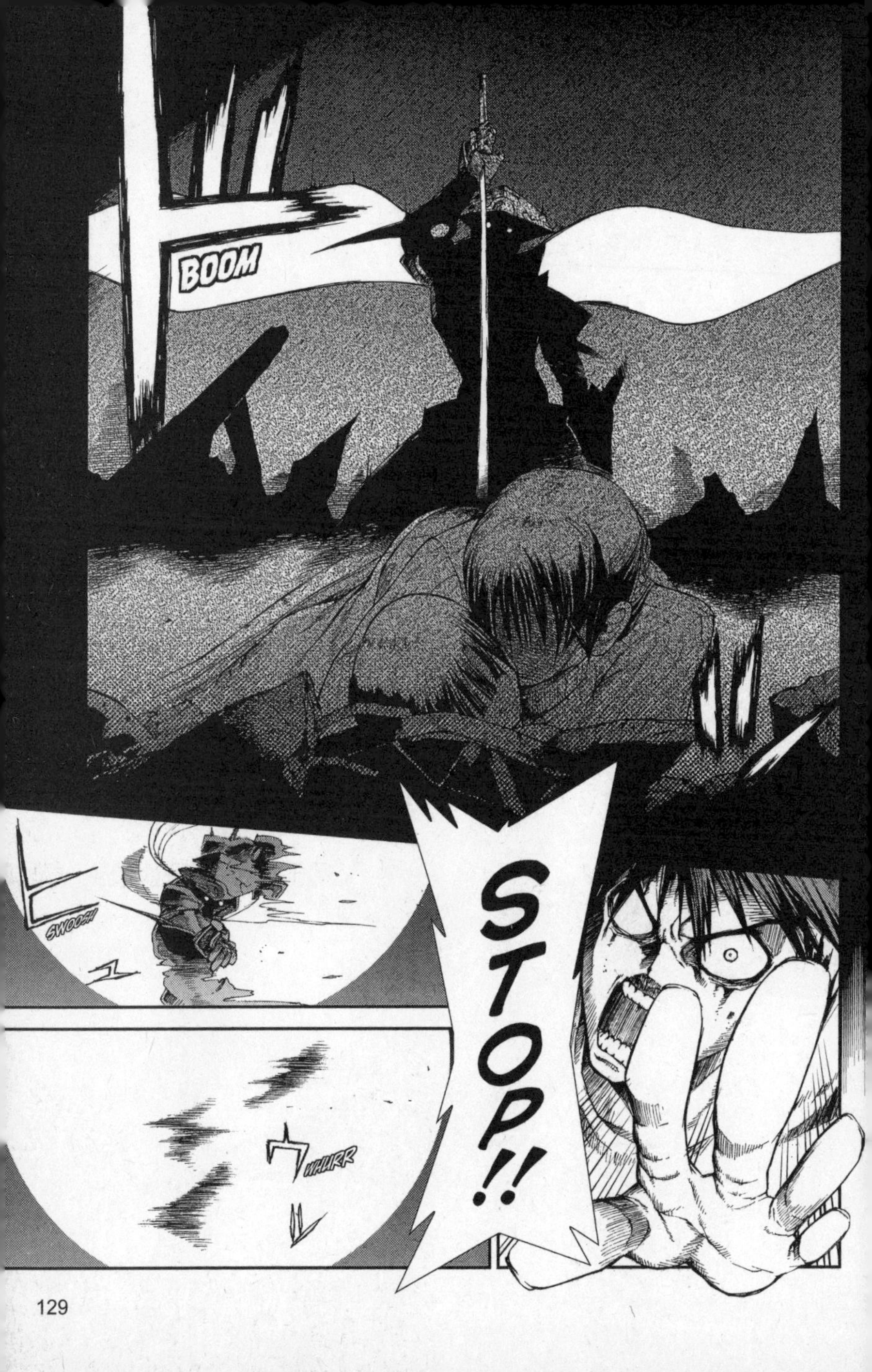
BOOM
STOP!!
SWOOSH
WHURR

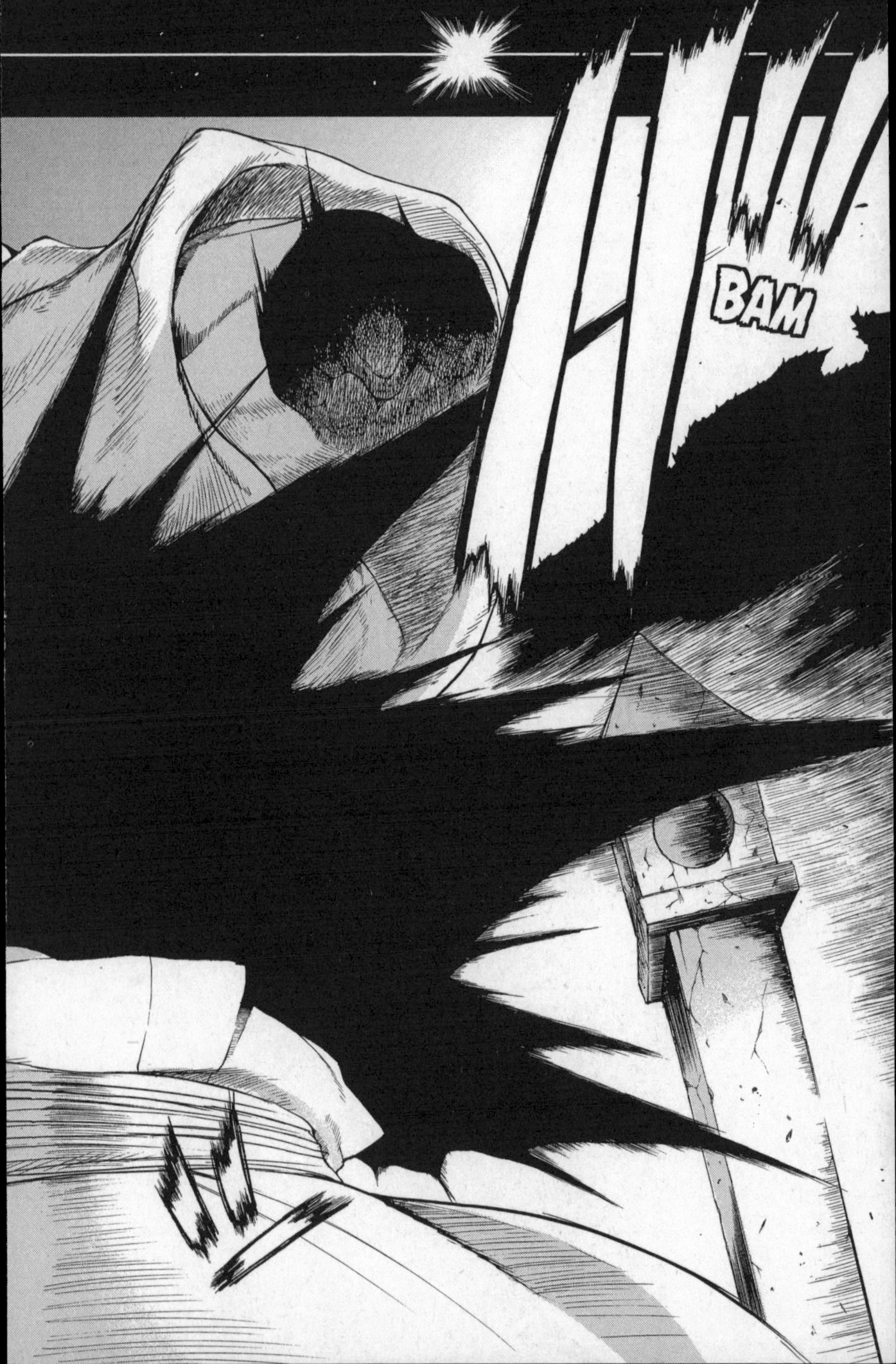
BAM

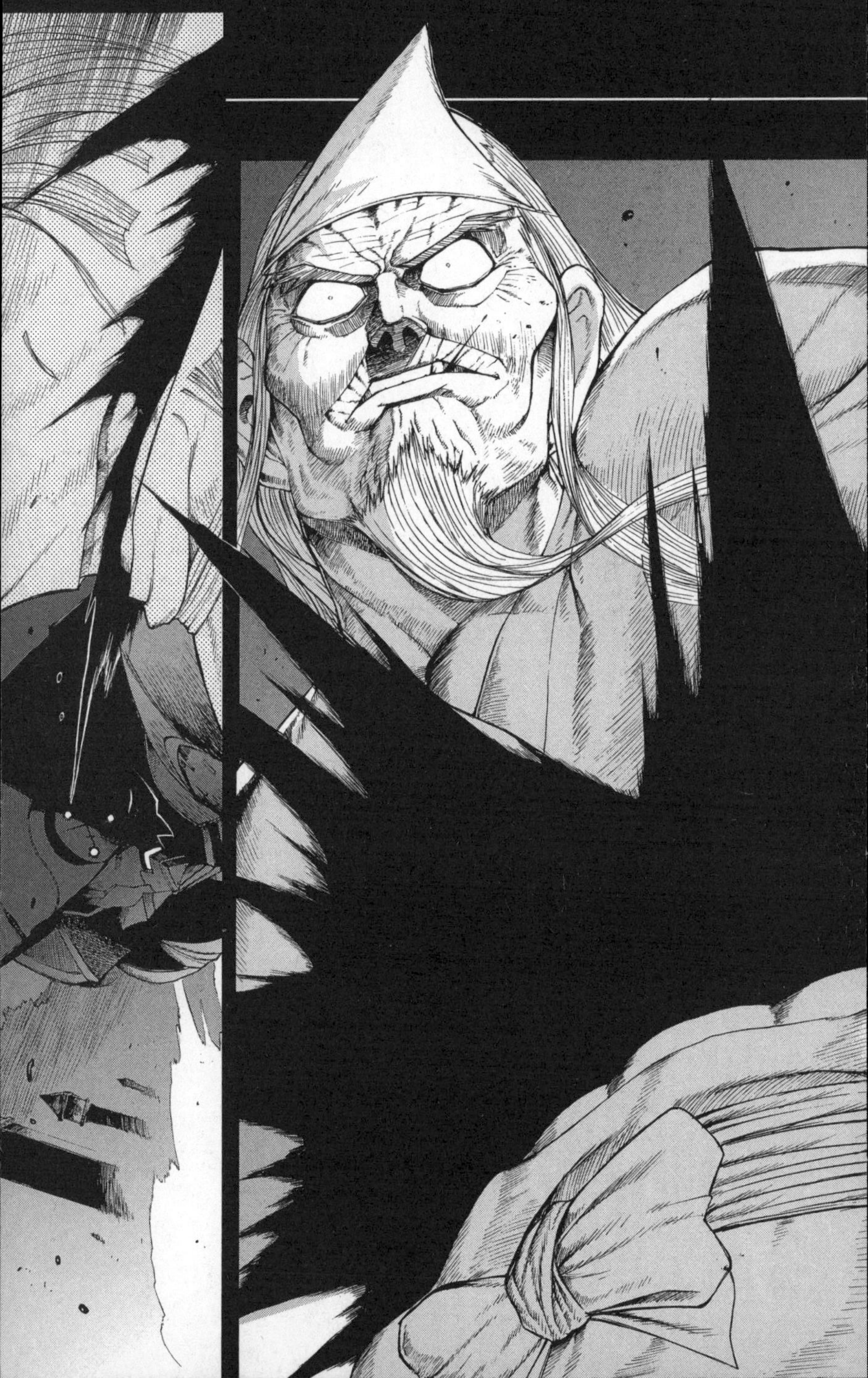

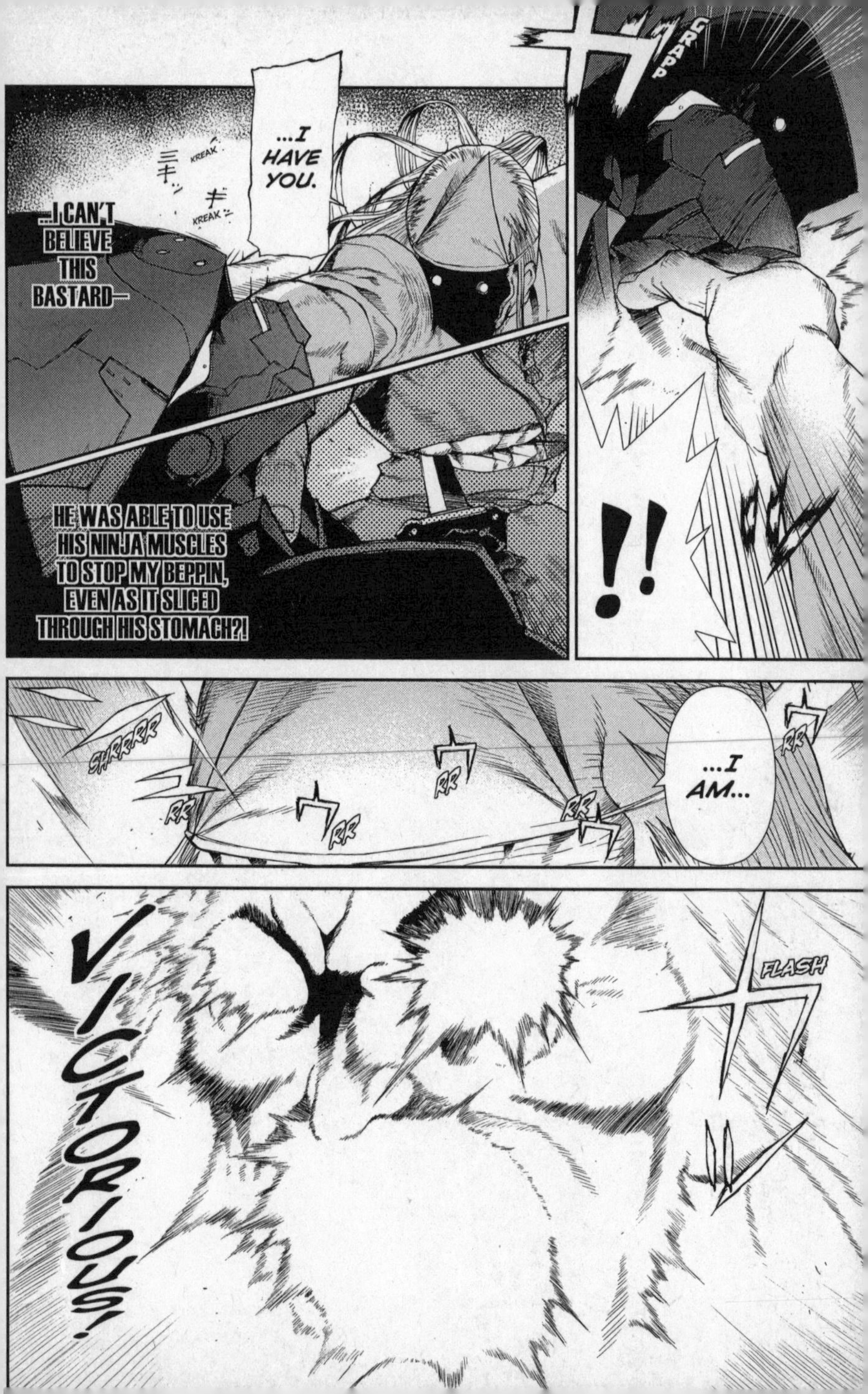
GRAPP
!!
...I HAVE YOU.
KREAK
KREAK
...I CAN'T BELIEVE THIS BASTARD—
HE WAS ABLE TO USE HIS NINJA MUSCLES TO STOP MY BEPPIN, EVEN AS IT SLICED THROUGH HIS STOMACH?!
...I AM...
RR
RR
RR
RR
SHRRRR
RR
FLASH
VICTORIOUS!

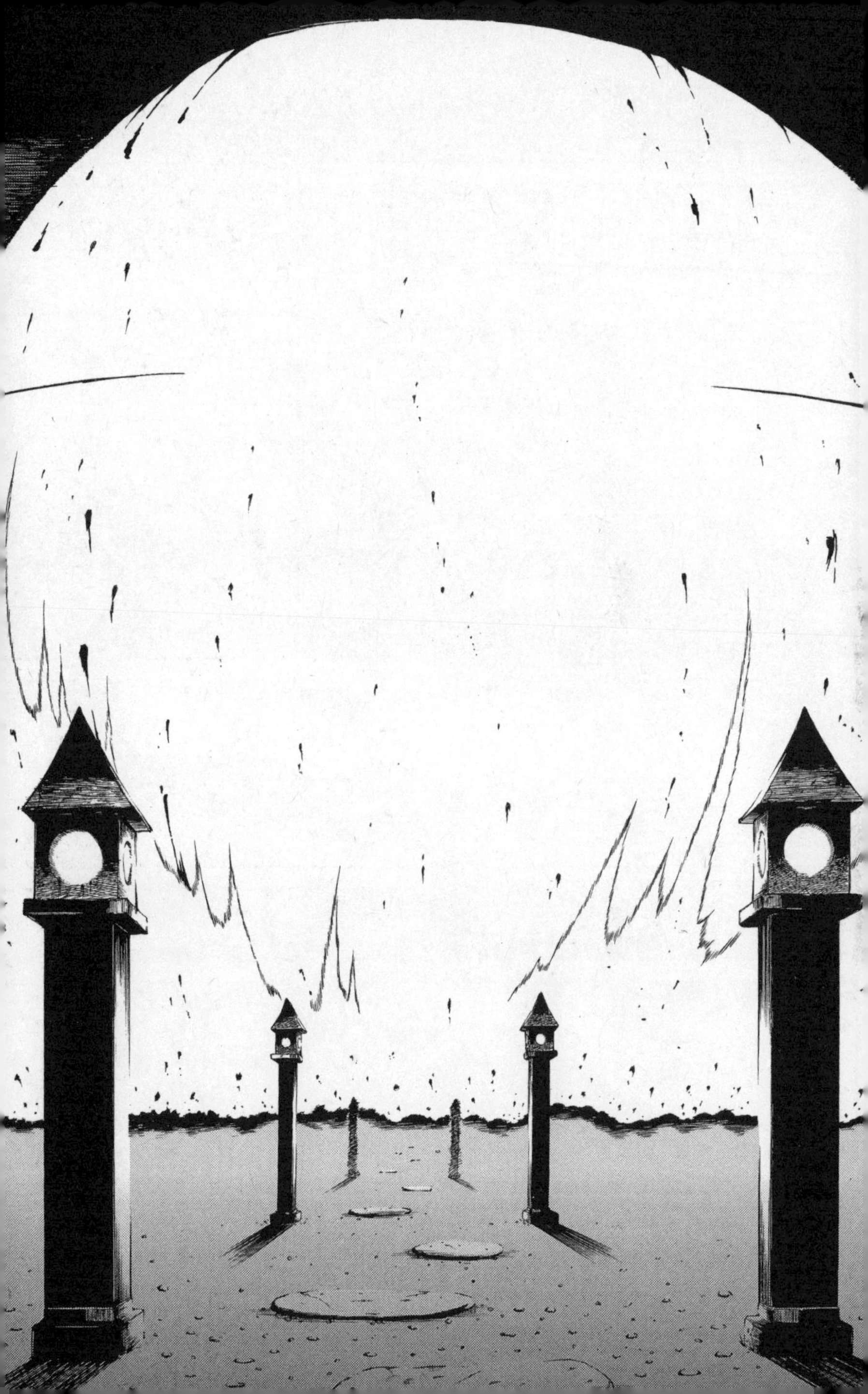

OOSH
OO
OO
OO
WHOO
GA-CHING
GA-CHING

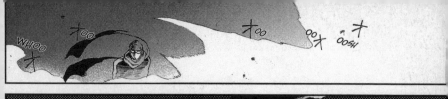

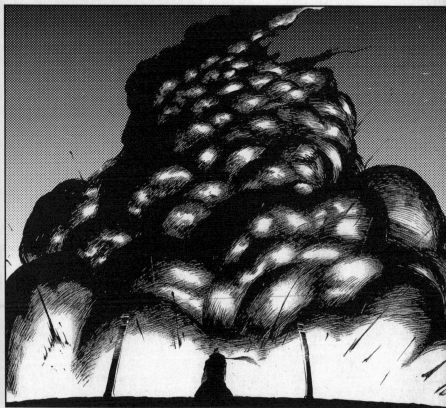

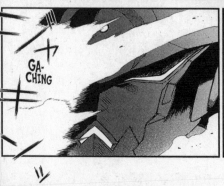

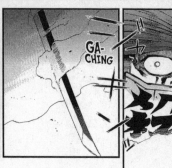

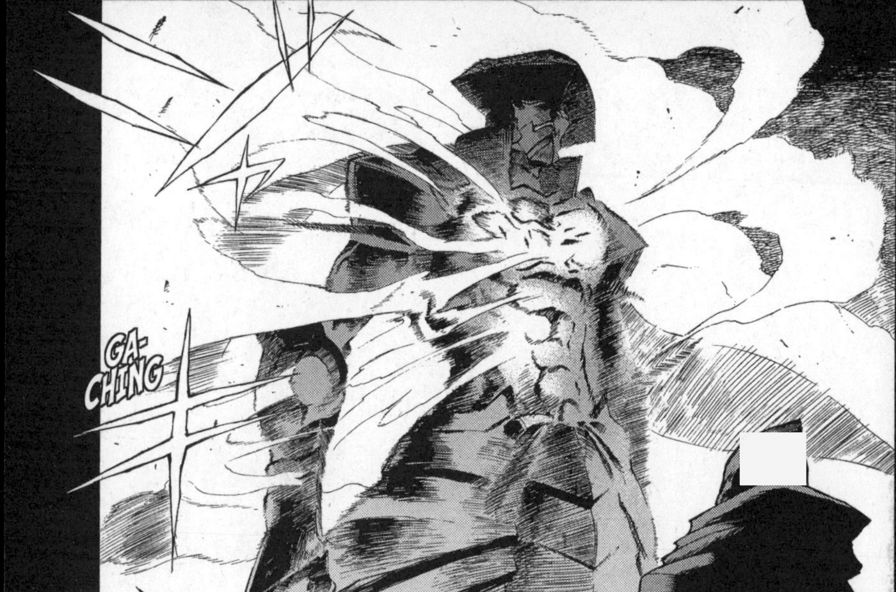
GA-CHING

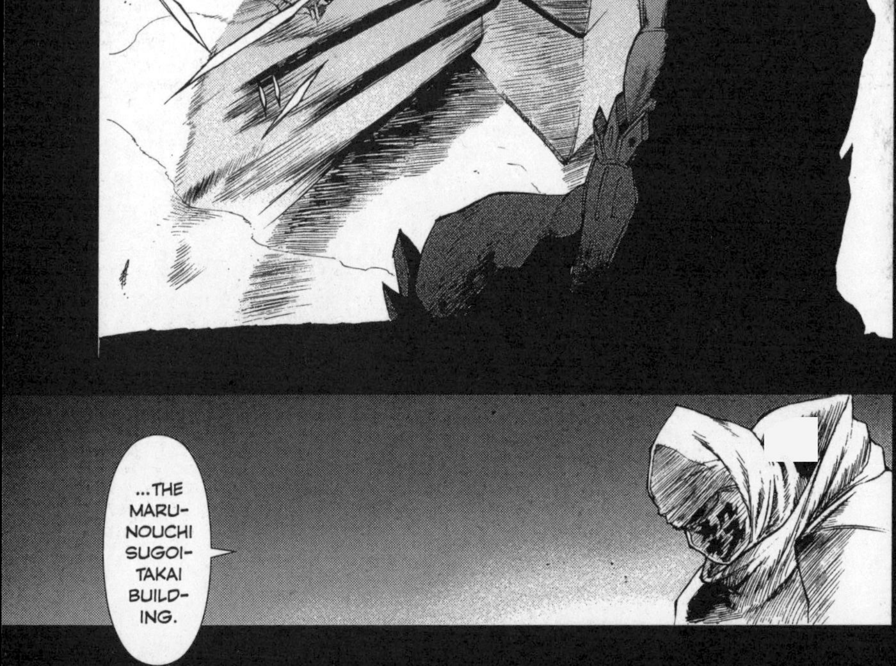
...THE MARUNOUCHI SUGOI-TAKAI BUILDING.

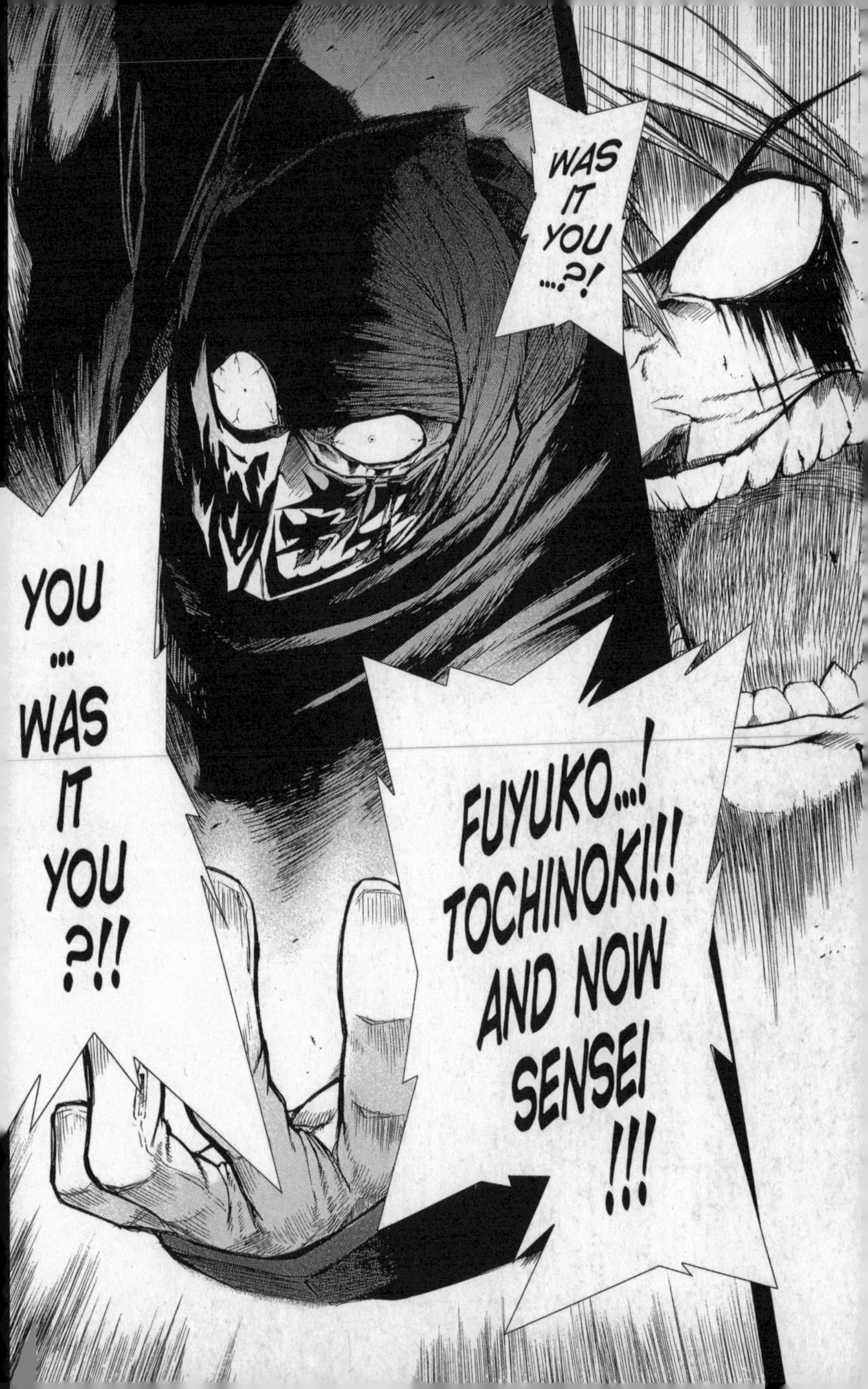
WAS IT YOU ...?!
FUYUKO...! TOCHINOKI!! AND NOW SENSEI!!!
YOU... WAS IT YOU?!!

I SEE.
SO YOU'RE THE WRETCHED WRAITH OF THE MARUNOUCHI CONFLICT— ONE OF THOSE CIVILIAN VICTIMS?
GH-
SHK
KILL!
KILL.
KILL!!

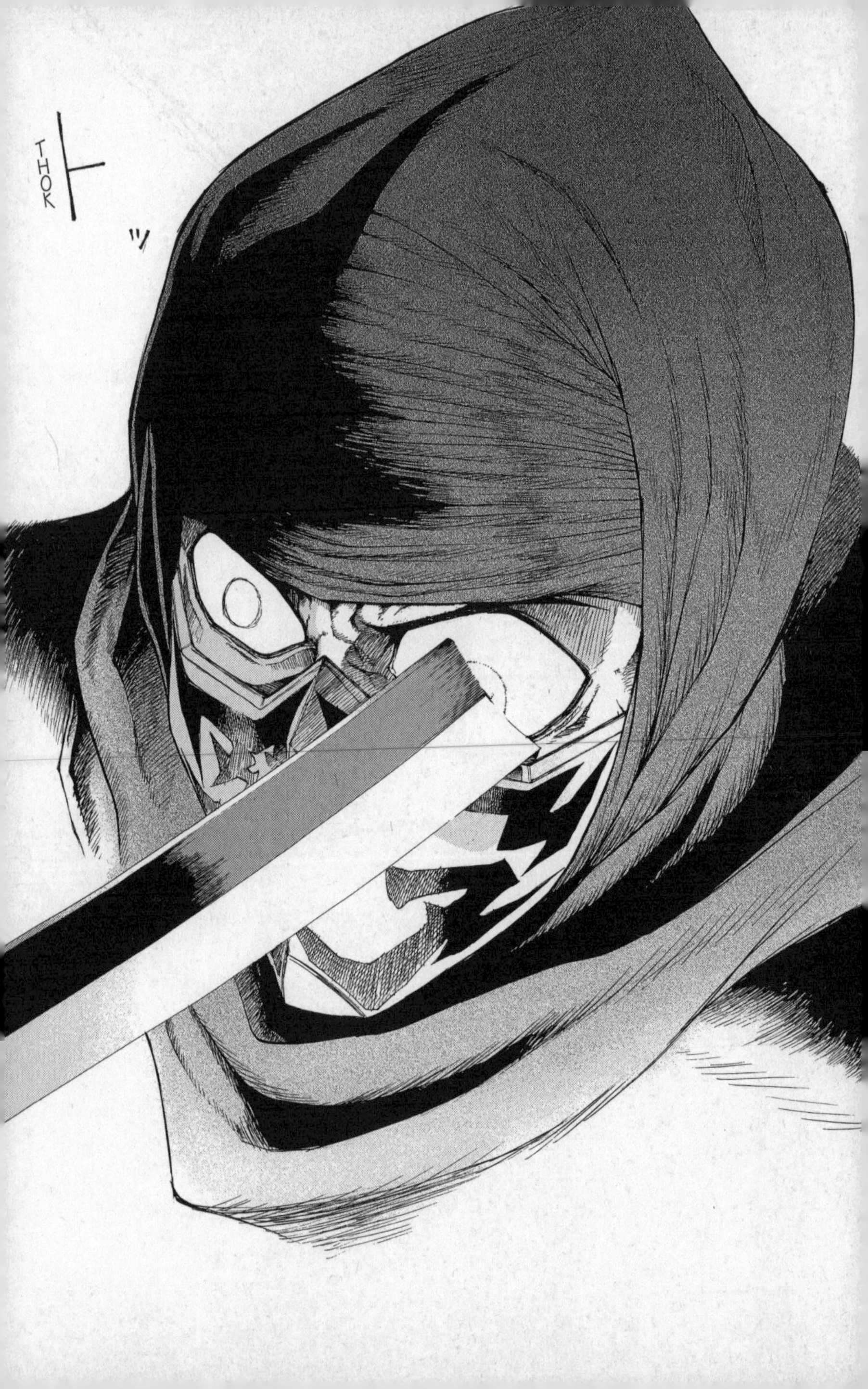
THOK

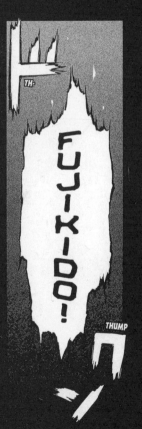

TH-

FUJIKIDO!

THUMP

KILL
...!!

KI...

SPLRT

K...I...

LL...

...KILL.

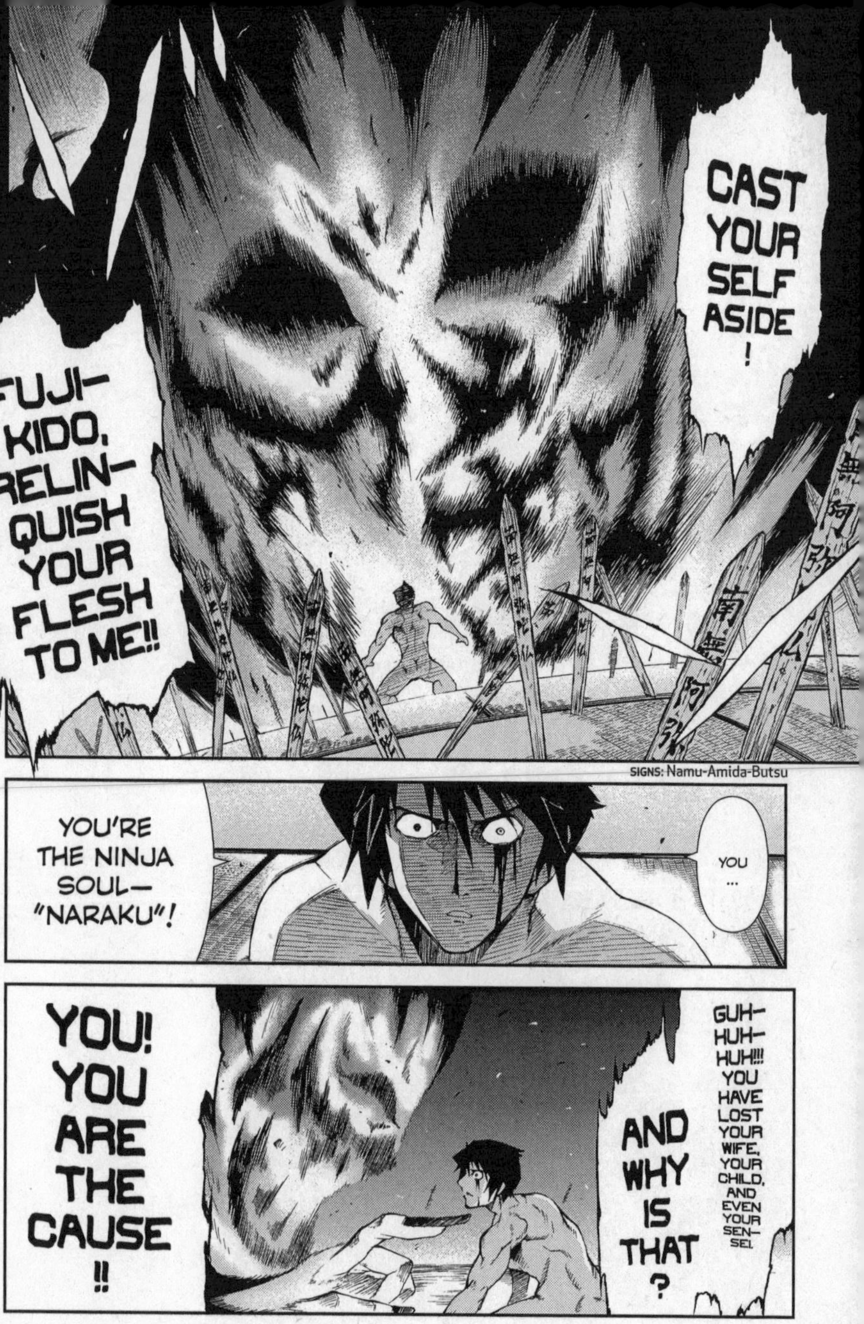
CAST YOURSELF ASIDE!
FUJIKIDO, RELINQUISH YOUR FLESH TO ME!!
SIGNS: Namu-Amida-Butsu
YOU ...
YOU'RE THE NINJA SOUL— "NARAKU"!
GUH-HUH-HUH!!! YOU HAVE LOST YOUR WIFE, YOUR CHILD, AND EVEN YOUR SENSEI.
AND WHY IS THAT?
YOU! YOU ARE THE CAUSE!!

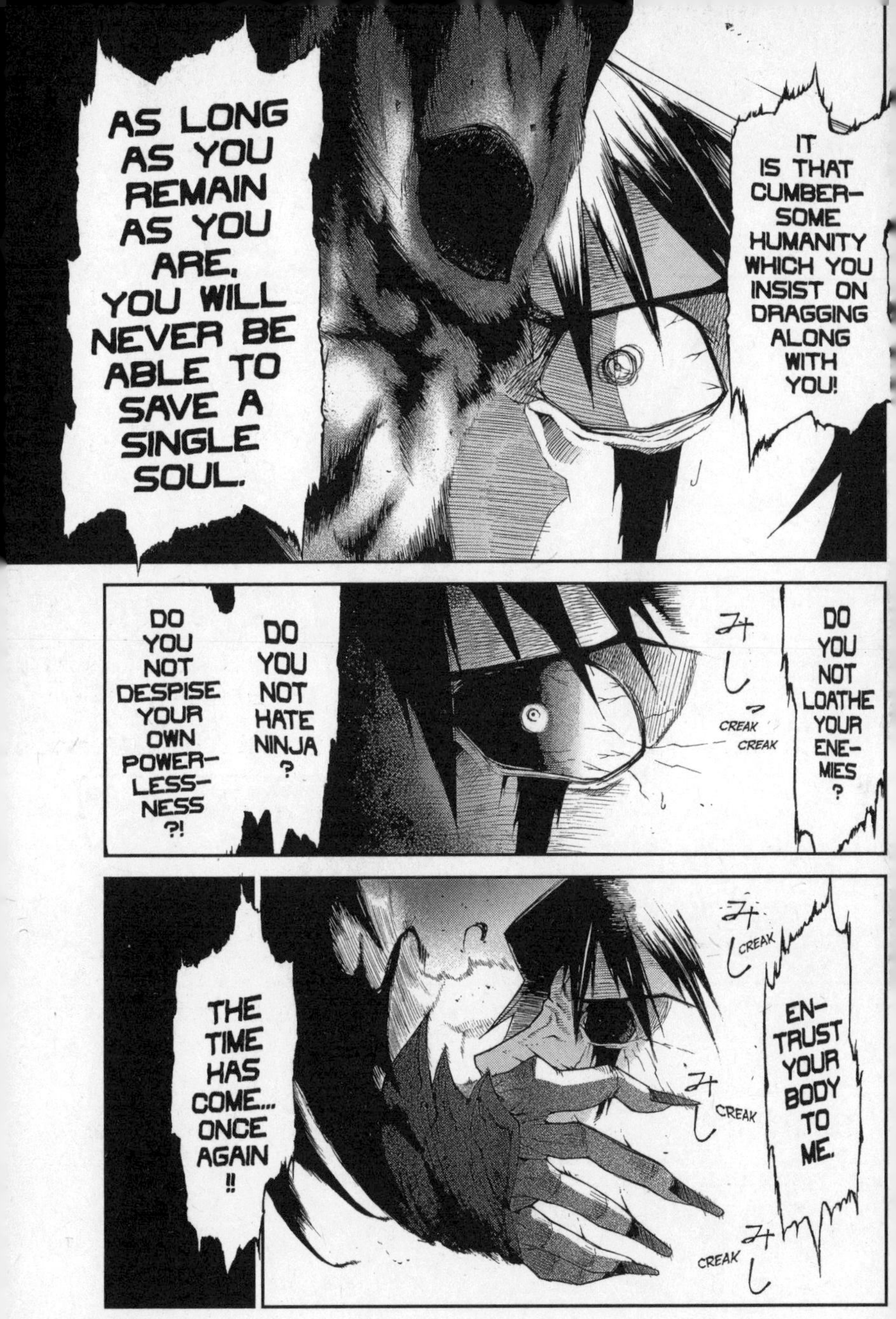
IT IS THAT CUMBER-SOME HUMANITY WHICH YOU INSIST ON DRAGGING ALONG WITH YOU!
AS LONG AS YOU REMAIN AS YOU ARE, YOU WILL NEVER BE ABLE TO SAVE A SINGLE SOUL.
DO YOU NOT LOATHE YOUR ENE-MIES?
みしっ
CREAK CREAK
DO YOU NOT HATE NINJA?
DO YOU NOT DESPISE YOUR OWN POWER-LESS-NESS?!
みし
CREAK
ENTRUST YOUR BODY TO ME.
みし
CREAK
みし
CREAK
THE TIME HAS COME... ONCE AGAIN!!

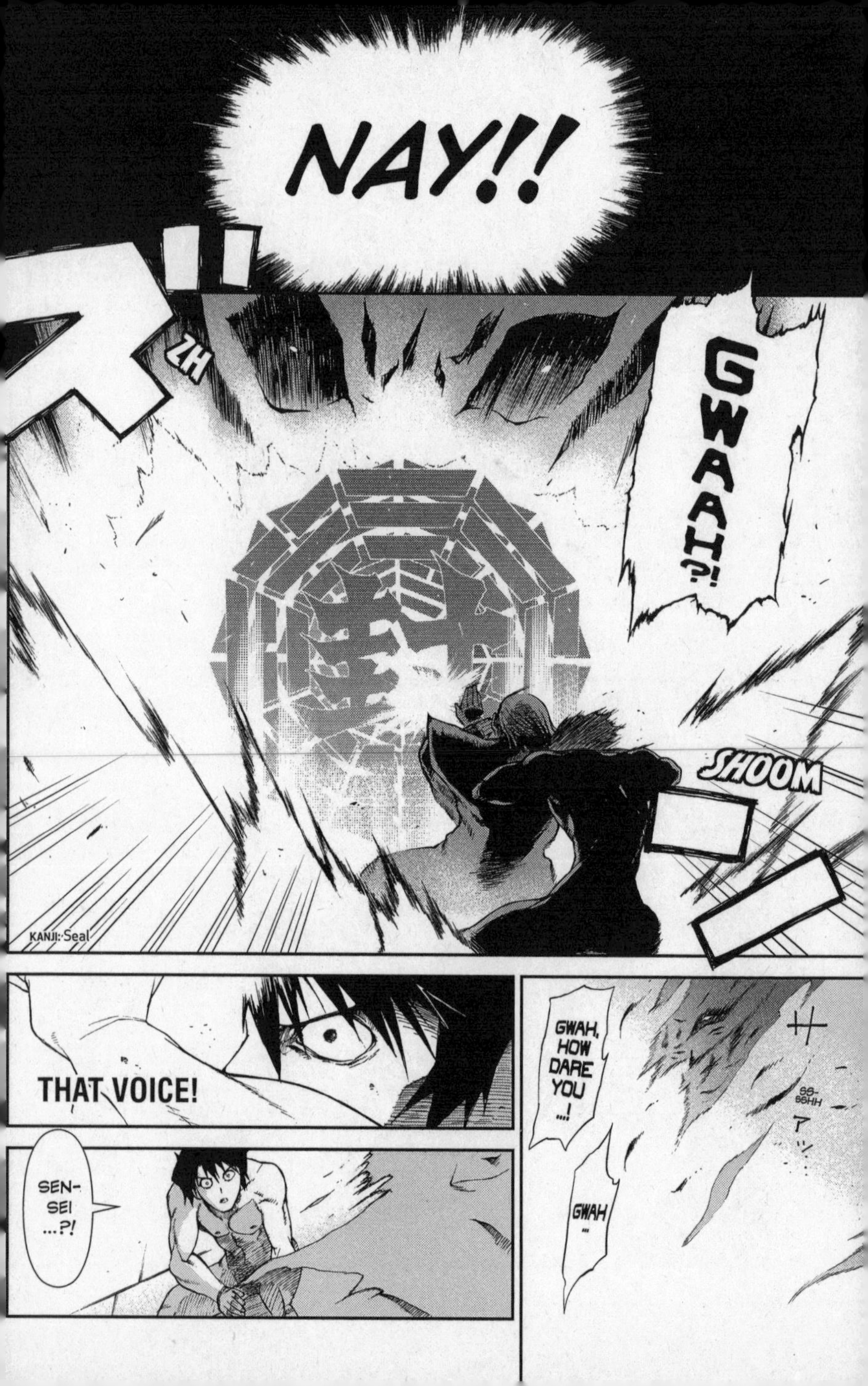
NAY!!
GWAAAH?!
ZH
SHOOM
KANJI: Seal
THAT VOICE!
GWAH, HOW DARE YOU ...!
SS-SSHH
GWAH ...
SEN-SEI ...?!

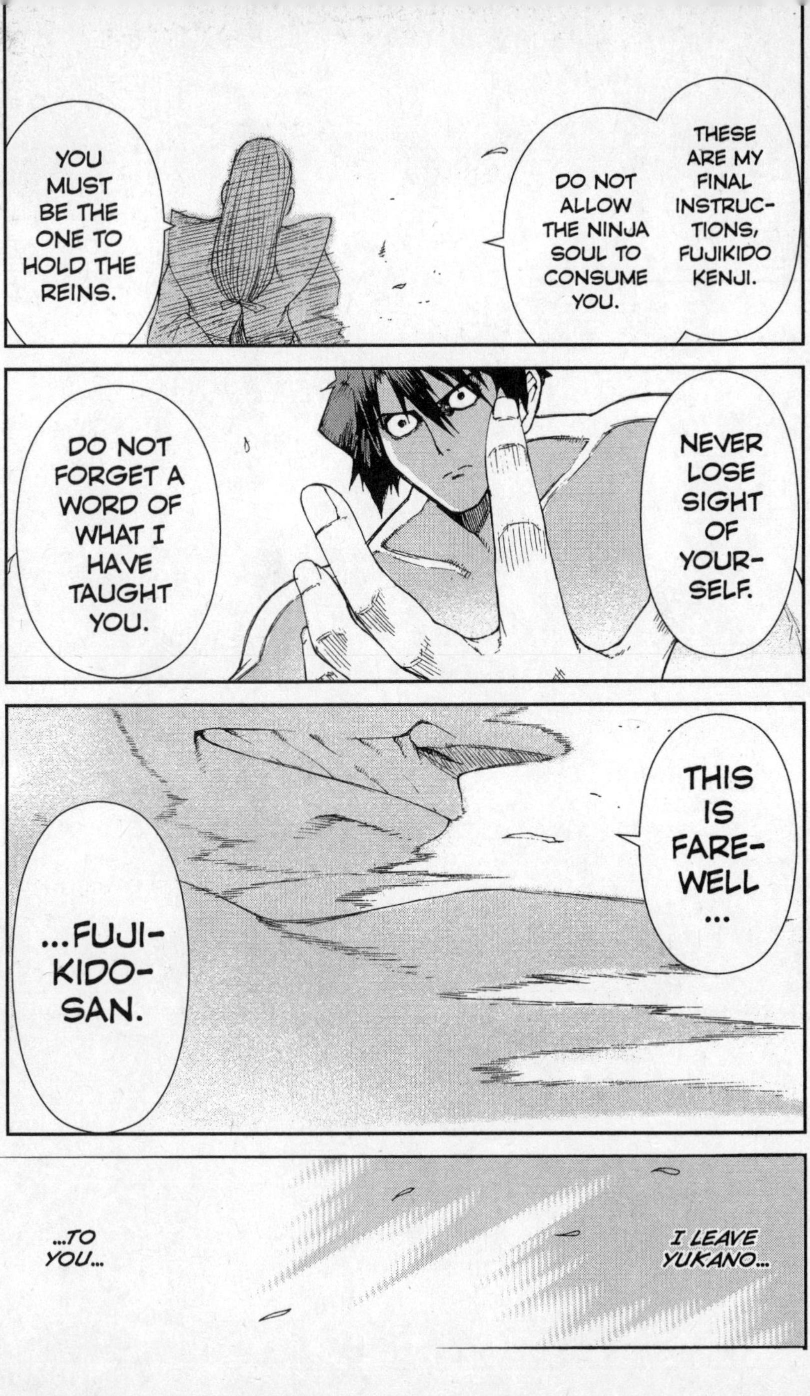
THESE ARE MY FINAL INSTRUCTIONS, FUJIKIDO KENJI.
DO NOT ALLOW THE NINJA SOUL TO CONSUME YOU.
YOU MUST BE THE ONE TO HOLD THE REINS.
NEVER LOSE SIGHT OF YOURSELF.
DO NOT FORGET A WORD OF WHAT I HAVE TAUGHT YOU.
THIS IS FAREWELL...
...FUJIKIDO-SAN.
I LEAVE YUKANO...
...TO YOU...

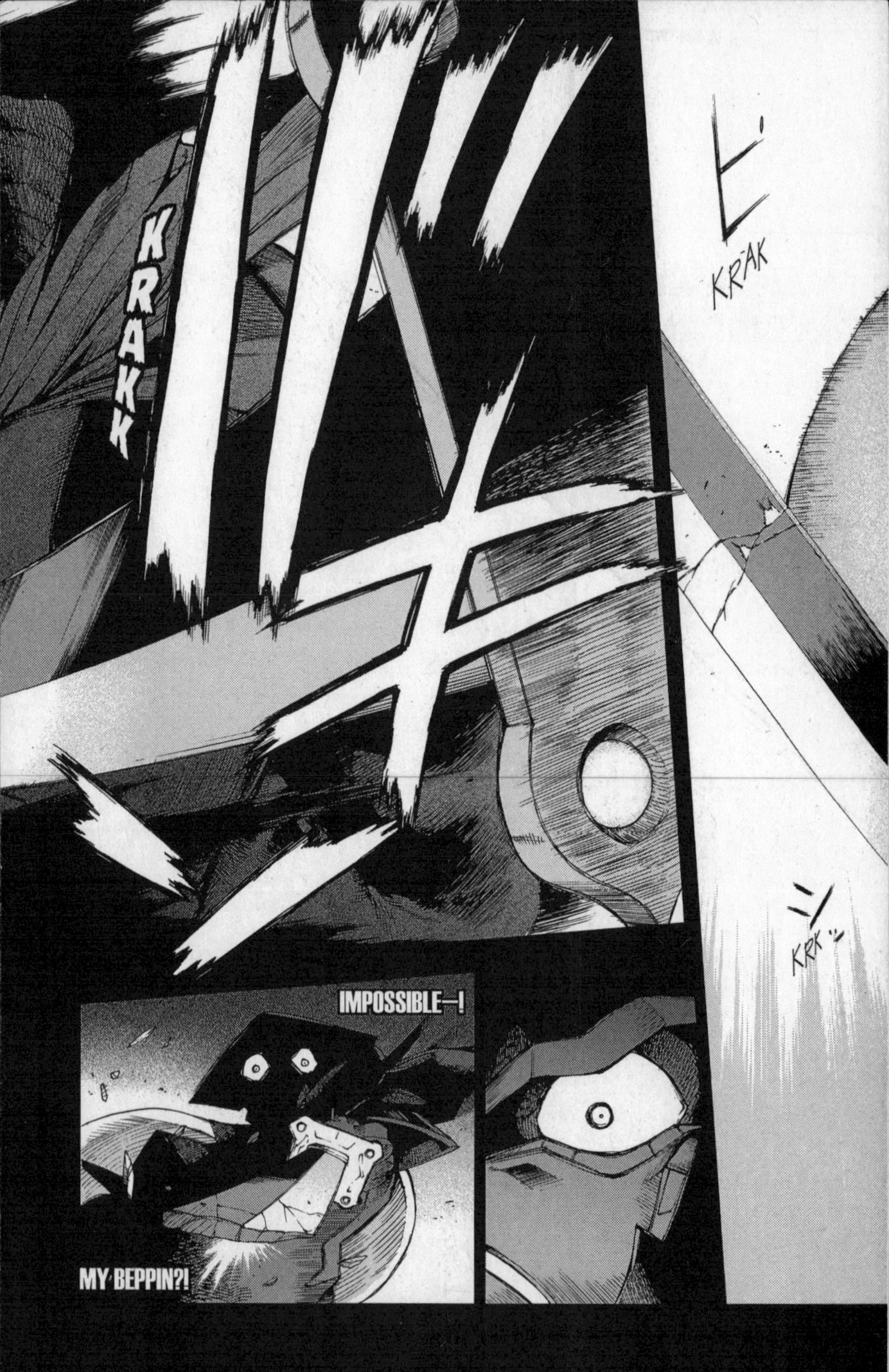
KRAK
KRAKK
KRK
IMPOSSIBLE—!
MY BEPPIN?!

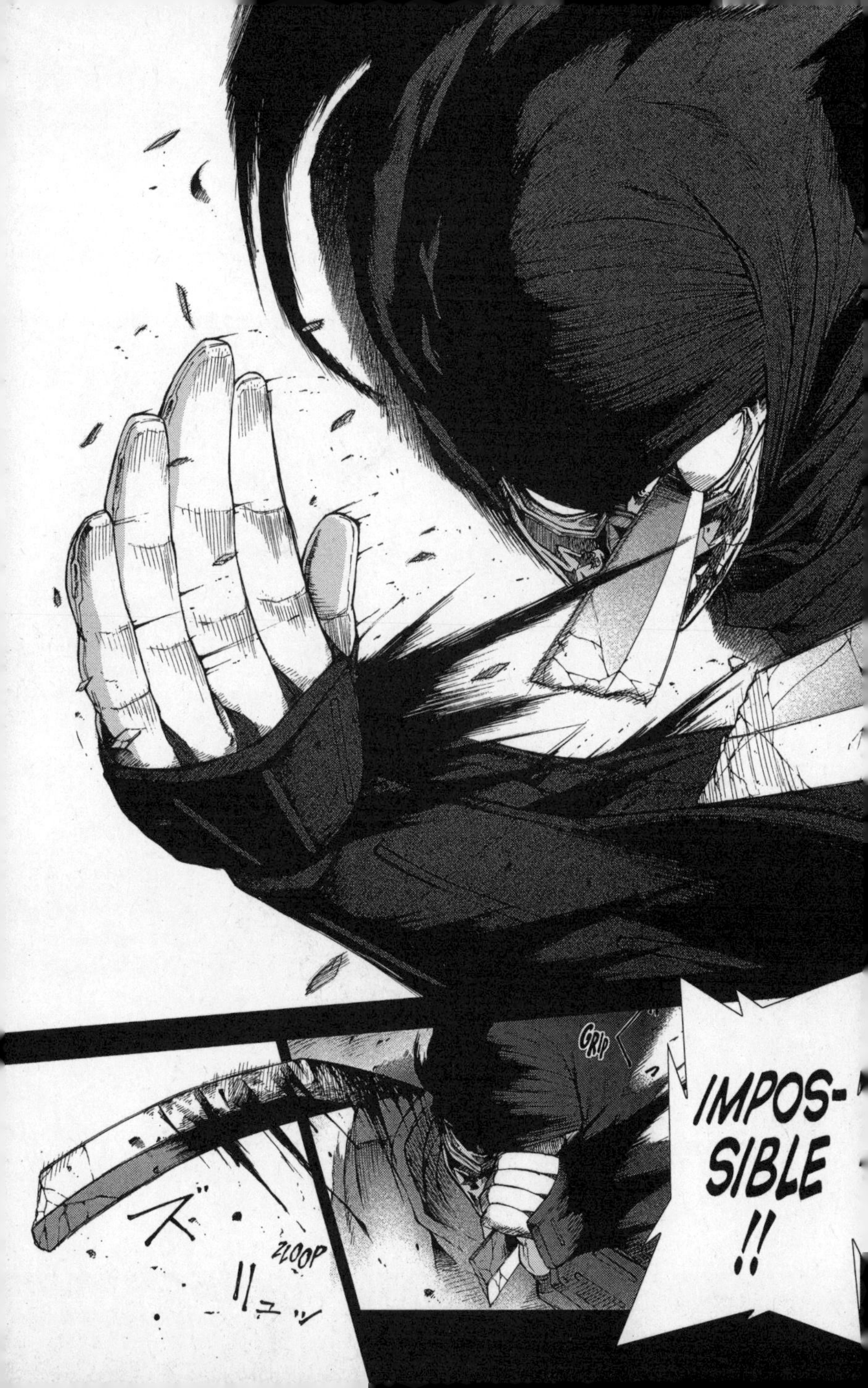
GRIP
IMPOS-
SIBLE
!!
ズリュッ
ZLOOP

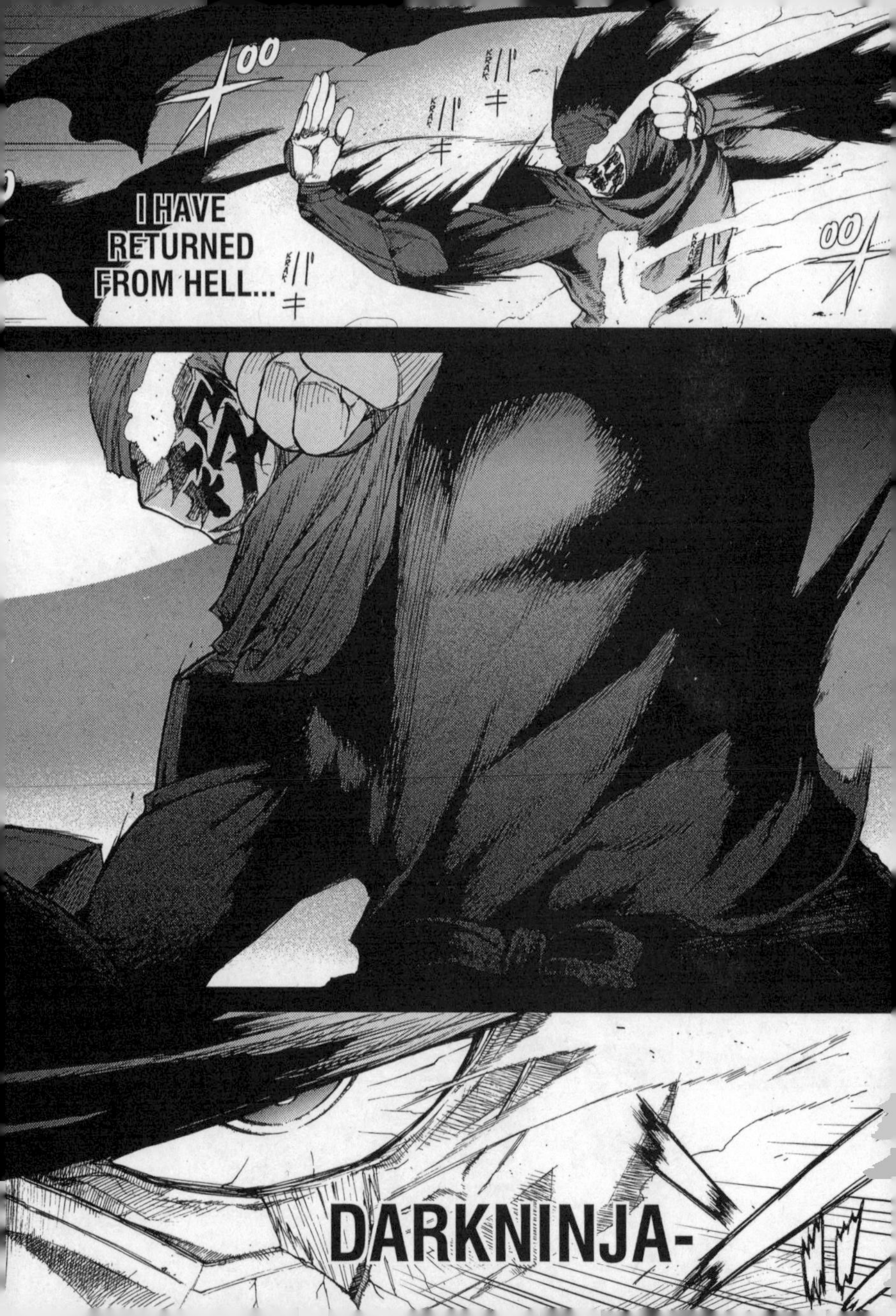
OO
KRAK
KRAK
KRAK
OO
I HAVE RETURNED FROM HELL...
KRAK
DARKNINJA-

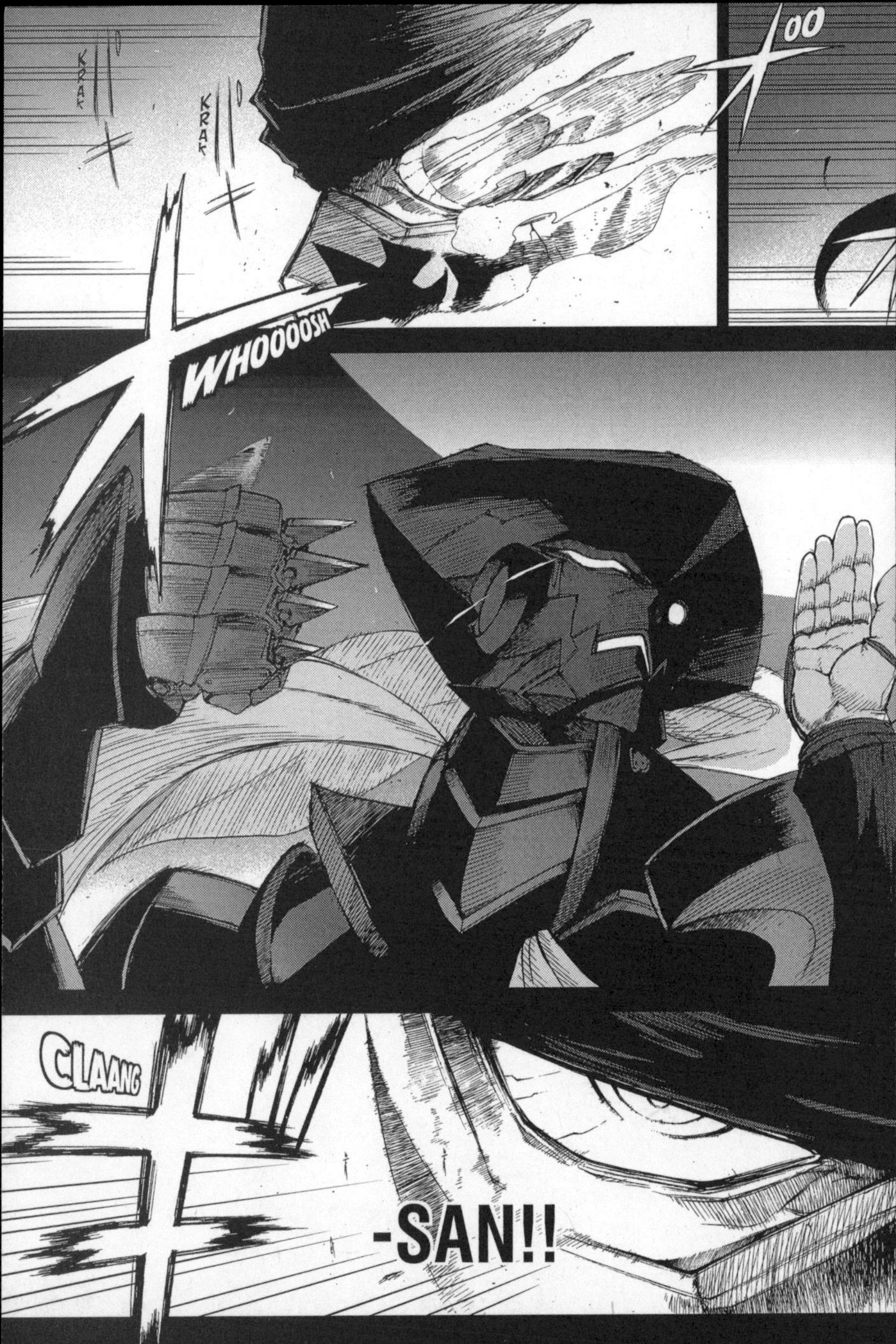
OO
KRAK
KRAK
WHOOOOSH
CLAANG
-SAN!!

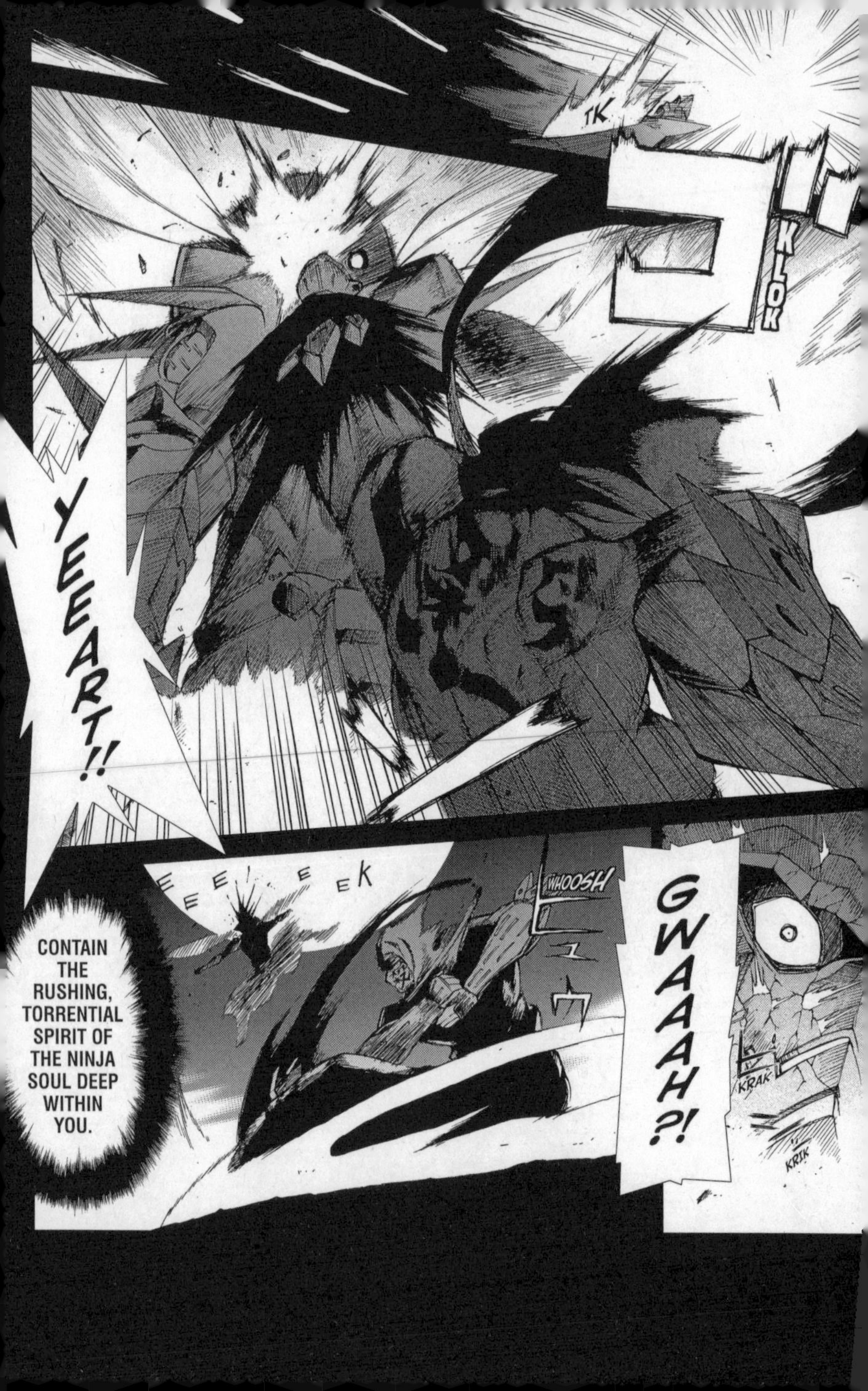
TK
KLOK
YEEART!!
GWAAAH?!
KRAK
KRIK
WHOOSH
EEEEEK
CONTAIN THE RUSHING, TORRENTIAL SPIRIT OF THE NINJA SOUL DEEP WITHIN YOU.

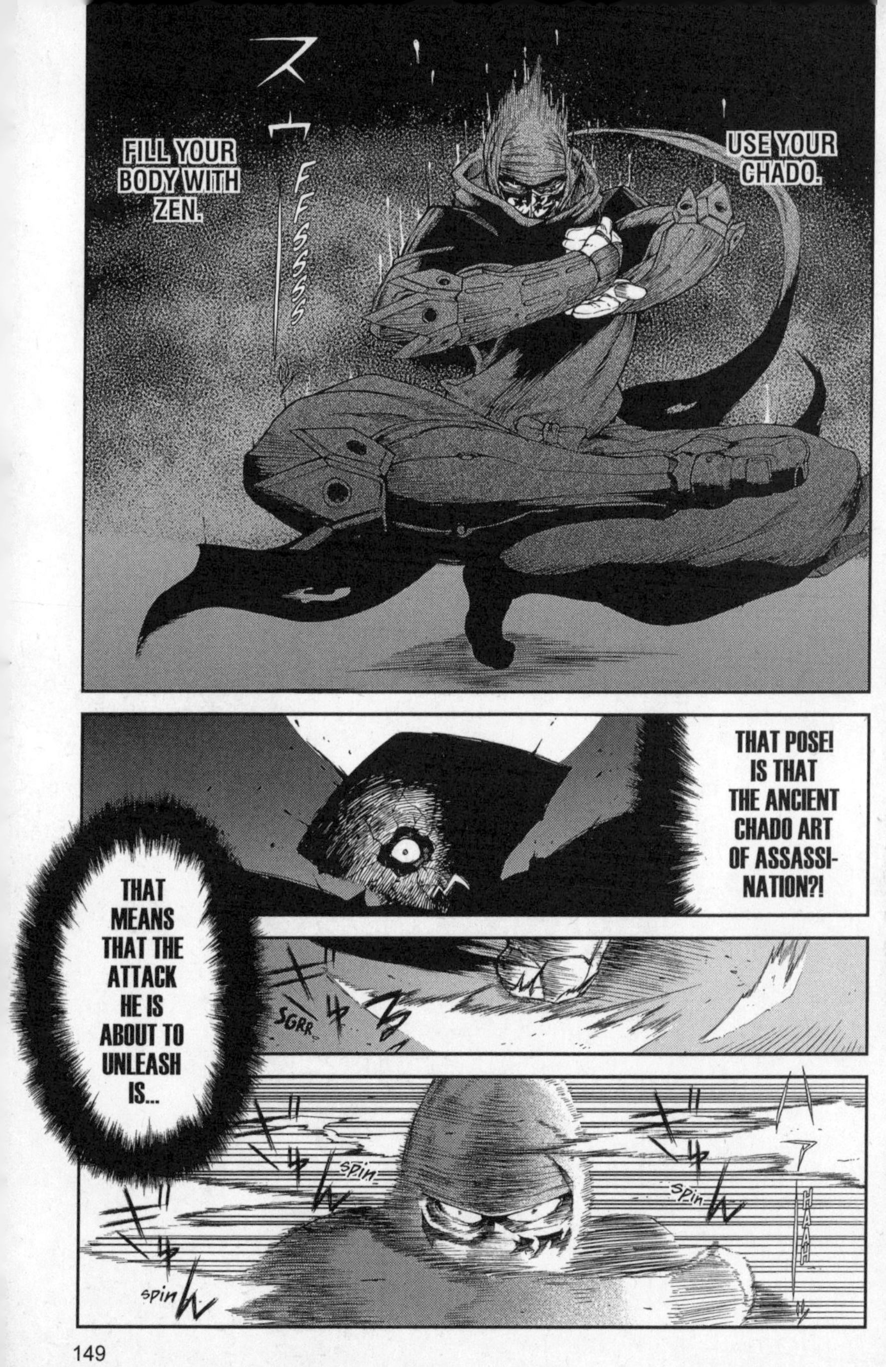
USE YOUR CHADO.
FILL YOUR BODY WITH ZEN.
FFSSSSS
THAT POSE! IS THAT THE ANCIENT CHADO ART OF ASSASSI-NATION?!
THAT MEANS THAT THE ATTACK HE IS ABOUT TO UNLEASH IS...
SGRR
spin
spin
spin
HAAAH

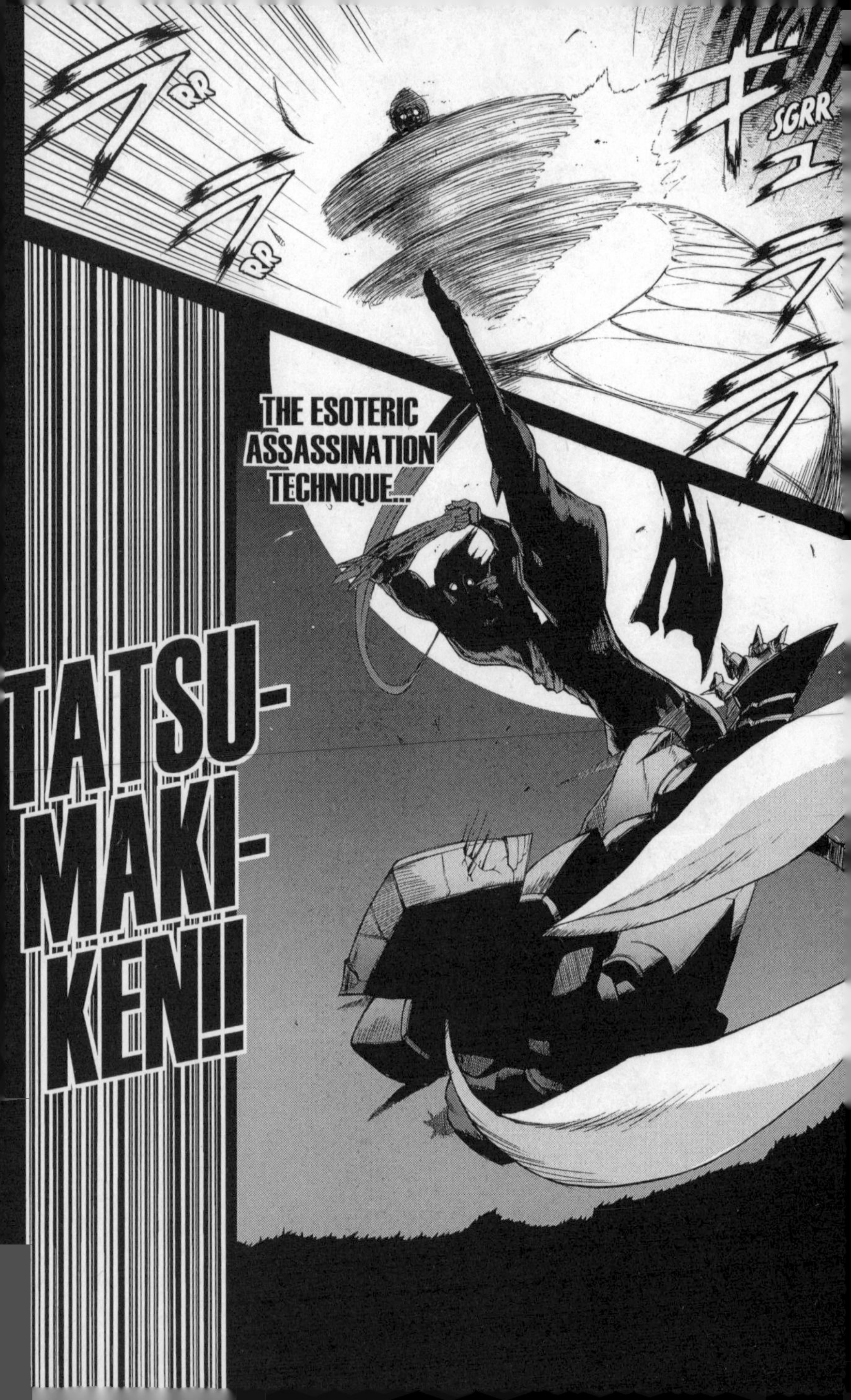
SGRR
RR
RR
THE ESOTERIC ASSASSINATION TECHNIQUE...
TATSU-MAKI-KEN!!

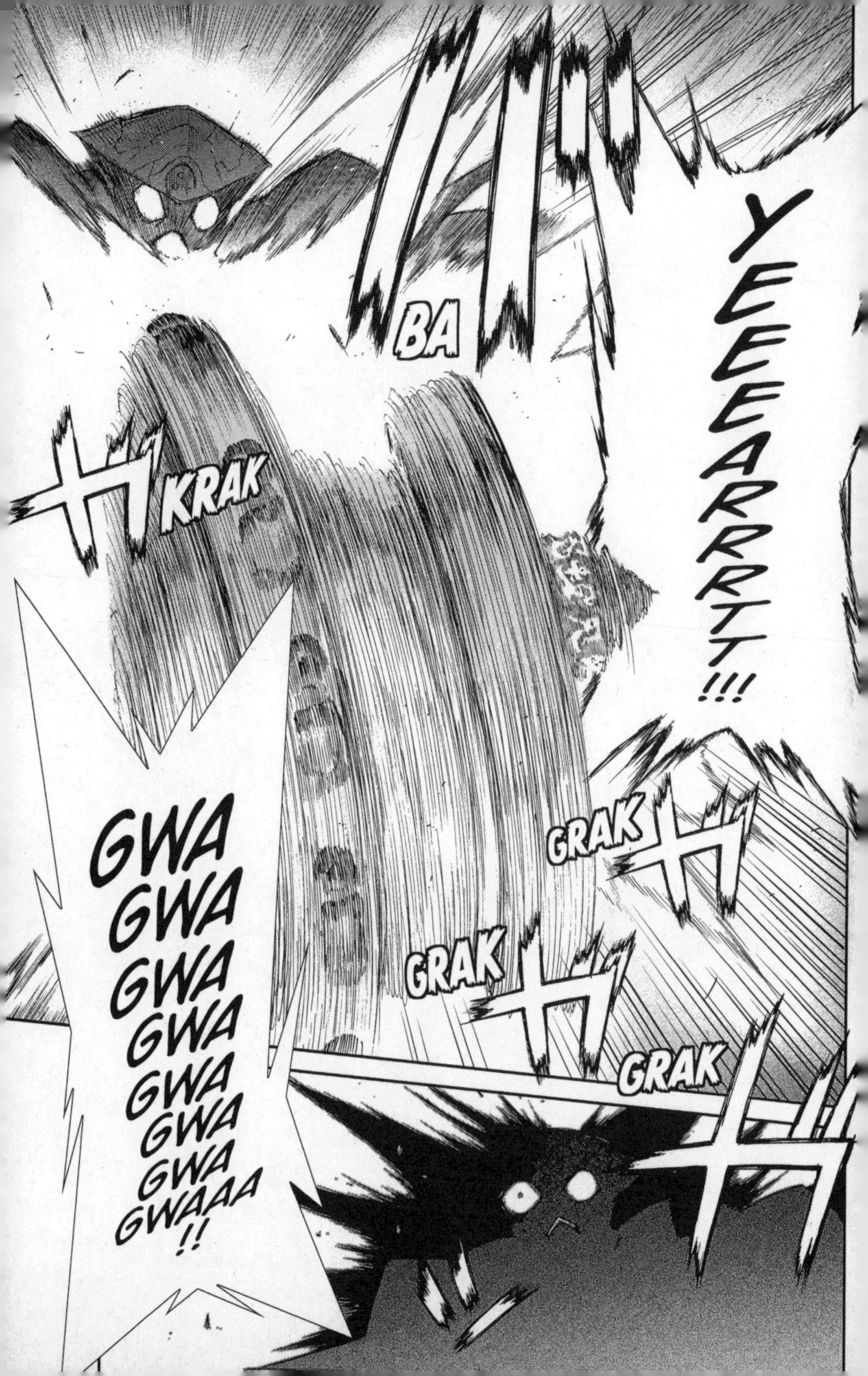
YEEEARRRTT!!!
BA
KRAK
GRAK
GRAK
GRAK
GWA GWA GWA GWA GWA GWA GWA GWA GWAAA!!

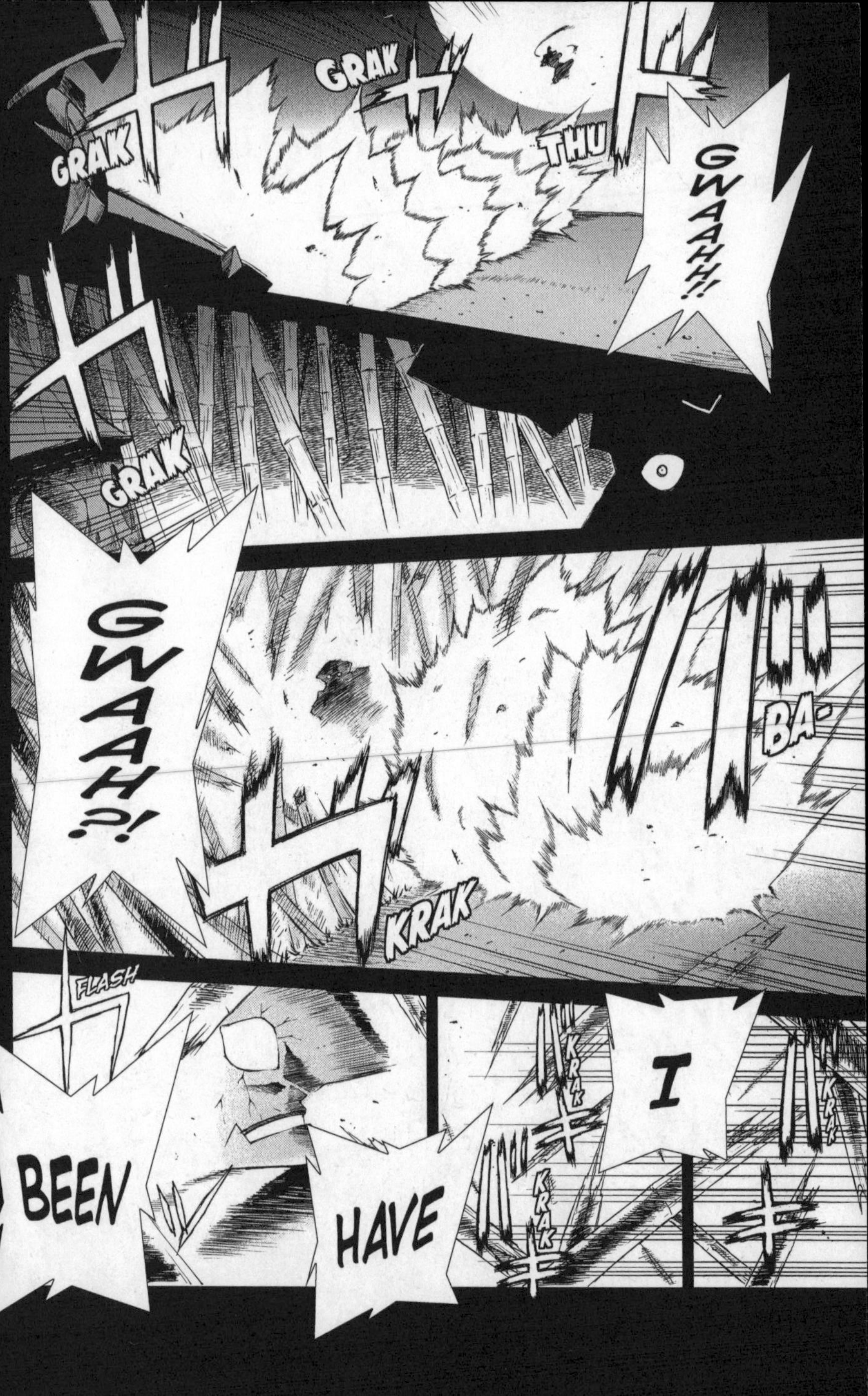
GWAAHH!!
THU
GRAK
GRAK
GRAK
BA-
GWAAH?!
KRAK
KRAK
I
KRAK
KRAK
HAVE
BEEN
FLASH

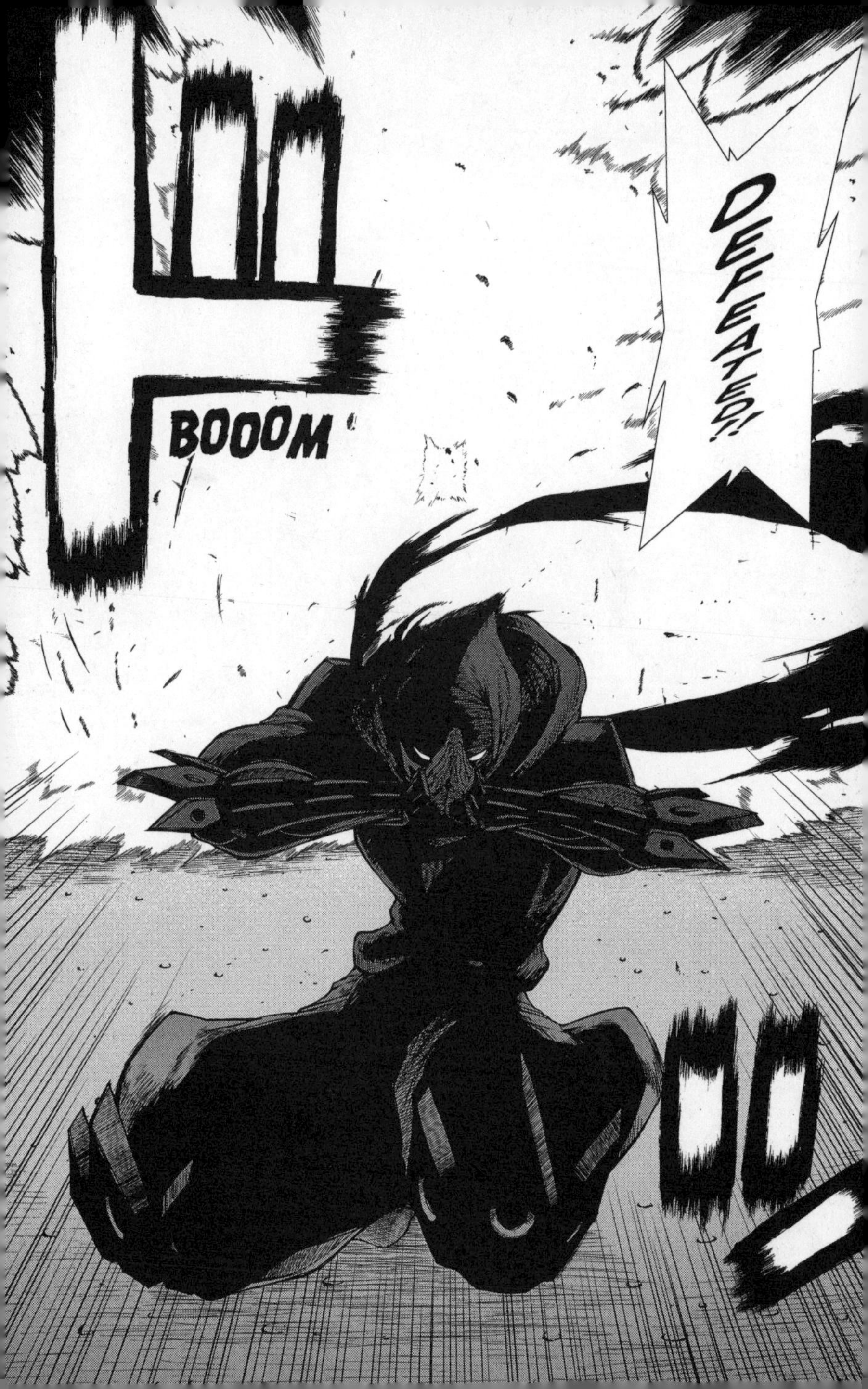
DEFEATED!!
BOOOM

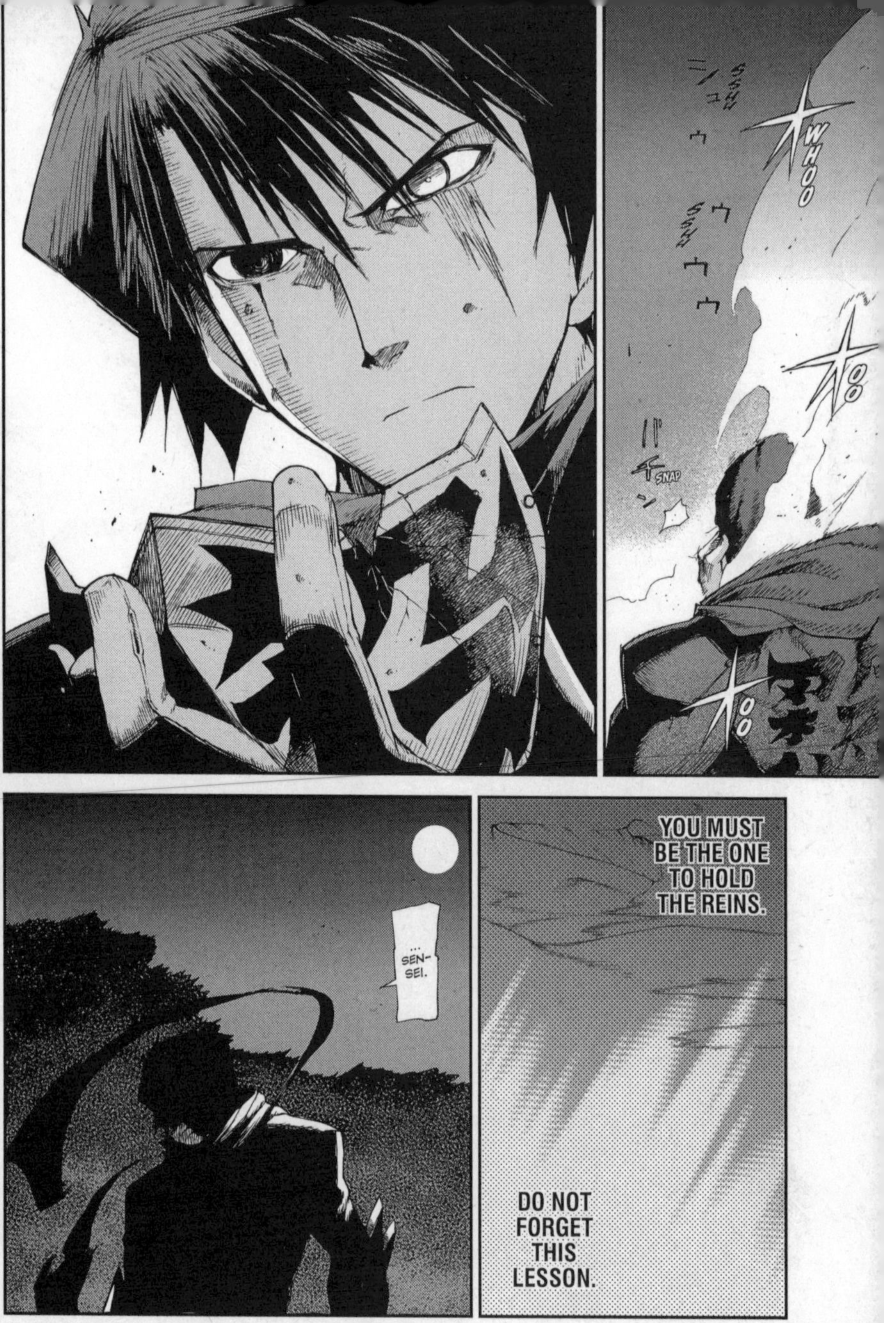
SSHH
SSHH
WHOO
OO
SNAP
OO
YOU MUST BE THE ONE TO HOLD THE REINS.
DO NOT FORGET THIS LESSON.
... SEN-SEI.

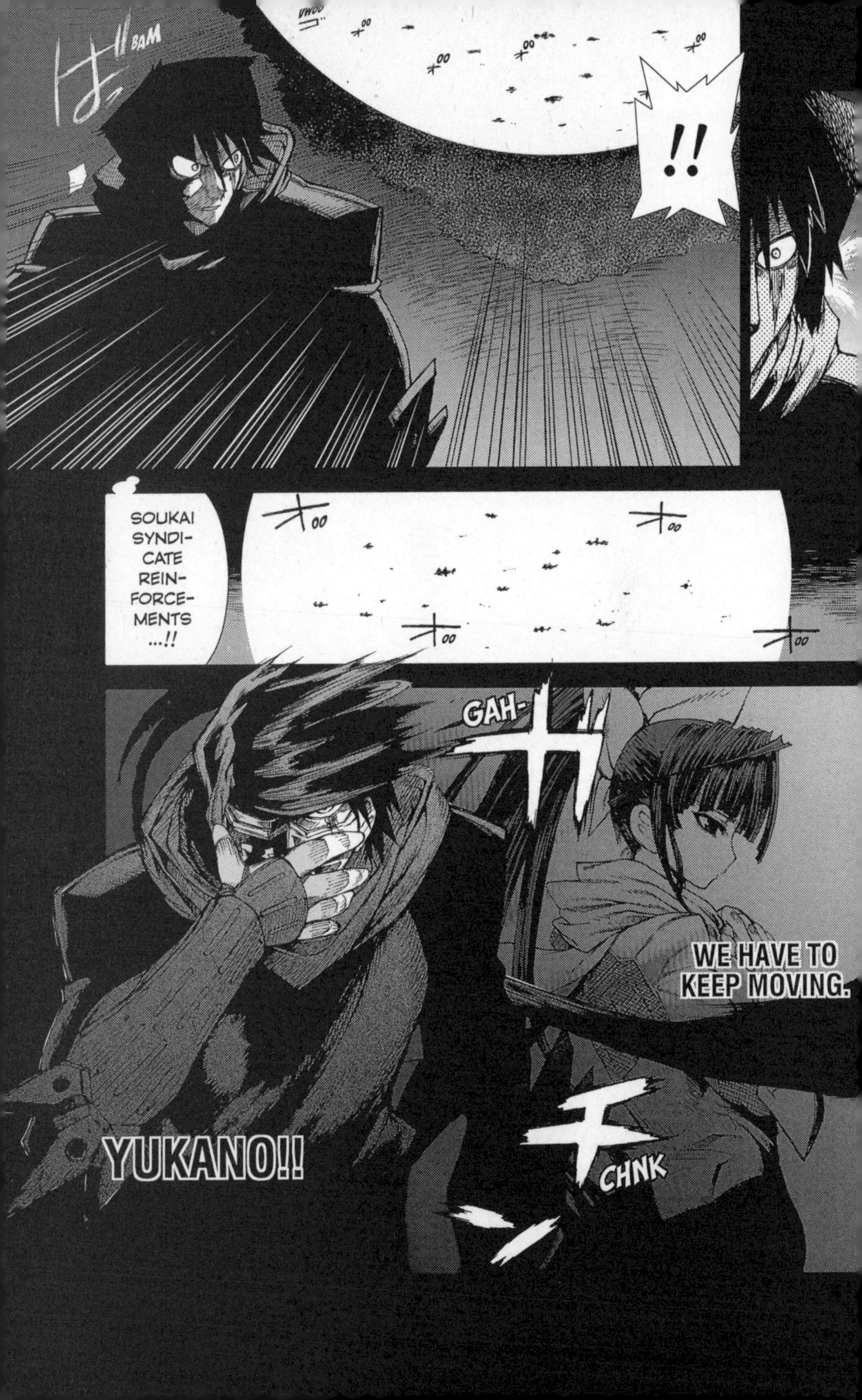
VWOO
!!
BAM
SOUKAI SYNDICATE REINFORCEMENTS ...!!
GAH-
WE HAVE TO KEEP MOVING.
YUKANO!!
CHNK

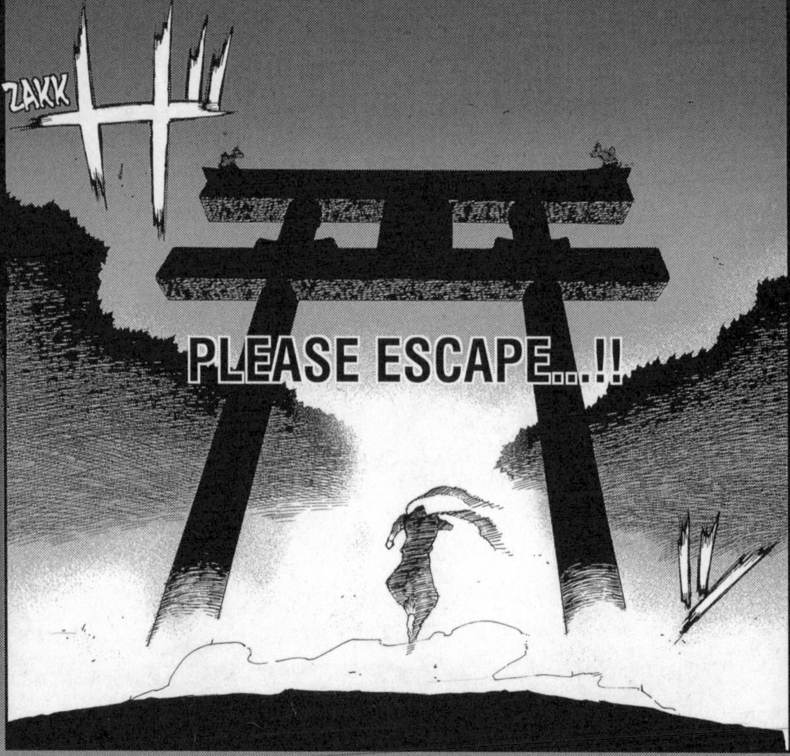
ZAKK
PLEASE ESCAPE...!!

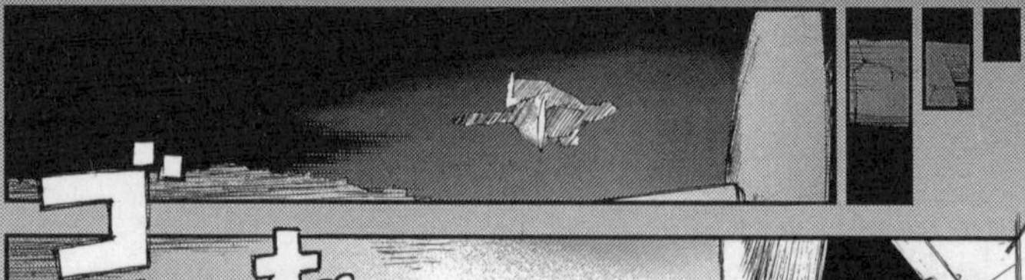

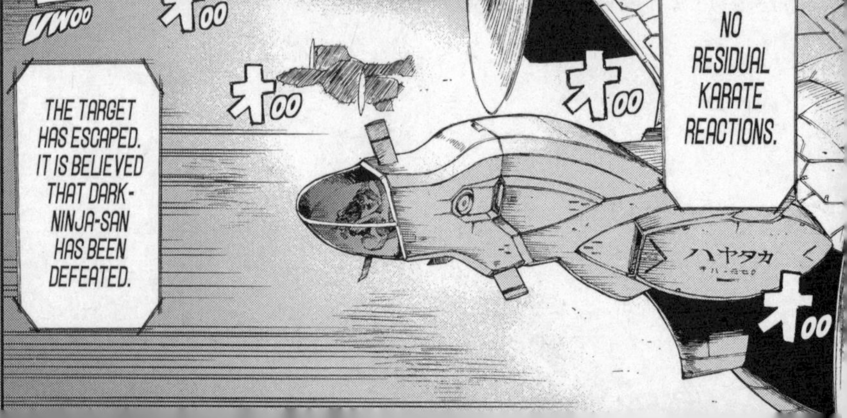
ゴ
VWOO
オOO
NO RESIDUAL KARATE REACTIONS.
オOO
オOO
THE TARGET HAS ESCAPED. IT IS BELIEVED THAT DARK-NINJA-SAN HAS BEEN DEFEATED.
ハヤタカ
オOO

SHIP: Hayataka

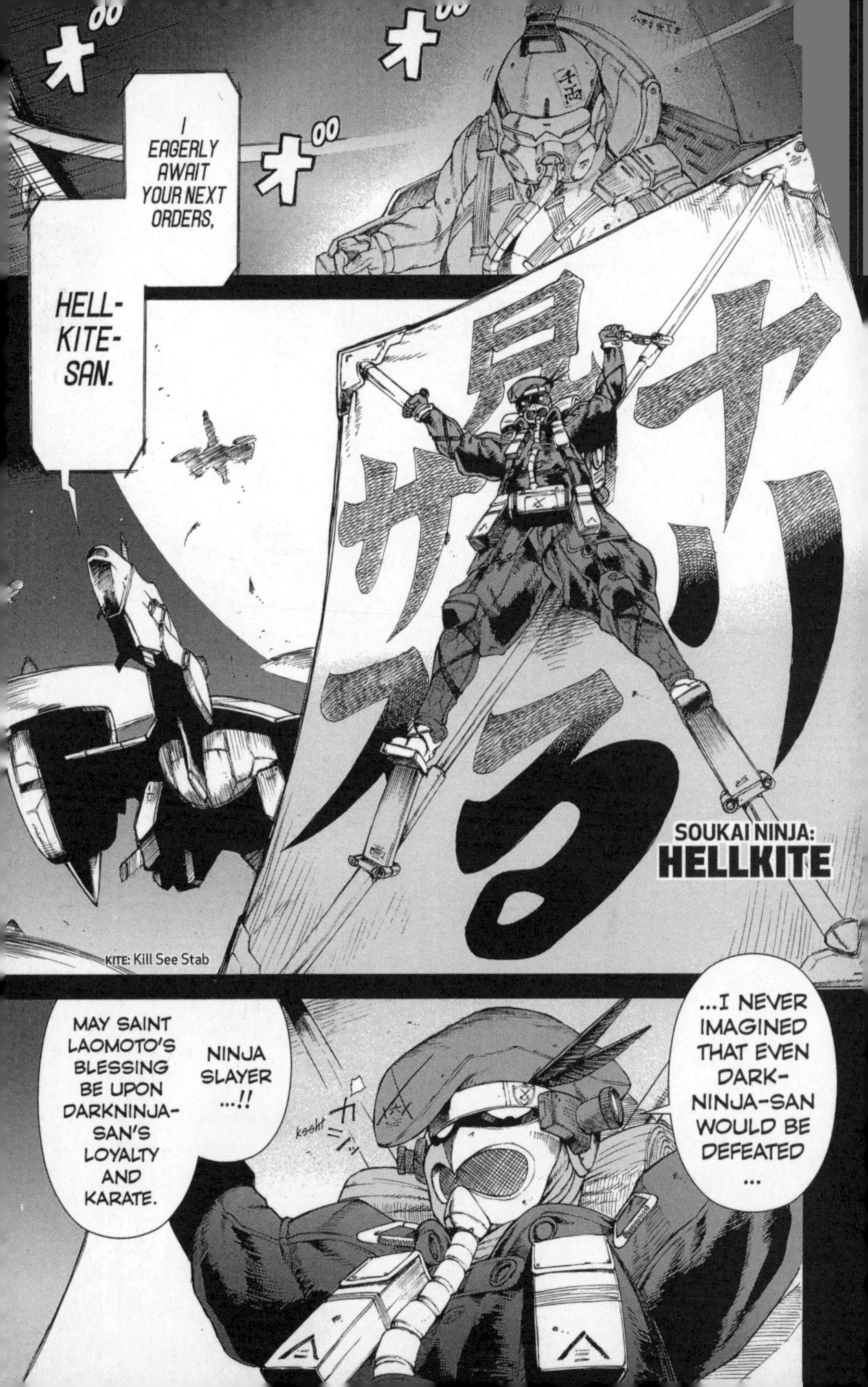

オOO
オOO
オOO
I EAGERLY AWAIT YOUR NEXT ORDERS,
HELL-KITE-SAN.
SOUKAI NINJA:
HELLKITE
KITE: Kill See Stab
...I NEVER IMAGINED THAT EVEN DARK-NINJA-SAN WOULD BE DEFEATED ...
kssht
NINJA SLAYER ...!!
MAY SAINT LAOMOTO'S BLESSING BE UPON DARKNINJA-SAN'S LOYALTY AND KARATE.

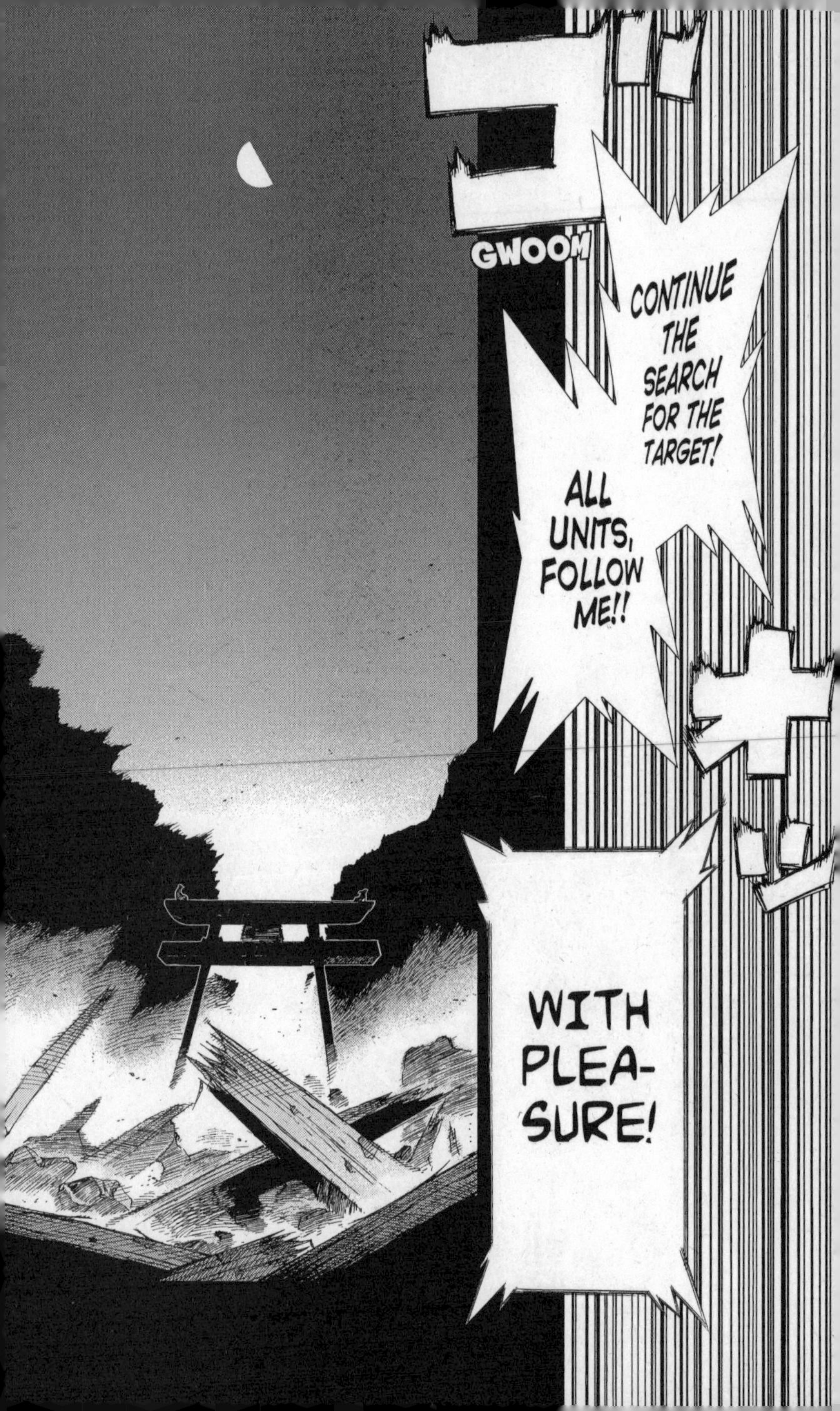
GWOOM
CONTINUE THE SEARCH FOR THE TARGET!
ALL UNITS, FOLLOW ME!!
WITH PLEA-SURE!

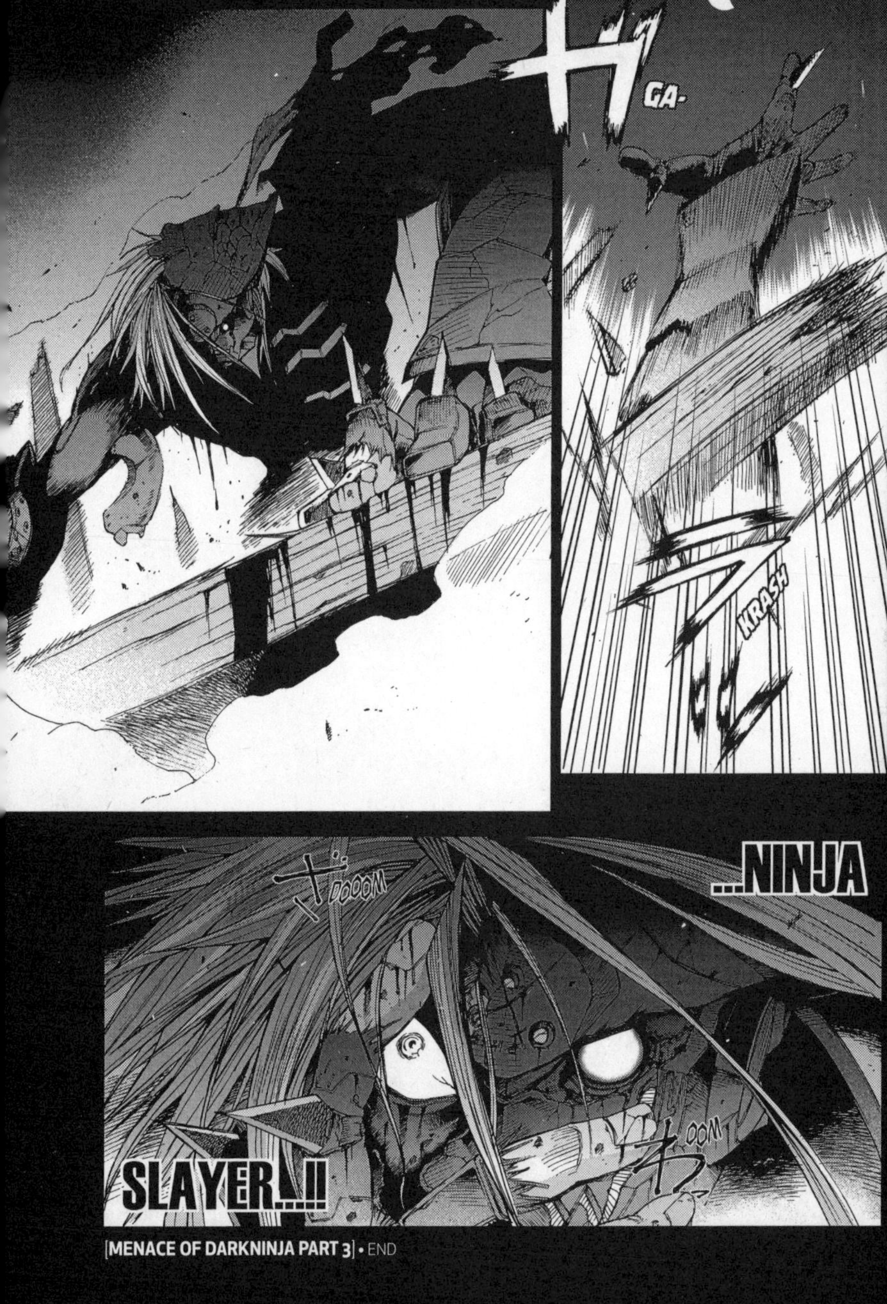
GA-
KRASH
...NINJA
DOOOM
OOM
SLAYER...!!

[MENACE OF DARKNINJA PART 3] • END

NINJA
ニンジャスレイヤー
SLAYER
KILLS!

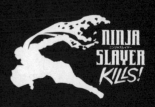

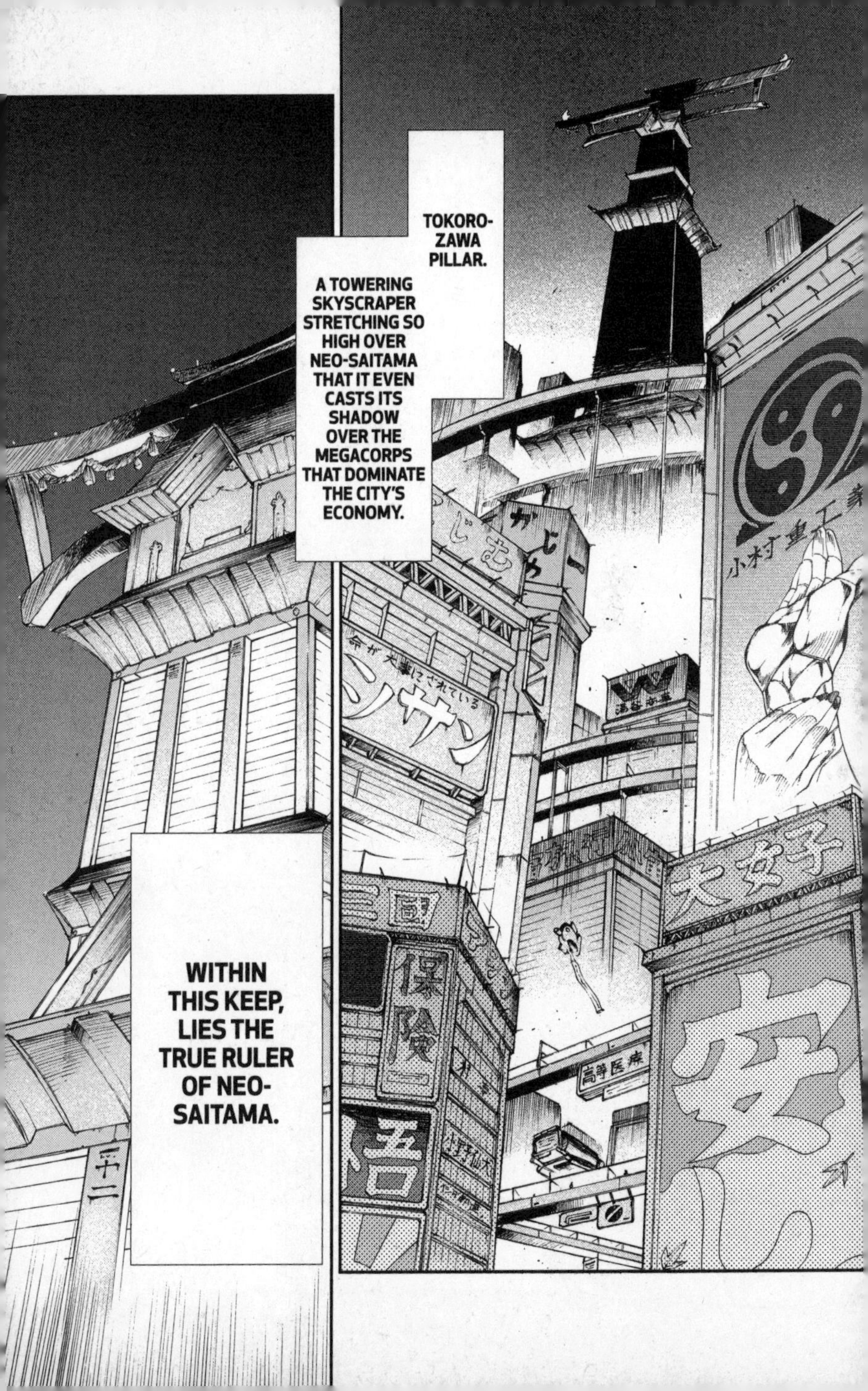
TOKORO-ZAWA PILLAR.
A TOWERING SKYSCRAPER STRETCHING SO HIGH OVER NEO-SAITAMA THAT IT EVEN CASTS ITS SHADOW OVER THE MEGACORPS THAT DOMINATE THE CITY'S ECONOMY.
WITHIN THIS KEEP, LIES THE TRUE RULER OF NEO-SAITAMA.

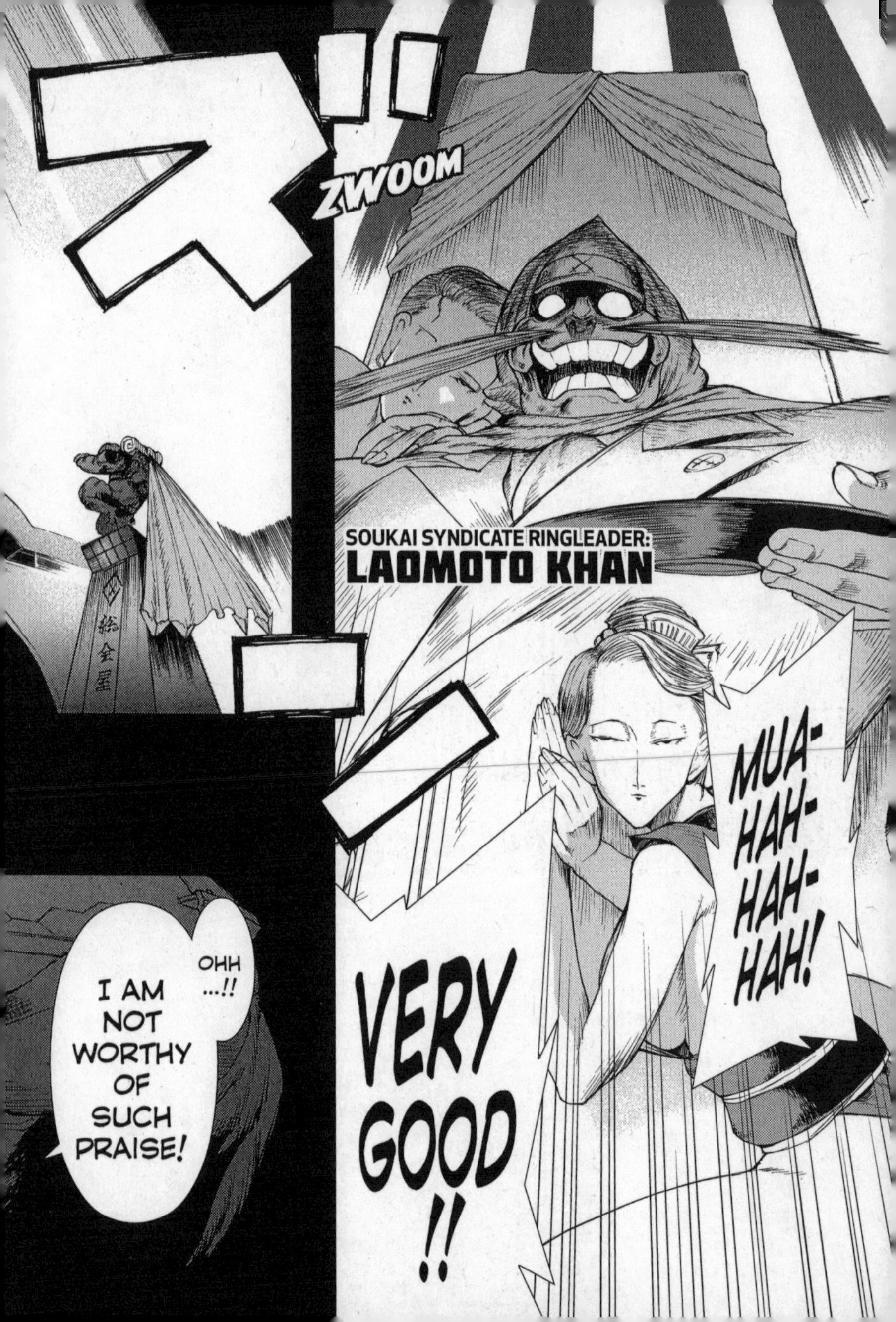
ZWOOM
SOUKAI SYNDICATE RINGLEADER: LAOMOTO KHAN
MUA-HAH-HAH-HAH-HAH!
VERY GOOD!!
OHH ...!!
I AM NOT WORTHY OF SUCH PRAISE!

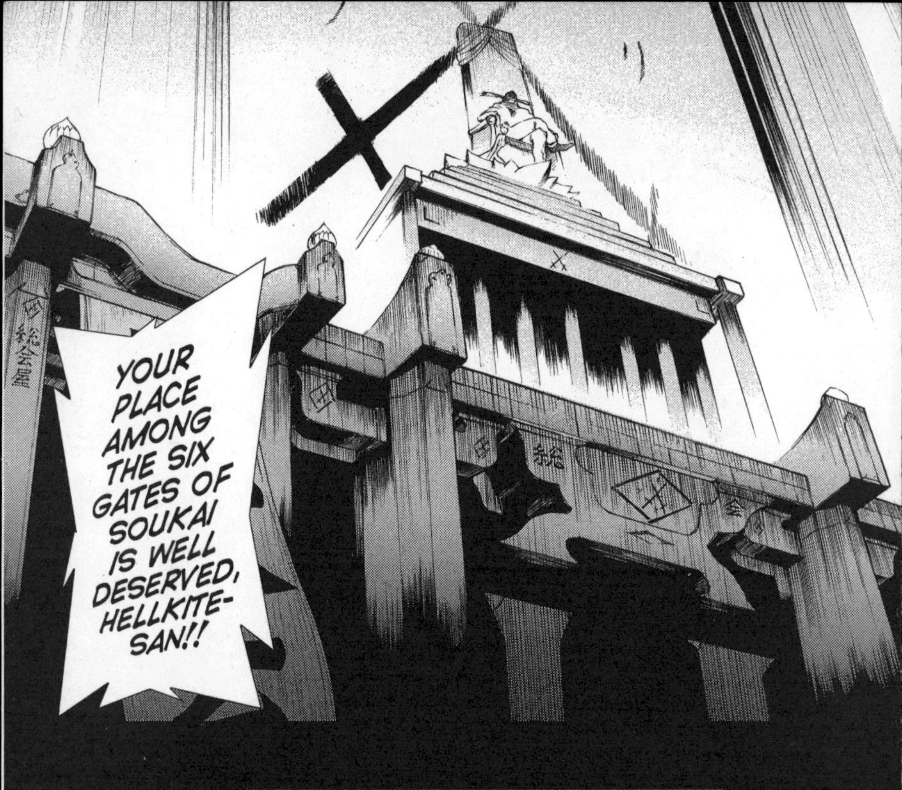
YOUR PLACE AMONG THE SIX GATES OF SOUKAI IS WELL DESERVED, HELLKITE-SAN!!

KILLs 006 ✦ DIVERGENCE AFTER DARK

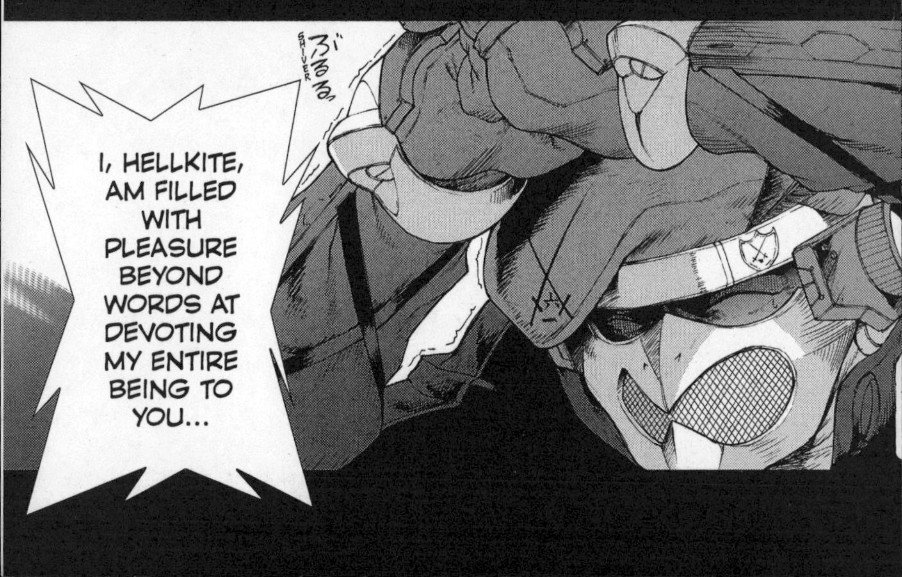
ぶるるっ
SHIVER
I, HELLKITE, AM FILLED WITH PLEASURE BEYOND WORDS AT DEVOTING MY ENTIRE BEING TO YOU...

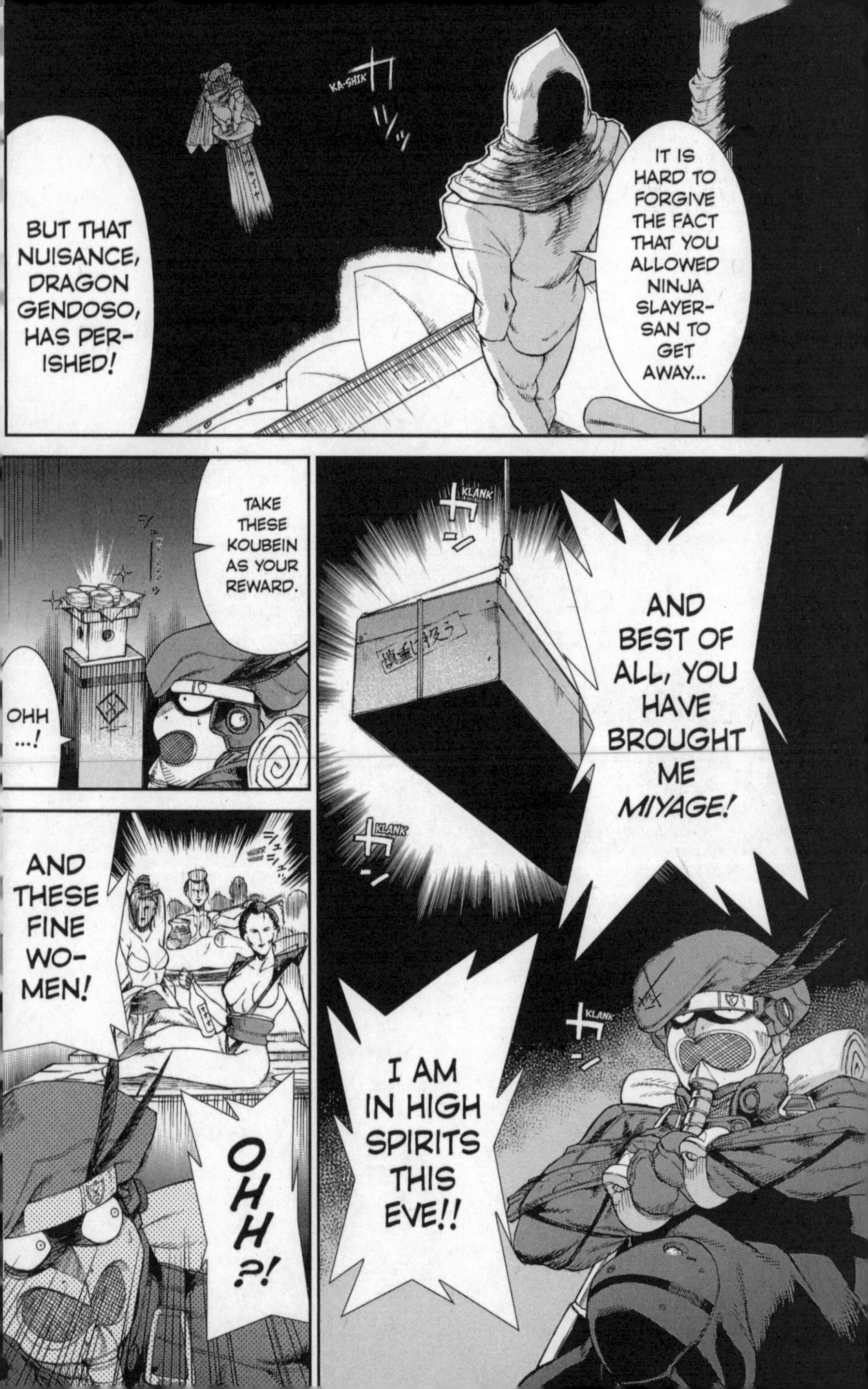
KA-SHIK
IT IS HARD TO FORGIVE THE FACT THAT YOU ALLOWED NINJA SLAYER-SAN TO GET AWAY...
BUT THAT NUISANCE, DRAGON GENDOSO, HAS PERISHED!
TAKE THESE KOUBEIN AS YOUR REWARD.
OHH ...!
WHIRR WHIRR
AND THESE FINE WOMEN!
OHH?!
KLANK
KLANK
AND BEST OF ALL, YOU HAVE BROUGHT ME *MIYAGE!*
KLANK
I AM IN HIGH SPIRITS THIS EVE!!

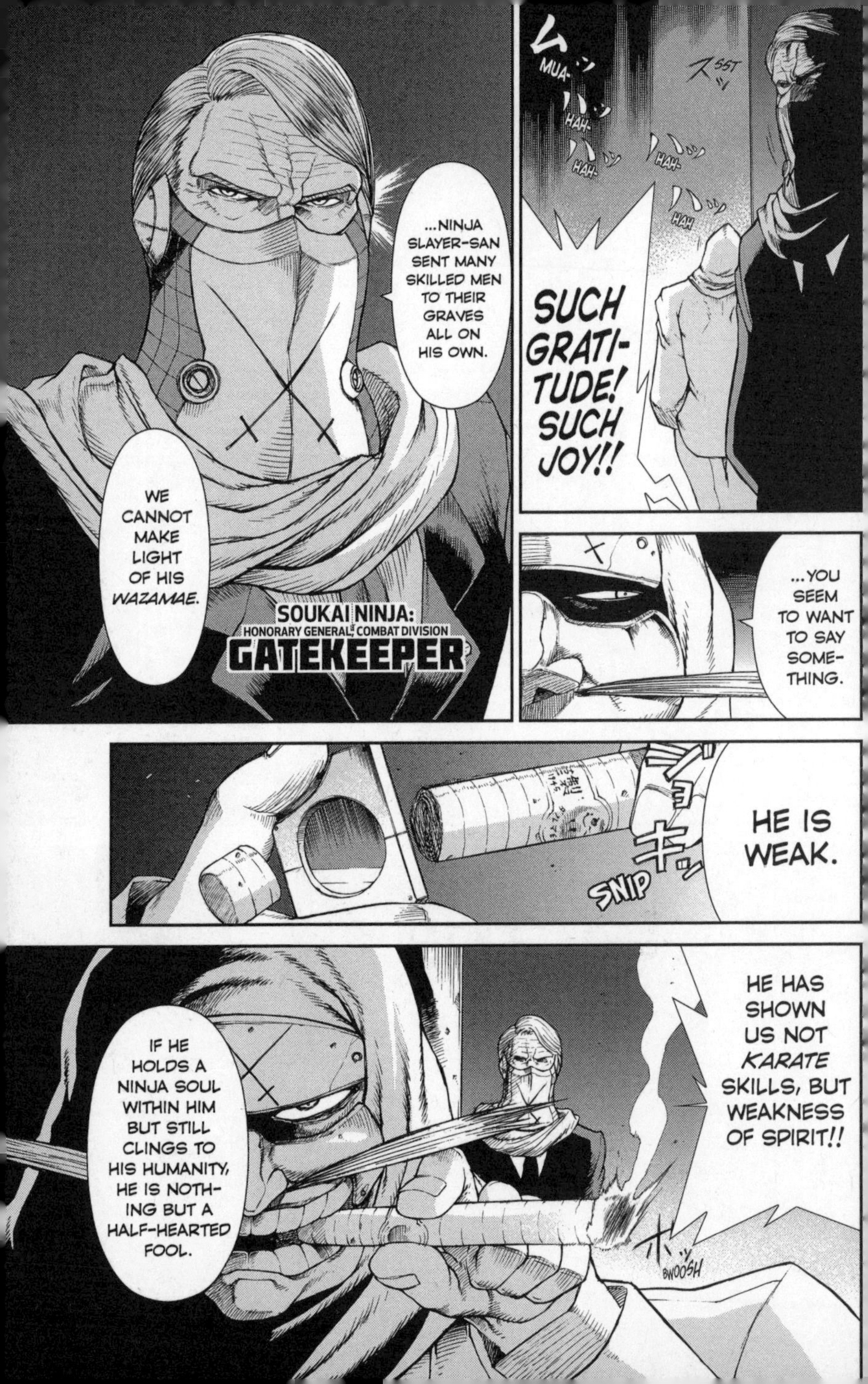

MUA-
SST
HAH-
HAH-
HAH-
HAH
SUCH GRATI-TUDE! SUCH JOY!!
...YOU SEEM TO WANT TO SAY SOME-THING.
...NINJA SLAYER-SAN SENT MANY SKILLED MEN TO THEIR GRAVES ALL ON HIS OWN.
WE CANNOT MAKE LIGHT OF HIS *WAZAMAE*.
SOUKAI NINJA:
HONORARY GENERAL, COMBAT DIVISION
GATEKEEPER
HE IS WEAK.
SNIP
HE HAS SHOWN US NOT *KARATE* SKILLS, BUT WEAKNESS OF SPIRIT!!
IF HE HOLDS A NINJA SOUL WITHIN HIM BUT STILL CLINGS TO HIS HUMANITY, HE IS NOTHING BUT A HALF-HEARTED FOOL.
BWOOSH

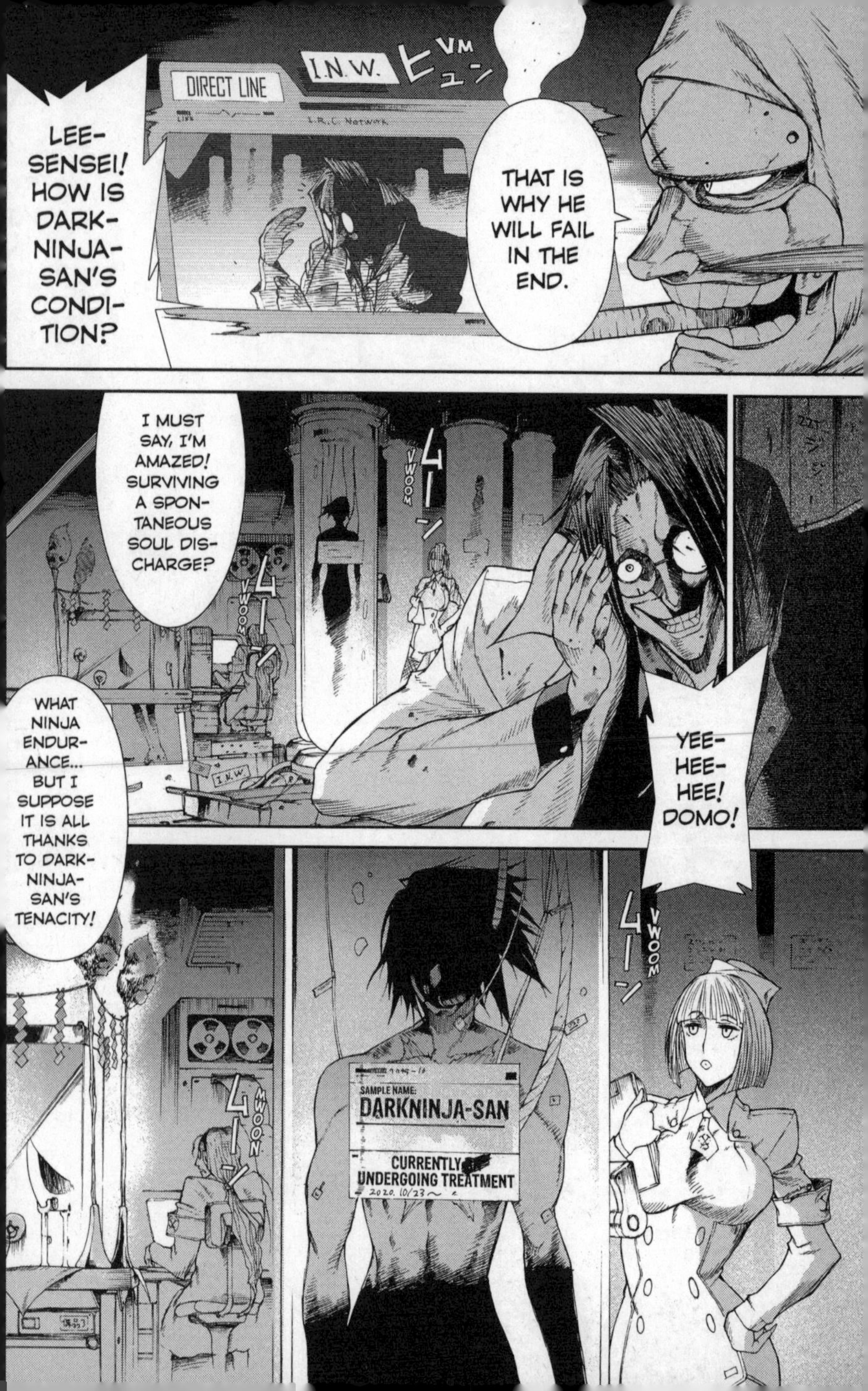
I.N.W.
DIRECT LINE
VM ヒュン
THAT IS WHY HE WILL FAIL IN THE END.
LEE-SENSEI! HOW IS DARK-NINJA-SAN'S CONDITION?
VWOOM
I MUST SAY, I'M AMAZED! SURVIVING A SPONTANEOUS SOUL DISCHARGE?
WHAT NINJA ENDURANCE... BUT I SUPPOSE IT IS ALL THANKS TO DARK-NINJA-SAN'S TENACITY!
YEE-HEE-HEE! DOMO!
VWOOM
SAMPLE NAME:
DARKNINJA-SAN
CURRENTLY UNDERGOING TREATMENT
2020. 10/23～

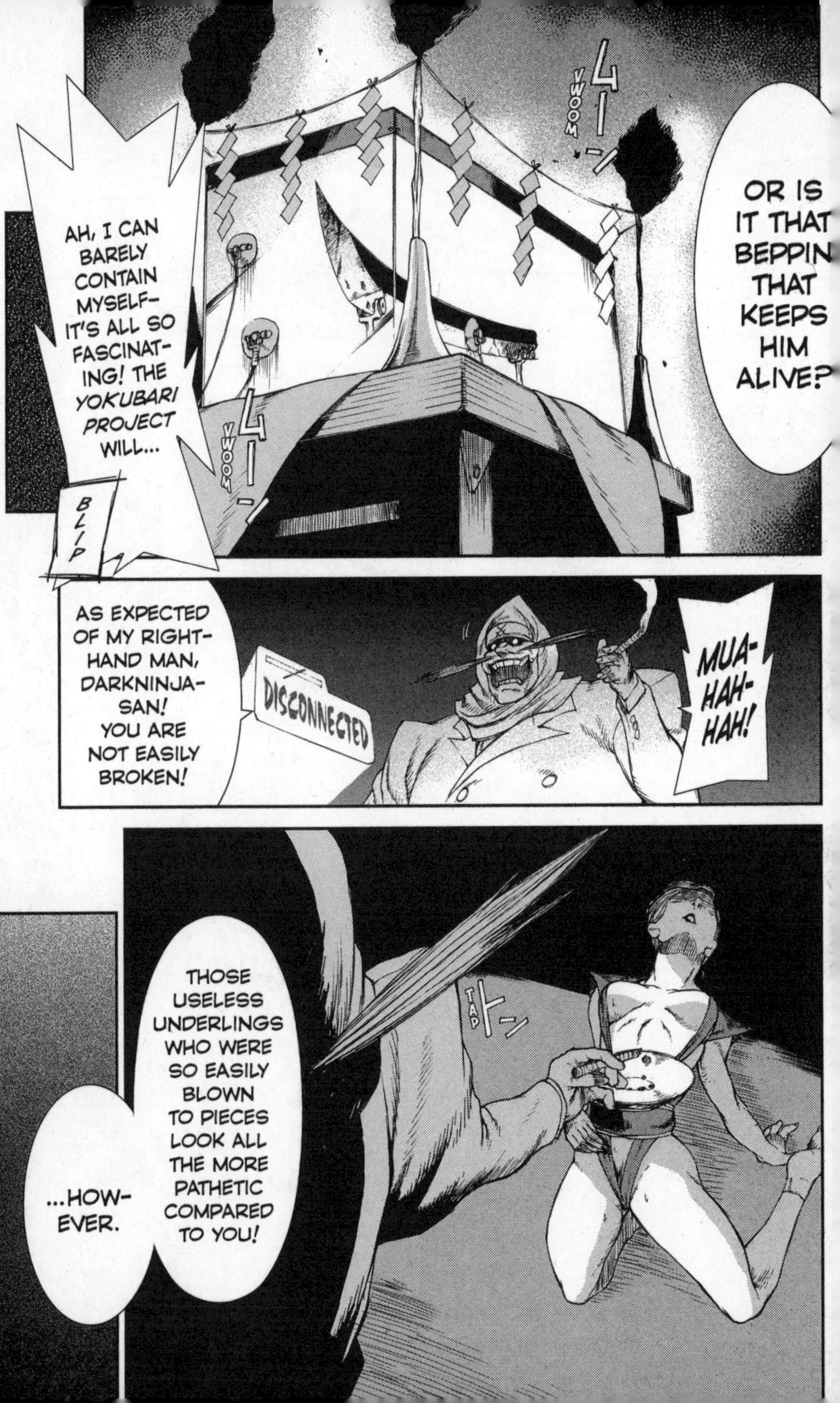
OR IS IT THAT BEPPIN THAT KEEPS HIM ALIVE?
VWOOM
VWOOM
AH, I CAN BARELY CONTAIN MYSELF– IT'S ALL SO FASCINATING! THE *YOKUBARI PROJECT* WILL...
BLIP
MUA-HAH-HAH!
DISCONNECTED
AS EXPECTED OF MY RIGHT-HAND MAN, DARKNINJA-SAN! YOU ARE NOT EASILY BROKEN!
TAP
THOSE USELESS UNDERLINGS WHO WERE SO EASILY BLOWN TO PIECES LOOK ALL THE MORE PATHETIC COMPARED TO YOU!
...HOWEVER.

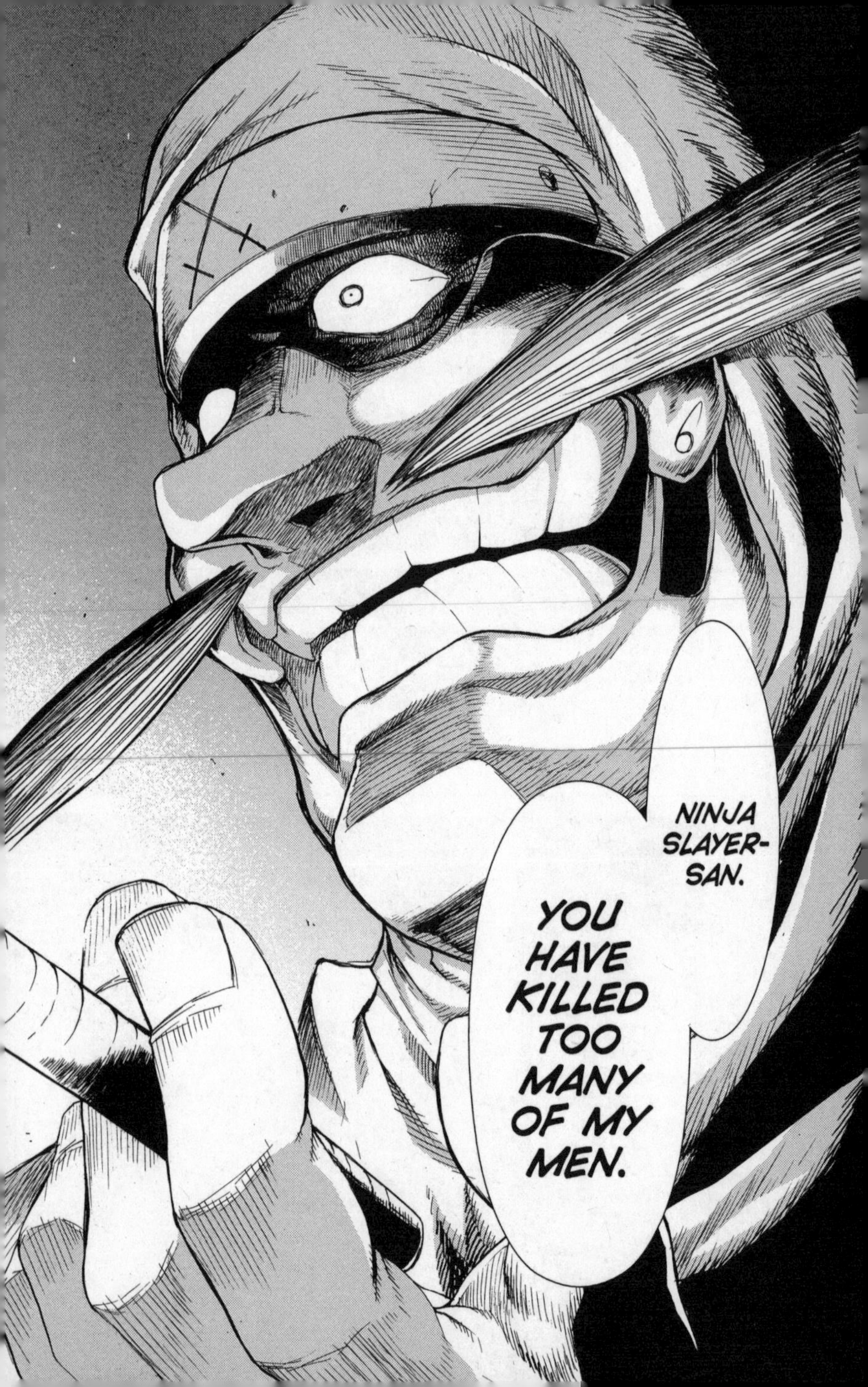
NINJA SLAYER-SAN.
YOU HAVE KILLED TOO MANY OF MY MEN.

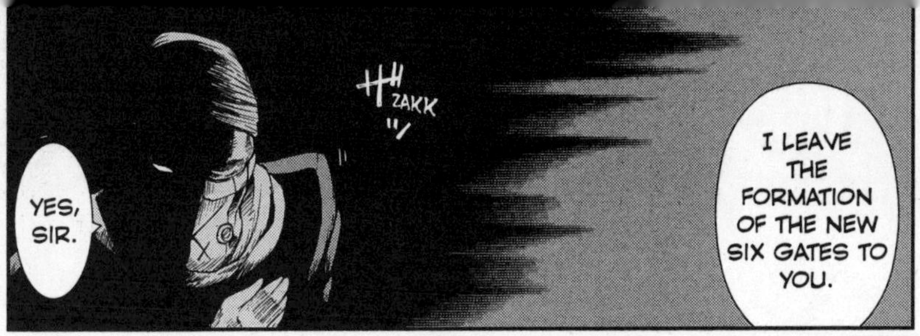
I LEAVE THE FORMATION OF THE NEW SIX GATES TO YOU.
ZAKK
YES, SIR.

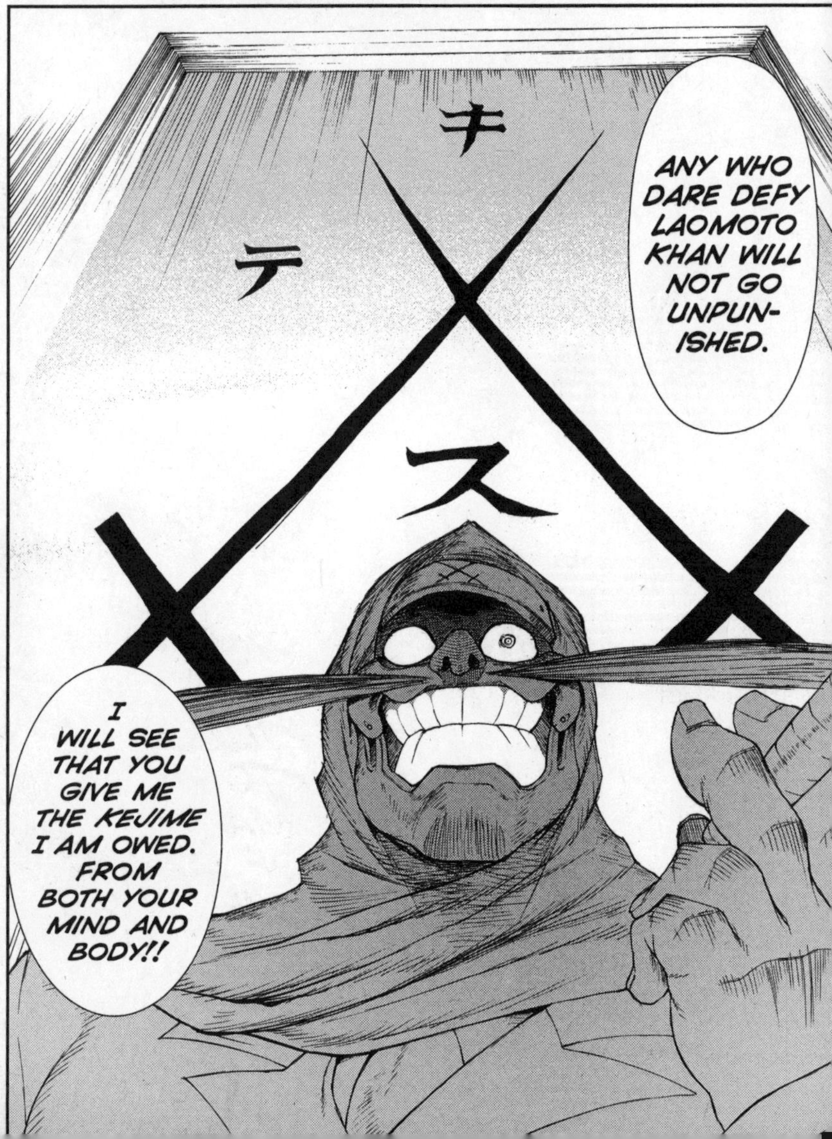
ANY WHO DARE DEFY LAOMOTO KHAN WILL NOT GO UNPUNISHED.
キ
テ
ス
I WILL SEE THAT YOU GIVE ME THE KEJIME I AM OWED. FROM BOTH YOUR MIND AND BODY!!

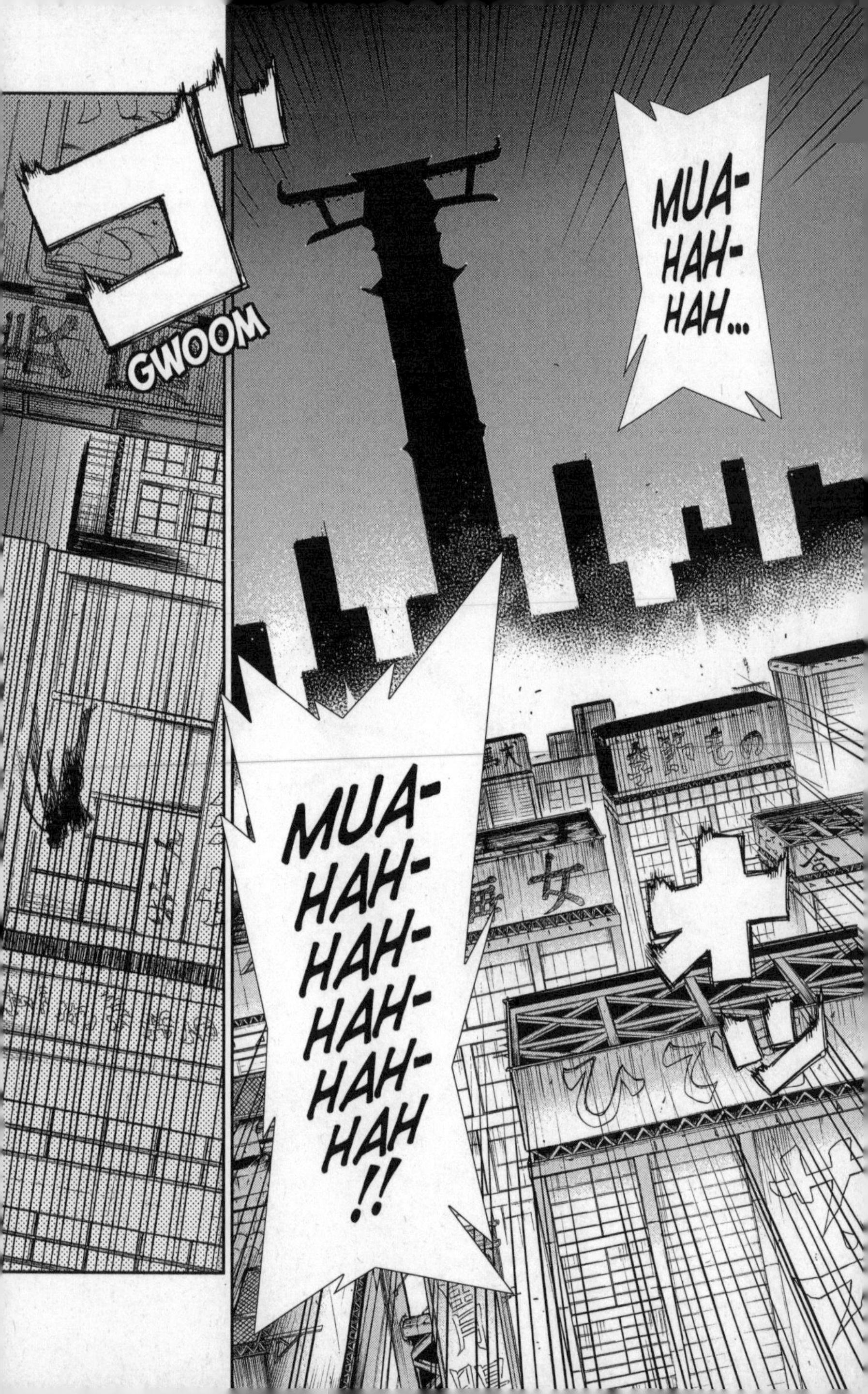
MUA-HAH-HAH...
MUA-HAH-HAH-HAH-HAH-HAH!!
GWOOM

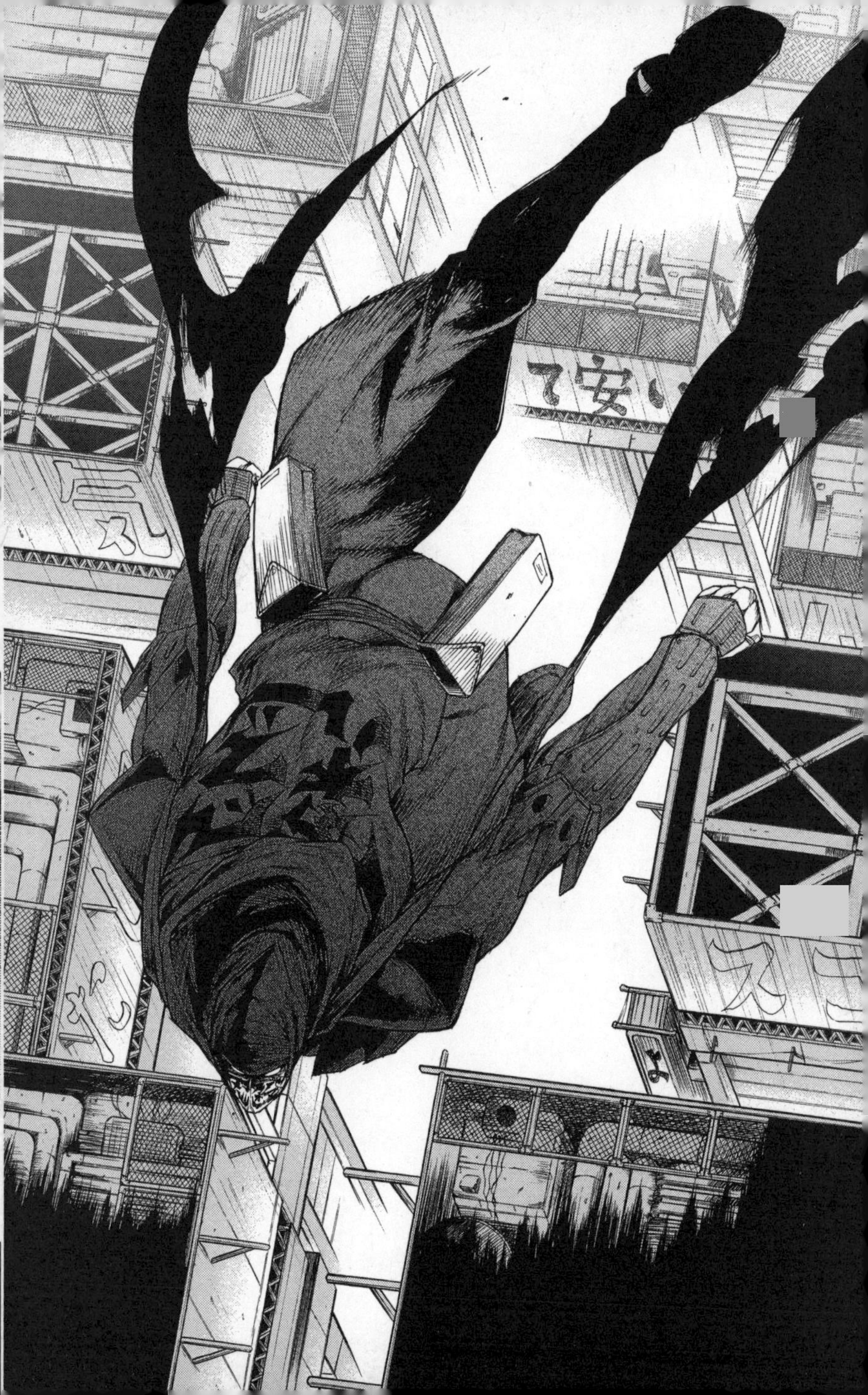
て安い

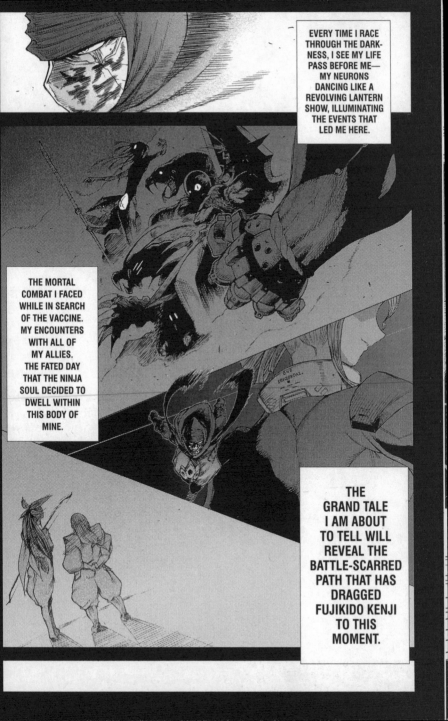

EVERY TIME I RACE THROUGH THE DARKNESS, I SEE MY LIFE PASS BEFORE ME—MY NEURONS DANCING LIKE A REVOLVING LANTERN SHOW, ILLUMINATING THE EVENTS THAT LED ME HERE.

THE MORTAL COMBAT I FACED WHILE IN SEARCH OF THE VACCINE. MY ENCOUNTERS WITH ALL OF MY ALLIES. THE FATED DAY THAT THE NINJA SOUL DECIDED TO DWELL WITHIN THIS BODY OF MINE.

THE GRAND TALE I AM ABOUT TO TELL WILL REVEAL THE BATTLE-SCARRED PATH THAT HAS DRAGGED FUJIKIDO KENJI TO THIS MOMENT.

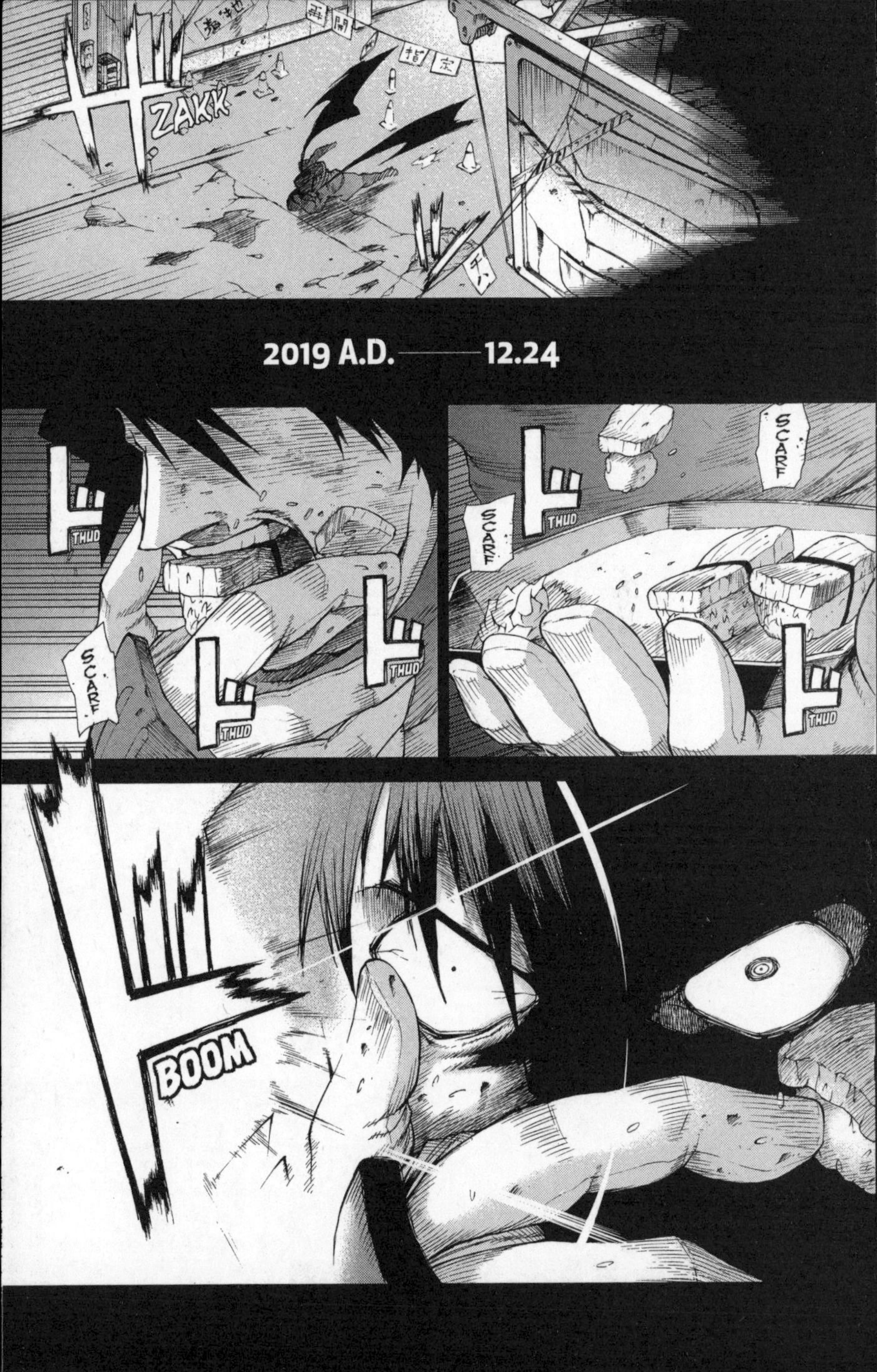
ZAKK
2019 A.D.——12.24
SCARF
THUD
SCARF
THUD
THUD
SCARF
THUD
THUD
BOOM

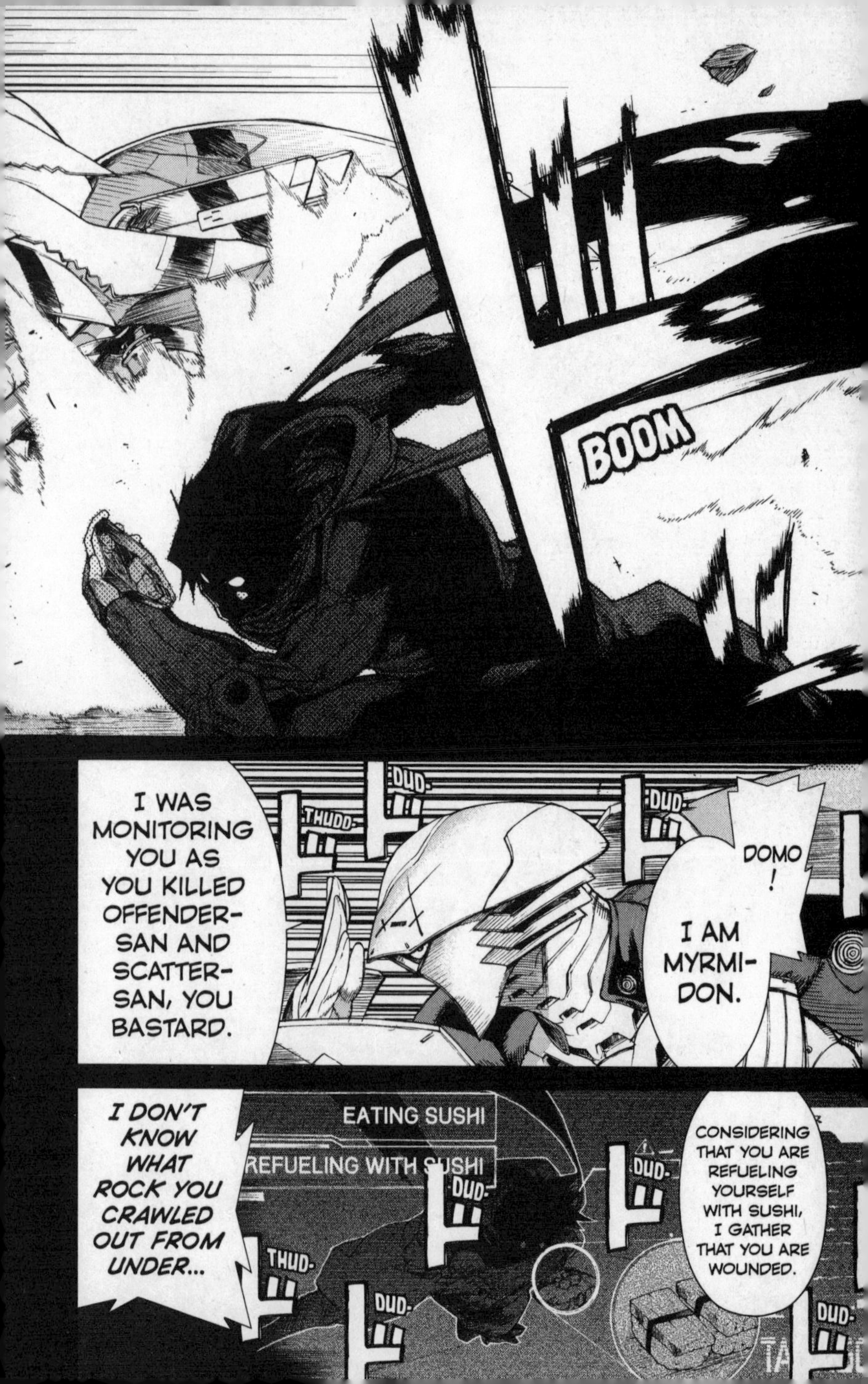
BOOM
DUD-
DUD-
THUDD-
DOMO!
I AM MYRMIDON.
I WAS MONITORING YOU AS YOU KILLED OFFENDER-SAN AND SCATTER-SAN, YOU BASTARD.
DUD-
CONSIDERING THAT YOU ARE REFUELING YOURSELF WITH SUSHI, I GATHER THAT YOU ARE WOUNDED.
DUD-
EATING SUSHI
REFUELING WITH SUSHI
DUD-
THUD-
DUD-
I DON'T KNOW WHAT ROCK YOU CRAWLED OUT FROM UNDER...

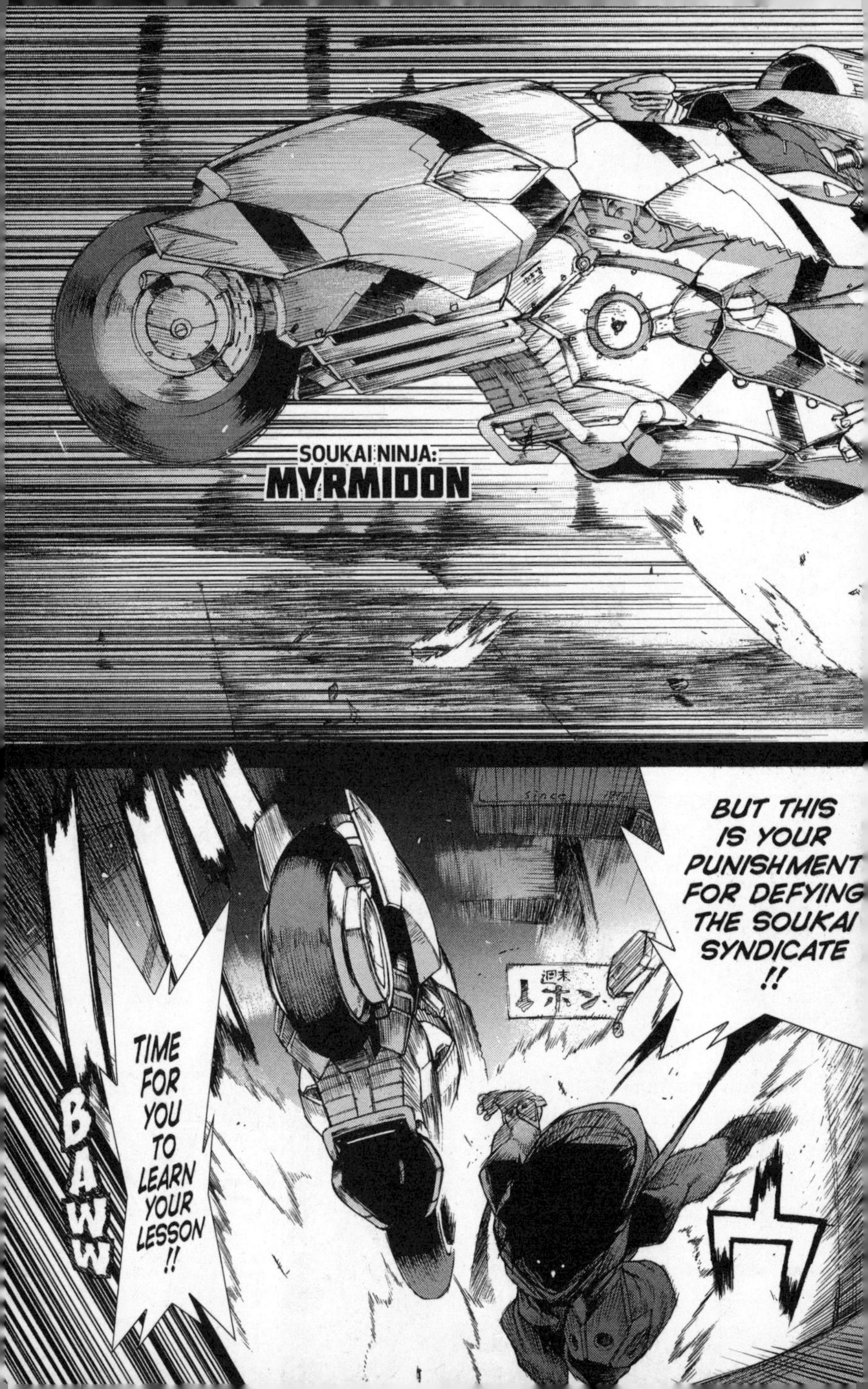
SOUKAI NINJA:
MYRMIDON
BUT THIS IS YOUR PUNISHMENT FOR DEFYING THE SOUKAI SYNDICATE !!
TIME FOR YOU TO LEARN YOUR LESSON !!
BAWW

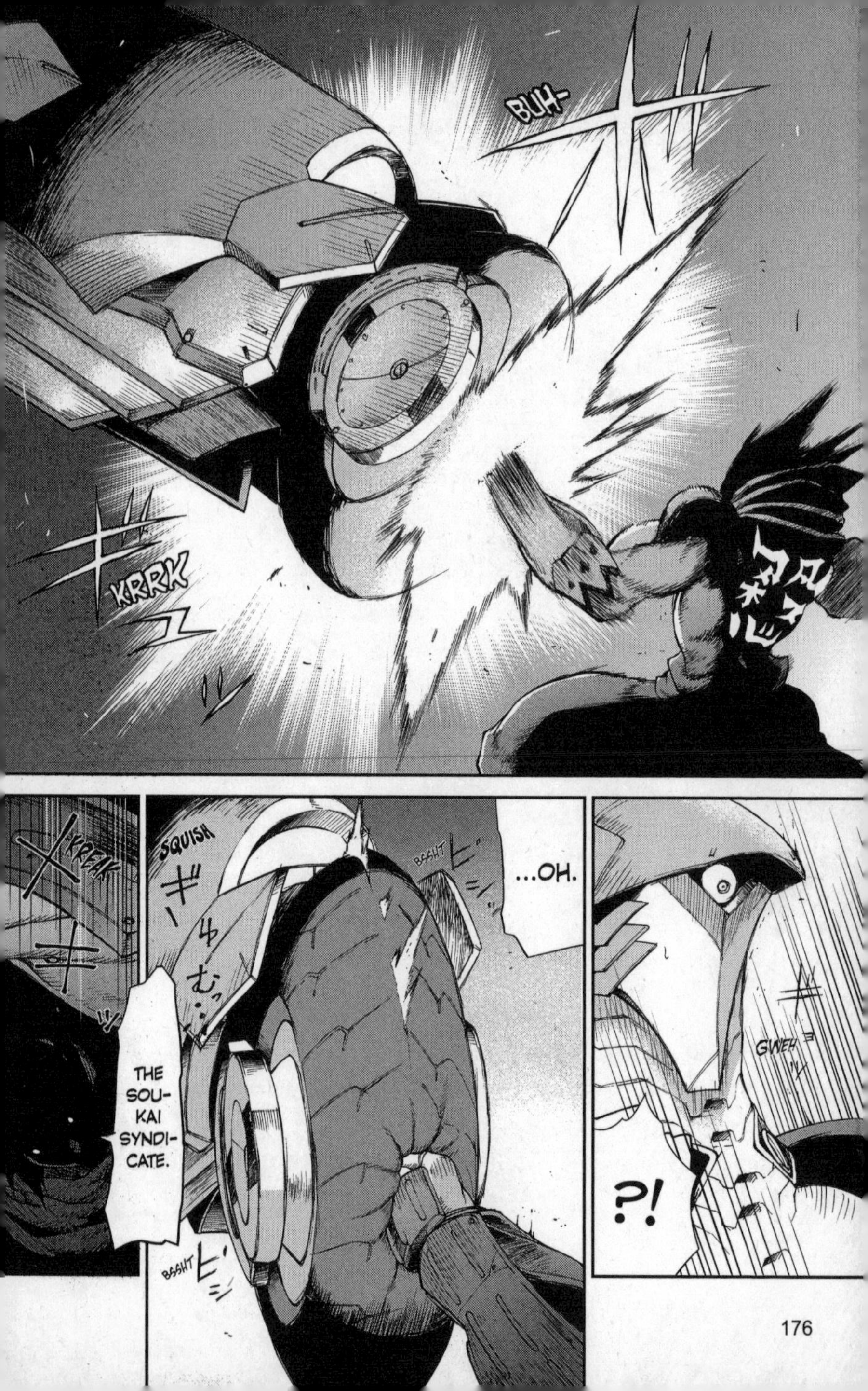
BUH-
KRRK
GWEH
?!
SQUISH
BASHT
...OH.
BASHT
KREAK
THE SOU-KAI SYNDI-CATE.

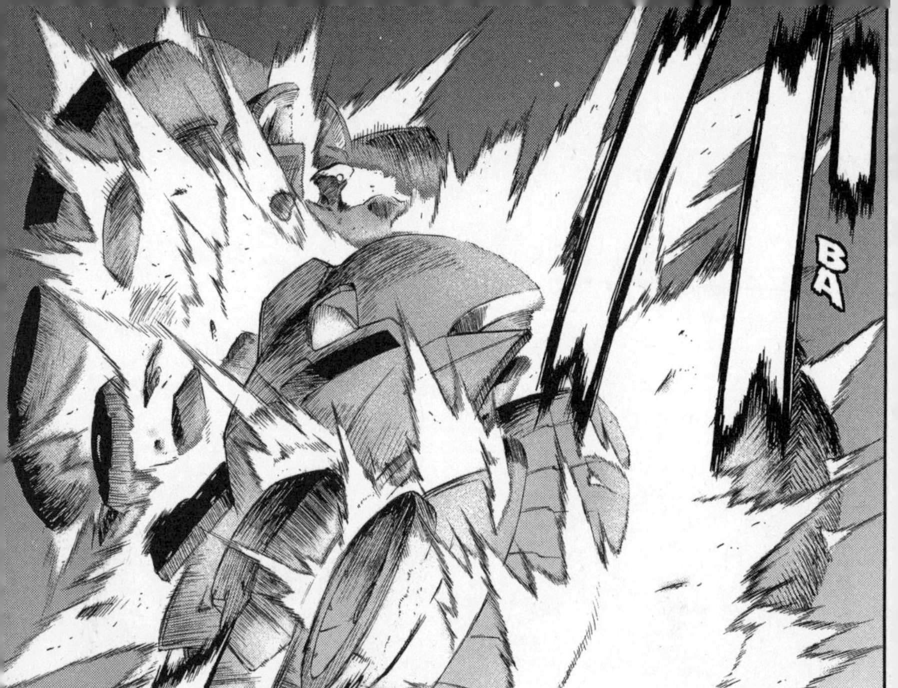
BA
ZOOK

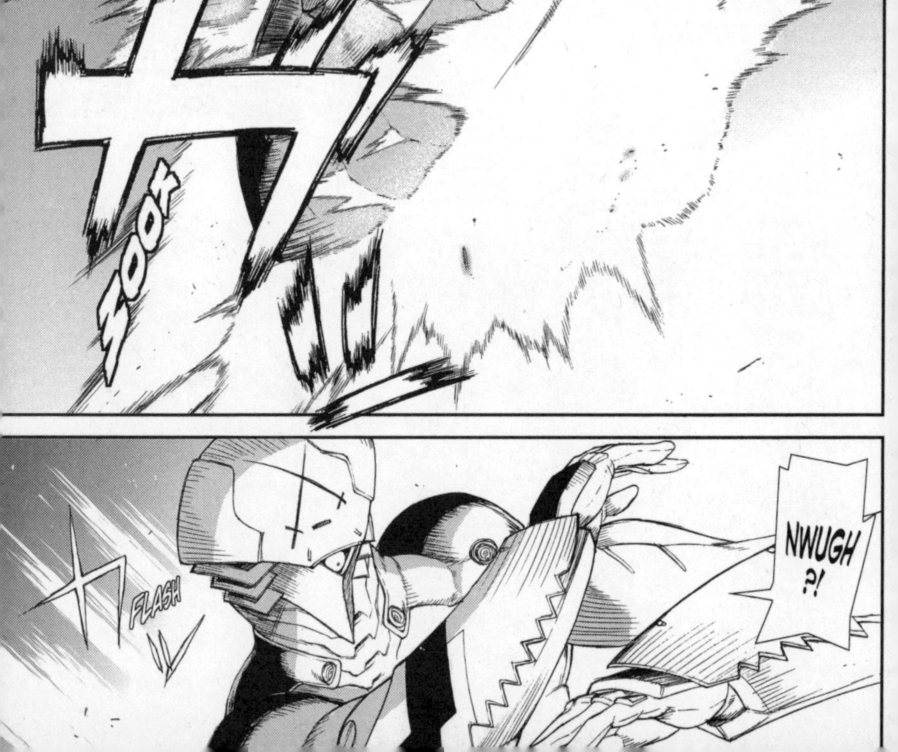
NWUGH ?!
FLASH

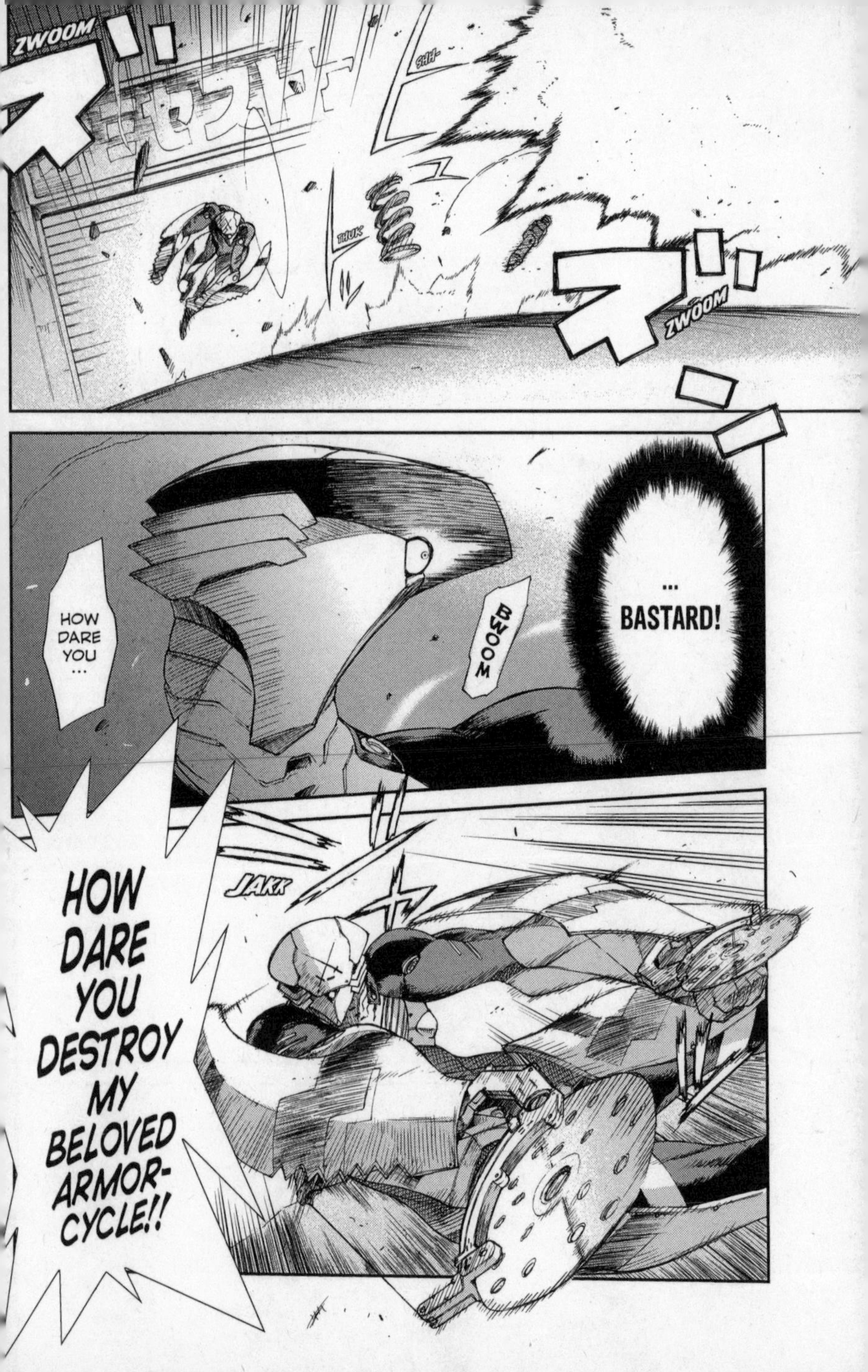
ZWOOM
SHH-
THUK
ZWOOM
BWOOM
... BASTARD!
HOW DARE YOU ...
JAKK
HOW DARE YOU DESTROY MY BELOVED ARMOR-CYCLE!!

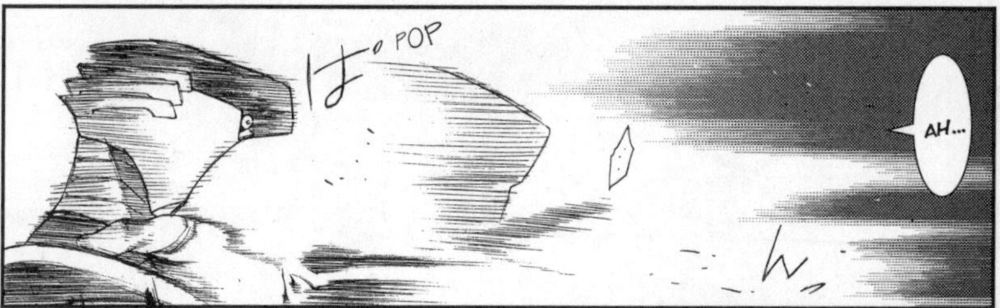
は POP
AH...
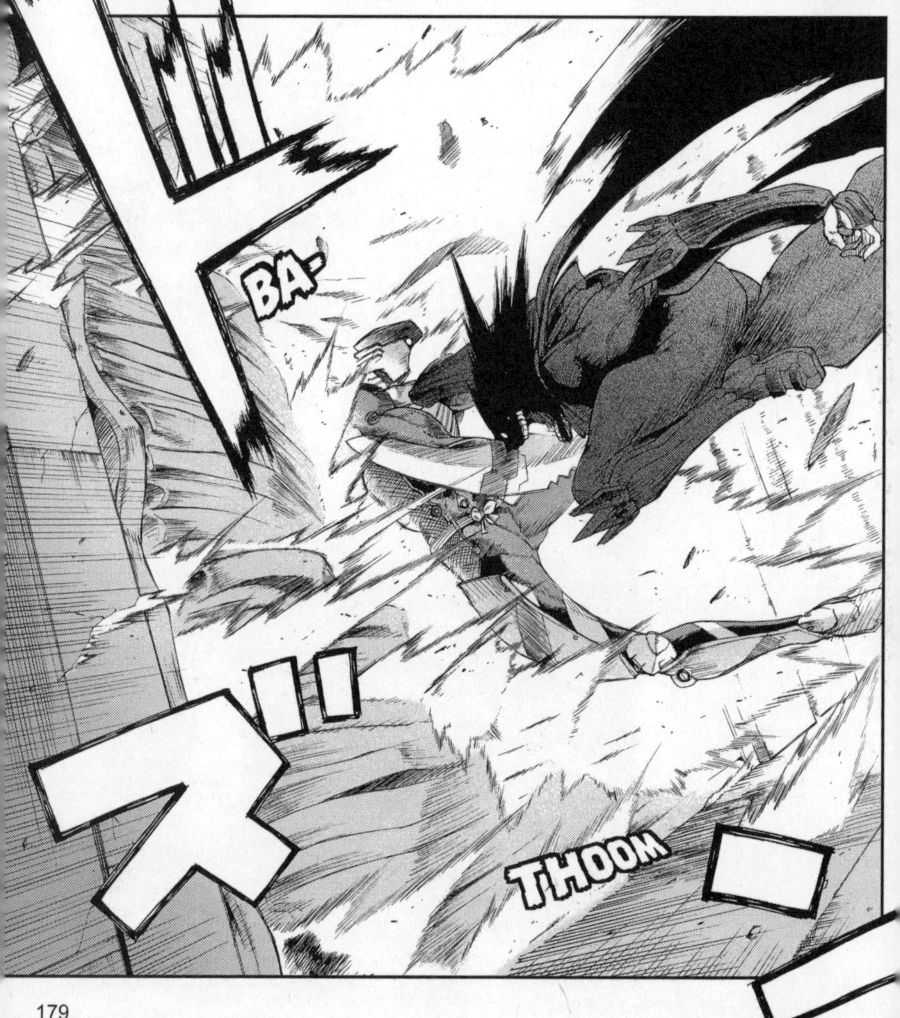
BA-
THOOM

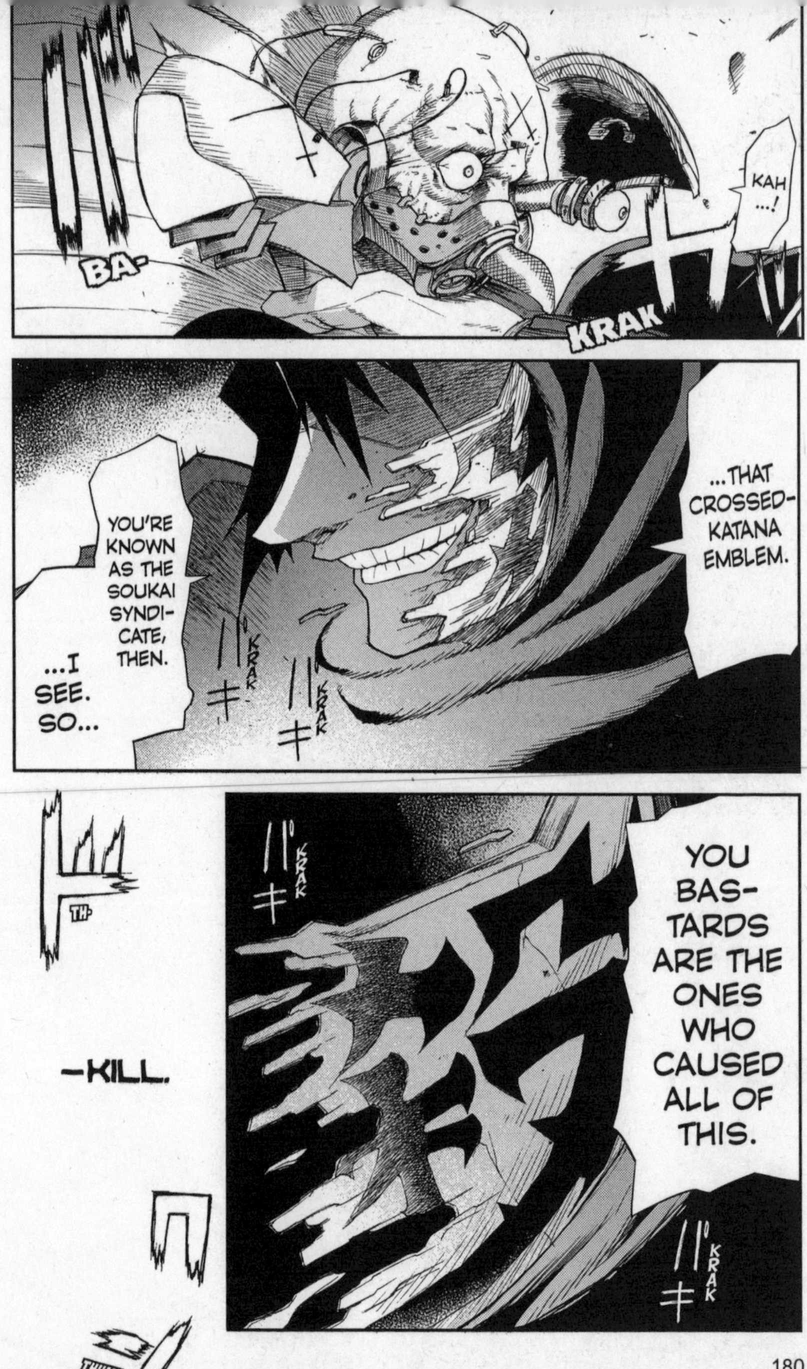
KAH ...!
KRAK
BA-
...THAT CROSSED-KATANA EMBLEM.
KRAK
KRAK
YOU'RE KNOWN AS THE SOUKAI SYNDICATE, THEN.
...I SEE. SO...
YOU BASTARDS ARE THE ONES WHO CAUSED ALL OF THIS.
KRAK
KRAK
TH-
-KILL.
THUMP

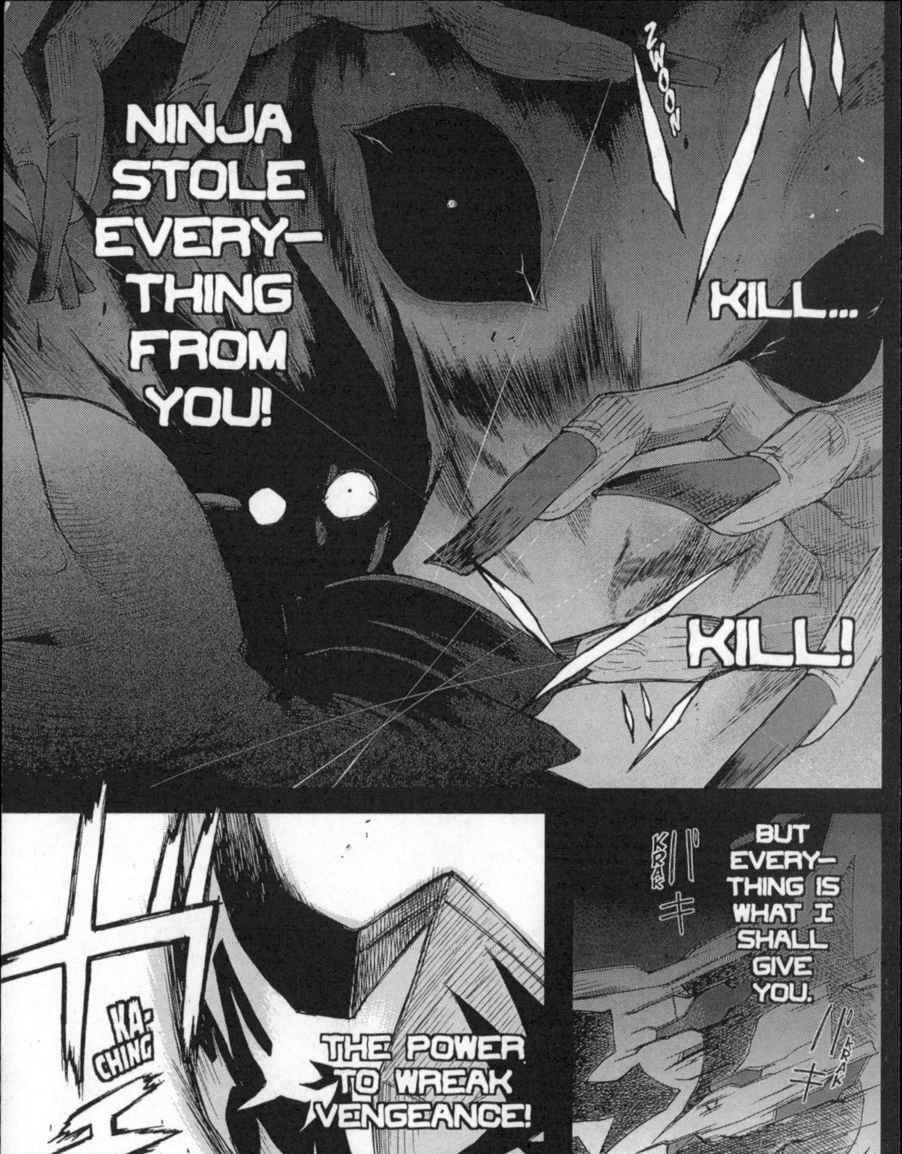
ZWOON
KILL...
NINJA STOLE EVERY-THING FROM YOU!
KILL!
パキ KRAK
BUT EVERY-THING IS WHAT I SHALL GIVE YOU.
パキ KRAK
パキ KRAK
KA-CHING
THE POWER TO WREAK VENGEANCE!

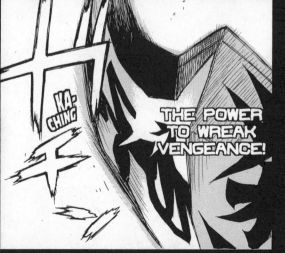

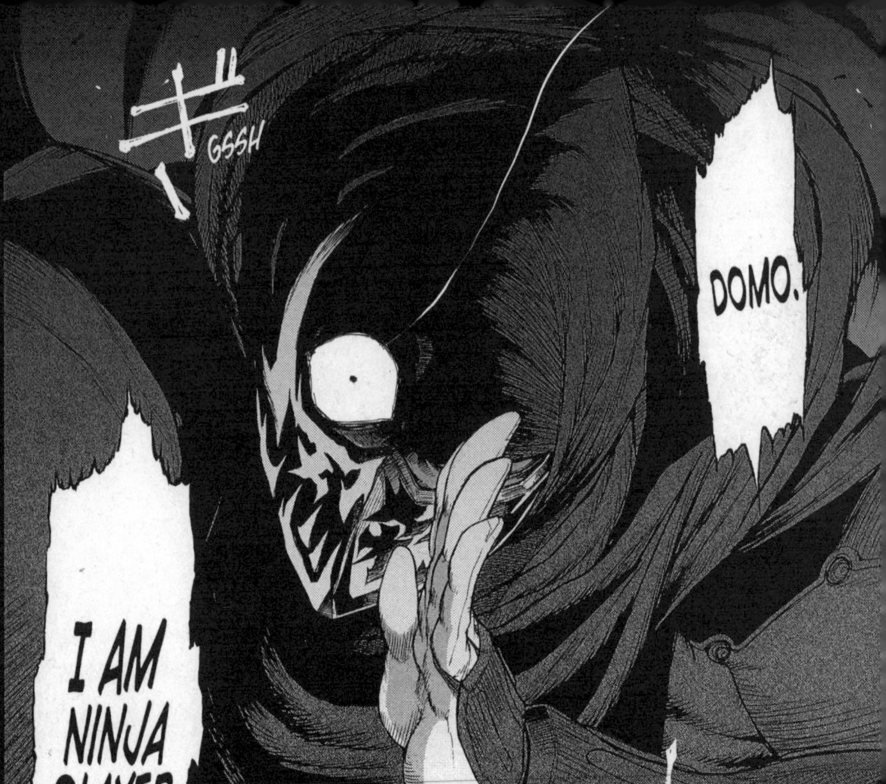
DOMO.
GSSH
I AM NINJA SLAYER.
SST

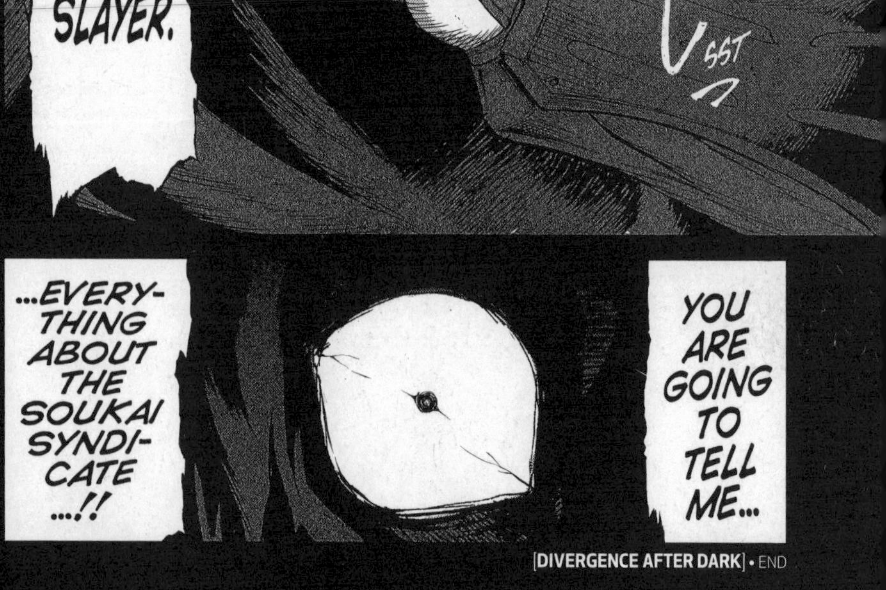
YOU ARE GOING TO TELL ME...
...EVERY-THING ABOUT THE SOUKAI SYNDI-CATE ...!!

[DIVERGENCE AFTER DARK] • END

TO BE CONTINUED

NINJA SLAYER
ニンジャスレイヤー
SLAYER
KILLS!

SETTING DESIGN COLLECTION

COMMENTARY: KOUTAROU SEKINE

NINJA SLAYER DARKNINJA MINUTE MAN

EQUATION MYRMIDON   SCATTER

OFFENDER

NINJA SLAYER

This work places emphasis on cybernetics and the qualities that define shonen manga, so the ninja that appear in *Kills* are designed along those lines. I felt that the plainness of our hero, Ninja Slayer, was important to his design, so I did not add any excess equipment to him and drew him with a sharp, edgy silhouette.

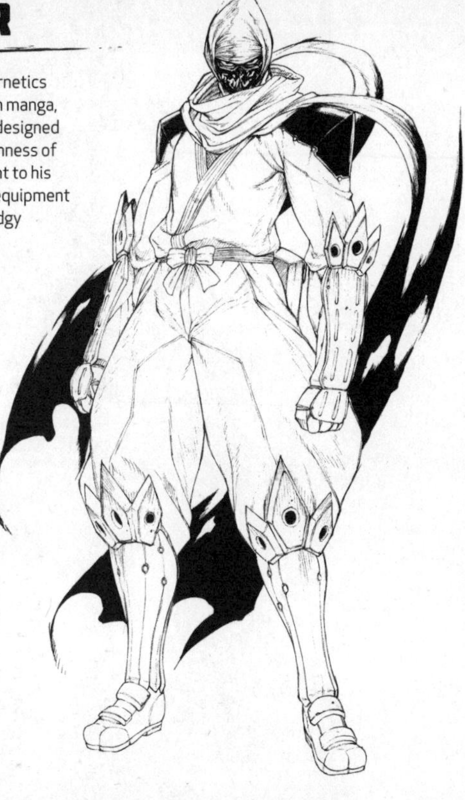

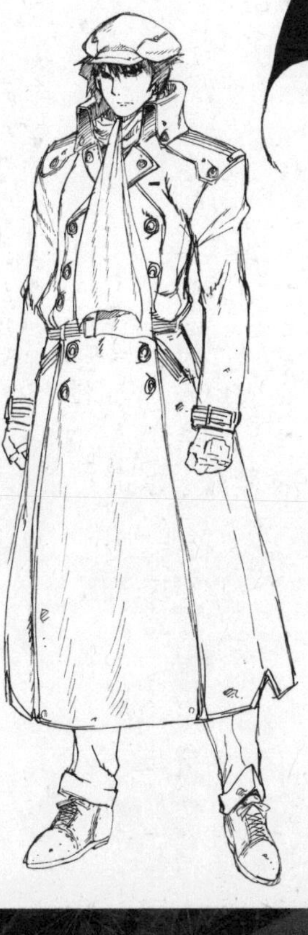

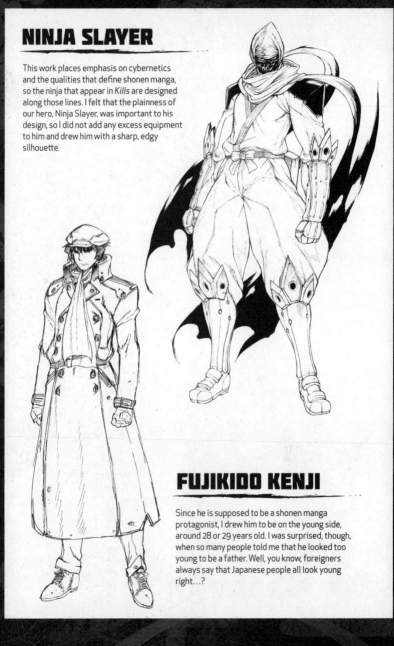

FUJIKIDO KENJI

Since he is supposed to be a shonen manga protagonist, I drew him to be on the young side, around 28 or 29 years old. I was surprised, though, when so many people told me that he looked too young to be a father. Well, you know, foreigners always say that Japanese people all look young right...?

I wanted the mashed-up kanji on the back of the costume to be an icon unique to *Kills*, so I came up with this one after rousing my inner foreign-born Japanese expert and drawing fully upon him.

I think it has some sort of emotional side to it that encompasses Fujikido, Naraku, and Ninja Slayer. You can't read it? Well, everyone says that. Even me.

DARKNINJA

This high-tech armor shines like brilliant obsidian as if to show off its heavy alloy construction. Its frame is made of cast bio-bamboo fibers and works to efficiently support Darkninja-san's *karate* techniques.

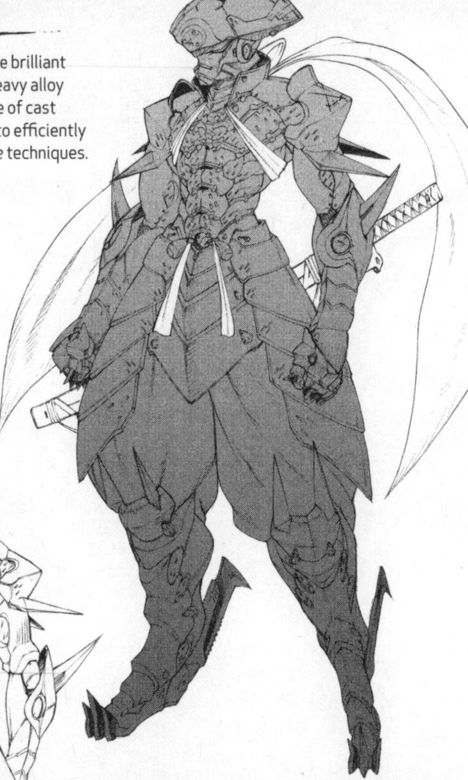

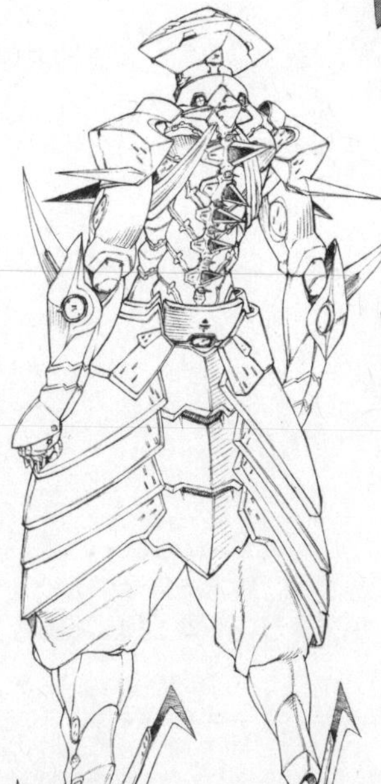

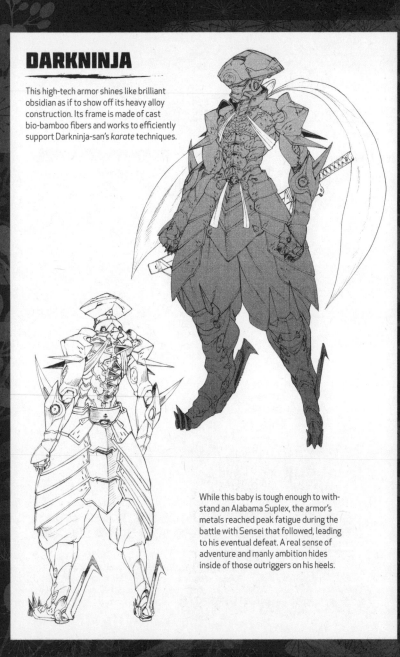

While this baby is tough enough to withstand an Alabama Suplex, the armor's metals reached peak fatigue during the battle with Sensei that followed, leading to his eventual defeat. A real sense of adventure and manly ambition hides inside of those outriggers on his heels.

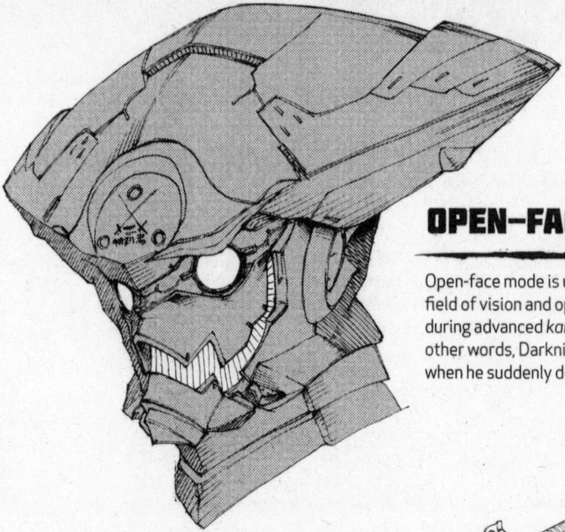

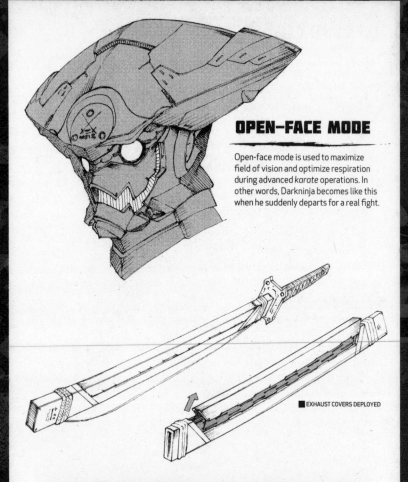

OPEN-FACE MODE

Open-face mode is used to maximize field of vision and optimize respiration during advanced *karate* operations. In other words, Darkninja becomes like this when he suddenly departs for a real fight.

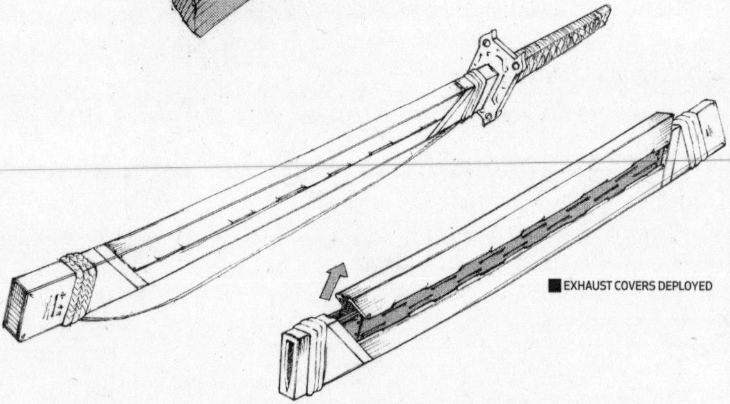
EXHAUST COVERS DEPLOYED

DEMON SWORD BEPPIN & OMURA INDUSTRIES-MADE PROTOTYPE BLAST-SCABBARD BLUE HAPPA SHI-3000

This scabbard allows for swords to be drawn at ultra-high speeds by causing an explosion inside of itself. After sprinkling explosives inside of the scabbard and then inserting Demon Sword Beppin, the ignition switch at the front of the scabbard can be pressed to create an explosion. So despite its sweet appearance, it works almost exactly like an old musket.

EQUATION

Along with Darkninja, this was one of the ninja I was free to design during the early stages of creation. While I did like him quite a bit, he dies right after appearing. What a harsh world this is.

The skin sewn onto his face is a "biotech skin-menpo" prototype. It squirms and shifts shapes, creating disguises by merging with his own skin. It would be bad news if a regular person tried to use it, because their body would attempt to reject the skin, but Equation is able to overcome that with his impressive ninja tenacity. Even so, it seems like it was hard for him to blend the bio-materials with his regular skin while walking around normally, so he's stuck going around with the menpo sewn onto his face.

MINUTE MAN

When I first saw his design in the novel version, I thought that his arm parts must clunk around a lot when they move, so I based the manga design on that. The story is that he lost both of his arms and his jaw in a previous fight and had them replaced with cybernetics.

A winch has been installed on his lower jaw, which is also used as reins when Equation rides him.

He found that the crawling propulsion support cybernetics on both of his arms were somewhat lacking, so he drew on his own experience and installed unique modifications such as ones that allow for faster suriken throwing speeds and secret attacks during close-quarters combat.

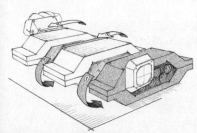

MINUTEMAN'S ARM CYBERNETICS

The blocks on his arms activate in stages during crawling propulsion. He moves his arms when blocks come into contact with the ground to make them spin at high speeds, pushing his body forward at cheetah-like crawling speeds.

MYRMIDON
& ARMORCYCLE

As his name means "ant man," I made
Myrmidon seem insectile when he merges
with his motorcycle, making sure that his
body would fit cleanly into his bike.

For fun, I designed him with splitter
camouflage, but I came to regret it later
when it just turned out to be annoying to
draw.

While he's full of little tricks and gimmicks
like disc-brake suriken, he's defeated
shortly after appearing without so much
as a chance to show off his powers. I at
least hope this helps you understand how
transient a ninja's life of battle can be.

When I drew the scene where he appears,
I was listening to the song "Kokubetsu
Toujou" from the Soukyu Gurentai (Terra
Diver) soundtrack in the background on
repeat.

Well, you know, considering the situation
and everything else, it's like he's a stage 1
boss, right…?

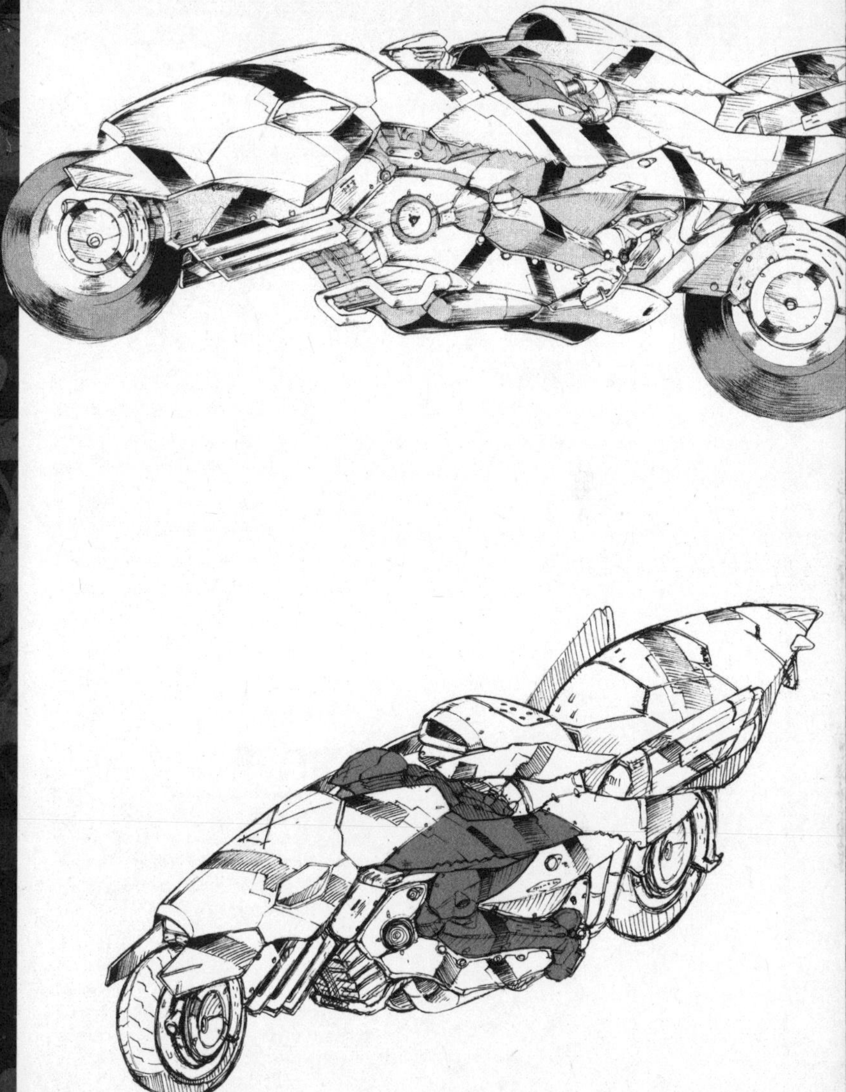

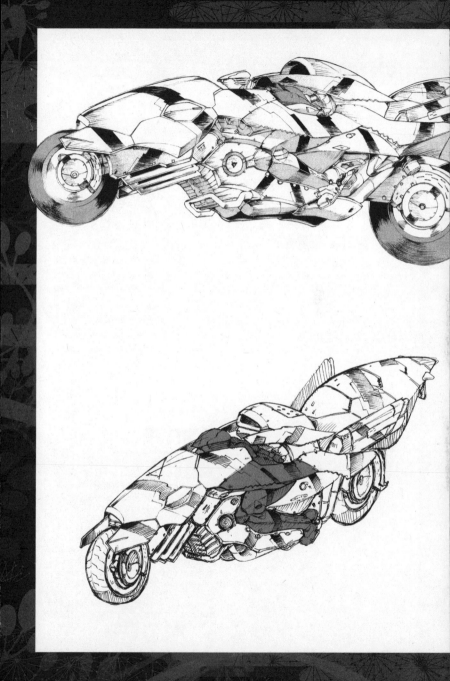

OFFENDER

Both Offender and Scatter show up first thing in *Born in Red Black*. Everything was decided on so suddenly that I didn't have much time to change their designs, so both of them were only slightly modified from the novel version before being quickly drawn.

I drew Offender thinking that he must have realized how much fun torture is when he was being tortured himself, turning him into a gross torture fetishist.

Then again, he suddenly sticks a machete straight into Fujikido's shoulder. I guess both he and I got a little carried away.

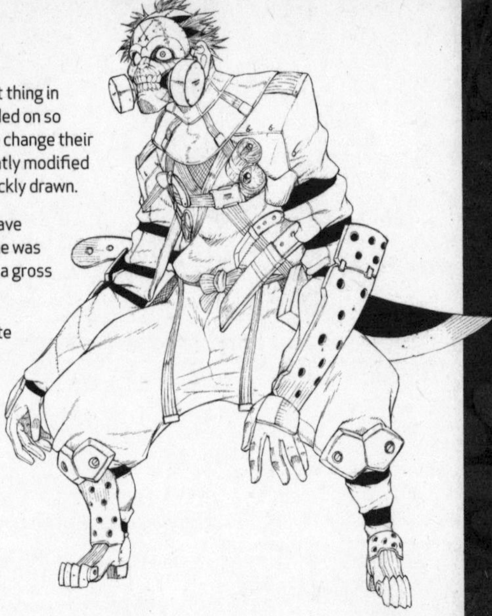

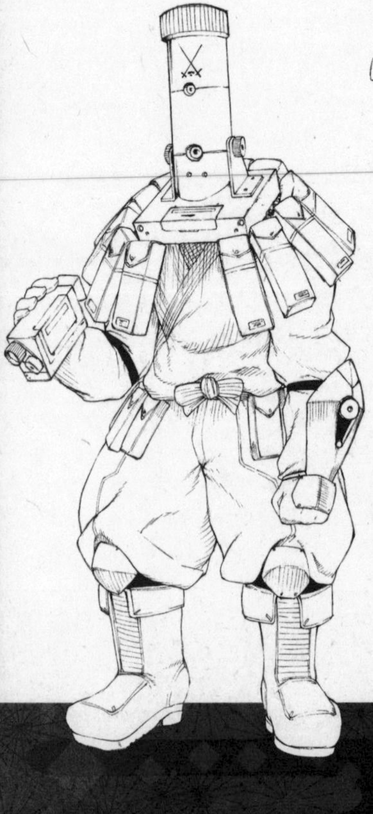

SCATTER

I tried drawing this character, then looked at it and thought that it looked like I'd drawn a monstrous microscope. Still, you'd agree that you wouldn't expect much at all in the way of *karate* skills from this guy, right? At least that part was accurate.

His head has been cybernetized for better detection abilities, but he still carries around an old video camera. Why? Because he personally thinks its best when gore videos are recorded on cheap quality videotape.

The pouches that cover his body are filled with batteries and tapes for his camcorder, making him totally unsuited for battle.

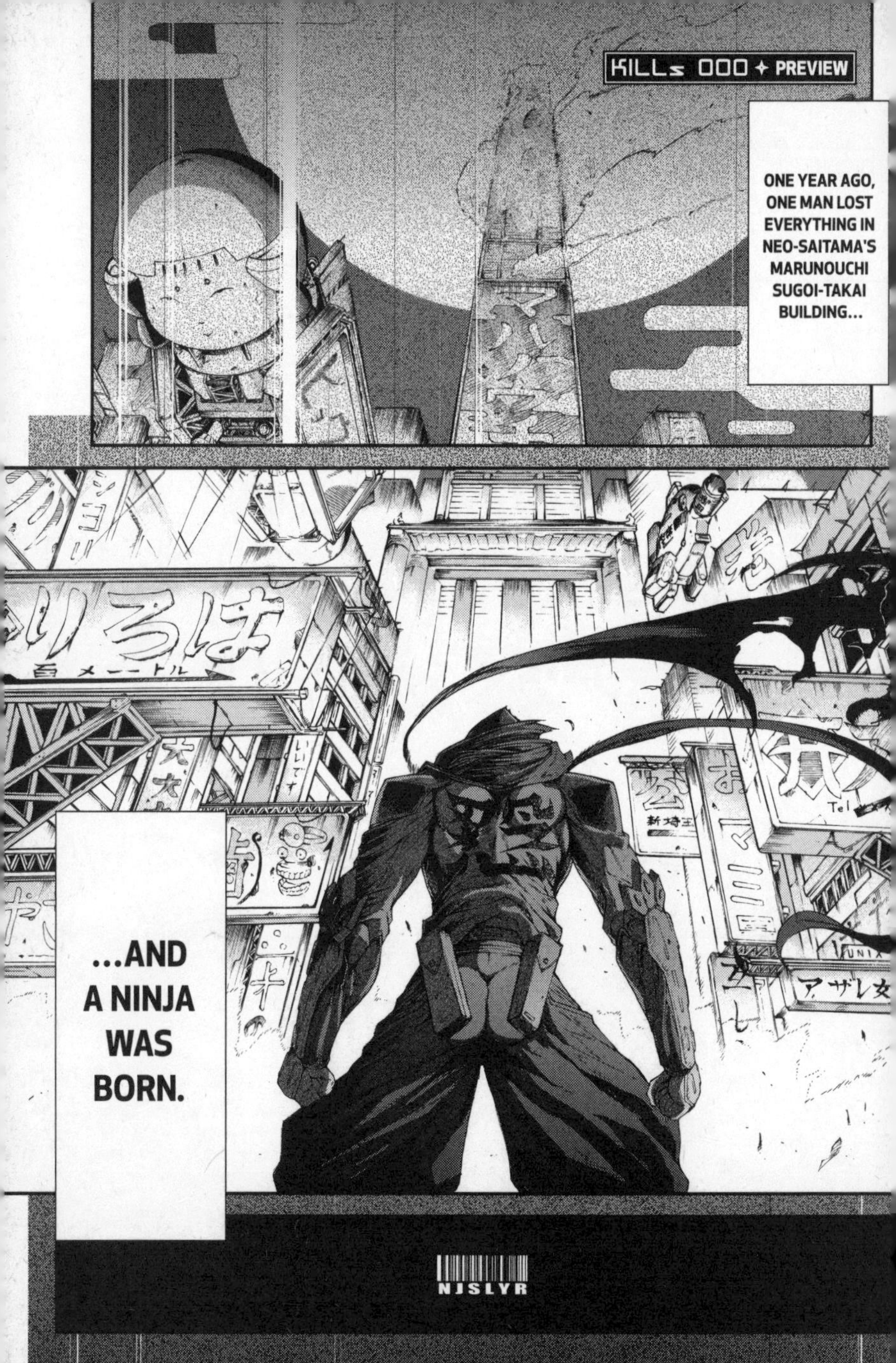
KILLs 000 ✦ PREVIEW
ONE YEAR AGO, ONE MAN LOST EVERYTHING IN NEO-SAITAMA'S MARUNOUCHI SUGOI-TAKAI BUILDING...
いろは
...AND A NINJA WAS BORN.
NJSLYR

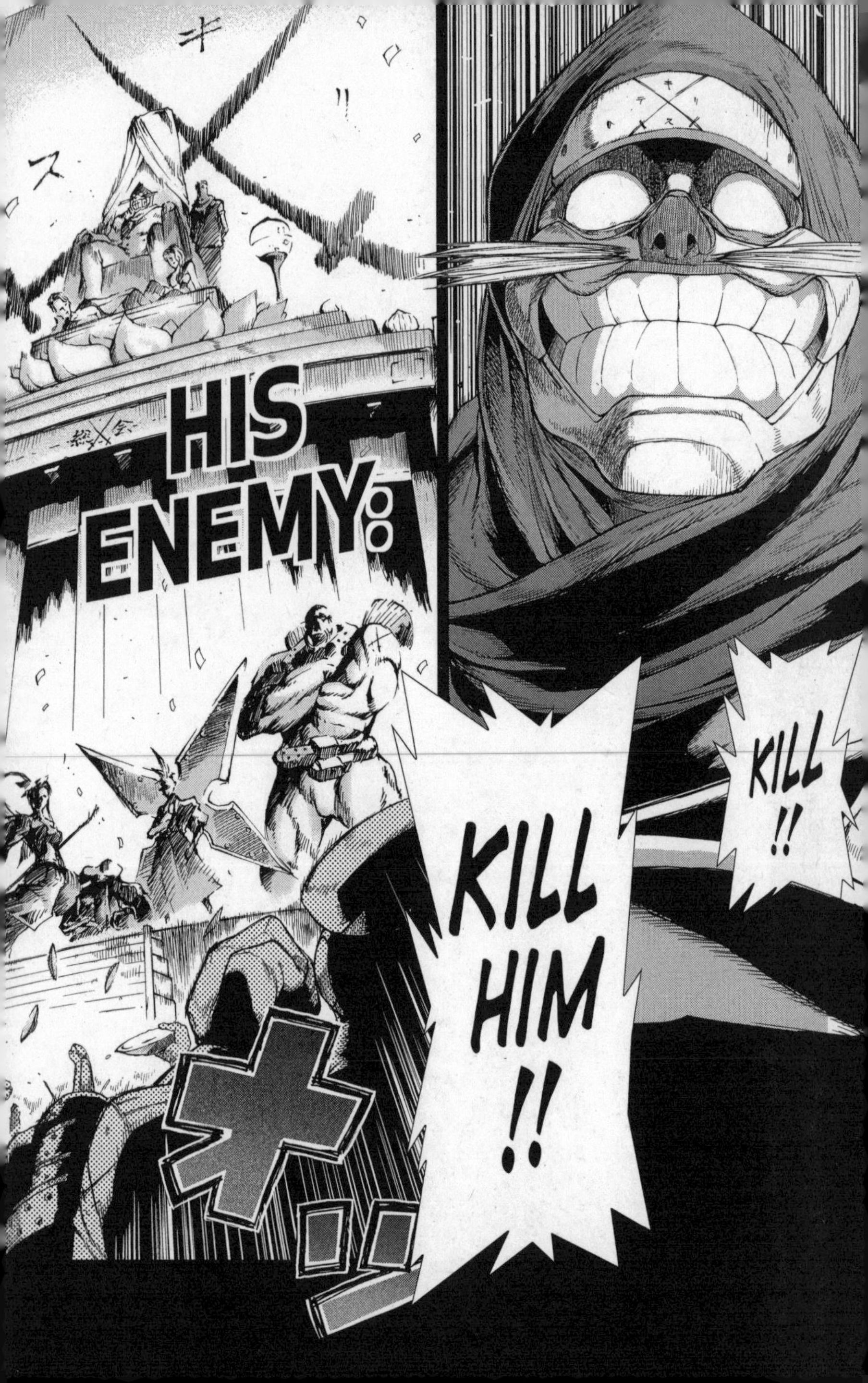
HIS ENEMY..
KILL HIM!!
KILL!!

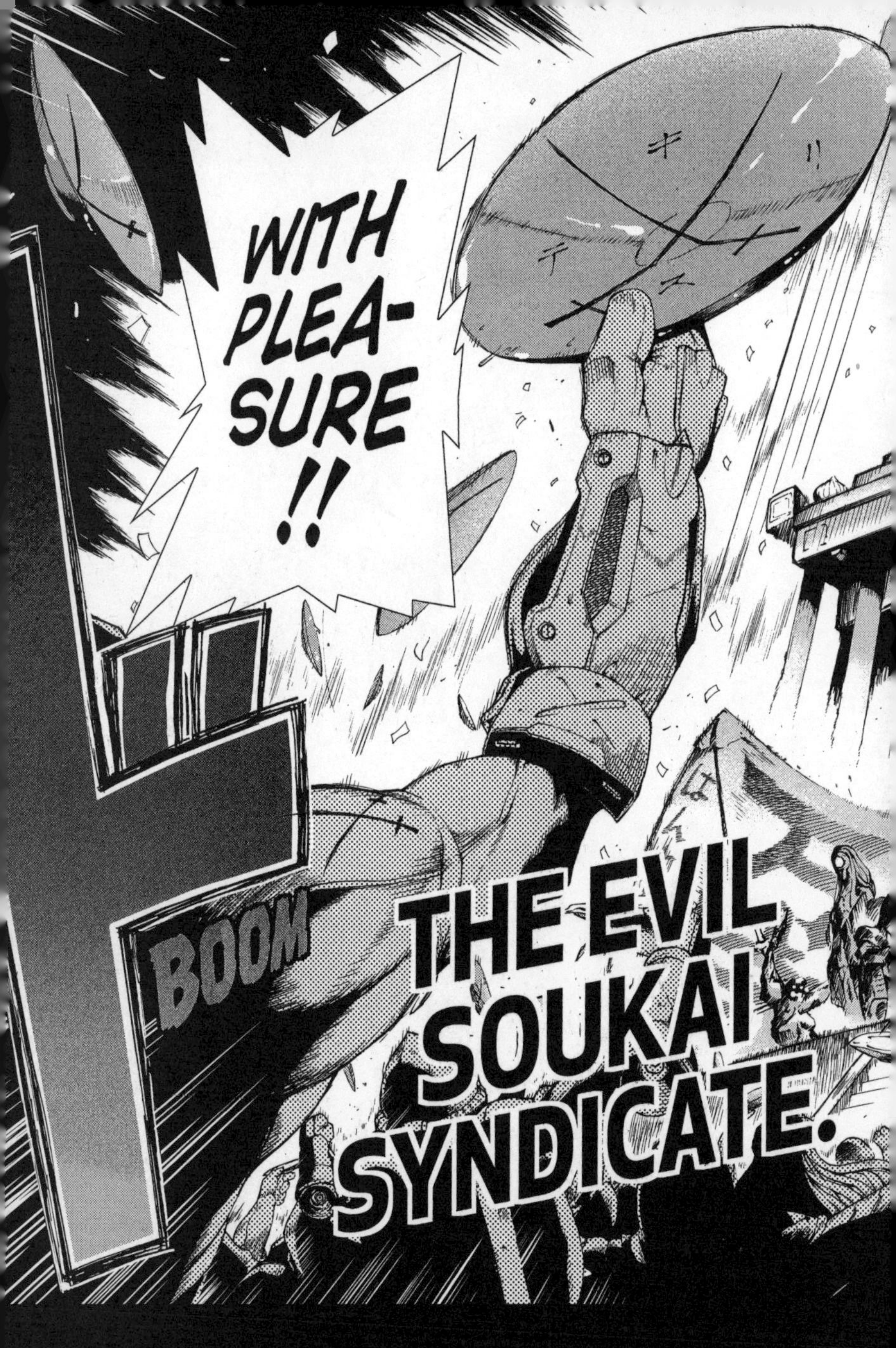
WITH PLEA-SURE!!
BOOM
THE EVIL SOUKAI SYNDICATE.

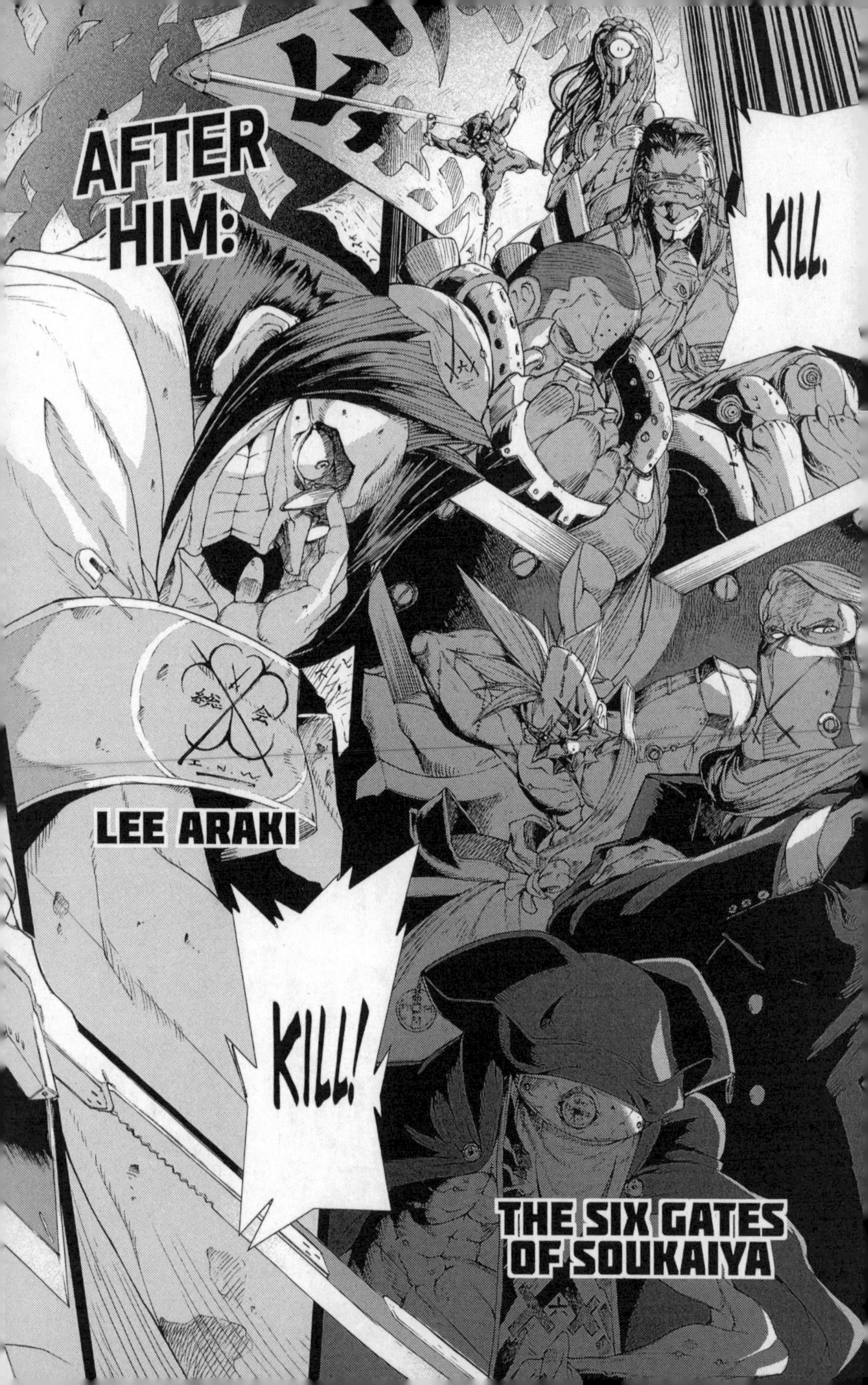
AFTER HIM!
KILL.
LEE ARAKI
KILL!
THE SIX GATES OF SOUKAIYA

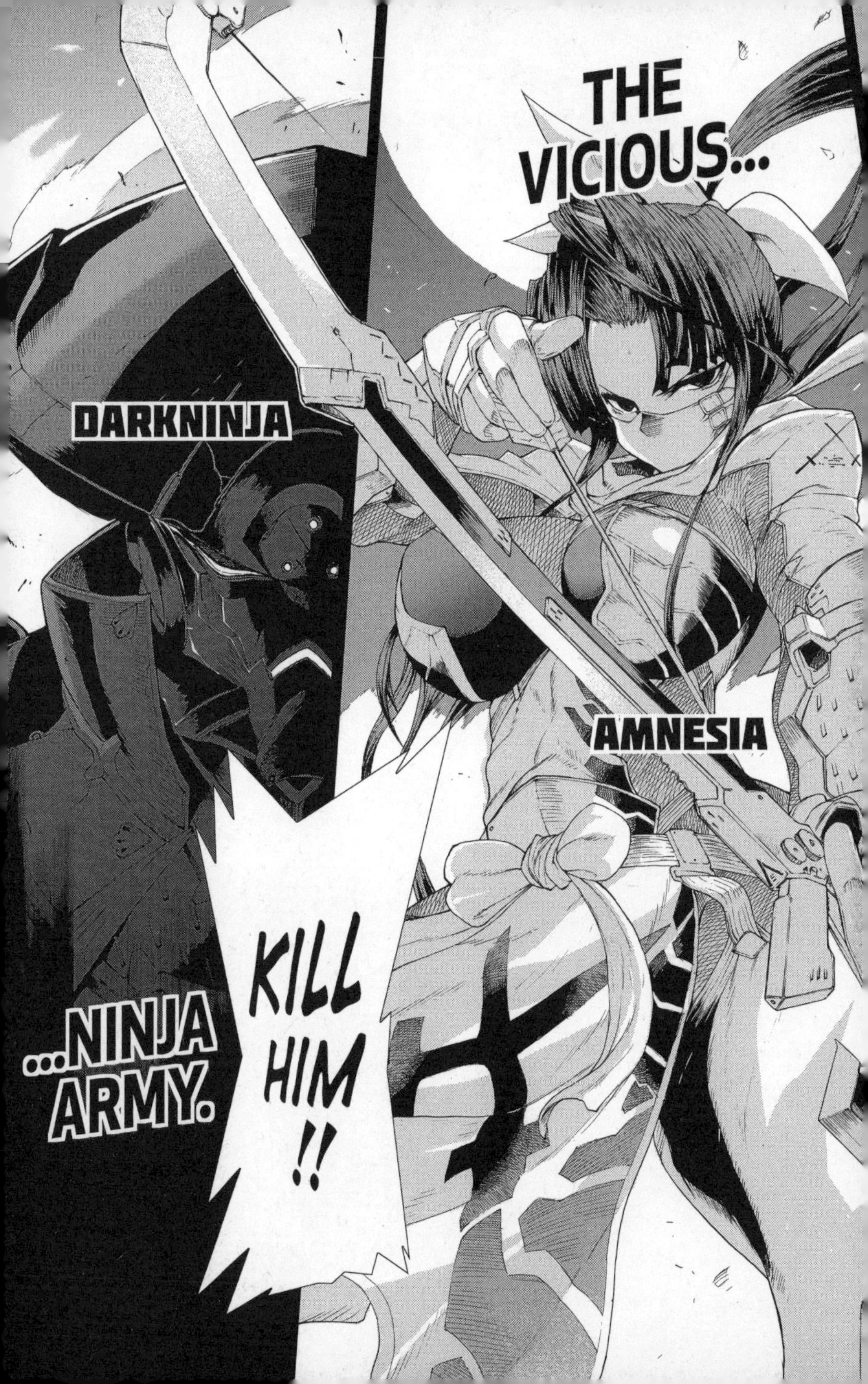
THE VICIOUS...
AMNESIA
DARKNINJA
KILL HIM !!
...NINJA ARMY.

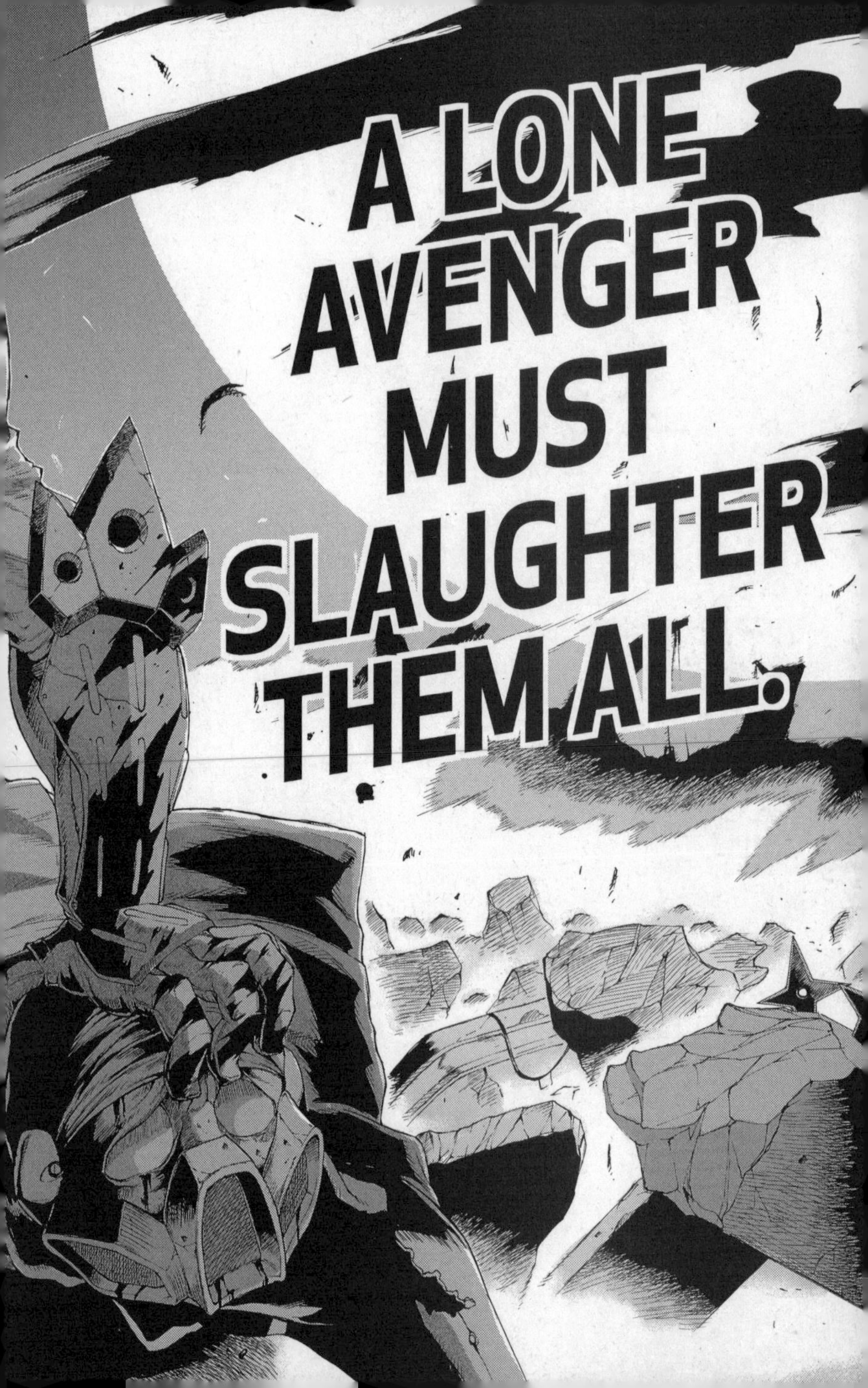
A LONE AVENGER MUST SLAUGHTER THEM ALL.

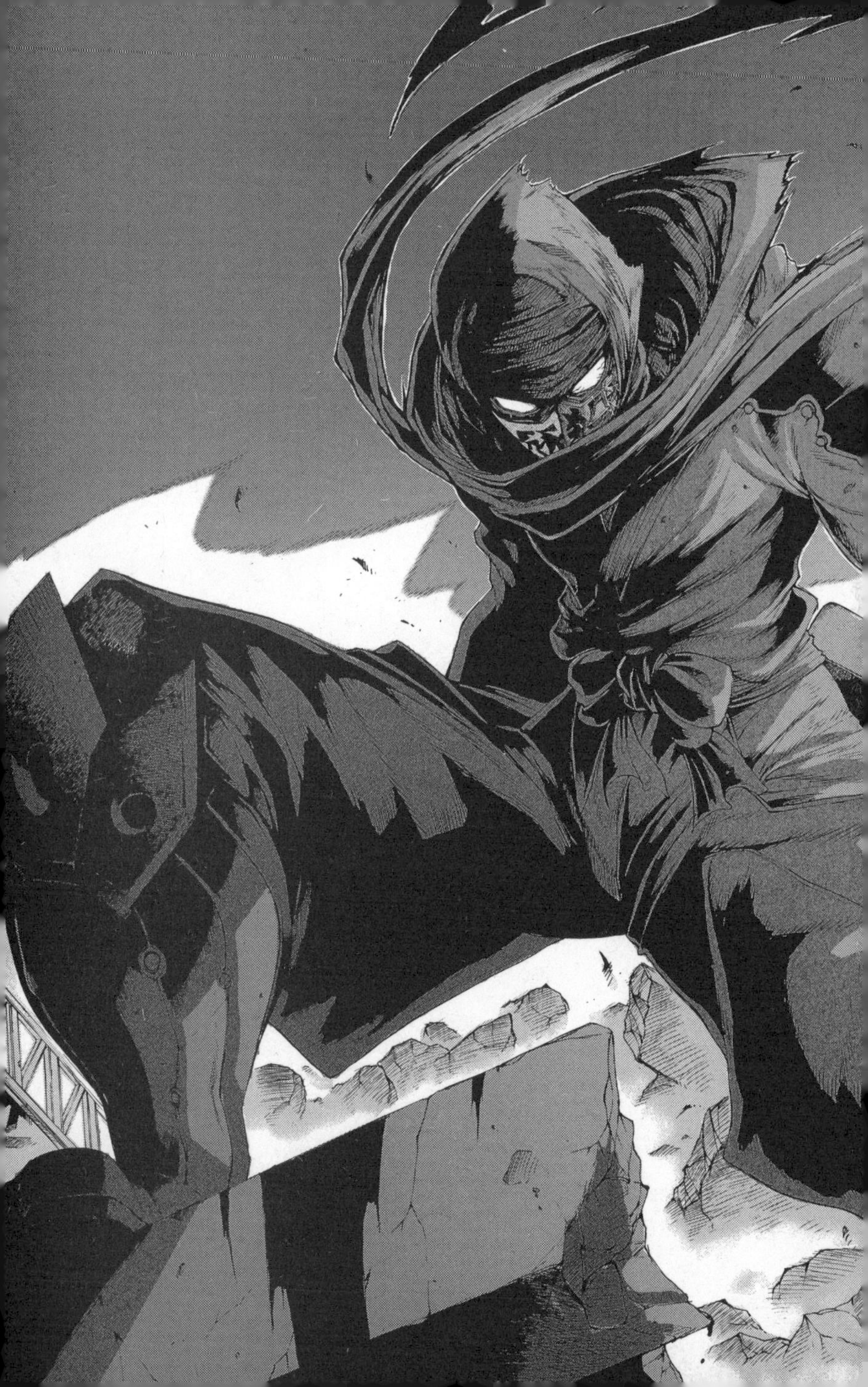

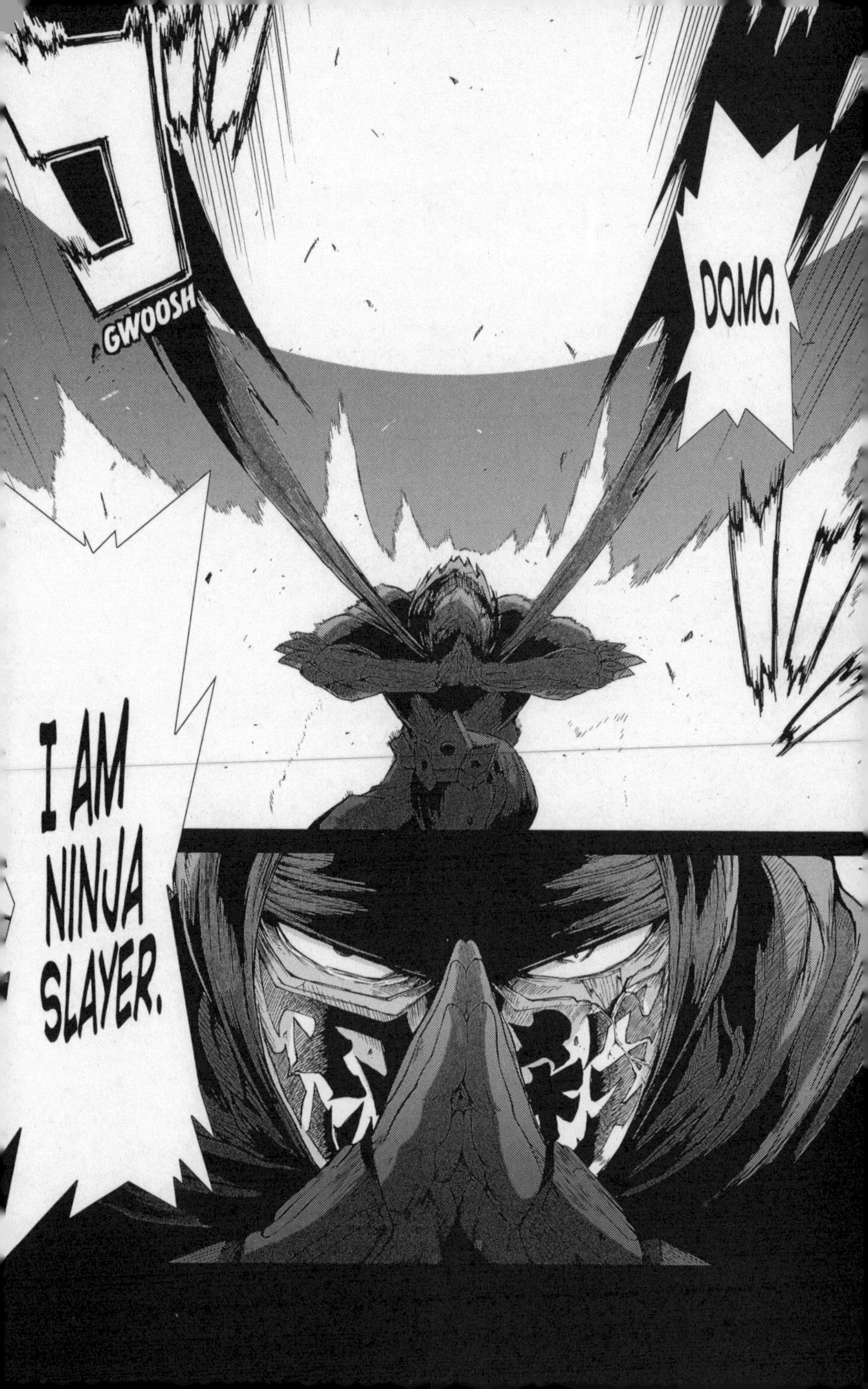
DOMO.
GWOOSH
I AM NINJA SLAYER.

AFTERWORD

A pleasure to meet you. My name is Koutarou Sekine. This release marks my first ever commercially published volume of manga. It's thanks to all of you readers and your support that I was able to create this book despite all the little bits of trouble I caused for everyone here and there. Reading your comments on Twitter and Nico Nico Seiga are my daily emotional respite. Thank you so much.

The original idea for Kills was that it was supposed to be a shonen manga-focused version of Ninja Slayer that even beginners could understand. What did you think? I was hooting in joy when I found out I'd be allowed to draw straight-up cybernetic ninjas battling it out in a cyberpunk world, so I just did whatever I felt like! Of course, I did wonder quite often if it'd really be all right for me to do some of these things, or if first-time Ninja Slayer readers would be able to follow along, but as long as you enjoyed this title, I'm happy.

The narration that is so unique to Ninja Slayer has been snipped right out due to the nature of the title. If you're a newbie who now feels familiar with the series after reading this manga, you should try reading the original novels, where you can get a taste of its rich charm.

Old-school ninja-heads will be able to get an idea of how I tend to work while drawing this series if they imagine Issei Masamune narrating the entire thing. Before you realize it, your body will want to transform and your brain will explode.

I just feel like saying sorry once again to the original authors, the translation team, and my editor K-san. Seriously...

Okay, see you next volume! Ciao!

KOUTAROU SEKINE

KOTODAMA

These words are more than just words, they have been brought to life on the breath of ninja since the Heian era and have been imbued with powers that bring them close to the heart and soul of ninja life. Know these words well, as they may tip the scales in your favor upon your next encounter with a ninja of exemplary *karate*.

WAZAMAE

A refined way to refer to one's ninja techniques or abilities, usually in reference to the great skill administered by a ninja.

KARATE

More than just the martial art that we have come to know through movies and other media, in the world of Ninja Slayer, *karate* encompasses the skills of all martial arts and can be used to describe the martial prowess that flows like blood in the veins of true ninja.

JITSU

Refers to various ninja techniques and practices.

HAIKU

In addition to being a form of Japanese poetry, in the world of Ninja Slayer, *haiku* are one's departing words upon imminent death. It is common courtesy among ninjas to allow one's opponent a moment to recite a *haiku* before dealing the final blow. Though there are rules that resemble the familiar 5-7-5 syllabic meter, uneducated ninjas have been known to recite *haiku* in poor form.

KIRISUTE

Literally "to cut and remove" this can sometimes be understood as "omission" but as the official motto of Soukai Syndicate, it is better interpreted as their mission to *slay and eradicate* all entities that stand in the way of the Soukai Syndicate's nefarious ways.

NAMUAMIDABUTSU

Also abbreviated to *namandabu*, this is a prayer and mantra from Pure Land Buddhism that can be interpreted as "may Buddha have mercy." It is often recited during meditation or at a funeral to send the departed to their next destination. Though different from Namusan, because it can be considered a phrase of exclamation, it can also be interpreted as, "oh my Buddha!"

NAMUSAN

An abbreviated version of *namu-sanpou*. This phrase can be interpreted as the "amen" of the Buddhist world, but is often used as an expression of shock, and thus is sometimes translated as "oh my Buddha!" In the grim world of Ninja Slayer, you will often hear *Namu-san* in response to the gory atrocities that one can see on an almost daily basis.

AISATSU

This refers to the common greetings that are practiced by true ninja. Politeness is close to godliness in the world of Ninja Slayer and before engaging in battle it is customary for ninja to introduce themselves with the word *Domo* (hello/greetings), followed by your ninja name.

SAYONARA

Japanese for goodbye or farewell. In the world of Ninja Slayer, this phrase is said upon a ninja's departure from this world and before a dying ninja explodes from the soon to escape ninja soul within.

IAIDO

Traditionally known as the art of drawing, striking with, and replacing a sword, in the world of Ninja Slayer, *iaido* encompasses all martial arts that make use of *katana*.

MIYAGE

A gift, offer, or souvenir.

KOUBEIN

Similar to the ancient Japanese form of currency called *koban*, *koubein* is a flat, oblong ingot of pure gold, thus making it very valuable.

KEJIME

Typically, this refers to settling an error committed by a *yakuza* or member of an organized crime group that usually culminates in the offender in question severing his or her finger in repentance. From this basic meaning, the word has spread to refer to any form of settlement and can even mean to dismember or kill someone.

HARAKIRI

Similar, yet different from *sepuku* (ritual suicide), in the world of Ninja Slayer, this is the ultimate form of *kejime*. Though it can result in killing oneself, it can also be expressed through social suicide or anything that would essentially harm oneself.

KAISHAKU

For those familiar with the practices of ritualistic suicide, *kaishaku* may be recognizable as the assistant who finishes the suicide by decapitating the one committing suicide. In a similar vein, to ninja, a *kaishaku* is the finishing blow dealt out of mercy for an opponent who has been utterly defeated.

WASSHOI!

To increase and focus the power of one's *jitsu*, Ninja use what are known as karate shouts. The most widely used *karate* shout is "yeee-art!" *Wasshoi* is primarily used by Ninja Slayer, though it has been heard on occasion from other ninja as well as a ninja-head or two.

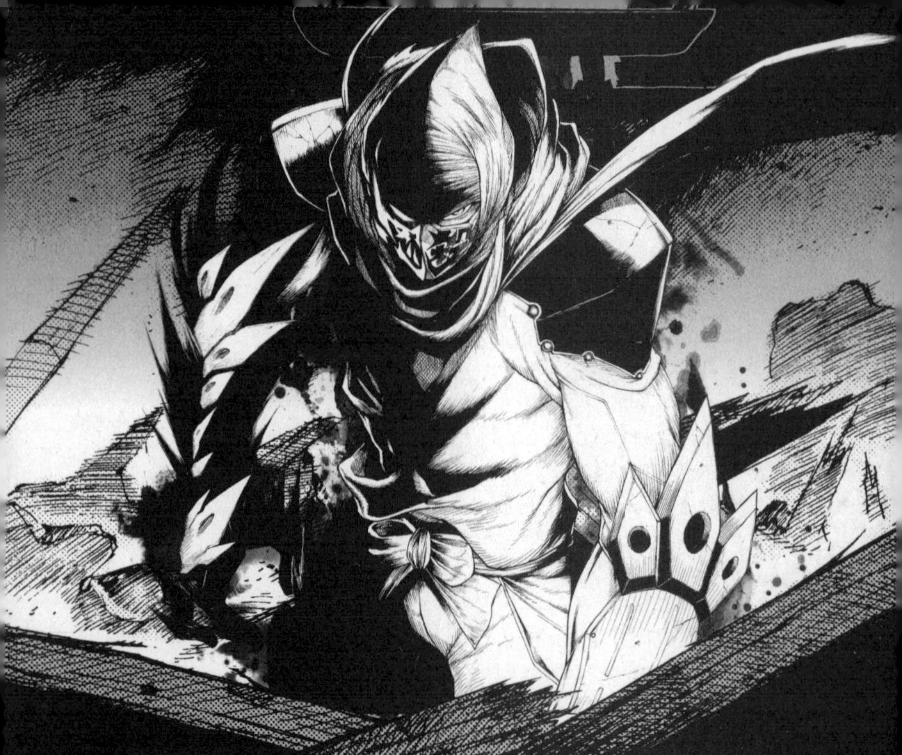

TRANSLATION NOTES

Neo-Saitama, page 3
In the dark future of Ninja Slayer, the capital of Japan is Neo-Saitama. In present day Japan, Saitama shares the same metropolitan area as Tokyo. However, it often functions as the more suburban part of the area, making it in some ways similar to New Jersey in contrast to New York City.

Kinkaku Temple, page 28
A temple that appears to be similar, but most likely different from the Golden Pavilion (kinkaku-ji), a zen-budhhist temple from Japan's Muromachi era and possibly one of the most recognizable landmarks in Kyoto.